MW01009771

DuANE S. ReVES
Box 295
BRuNo, SK
SoK 0S0

March 29, 1999

The Denver and Rio Grande Western Railroad

Rebel of the Rockies

by

Robert G. Athearn

University of Nebraska Press

Lincoln   London

First Bison Book printing: 1977
Most recent printing indicated by first digit below:
                             7   8   9   10

Library of Congress Cataloging in Publication Data

Athearn, Robert G.
   The Denver and Rio Grande Western Railroad.

   Reprint of the 1967 issue of the work published by Yale
University Press, New Haven, which was issued as no. 2 of
the Yale Western Americana series, under title: Rebel of
the Rockies.
   Bibliography: p. 361
   1.   Denver and Rio Grande Western Railroad—History.
I. Title.   II. Series: Yale Western Americana
series; 2.
[HE2791.D442364 1977]   385'.09788   76–30296
ISBN 0–8032–0920–7
ISBN 0–8032–5861–5 pbk.

This book was originally published under the title *Rebel of
the Rockies: A History of the Denver and Rio Grande Western
Railroad.*

For James L. Athearn, a Westerner
and onetime railroader

Preface

MUCH HAS BEEN PUBLISHED about the nation's railroads and the men who ran them. In recent years the attention of writers often has turned to some of the smaller and more colorful roads now out of existence. There is a mounting interest in the "age of steam," an era remembered by many older people but one that is history to some of the younger folk. The story of railroading in the Colorado Rockies has been the subject of several recently published books, yet none has been about the Denver and Rio Grande, a railroad that provided all the glamour and excitement of the Frontier, and today is one of the most modern and up-to-date lines in the nation.

It was the desire of the late Wilson McCarthy, president of the Denver and Rio Grande Western, that the story of his company be told, and with that in mind one of his representatives came to the University of Colorado history department to find a person who would undertake the work. I agreed to complete such a study provided no control of any kind would be exercised and that all interpretations and conclusions would be mine alone. During the period of research and writing, the company provided me with subsistence and ordinary expenses, much in the manner that foundations offer grants to those engaged in similar projects. It provided every possible assistance in the search for materials. Most of the original sources required for such a book as this are housed in the State Archives and Public Records of Colorado and are available to the general public. Documents still in the possession of the company were placed at my disposal without hesitation, and no door was closed. G. B. Aydelott, president of the Railroad, was exceedingly frank on this point: "If you find any skeletons in our closet, drag 'em out." Carlton T. Sills, director of publicity and the man with whom I worked most closely, took a similar point of view. "Tell the truth," he urged. "We can stand it." It is a pleasure to be able to record that none of the company officers whom I came to know ever showed the slightest desire to color the story.

They were interested in providing factual information and correcting obvious errors, but at no time did anyone try to do more. The viewpoints, the organization of the book, and the selection of a publisher were matters left entirely in my hands. "It wouldn't do any good to try to 'sell' you on the railroad," one of the officials told me with a grin. "College professors are such damned contrary critters you'd probably take the other side if we did." So the book took shape as the professor roamed the railroad property at will, from the offices of the chairman of the board and the president, down to the friendly cabs of the locomotive engineers with whom I rode. The only question ever asked was: "What can we do for you?"

I owe my thanks also to the University of Colorado not only for its generosity in relieving me of my teaching duties so that I might go railroading each summer but also to its Council on Research and Creative Work for a leave of absence that provided time for writing. Jerome DeSanto, Billie Barnes Jensen, Jane Furey, and Duane Smith helped in the arduous search through newspaper files, as did my colleagues Howard Lee Scamehorn and William Petrowski, who were at work on related topics. Virginia Grieder kept her typewriter going to turn out copy as fast as it came to hand, as did Robert Clendenen, who also made valuable editorial suggestions.

Marcus "Mike" Bosco and Mrs. Perry Malaby, both of Glenwood Springs, Colorado, were patient about giving interviews. Mrs. Malaby, who as a young bride had come over Independence Pass to Aspen in a stagecoach, watched the first D&RG train enter Glenwood Springs in 1887. Maurice Leckenby, of Steamboat Springs, offered both the files of his newspaper, the *Pilot*, and his personal knowledge of the railroad that serves his community. Richard Overton, author of several notable railroad histories, and the late Ralph Budd, former president of the Burlington Railroad, answered a number of questions and helped to make clear several complicated problems pertaining to Rio Grande history. S. J. Norris, consulting engineer, now living at Oroville, California, provided fresh information about the origins of the Western Pacific Railroad and its relations with the Rio Grande, as did Gilbert H. Kneiss of the Western Pacific.

Of course, it is to the librarians and archivists, that rare breed of people, that I owe much more than thanks. A. Russell Mortensen, formerly director of the Historical Society of Utah, and A. William Lund, assistant church historian, Church of Jesus Christ of Latter

Day Saints Library, Salt Lake City, were extremely friendly toward the project. So were Dolores Renze, State Archivist of Colorado; Alys Freeze, Denver Public Library; and Lucile Fry, University of Colorado Western History Collections librarian. Gertrude Hill of the Museum of New Mexico Library made available the William Blackmore papers and other pertinent documents. I wish to thank also those kind people at the British Museum who offered both a warm welcome and a helping hand in the search for materials relating to British interests in the Rio Grande. Also in Britain, Professor Charles Mowat of the University College of North Wales was helpful in locating material relating to the Festiniog Railway of Wales.

In the search for pictures I enlisted the help of Laura A. Ekstrom, State Historical Society Library, Denver; Gil W. Bauer, Colorado State Archives and Public Records; and Margaret Shepherd, Curator of Photographs, Utah State Historical Society. Jackson C. Thode, Rio Grande railroader, found a number of excellent items in the railroad's archives.

Map-maker Clarence O. Froid of the Rio Grande engineering staff spent an untold number of hours laboring over maps that would help tell the Colorado railroad story. William G. Prescott, secretary to the company, explained a number of points not made entirely clear by the documentary evidence at hand. Finally, my sincere thanks go to artists Dale R. Roylance and Howard L. Fogg, Jr., for their close cooperation in providing chapter illustrations and a dust jacket for the book.

Several of the earlier chapters were published as articles in the *Colorado Magazine,* the *Utah Historical Quarterly,* and the *University of Colorado Studies in History.*

ROBERT G. ATHEARN

University of Colorado
July 17, 1962

Contents

List of illustrations

Maps

1. The road to Little London

AT PRECISELY EIGHT O'CLOCK on a bright autumn morning in 1871, the people of Denver watched a shiny new train move along the edge of the city, pause at Fifteenth and Wynkoop Streets, then disappear southward along the Platte River. As it passed, they could see the name "Montezuma" painted on the cab of the thirty-nine-foot engine and the words "Denver & Rio Grande" spread the full length of its tender. Then came a baggage car, followed by "two elegant passenger coaches," one bearing the name "Denver," the other, "El Paso." In that fleeting moment a whole story of railroad enterprise passed in review. The words on the coaches and tender explained the road's projected termini, and the engine's name revealed a hope that it would one day enter the city of the Aztec kings. But on this 26th day of October the train was going only to Colorado Springs —a village that was barely three months old.

The passengers were neither the paying variety nor just ordinary folk. This was "show day," and to display its accomplishments the management had invited members of the local press to enjoy an excursion at its expense. Among them were such men as Nathan C. Meeker of the *Greeley Tribune,* whose massacre at the White River agency would make national news before the decade was out; O. J. Goldrick, Denver's first schoolmaster, representing the Denver *Herald;* and *Rocky Mountain News* editor William N. Byers. The latter was undoubtedly the most enthusiastic member of the group. His newspaper, destined to become a Denver institution, strongly supported Colorado's first home railroad as a major contribution to the young community's economic well-being. As the train moved along at a steady fifteen miles per hour, the *News* reporter admired the clear, blue atmosphere marred only by a few thunderheads in the distance, and indulged himself in a brief but glowing essay on Colorado's climate. Meanwhile, the little engine, weighing only twenty-five thousand pounds, tugged its load along a grade that gradually increased to seventy-five feet per mile as it scaled what was known as "Lake Pass." Beyond the right-of-way were stands of excellent timber, and piled along the road lay a half-million feet of lumber awaiting shipment.

Five hours later, and seventy-six miles south of Denver, the train came to a station labeled Colorado Springs, where a railroad chef had a meal ready. Their host, young and personable road-president William Jackson Palmer, and his right-hand man, former territorial governor Alexander C. Hunt, were waiting to escort the party to the site of the new colony town. After lunch, members of the excursion inspected the tract, upon which the first house had been built that August, and then went back to the railroad cars for the return trip to Denver.[1]

---

1. Denver *Daily Rocky Mountain News,* Oct. 28, 1871. The same story appears in the weekly *Rocky Mountain News,* Nov. 1, 1871.

During these years there were a number of such young men as Palmer in the plains and Rocky Mountain West—veterans of the Civil War in search of fresh economic opportunities in a land that was new and as yet relatively undeveloped. Some of them sought the gold fields as the most obvious source of wealth, others aspired to the title of cattle baron or merchant prince, but Palmer cast his lot with the railroad builders, believing that transportation was the key to success in the limitless stretches of public domain beyond the Missouri. Like General Grenville Dodge, chief engineer of the Union Pacific, or former Confederate General Thomas L. Rosser, who had a similar position with the Northern Pacific, General Palmer was anxious to start life anew with what appeared to be a very promising Western industry.

Few, if any, of the former soldiers returned to civilian life with better prospects. Using his previous railroad experience as private secretary to J. Edgar Thomson of the Pennsylvania line, Palmer made himself available to a business whose expansion would match any other in the postwar boom. It was with careful consideration that he chose the Union Pacific's Eastern Division, a road being built across the plains of Kansas and one that soon would adopt the optimistic name of Kansas Pacific. Because he foresaw, quite correctly, that the West offered enormous opportunities for enterprising individuals who were qualified to act as agents for eastern capitalists, he accepted the treasurership of the road, along with the post of secretary-treasurer of the construction company that proposed to build it.

Originally, it was planned that the Union Pacific's Eastern Division would connect with the main line at the Hundredth Parallel, somewhere in the vicinity of Fort Kearny, Nebraska, but the enthusiasm of the road builders, spurred by the pleas of Denver for a direct connection with the East, resulted in the decision to build to that mining capital. During 1867 surveys were made across the plains; and that fall, advance parties, over which Palmer had general charge, were sent forth to choose a route west of the Rio Grande River to the Pacific coast in anticipation of a transcontinental road. It was here, while trying to choose between a route along the Thirty-Second Parallel or the Thirty-Fifth Parallel, that he became acquainted with the American Southwest. This region of the arid West was still a victim of the "desert theory" fixed upon the land by army explorers Zebulon Pike and Stephen Long over a half-century earlier. Palmer freely admitted that "the western half of the continent is not an agricultural Paradise," but he held that "it is far from being a desert, as many have supposed." Although much of the plains and mountain country was regarded as unsuitable for agriculture, the General believed that "there are frequent and extensive districts of great attraction to the farmer." He correctly foresaw the possibilities of irrigation, and even recognized the potential for "dry land" farming. His statement that "the quality of wheat grown in these elevated valleys and dry atmosphere is most highly prized" anticipated the later development of hard, high-protein wheat so much in demand by a milling industry that was to expand enormously in the years to come.

More generally accepted at the time was his assertion that there existed "one vast, uninterrupted belt of uniformly superior pasturage, extending from Kansas to the Pacific Ocean, on which horses, mules, cattle, and sheep can be raised in countless herds, as cheaply, perhaps, as anywhere in the world." In the early seventies this was being demonstrated by the rapid spread of the cattleman's frontier. Well recognized, too, was the vast mineral wealth of the West; but Palmer was interested in that which he called the "useful" as well as the "precious," and he spoke of the coal and iron to be had in this mountain fastness. As a railroad man interested in a long-term investment, he pondered the extent of this wealth: "When it is remembered how little and how carelessly this vast territory, the home of savage Indians, has been explored by white men, and that, even in the small and old-settled district of Cornwall, where mining was carried on before the Christian era, and where the earth has been burrowed for ages at a great depth, new discoveries are still made of tin and copper lodes, we may well wonder at the amount of hidden treasures which the few disclosures already made would indicate."[2] Enthusiastically, he reported that while the population of these parts was still small, the potential was great. Certainly, he argued, a line built through a country that was possessed of both agricultural and mining resources would be profitable.

Congress did not share the road projectors' enthusiasms and declined to provide the necessary subsidy to build on to the Pacific along the Thirty-Fifth Parallel, as Palmer had urged. Nevertheless, by the fall of 1870 Denver had welcomed the tracks of the Kansas Pacific and

2. William A. Bell, *New Tracks in North America* (London, 1870), pp. 497–98, quoting Gen. Palmer.

realized its ambition of a connection with the Missouri River. The "Queen City of the Plains" would have to wait another sixty-four years for the opening of a line due west to California. Meanwhile, the Kansas Pacific people were obliged to satisfy their desires for a transcontinental route by making a connection with the Union Pacific, at Cheyenne.

Palmer, who was not yet thirty-five years old, cut himself loose from his employers and struck out on his own. His almost passionate defense of the country south of Denver, offered in the official report on the Thirty-Fifth Parallel route, had revealed him as a man of vision reminiscent of Colorado's former Governor Gilpin, who had for years talked in glowing terms of railroad opportunities in the West. In Palmer the business leaders of Denver found a friend and an earnest booster. Alexander Hunt and former Governor John Evans welcomed him and shared his excitement over the prospects for Colorado. The latter quite frankly admitted that "Colorado without railroads, is comparatively worthless."[3]

Palmer's desire to build a road along the mountain front south of Denver was revealed privately months before the Kansas Pacific line reached that city. After trying, without avail, to persuade the directors of the company to build up the rich Arkansas valley to Pueblo and then north to Denver, the enthusiastic promoter determined to stake out the claim for himself. It was a man-sized undertaking for the slender young war veteran, one that would run into millions of dollars, and all he had to offer was the burning zeal of a crusader and a hope that those with funds to invest would see the light and sign the pledge. There was no difficulty in obtaining an enthusiastic hearing in Colorado, but what was most needed now was eastern or European

3. The best account of Palmer's early days in the West is found in George L. Anderson, *General William J. Palmer: A Decade of Colorado Railroad Building, 1870–1880* (Colorado Springs, 1936). See also Owen Meredith Wilson, "A History of the Denver and Rio Grande Project, 1870–1901" (dissertation, University of California, 1942); Samuel Donald Mock, "Railroad Development in the Colorado Region to 1880" (dissertation, University of Nebraska, 1938); Paul Stewart Logan, "The History of the Denver and Rio Grande Railway, 1871–1881" (master's thesis, University of Colorado, 1931). Part of this last work appeared in Paul S. Logan, "Building the Narrow Gauge from Denver to Pueblo," *Colorado Magazine*, 8 (1931), 201–08. The Colorado Springs *Weekly Gazette* for Aug. 6, 1896, devotes the entire issue to an historical reminiscence of the town's founding. One of the articles was written by W. J. Palmer. Herbert O. Brayer's *William Blackmore: Early Financing of the Denver & Rio Grande Railway and Ancillary Land Companies, 1871–1878* (Denver, 1949) describes initial financing efforts.

money, in quantity. With this in mind Palmer traveled eastward in
the spring of 1869.

As his train left St. Louis and angled across Illinois, Palmer fell
into conversation with a well-dressed fellow passenger who displayed
a willingness to listen and to talk about the West. In the course of the
talk the stranger introduced himself as William Proctor Mellen, a New
York attorney and a man of many connections. For example, Mellen
was closely acquainted with Salmon Chase, who had been Lincoln's
wartime Secretary of the Treasury. Both Mellen and Chase knew
William Blackmore, the British financier who had invested some of
his money in Southern Colorado real estate. There were possibilities
out in the Rockies, the attorney admitted; perhaps he could be of
some assistance to the young man suffering from railroaditis.

It was a casual offer which might never have come to anything had
it not been for an additional quirk of fate. As the men fell deeper into
railroad talk, they were joined by Mellen's nineteen-year-old daughter, "a small demurely-elegant, snub-nosed creature with a low musical
voice," who was introduced to the dapper young bachelor lately from
Colorado.[4] Her name was Mary Lincoln Mellen, but she went by the
nickname Queen. Palmer, who was aspiring to the title Railroad
King, took one long look and decided that royal life wouldn't be
worth living without this particular queen. Before the train reached
Cincinnati, Mellen's daughter had acquired another ardent suitor,
one who knew what he wanted and who in this case pursued his quest
until he won it. He followed the Mellens all the way to their home in
Flushing, Long Island, and stayed on as a house guest until Queen
consented to an engagement. Then he headed west once more, his
brain awhirl with plans for a railroad of his own and a castle for Queen
at the foot of the Rockies. No wonder folk in Colorado said the young
veteran was a go-getter.

During the remaining months of 1869 he crisscrossed the plains,
finishing his work with the Kansas Pacific, and with each view of the
land along the Rockies he became more enamored with the idea of
a north–south line in that vicinity. His letters to Queen were filled
with talk of the West. "Life has never seemed *straighter* to me than
when, not for recreation but in the course of regular duties, I have
been thrown on the Plains," he told her. And the mountains. He de-

4. Marshall Sprague, *Newport in the Rockies: The Life and Good Times of Colorado
Springs* (Denver, Sage Books, 1961), p. 21.

1. General William Jackson Palmer. Builder of the Denver and Rio Grande Railway.

scribed a recent morning when he had arisen, approached the window, and "a sight burst upon me which was worthy of God's own day. The Range, all covered with snow, arose, pure and grand, from the brown plains. As I looked I thought, 'Could one live in constant view of these grand mountains without being elevated by them into a lofty plane of thought and purpose?' "

Covetously, he eyed the country around the tawdry little village of Colorado City and foresaw much more than a group of men grubbing the land for a living. "Near here are the finest springs of soda—and the most enticing scenery. I am sure there will be a famous resort here soon after the R.Rd. reaches Denver. The scenery is even finer South of Denver than North of it, and -besides, the grass is greener, there is more water, a little forest of pine occasionally, and the sight is gladdened by the rude but comfortable farm houses, which are dotted almost continuously from the Arkansas to the Platte."[5]

The idea of living in this new country became an obsession with him. He had, as the Texans called it, "Mustang Fever." The West was in his blood; his mind was filled with the future of this relatively untouched land of promise. On January 17, 1870, he finally came out with it, fixed his plans on paper, and set a course from which he never strayed. "I had a dream last evening while sitting in the gloaming at the car window," he wrote to Queen. "I mean a wide-awake dream. Shall I tell it to you? I thought how fine it would be to have a little railroad a few hundred miles in length, all under one's own control with one's friends, to have no jealousies and contests and differing policies, but to be able to carry out unimpeded and harmoniously one's views in regard to what ought and ought not to be done. In this ideal railroad all my friends should be interested, the most fitting men should be chosen for different positions, and all would work heartedly and unitedly towards the common end."

He went on, listing old comrades-in-arms, personal acquaintances, and men whose qualities he admired, who would serve in administrative capacities. Then there were the lower ranks, the workers who would operate the equipment, "a host of good fellows from my regiment," to become engineers, mechanics, conductors, brakemen, clerks, agents. "Then I would have every one of these, as well as every other employee on the Road, no matter how low his rank, interested in the

5. John S. Fisher, *Builder of the West: The Life of General William Jackson Palmer* (Caldwell, Idaho, Caxton Printers, 1939), pp. 162, 178.

stock and profits of the line—so that each and all should feel as if it were their own business and that they were adding to their store and growing more prosperous along with the Road. They should feel as if it were their own Road and not some stranger soulless corporation. How impossible would be peculation, waste, careless management on 'Our Road.' "[6]

Palmer, the businessman, was also a social planner, and out West he would build his Utopian society. There would be, he promised Queen, "a nice house-car made, just convenient for you and me . . . to travel up and down when business demanded, and this car should contain every convenience of living while in motion; but everything would go along so smoothly that it would not be necessary to devote a very large proportion of the time to business. About five hours each day would suffice." This was not all. The whole organization would be a happy one. "It would be quite a little family," he dreamed on, "and everybody should be looked after to see that there was no distress among the workmen and their families—and schools should be put up for them, and bath-houses, and there should be libraries and lectures, and there would never be any strikes or hard feelings among the labourers toward the capitalists, for they would all be capitalists themselves in a small way, and those savings they should be furnished with opportunities of investing in and along the Road, so that all their interests should be the same as their employers'. " He set himself apart from many an exploiter of natural resources of the late nineteenth century when he concluded: "But my dream was not all of a new mode of making money, but of a model way of conjoining that with usefulness on a large scale, solving with it a good many vexed social problems."[7]

By the spring of 1870 Palmer had persuaded Mellen and Queen to come out and have a look. Colonel William H. Greenwood, chief engineer of the Kansas Pacific, joined the party and together they visited Colorado City near the future location of Colorado Springs. Enthusiastically, the dreamer of railroads pointed out to his guests that a line along the canyon mouths that opened from the mountains onto the plains, with branches reaching into the valleys, was certain to catch the traffic passing to and from the mines. His arguments were so powerful that he convinced himself all over again of the invulner-

6. Ibid., p. 177.
7. Ibid., pp. 177–78.

ability of his scheme. He was more than ever determined to push ahead with it.

When the party returned to Denver, Palmer persuaded his friends A. C. Hunt, F. Z. Salomon, and Irving Howbert to organize a dummy railroad company to hold the field for him until he was in a position to perfect his own plans. Next, he turned to the acquisition of land. Much of the country along the mountains was "offered land"—that is, subject to private entry—and on some of it people had already taken up claims. Since land, the value of which would rise with the coming of the road, was to be one of the bases for financial support of the whole project, it was necessary to acquire title to as much of it as possible before publicly announcing his plan. Accordingly, Hunt and Howbert covered the ground between Denver and Colorado City, to determine what part of it would be valuable, after which the latter embarked upon a buying trip, obtaining the necessary relinquishments for next to nothing. Then the property was purchased from the federal government with agricultural scrip, which was also very cheap. The site upon which Colorado Springs was built sold for eighty cents an acre.[8] The right of way for the roadbed itself was gained from the United States government by a direct charter conveying to the company a strip two hundred feet wide with twenty-acre tracts for depot purposes at ten-mile intervals.

By the late summer of 1870, with the Kansas Pacific finished to Denver, Palmer was ready to pursue actively his plans for the construction of his own railroad running south of Denver to El Paso. On October 24 he wrote to William Mellen, "We are determined to put through the N. and S. Line immediately . . . I have a very tempting plan of Pool ready, and will vouch for the ready paying from the start; expecting to live along this line and to make a speciality of this railroad system, I shall undertake to make it a success."[9] To show he had something more to offer than enthusiasm, Palmer revealed that Wilson Waddingham, a New Mexico land speculator, had just called upon him, at which time the young railroader "invited him to put in his money, which he did at once to the extent of $50,000, and authorized me besides to sell his Maxwell [Land Grant] stock while abroad and

8. Irving Howbert, *Memories of a Lifetime in the Pike's Peak Region* (New York, 1925), pp. 220–22.

9. Fisher, *Builder of the West*, pp. 192–93. Anderson, pp. 53–54.

put the proceeds into our little railroad." This would raise perhaps another quarter of a million dollars, enough to assure a successful beginning.

With Waddingham's cooperation secured, Palmer returned to Philadelphia to talk to some wealthy Quakers of his acquaintance. On November 5 he sat down with a group calling itself, quite appropriately, the "Colorado Construction Company, Friends," and discussed the progress of the new railroad venture in the Rockies. Then he hurried on to Flushing, where Queen was waiting, and there they were married. Two days later he and his bride were aboard the SS *Scotia* bound for Liverpool, where Dr. William A. Bell was anxiously awaiting them.

Young Dr. Bell, along with thousands of other nineteenth-century Britishers, was fascinated by the American West. He had turned up at St. Louis about the time the Kansas Pacific surveys were getting under way and, through the influence of some of his friends in Philadelphia, had "managed" a place on the expedition. By the time he had made his wishes known, the only vacancy was that of photographer, but determined not to be left behind, he utilized the two weeks available to him to learn something about his new profession. Fortunately, he did not have to show the results of his efforts, for after the group was in the field only a few days, the expedition physician went home, leaving that post open. It was at St. Louis, while preparing for the Western adventure, that Bell and Palmer first met. They became lifelong friends.

Bell left the surveying parties at Camp Grant, Arizona, in the fall of 1867 to visit the Mexican state of Sonora and to determine "the feasibility or otherwise of constructing a branch railway through it to Guaymas." Already, the railroad bug had bitten the adventurous physician. That winter he rejoined the surveying parties at San Francisco, and in February of 1868 he started back across the continent, bound for home. It was almost impossible for the average British traveler in the American West to refrain from writing a book, and Bell was no exception. In the spring of 1869 he completed his, calling it *New Tracks in North America: A Journal of Travel and Adventure Whilst Engaged in the Survey for a Southern Railroad to the Pacific in 1866–68*. It was dedicated to his father, a wealthy London physician, and to General Palmer.

During the months that followed Bell's travels in the Rockies he

2. D&RG Locomotive Shou-wa-no. One of the D&RG's first freight locomotives, it cost the company $8,500.

3. D&RG's First Passenger Coach, 1871. A woodcut illustration of the *Denver*, widely used by Palmer for publicizing the "Baby Road" in America and Europe.

was in close touch with his American friend in Colorado, determined to be a part of the new and exciting project for a narrow gauge along the mountains. The concluding chapter of *New Tracks*, entitled "Emigration," clearly suggested the need for strong backs and alert minds in the new West, a place where British artisans would be welcome. Great Britain required a new equilibrium between the demand and supply of labor, said the author, "and wholesale emigration is the only means by which this can be accomplished." He suggested the establishment of a central bureau at London, to help those who wanted new homes, and the creation of a newspaper to be called "The Emigrant," whose function would be to publicize opportunities elsewhere. When Bell was not engaged in promoting emigration, he was circulating among his father's rich clients, attempting to interest them in a promising Western railroad investment sponsored by his friend Palmer. To those who were not interested in rails he described a proposed colony near the south of Denver, close to a little village called Colorado City. He wanted to raise a half-million dollars to create this residential outpost in the West, where Britons could settle down and enjoy a remarkably healthful climate in peace and quiet. In turn, he and Palmer planned to utilize the real estate operation in their railroad plans. This colony and other municipal creations would make excellent collateral for borrowing more money to lay more rails. It was of such things that Bell and Palmer wanted to talk when the *Scotia* reached Liverpool.[10]

Before Palmer made his trip back east and to Europe, he made serious study of the probabilities of success for his new venture. His close friend W. H. Greenwood of the Kansas Pacific, who was anxious to take part in the grand plan, assured him that the conception of a north–south railroad was both feasible and logical. The Rocky Mountain front, said the engineer, would cause all transcontinental railroads, except the Union Pacific, to alter their westbound direction in seeking an outlet to the Pacific. The new road, lying athwart these routes, would be in a perfect position to collect both through and local traffic from the large lines.

Alexander C. Hunt, now removed as territorial governor to make room for one of President Grant's favorites but still very close to

---

10. Bell's friendship with Palmer is discussed in the opening chapters of Sprague, *Newport in the Rockies*.

Palmer, supported Greenwood's notion that the country south of Denver was ideally situated for a railroad. From it came much of the lumber used in that city as well as by communities along the other railroads entering that place. Not only did the route intersect numerous roads into the gold mines, but along it were deposits of gypsum, as well as known coal veins. The climate, varying sharply as one proceeded south, was bound to attract pleasure seekers, and it certainly would yield a wide range of agricultural products. Finally, the line would tap the southern cattle ranges and offer transportation to remote military posts. Hunt, whose enthusiasm matched Palmer's, was quite excited about the promise of Colorado's future.[11]

Company officers agreed that the road's width should be three feet as opposed to the four-foot eight and one-half inch gauge used on most other American railroads. Their thinking stemmed from several sources. They knew that much of the line would run through mining country, where some of its branches had, of necessity, to be built by individual mining companies desiring service. By so constructing the entire line, there would be no break in service between points of supply and the mines. The narrow gauge also would mean cheaper construction costs in a terrain requiring considerable rock work, expensive excavation, and frequent tunneling. This factor was believed to be of interest to foreign investors—particularly British—who were familiar with this gauge. Since there were no other roads south of Denver, Greenwood pointed out that the initial use of narrow gauge by the Denver and Rio Grande Railway Company, as the road was to be known, would dictate its use by all subsequent lines in the region.

Captain Howard Schuyler, who was with Palmer on the Kansas Pacific project, helped to sell the projectors on the narrow gauge. During a recent visit to Great Britain he had interested himself in the Festiniog Railway of North Wales, whose short but steep ascent through the rugged Welsh terrain from Portmadoc on the sea to the slate mines at Blaenau Ffestiniog closely approximated the kind of construction the Rio Grande contemplated. That little line, part of which is still in use as a tourist attraction, was at the time receiving a good deal of attention from railroad engineers, who came from as far away as India and Russia to watch it in operation. Its chief engineer,

11. A. C. Hunt to W. J. Palmer, Oct. 30, 1870, in *The Denver and Rio Grande Railway of Colorado and New Mexico* (London, 1871), pp. 14–16.

Charles E. Spooner, had written extensively about the Festiniog, a two-foot gauge road, and had incorporated most of the information in his *Narrow Gauge Railways,* published at London in 1871. His favorable comments about the utility of a somewhat wider gauge than that used on the Festiniog—three feet, for example—encouraged Rio Grande projectors in their search for the ideal dimension. Robert Fairlie, an internationally known British railway expert, also wrote in glowing terms of the feasibility and economy of the "slim gauge," as American railroad men came to call it. Two feet or three feet, those who believed in it felt it was more efficient than that which later became known as standard.

Having settled upon the physical approach to the problem, Palmer next sought the advice of Samuel E. Brown, attorney, and engaged him to study the articles of incorporation to make sure no conflicting interests might rise up to complicate his plan. The field was clear, Brown reported. The Denver and Rio Grande had complied with the law and there were no legal obstacles in its path.[12] Satisfied, the General proceeded with formal organization.

On October 27, 1870, the certificate of incorporation for the railroad was filed. It had a capital stock of $2,500,000 and the main office was located at Denver. The board of directors consisted of William P. Mellen, New York; Robert Henry Lamborn, a Philadelphian who had served with Palmer during the war; Alexander Cameron Hunt, Denver; Captain Howard Schuyler; and Palmer himself. The announced route of the main line—to be very important in later litigation—was south from Denver to the Arkansas River near Pueblo, westward through the "Big Canon of the Arkansas," across Poncha Pass into the San Luis Valley to the Rio Grande River, and thence along it to El Paso. Seven branches were proposed, covering a good portion of the mining country and including one to Salt Lake City.[13]

A contract to build was let to the North and South Construction Company, of Philadelphia, on December 1, 1870. During that month it was succeeded by the Union Contract Company, a firm chartered by the Pennsylvania legislature and headed by Palmer's wartime friend Charles S. Hinchman. In return for building the estimated 875 miles between Denver and El Paso, the Union Contract Company

---

12. Samuel E. Brown to Palmer, Oct. 28, 1870, ibid., pp. 21–23.
13. Anderson, *Palmer,* pp. 54–55. Wilson, "Denver and Rio Grande," pp. 16–18.

was to receive $14,000,000 in first-mortgage 7 per-cent gold bonds, less $16,000 for each mile it failed to complete. It was agreed that the Denver and Rio Grande could also pay in its own capital stock or in any municipal, county, state, or federal bonds it could secure.[14]

Energetically, the management of the new road set about its task. Dr. Bell, busily seeking out prospective investors abroad, wrote to the English land speculator William Blackmore, in January 1871, "We are thoroughly in earnest about this enterprise, the grading has *already commenced . . .*"[15] During the same month Palmer published in London a twenty-nine page pamphlet entitled *The Denver and Rio Grande Railway of Colorado and New Mexico,* in which he told potential stockholders about the advantages of his railroad. The land along the Rockies was arable and well watered. It also contained coal, iron ore, fire clay, limestone, and building materials, not to mention the well-known deposits of precious metals. The road was bound to be valuable in supplying miners. "A population engaged in mining," he explained, "is by far the most profitable of any to a railway. A hundred miners, from their wandering habits and many wants, are better customers than four times that number otherwise employed." The high price of foodstuffs paid by these men would make farming very profitable to those who would come to till the soil.

It was something more than their "wandering habits and many wants" that interested mining men in rail transportation. The latter years of the '60s had seen the extractive industry sink into the doldrums as placer, or "pick 'n' pan," mining petered out and many an individual found himself unable to buy machinery to engage in quartz mining. As corporate organization took over, frequently sponsored and financed by British capital, transportation took on new importance. Heavy machinery, such as hoists, pumping equipment, and drilling equipment, was very expensive to transport by wagon; equally costly to move by such means was low-grade ore, bound for smelting

---

14. Denver and Rio Grande Railway subscription schedule, in William Jackson Palmer Papers, copies in Division of State Archives and Public Records, Denver. Copy of agreement with the Union Contract Co., in D&RG Archives, Division of State Archives and Public Records, Denver. (Note: Rio Grande archival material is found in two locations: the Railroad's general offices, and at the State Archives and Public Records. Unless the Railroad's offices are specified, all references to the D&RG Archives refer to the holdings in S.A. and P.R.)

15. William Bell to William Blackmore, Jan. 3, 1871, item 0158, William Blackmore Papers, Museum of New Mexico Library, Santa Fe.

4. First Building in Colorado Springs, 1871. "Little London," as Colorado Springs became known, started off in a modest way. This first building might well be called "Early American" architecture.

Dinner.

Monday   Dec. 25th 1871.

Soup.

Oyster.   Mock Turtle.

Fish.

Baked Mountain Trout.

Boiled.

Leg of Mutton, Turnipsauce. Corned Beef.
Puppee Ham, Champagnesauce. Tongue, Caper Sce.

Roast.

Turkey stuffed   Turkey, Cranberry sauce.
Beef. Chicken.   Ribbs of Beef Apple.
Elk, Cranberry sauce.   Pork with
Venison, Currant Jelly.   Loin of Beef Larded.
Leg of Mutton stuffed.   Veal stuffed.

Cold Dishes.

Aspect of Oysters in Jelly.
Corned Beef Pressed. Tripe with Jelly.
Tripe Salad. Chicken Salad, Potatoes Salad.
Lobster Salad.
Cold Slaw.

Entrées.

Filet de Mouton. Oyster Pates à la Royale.
Beef Tongue à la Britannic Mutton chop breaded.
Timbal, Macaroni with Cheese Beef à la Mode.

Relishes.

Worcestershire Sauce. English Club Sauce.
Tomatoe Catsup. Hardford Club Sauce.
Cucumber Pickled. Beets.

Vegetables.

Boston Browned and mashed Potatoes.
Tomatoes, Lima Beans, Green Corn, Succotash.
String Beans, Green Peas.

Pastry.

Cocoanut, Mince and Lemon Pies.
Sallielon Pudding, Tapioca Pudding Lemon Sauce.
Sherry sauce. Strawberry Meringues. Favorites,
Jelly Tarts, Silver, Fruit and Jelly Cakes. Strawberry Rolls.

Dessert.

Madeira Jelly. Blanc Mange. Apples, Almonds,
Walnuts, Raisins. Tea, Coffee and Chocolate.
English Tea Rolls.

260

5. D&RG Eating House Menu, 1871. Many of the early travelers complained of the fare offered in western railroad eateries. This one should have satisfied even the most particular. It is from the Rio Grande Railroad restaurant at Colorado Springs.

centers. In the new mineral frontier, railroads were to play an extremely significant role.[16]

Because of delay in receiving iron rails from Great Britain, the
first spike was not driven until July 28. Appropriately, it was Colonel
Greenwood, general manager of construction, who put it down, after
which solicitor Samuel Brown told the gathering, in a somewhat defensive vein, that the rest of the nation's railroad builders were using
too broad a gauge. He predicted that in twenty years the three-foot
width would be standard.[17] Behind his argument lay the sensitivity of
the company toward the constant criticism of the gauge it proposed
to use. It was so widespread that in the spring of 1871 the road's promoters found it necessary to print and distribute a circular defending
the three-foot width. On February 17, 1871, the *Daily Rocky Mountain News* not only reprinted the circular but wrote a sharp editorial
in its behalf. One of the principal criticisms of the narrow gauge was
the belief that it could not haul cattle successfully. The *News* denied
this assertion.

The ceremonies dispensed with, the tracklaying began in earnest.
By the first of September the little iron rails, weighing only thirty
pounds to the yard, reached out from Denver some twenty-three miles.
On October 21 they came to the brand new colony town of Colorado
Springs, and the seventy-six-mile first division of the Denver and Rio
Grande was presumably ready for business. All it needed was traffic.

Palmer already had thought about that matter. From the outset
he planned to participate in the establishment of a colony town near
Colorado City and to use it in support of his project. On June 21, 1871,
he signed an agreement with General R. A. Cameron, lately of the
Greeley Colony, providing for the establishment of a joint stock company with a capital stock of $300,000, to be divided into shares of $100
each. Property at and around the Springs, owned by Palmer, was then
to be sold to the new company, which, in turn, would sell a thousand
shares for cash and pay the proceeds to Palmer, who promised to loan
one-half of it to the company for three years at 7 per cent.[18] The president of the Colorado Springs Company was William Jackson Palmer.

16. Clark Christian Spence, "Robert Orchard Old and the British and Colorado Mining
Bureau" (Master's thesis, University of Colorado, 1951).

17. *Daily Rocky Mountain News*, July 29, 1871. Logan, *Colorado Magazine, 8,* 202.

18. Memorandum Agreement of June 21, 1871, signed by William J. Palmer and R. A.
Cameron, D&RG Archives, Division of State Archives and Public Records, Denver.

MAP 1

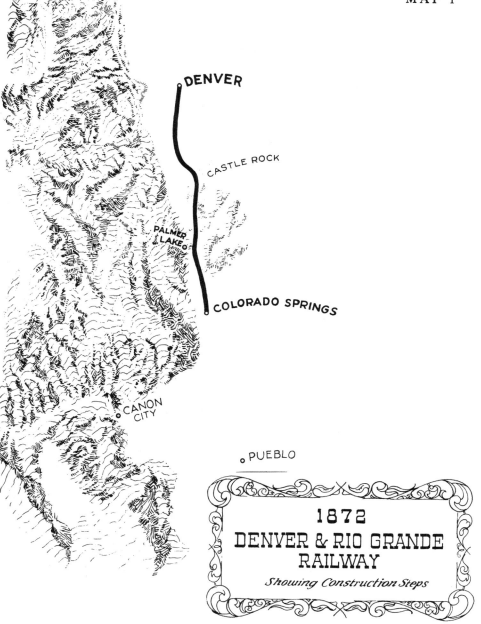

DENVER

CASTLE ROCK

PALMER LAKE

COLORADO SPRINGS

CANON CITY

PUEBLO

1872
DENVER & RIO GRANDE
RAILWAY
Showing Construction Steps

The colony's pamphlet propaganda was so successful, particularly in England, that the new village was soon to be dubbed "Little London." So rapidly did the newcomers arrive that manager Cameron had to send a rush order to Chicago for 150 portable houses to prevent suffering during the first winter. By early 1872, two months after the completion of the road's first division, Colorado Springs claimed a population of almost 800. Already there were a number of business houses, a newspaper, two churches, a reading room, and a proposed schoolhouse.

As they watched the Colorado Springs colony grow, the promoters made plans to duplicate the success all along the line. During 1872 Hunt reminded Palmer that they had connected with their own enterprise, "over a million and a half acres of land. The ostensible purpose for which these lands were purchased was for colonization." Why not send agents abroad, to Switzerland, Sweden, Germany, and particularly to troubled Alsace-Lorraine, to seek out "hardy husbandmen" for further colonization? Follow the example of the Mormons, Hunt advised. Offer the newcomers half-fare tickets, cheap lands, a healthful climate, rich soil, and a place to settle among friends. He thought company holdings along the Arkansas and in the upper Rio Grande country ideally situated for the land-hungry farmers of Europe.[19]

Regular business on the small railroad began on the first day of 1872, when the Union Contract Company turned it over to the new owners. It was an immediate success. Before the day of rail travel, a triweekly stagecoach, carrying an average of five passengers per trip, ran between Denver and the Colorado Springs area. During 1872 the Denver and Rio Grande carried 25,168 passengers, an average of 484 weekly. With a great deal of pride, General Palmer pointed out that this was an increase of 1500 per cent. During that year the road hauled over 46,000 tons of freight, most of which was commercial, the rest construction materials. Among the freight items were wool, hides, furniture, hay, wagons, agricultural implements, groceries, iron, nails, hardware, grain, lumber, cordwood, stone, lime, cattle, sheep, coal, and mining machinery. The pineries along the divide, south of Denver, added a good deal to the traffic. Palmer wrote: "Their produce is shipped both ways over the railroad, and the demand is rapidly in-

19. A. C. Hunt to W. J. Palmer, Nov. 9, 1872, William A. Bell Papers, Division of State Archives and Public Records, Denver.

creasing for all the requirements of a new country without trees on the plain, and rapidly filling up with towns and farmhouses. There are about 20 saw-mills along the completed line." Then, there were the coal mines near Canon City, not quite reached during 1872. They held great promise as a source of locomotive fuel. Palmer never tired of essaying upon Colorado's resources and its brilliant future.[20]

The General had a right to boast. When he began his project in 1870, Denver was a small place of 4800 people. North and west of the city lay Golden and Boulder, little towns that would grow slowly. To the south there was Colorado City, with perhaps 300 residents, with another five or six hundred scattered along the mountain base toward Trinidad. The region's real metropolis was Santa Fe, an old and well-established commercial point of around 8,000 residents.[21]

By the end of 1872 Palmer claimed that in two years Pueblo's population had jumped from 500 to 3500, and that Colorado Springs was already a thriving city of 1500, having grown almost 100 per cent during the year. Trinidad, he said, now had 1100 people, while Denver was a relatively large city of 15,000. Even with allowance for some exaggeration on the promoter's part, population figures had mounted noticeably with the coming of the major railroads to the Denver area. Unquestionably, the plans of the Rio Grande and the excellence of its projectors' salesmanship had advertised the region south of Denver. All over the West, emigrant families followed the rail routes to make their new homes. They would come in great numbers to live along the little narrow gauge.

Newcomers watched the operations of the new road with interest. It gave them a feeling of satisfaction to see the tiny *Montezuma* or the *Cortez* moving across the foothills, pulling their thirty-five-foot by seven-foot passenger cars. Divided into two apartments, the cars had double seats on one side of the aisle and single seats on the other, with the arrangement reversed in each apartment to preserve balance. They weighed only 12,000 pounds. Interesting also were the somewhat larger freight engines, with names like *Tabi-wachi, Ouray, Shou-wa-no*, costing $8500 each. They pulled either the eight-wheeled truck-

20. *First Annual Report of the Board of Directors of the Denver and Rio Grande Railway to the Stockholders* (April 1, 1873), p. 9.

21. Arthur Ridgway, "Denver and Rio Grande: Development of Physical Property in Chronological Narrative" (MS, 1921), p. 2.

type freight car, twenty-four feet in length or the tiny, twelve-foot four-wheeled cars.

These were small beginnings, but Coloradans were proud of what they called "the Baby Road." Even though it used a mule instead of a switch engine and its first schedule was no more than a plain piece of paper upon which the superintendent of the road himself affixed departure and arrival times, a start had been made. And it was not an easy beginning. Tracklaying to Colorado Springs was completed in the fall of 1871, but before it could be ballasted or surfaced, severe winter weather had stopped the work. Even after the first of the year, when trains began running regularly, the roadbed was soft and unreliable. Added to these difficulties, the gradient on the first division was heavy and the curvature sharp. The ascent of 2,000 feet and descent of 1300 made construction more costly than had been anticipated. The newness of track, the experimental character of the rolling stock, high shop and other labor costs, and the expensive, inferior coal that had to be used before the Canon City area mines were reached added to the complexities surrounding the initiation of the venture.

On January 1, 1872, the day regular service to Colorado Springs was inaugurated, grading commenced on the second division toward Pueblo, 118 miles south of Denver. Connection with Pueblo was not an announced part of the original plan. The charter talked of building south toward the Arkansas River, to the Labran coal fields in the vicinity of Canon City and "near Pueblo," after which the rails would pass through the Grand Canon of the Arkansas and seek the headwaters of the Rio Grande. Even after grading south of Colorado Springs began, the railroad company declined to reveal publicly its next immediate goal.

For over a year Palmer and his associates had studied the country to the south. Meanwhile, in March 1871, a mass meeting was held in Pueblo to discuss the possibility of a rail connection with Denver by means of the new line. Townsmen were agitated when they listened to a letter written by Alexander Hunt explaining that Pueblo was not on the main line because it would lengthen the route by twenty-five miles. The inference was clear that if they wanted a road, they would have to do something about raising money to assist in its building.[22]

22. *Daily Rocky Mountain News*, March 5, 1871.

During that summer, as southern Colorado pondered its railroad future, Palmer and Hunt continued their appraisal of the situation. In November, Palmer, Mellen, Lamborn, Greenwood, and Josiah C. Reiff organized a new land company called The Central Colorado Improvement Company, the purpose of which was to buy the Nolan Grant and other land. This large tract lying south of the Arkansas River, near Pueblo, originally was granted to Gervacio Nolan by Mexico. On July 1, 1870, Congress confirmed its title, but only to the extent of some 40,000 acres. Palmer and his associates bought it from Charles Goodnight, Peter K. Dotson, and Charles Blake.[23]

Excited by the knowledge that Canon City had approved a $50,000 bond issue to bring the road from Colorado Springs, and fearful of being left out, the people of Pueblo went to the polls in late June 1871 and voted overwhelmingly to assist the Denver and Rio Grande. During the following months, as the railroad officials negotiated for the Nolan Grant, nothing was said about the direction of their proposed construction. Stories made the rounds that the $100,000 voted in June by Pueblo was not a large enough sum. When a committee was appointed to press for a decision and word leaked out that it might even flirt with other railroads, Palmer was forced into action. Toward the end of November, Hunt came to Pueblo and announced that the narrow gauge would build into that city if another $50,000 in municipal bonds was forthcoming. This, he said, was needed to build a branch line to the Labran (Florence) coal fields. Reluctantly, on January 30, 1872, voters agreed to the final stipulation.[24]

Meanwhile, apparently certain of a favorable vote, the railroad had, on January first, arranged with the Union Contract Company for the laying of tracks to within a mile of the Pueblo Courthouse. On June 19, 1872, the first train entered the old Santa Fe Trail trading center. Shamefacedly, the *Colorado Chieftain* confessed that the Rio Grande's arrival was "accomplished so quickly and so cleverly, that but few of our citizens were aware that the road had reached town." However, Pueblo made up for its civic laxity on July 3, when an excursion train filled with Denver dignitaries arrived amid a thunder of welcome. The passengers were promptly escorted to the courthouse, where a banquet was served, and for those who could stay on there was a grand

23. Irving W. Stanton, *Sixty Years in Colorado: Reminiscences and Reflections of a Pioneer of 1860* (Denver, 1922), p. 178.
24. Wilson, "Denver and Rio Grande," pp. 42–45.

MAP 2

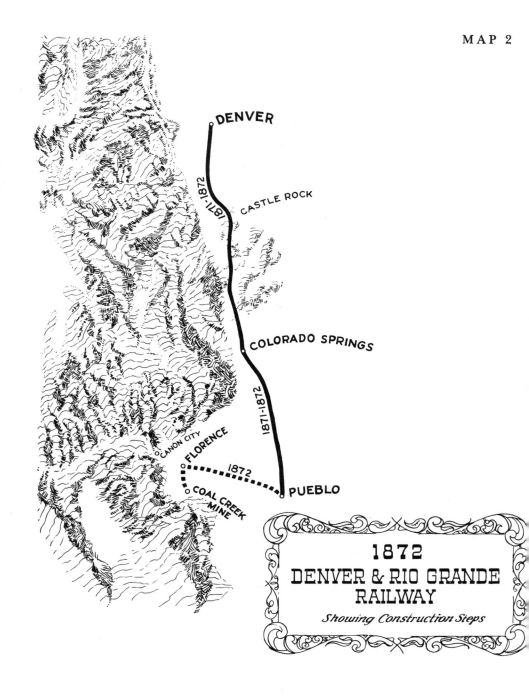

DENVER

CASTLE ROCK

1871-1872

COLORADO SPRINGS

1871-1872

CANON CITY

FLORENCE

1872

COAL CREEK
MINE

PUEBLO

1872
DENVER & RIO GRANDE
RAILWAY
Showing Construction Steps

ball. The whole affair, said the paper, "served to place Pueblo and Denver in closer and more endearing bonds of fellowship."[25]

The bonds of fellowship did not get a chance to cement. Palmer's organization, now in possession of the Nolan Grant, decided to move the Pueblo depot across the river to a new and favored company town called South Pueblo. Deeply angered by what they regarded as both an act of duplicity and a breach of agreement, the people of the county declined to honor the promised bonds. The railroad at once instituted suit, but the decision was unfavorable and the delivery never made.[26]

Despite what they felt to be a betrayal, Pueblo businessmen had to admit that the road was highly beneficial. With its approach, that sleepy municipality sprang into life and experienced a sharp boom. During 1872, 185 new buildings, worth approximately $621,000, were built. Forty acres on the north side of town were brought into the city, and South Pueblo, that child of the Central Colorado Improvement Company, attracted new settlers to the community. The latter addition was particularly stimulated by the railroad extension to the coal fields of Fremont County.[27]

Building the branch to the Labran coal mines, near Canon City, was commenced before the main line reached Pueblo. At a meeting of May 1, 1872, it was agreed that the Central Colorado Improvement Company would purchase $1,040,000 worth of the railroad's bonds and pay, upon receipt thereof, $825,000 in cash, or just under 80 per cent of the face value. The road builders promised to construct a sixty-five-mile railroad and telegraph line from Canon City, down the Arkansas Valley to the mouth of the Huerfano, east of Pueblo. That portion between Pueblo and the coal mines was to be in operation within a year; the remainder, by May 1, 1874. The Rio Grande further agreed to haul coal for the Improvement Company for 15 per cent less than that charged anyone else for coal haulage over its tracks for a period of thirty years.[28]

Dirt flew, and by the end of October 1872 a thirty-six-mile spur called the Canon Coal Railway Company reached the coal fields, ful-

25. *Colorado Chieftain,* June 20, July 4, 1872.

26. Stanton, *Sixty Years in Colorado,* p. 179.

27. Milo L. Whittaker, *Pathbreakers and Pioneers of the Pueblo Region* (Philadelphia, 1917), p. 110.

28. Minutes of the Board of Directors of the Denver and Rio Grande Railway, May 1, 1872, in D&RG Archives. Whittaker, pp. 108-09.

filling the long-desired connection with fuel supplies and an additional source of traffic. But the Denver and Rio Grande's eyes were bigger
than its pocketbook. When the Union Contract Company prepared
to turn over the new branch, Palmer and Company could not pay, so
the contract company retained possession of it until 1874. It was the
construction company, using its own funds, that finally finished the
stretch into Canon City.[29]

Completion of the branch to Labran in 1872 ought to have made
the residents of Canon City happy. It did not. They complained bitterly that instead of building on into the city, the Rio Grande graded
the road that far and then, with what appeared to be stubborn arbi-
trariness, refused to lay the necessary rails, apparently wishing to
spend the money capturing new and unclaimed territory elsewhere.
Palmer, of course, would not confess to them that he was unable to
pay for the already constructed part of the branch.

For about a year and a half Canon City experienced a depression,
and like a man dying of thirst with water just beyond his reach, its
people angrily viewed the nine-mile stretch of graded but trackless
space that separated them from a rail connection with Pueblo. Fremont County, which in 1871 had voted a $50,000 bond issue, was now
asked to confirm that decision and to add a like amount, as the price
of rail service. Rural inhabitants doubted that a railroad into Canon
City was worth that much, and even some of the townsmen objected
to the railroad's tactics. Nevertheless, in March 1873 a county election
was held, and while the result was favorable, the county commissioners
did not regard a majority of two votes as sufficiently popular enthusiasm to give their approval. Finally, in March 1874, the city held its
own election and agreed to the railroad's demands: $50,000 in bonds
and $50,000 worth of adjacent lands. Four months later, on July 6,
the first locomotive entered Canon City. The Rio Grande had held
out for its price and it had been paid, albeit with great reluctance.

Two of southern Colorado's important cities now had rail service.
But in gaining it a good many people in that part of the country felt
they had paid dearly. Time would reveal that the Denver and Rio
Grande's greediness was expensive, for the decision to go south,
through Pueblo, deeply disappointed Canon City. The die was cast
at a meeting of the Board of Directors, held on January 30, 1872, when

29. Minutes of the Board of Directors, July 17, 1874.

William Mellen offered a resolution to the effect that at least a hundred miles could be saved in building the main line by running south from Pueblo across the Spanish range, near the headwaters of the Huerfano or Purgatoire, instead of "going by the route originally contemplated up the Arkansas River by Canon City."[30]

Within a half-dozen years the whole picture was to change, and the Rio Grande, then extremely anxious to lay its tracks through the Grand Canon of the Arkansas, or what was later called the "Royal Gorge," was to discover that it had few friends in Canon City. Confronted by vicious competition from the Atchison, Topeka, and Santa Fe, Palmer would have to make the fight of his life to retain the narrow defile that offered the only logical passageway into the mountains for some distance. When the General looked back upon the events surrounding the entrance of his road into Pueblo and Canon City, he may have recalled a remark he had made in a letter written to his wife during their courtship days: "One thing I feel certain of—that amidst all the hot competition of this American business life there is a great temptation to be a little unscrupulous."[31] Southern Colorado felt that he had indeed yielded to the temptation.

30. Ibid., Jan. 30, 1872.
31. Palmer to Queen Mellen, June 11, 1869, in Fisher, *Builder of the West*, p. 154.

2. *I communicate with everybody I ever knew*

DURING THE DAYS of restless discontent, while the Canon City people looked in vain for their railroad, the Rio Grande management suffered from growing pains and financial depression.

The year 1872 was one of rapid expansion, and while the road netted over $100,000 in passenger and freight traffic, construction costs were enormous. Dr. William Bell did his best to raise money in

Europe, but had to admit to William Blackmore that "I find I cannot possibly obtain more than $250,000 (say £50,000) for subscription in England."[1] In his first annual report President Palmer fretted at the delay caused by building branches, necessary as they might be. "It would be better to finish the whole line to El Paso, on the Mexican frontier, as it could rapidly be done in two to three years," he told stockholders. "It takes practically no longer to get 650 miles of iron rails and joints out from Europe than 76 [the distance between Denver and Colorado Springs]; and this is the measure of the rapidity of building a road."[2] Like a small boy turned loose in a candy store, he was anxious to secure all the territory he could while the getting was good. If the people of Canon City were up in arms over delays, they would have to get over it and pay the price demanded for a branch line; Palmer was headed for Mexico.

From his standpoint there was good reason for haste. In September 1872, a scant three months after the Rio Grande entered Pueblo and while the Arkansas Valley branch was being built westward to the coal fields, the Kansas Pacific Railway had organized a subsidiary known as the Arkansas Valley Railway Company and asked Pueblo to support it so that the mainline might reach that city from eastern Colorado. Hardly had that proposition been received than representatives of the Atchison, Topeka, and Santa Fe turned up, under the name Kansas and Colorado Railroad Company, and promised to build into Pueblo much faster than the Kansas Pacific, with the help of local money. The result was that in January 1873 both propositions were voted upon, and to the surprise of the taxpayers, both bond issues carried, adding $400,000 to the burden already assumed.[3] Pueblo, like many a prairie town to the east, envisaged itself as soon bearing the title G.R.C., or Great Railroad Center. The railroad virus had struck the southern Colorado towns, and hard.

Ironically, what at first appeared to save the day for worried General Palmer was the panic of 1873 that struck down many major eastern corporations. The Kansas Pacific became so distressed financially that it had to drop out of the race, while the Atchison, as it was then generally known, was stopped at the Colorado line to await the

1. W. A. Bell to William Blackmore, Feb. 26, 1872, item 0478, William Blackmore Papers.
2. *First Annual Report*, p. 12.
3. Whittaker, *Pathbreakers and Pioneers*, pp. 110–11. Minutes D&RG Board of Directors, July 17, 1874, D&RG Archives.

abatement of financial storms. Many years later, Dr. Bell recalled that the period from 1870 to 1873 was a time of great prosperity for the young territory of Colorado. The assessed property value of the four counties through which the Denver and Rio Grande had passed jumped from approximately seven million in 1870 to over eighteen million in 1873: "Mining was active and the receipts of the new railway were entirely satisfactory. Immediately following this hopeful outlook came the panic of that year, which did not seriously affect Colorado until '74 and '75."[4]

Palmer admitted that the first eight months of the year were very good, the remainder being about as remunerative as the same period in the first year of operation. From January to August net earnings increased 160 per cent, but the late months seriously cut anticipated profits. The panic, he said, had not hit Colorado business drastically. Only one bank was unable to meet its obligation and it later paid off every dollar. While the business of transportation suffered because of the natural check upon immigration in hard times, the picture was not at all dark. Or so the president said. At a time when seventy-seven American railroads had failed, he was proud that his was able to meet all obligations and to show net earnings of nearly $200,000 during the panic year.[5] Privately, he hoped that while the Kansas Pacific and the Atchison were obliged to delay their expansion, his road could claim the territory south and west of Pueblo.

Publicly, the Rio Grande president revealed no worry about the approach of competing lines. In his report of April 1, 1873, he said that their arrival would merely settle country to the east and create additional markets for coal, lumber, and other mountain products. He reiterated the idea the following year, asserting that his line was built to tap the mountain trade and he had no objection to the coming of eastern roads:

> So far from feeling that this was objectionable we have considered it always as a decidedly advantageous feature in our case. The several east and west lines can only get this Eastern trade from and to its markets by passing it over a certain distance of the

4. Address by Dr. William A. Bell at a dinner given for the employees of the D&RG at the Union Station, Denver, Jan. 28, 1920. In William Jackson Palmer Papers, microfilm, Division of State Archives and Public Records, Denver.

5. *Second Annual Report of the Board of Directors of the Denver and Rio Grande Railway to the Stockholders for the year 1873* (July 31, 1874), p. 5.

Denver and Rio Grande lines. Preserving a strict impartiality, the temptation to local aggression by either of those companies would naturally be greatly diminished, and all would be benefitted. We have no quarrel to make, therefore, with any east and west line, and, so far from fearing their effects, we welcome them all, and will treat each as the most favored.[6]

Despite such professions of friendship, Palmer was very anxious to push on toward Santa Fe before any other road decided it was able to tap the New Mexican trade. In the spring of 1873 he wrote that New Mexico already had a population of 110,000, which was perhaps twice that of Colorado when the road was begun. Just beyond reach lay the Santa Fe traffic, which, he said, would nearly double the net earnings of the road if it could be reached. The extension of tracks south to Trinidad would attract a good deal of traffic, for that place was a common point on the Santa Fe trail and only ninety miles from Pueblo. But to insure the complete control desired, Santa Fe had to be reached.

Businessmen of New Mexico were more than enthusiastic about such plans. The Santa Fe *Weekly New Mexican* called Palmer a "gentleman of intelligence, character, wealth and large community interest with the Rocky Mountain section," and it watched the development of his plans with intense interest.[7] In the fall of 1874 Palmer and A. C. Hunt visited Santa Fe, giving assurances that the Denver and Rio Grande would be completed to Trinidad by the following spring and New Mexico could expect a railroad shortly thereafter. While the people of the region were said to favor the Kansas Pacific or the Atchison, either of which would furnish a direct connection with the East, they believed that the Denver and Rio Grande would be the first line to reach them. While this road would give New Mexico a more roundabout connection with the major roads, for the moment it was the most active one in the mountain West.[8] Already it advertised in the Santa Fe *New Mexican* that it was the "direct and only railroad to Southern Colorado and New Mexico, connecting with Barlow and Sanderson's stage line at Pueblo."[9] Santa Fe was calling.

6. Ibid., p. 13.
7. Santa Fe *Weekly New Mexican*, June 18, 1872.
8. Ibid., Nov. 3, 1874.
9. Ibid., April 21, 1874.

So were Galveston and Houston, Texas, both of which cities sought a connection with the Denver and Rio Grande. Such interest excited the railroad's promoters to renewed activity, and during 1874 plans were made to push on toward Trinidad.

The prospects were encouraging, President Palmer told his company's stockholders. By March of that year 156 miles of track were in operation between Denver and New Mexico. The five counties served had trebled, perhaps quadrupled, in wealth and population since 1870.[10] So far as home credit was concerned, no railroad in the western half of the United States exceeded that of the Rio Grande. Never, except for one month, had the road been obliged to postpone a payday and it always met its bills promptly.

By July 1874 forty miles of roadbed were graded between Pueblo and Cucharas. The Trinidad extension, when finished, would double the line's gross business at a cost of a mere $125,000 annual interest, wrote the president. Admittedly, the prospect for passenger travel on the new division was not as great as that farther north, but it ran through rich valleys such as the San Carlos, Greenhorn, Huerfano, Cucharas, Santa Clara, and Purgatoire, whose local traffic would no doubt be lucrative. The country south of Pueblo, between the Arkansas and the Raton mountains, was regarded as "probably the greatest grazing field in Colorado, already containing over 100,000 head of cattle, and nearly doubling annually." This, added to the coal, coke, and iron traffic originating at Cucharas and Trinidad, promised rich returns.

Already the Canon City steam coal was well known. In February, R. Neilson Clark, a mining engineer, reported that the Denver and Rio Grande used only a ton for an 85.29 mile run, while the Kansas Pacific, using Fort Scott coal, used a ton every 39.87 miles. But the Trinidad field, when opened, promised even greater things. Its excellent coking coal could be the basis for a whole industrial development in Colorado. "I have never seen a more valuable deposit of coal west of the anthracite region of Pennsylvania," the engineer told Palmer. It was Clark's belief that the Trinidad field contained the only coal that would coke between the Ohio Valley and the Pacific

10. William J. Palmer, *The Westward March of Emigration in the United States, Considered in its Bearing upon the Near Future of Colorado and New Mexico* (Lancaster, Pa., 1874), pp. 39–40.

Ocean, with the possible exception of the anthracite beds near Santa Fe.[11]

The most important immediate advantage of the Trinidad extension was the promise of all the passenger traffic and much of the freight business passing between New Mexico and the East, the freight alone being estimated at 10,000 tons. As a specific example of the need for additional trackage, Palmer related that in a single day his road had carried almost $1500 in government troop fares from Denver to Pueblo. Bound for New Mexico, these troops would have gone on to Trinidad, yielding another thousand dollars in revenue, had the road been extended that far.[12]

Friends of the Rio Grande agreed with all Palmer had to say about the urgent necessity of expansion. But despite brave talk about Colorado's immunity to the panic, it was a time of national financial distress, bound to affect such local enterprises. Fortunately, the railroad's traffic was largely local. This and the fact that it was assisted by the Union Contract Company and the Central Colorado Improvement Company made survival possible. Despite financial troubles, snow blockades in Colorado's capricious winters, and, in one instance, damage done by a wind that lifted a train car completely off the tracks, the little road maintained its schedules and offered the service it had promised.

There were those, of course, who thought the price was too high. The traveler and author J. H. Beadle said the railroad was familiarly known in Colorado as the "Narrow Gouge," in complaint of its passenger rate of ten cents a mile.[13] He and others preferred this to the more expensive and uncomfortable stagecoach, but criticism of railroads was coming into vogue as the national indoor sport and it made good reading.

Complaints against the narrow gauge were not reserved for more critical outsiders. As early as autumn 1871, at a time when formal service on the D&RG had not yet begun, farmer N. Z. Cozens told his brother that he thought "the Narrow Gauge is the poorest" and that the stage lines could make better and more correct time than the new railroad. He complained that every time the locomotive passed,

11. Report of R. Neilson Clark, Feb. 10, 1874, in *Second Annual Report*, pp. 26, 83, 84.

12. *Second Annual Report*, p. 63.

13. J. H. Beadle, *The Undeveloped West; or, Five Years in the Territories* (Philadelphia, 1873), p. 443.

it set fire to some of the bridges, "and it takes the ranch men, along the line, nearly all the time putting out fires." He saw no future for the road. "I think they cut a hog in the ass when they built this road, and I believe the Mexicans will run the road out of the country with their *Bull* teems. They can haul cheeper and can make about as good time, and are not running off the track all the time." He, too, was disturbed by the high rates and added that, in addition, "you must run all the risks of getting your neck broke." Still, he had to admit: "Ranches are selling up in the thousands, especially along the RR. We could take $3,000 for our 320 acres—nothing short up to 5 thousand will buy it."[14]

Nor did Colorado critics reserve their opinions for private correspondence. One of them, signing himself "G.B.H.," wrote from Colorado Springs that Palmer's road was not the unqualified success it was made out to be. The train to Denver was then (January 1873) running but one passenger car most of the time and it was frequently only partly filled. This, said the letter writer, was because half-fare on the D&RG was higher than full fare east of the Missouri. It was asserted that two men could go from Colorado Springs to Denver with a livery outfit and be gone two days, at the same expense as if they had traveled by rail, or they could go to Canon City from the Springs for two-thirds the cost of railway tickets. The letter disturbed editor Byers of the *Rocky Mountain News*, a strong D&RG supporter. He commented that if this were true, livery rates at Colorado Springs were no doubt a good deal lower than when he was last there.[15]

The hostile penman from Colorado Springs came storming back into the *News* columns a few days later, with facts and figures to prove his assertion. What use was the railroad, he inquired? Colorado businessmen simply could not afford to travel by rail at the present outrageous rates. He quoted the presiding elder of the Methodist Episcopal Church, whose work was primarily along the D&RG, as saying he would no longer travel by steam, so costly had it become. Mercantile men were said to agree with him. Rail-freight rates were so exorbitant that the dealers were going back to mule and bull teams to transport their wares. Finally, the local muckraker charged that the coal

14. N. Z. Cozens to William Z. Cozens, Nov. 5, 1871, in N. Z. Cozens Letters 1870–76, State Historical Society of Colorado. The comment on land prices comes from a letter of July 27, 1871, ibid.

15. *Daily Rocky Mountain News*, Jan. 23, 1873.

company at the Labran fields, a railroad affiliate, was charging $5.00 a ton to haul fuel to Pueblo, a distance of thirty-odd miles, but only $1.00 a ton to carry it north, and upgrade, the forty-five miles from Pueblo to Colorado Springs. No wonder Pueblo had grievances against Palmer's road, he said. Byers, always faithful to the railroad, again felt obliged to answer, but he had to admit, "We think their rates excessive, and their policy not as conducive to the development of the country as it might be." Nevertheless, he stoutly contended that the narrow gauge had contributed more to southern Colorado than any other single factor.[16]

That the feeling was persistent, and that "G.B.H." was not just a crank letter-writer, is indicated by the writings of an "Interested Spectator," who boldly attacked the Rio Grande in Colorado Springs' own *Gazette* during 1875. Some of that city's philanthropic men, he wrote, were so tired of the Denver and Rio Grande, which was "like a leech sucking the life blood of the town and caring not but to draw from it the last possible drop," that they had formed the River Bend, Colorado Springs, and San Juan Railroad, whose purpose it was to make a direct connection with the East by the Kansas Pacific Railroad. Such a connection, never actually accomplished, might have offered Colorado Springs more direct service, but it did not necessarily promise low freight rates. The entire West was paying a disproportionate amount for such haulage, and for the remainder of the century that fact would be a leading political issue.[17]

Complaints about the Rio Grande, in particular, continued on into the next decade. An Englishman who settled a few miles from Colorado Springs in the early 1880s wrote that the line's rates were so high that no particular benefit resulted from being near it. Farming was not profitable because it cost so much to market the produce. He repeated the charge that it was cheaper for passengers to hire a livery rig than to go by rail, and complained that while most roads tended to increase and foster travel, the D&RG was a notable exception. The

16. Ibid., Feb. 2, 1873.

17. *Colorado Springs Gazette and El Paso County News*, Dec. 11, 1875. In the fall of 1871, Foster Nichols, general agent of the DuPont Powder Co., wrote to D. C. Dodge, then general western agent for the Kansas Pacific, quoting an article in a Denver paper which said the freight rate from New York to Kansas City was 48¢ a hundred and from Kansas City to Denver it was $2.40 a hundred. He was willing to send 2 or 3 carloads of gunpowder from New York to Denver at those prices. Foster Nichols to D. C. Dodge, Sept. 5, 1871, D. C. Dodge Letter Books, Denver Public Library.

newcomer was undisguisedly disappointed in the management of the new road and did not hesitate to publicize his antipathies toward it.[18]

Palmer's enthusiasm was not dulled by all the tumult and shouting. He was a man with a mission, and he was determined to make his dream of a north–south railway come true. As early as the summer of 1874 he announced optimistically that the "panic is now over, and the outlook for the future is altogether hopeful." Colorado's extraordinary growth, only momentarily checked, was once again evident to him. Anticipating historian Frederick Jackson Turner's "safety valve" theory of the frontier's attraction during times of depression, Palmer expressed the belief that immigration actually had been helped by the panic.[19] He was certain that by the following year the eight hotels at Manitou would be unable to handle the flow of tourist travel.

The optimism was infectious. The Colorado Springs *Gazette* might print indignant letters such as those from the "Interested Spectator," but its editorial faithfulness to Palmer never wavered. Even in 1874, when times were still hard, the paper eulogized the narrow gauge, maintaining that in "every way . . . it has fostered the growth and prosperity of the Town, doing more for it than it is ever likely to do for any other place. . . . The self interest of the Railway Co. is the surest protection for the town."[20] A few months later the editor described an exhibition of fruit, received by General Palmer from New Mexico, and he predicted that "so soon as the Denver and Rio Grande gets into New Mexico, we shall doubtless have an abundance of cheap fruit, for a few hundred miles will take it into a semi-tropical climate."[21] On occasion, papers such as the Chicago *Evening Journal* printed flattering accounts about the road, and the *Gazette* was quick to publish them.[22]

Talk was not enough. It seemed clear to most people in Colorado that the D&RG was charging all that the traffic would bear—some said more—but still its income was not commensurate with its needs. Palmer had estimated that earnings for 1873 would reach $250,000, but "in consequence of the panic" they were actually just over $195,000. During 1874 earnings continued to slump with the annual

18. Edward Money, *The Truth about America* (London, 1886), pp. 67–68.
19. *Second Annual Report*, p. 10.
20. Colorado Springs *Gazette*, May 16, 1874.
21. Ibid., Sept. 19, 1874.
22. Ibid., Nov. 7, 1874.

return showing a net of slightly over $182,000. Even if the estimated earnings figure of 1873 had been reached, the Rio Grande would have barely broken even. Interest obligations on the main line alone amounted to $20,000 a month, or $240,000 annually.[23] With income falling behind interest demands by nearly $60,000 a year, rough financial weather ahead was indicated.

Curiously enough, Palmer showed no signs of shortening his sails. While he quite mistakenly supposed that failure on the part of the Kansas Pacific and the Atchison, Topeka, and Santa Fe to meet their own interest obligations precluded any early extension into the Southwest by them, he seemed convinced that he must expand, even in the face of financial difficulties. His work was at a critical point. He had the basis of a railroad system, but it was not yet extensive enough to attract sufficient traffic. He viewed the building of branch lines with mixed feelings. While they hindered the growth of the main line, they were necessary to it, for it was such traffic that Palmer originally had supposed would support his endeavor.

The larger dilemma, of course, was whether to retrench and ride out the financial storm, hoping to survive on what amounted to a monopoly of local business, or to keep building. Whatever thoughts he may have had about pursuing the more conservative course were quickly dismissed. To the east lay a twin-headed monster in the form of the Kansas Pacific and the Atchison roads, dormant for the moment but potentially dangerous. And then there was Palmer himself. He was not a close-to-the-vest player; it was his nature to plunge. There appeared to be no other choice but to go ahead and add enough territory to the line to assure success for the whole venture. He took that alternative without the slightest hesitation.

Early in 1875 the General and his wife went to Paris, where he hoped to interest the French in his railroad plans. The usual prospectus was formulated and publicity was commenced. At first it appeared that money would be forthcoming, but by summer it was evident that the new promotion plan was a failure. Returning to Philadelphia, Palmer continued his efforts, trying to raise a "pool" for the Trinidad extension. A prospectus marked "confidential" was prepared for Americans who had money to invest. It told, in glowing terms, of the rich and arable country that stretched for a hundred miles south of

23. *Second Annual Report*, pp. 6, 29. Colorado Springs *Gazette*, Aug. 14, 1875. *Railroad Gazette*, Sept. 15, 1876.

Pueblo, of its coal deposits, and of a great trade potential. At Trinidad the railroad would intersect a profitable wagon traffic that had to pay an average rate of about twenty-five cents a ton mile. Then there was the rich San Juan country of southwestern Colorado: "More rich silver lodes have been discovered there than elsewhere in Colorado or in any of the Western States or Territories."[24]

Undoubtedly, Palmer drew heavily upon Dr. Bell for his information about the San Juan region. Bell and the others were constantly probing the land along the projected route. The doctor wrote that the recent mining boom there had doubled local trade and had added at least 50 per cent to the trade of New Mexico for the year 1875: "Indeed, the trade of these counties had yielded to the freighters and stage coach proprietors that carried it during the past year, enough money to enable a railroad to either district to pay from its net receipts 7 per cent interest on bonds to the amount of $20,000 per mile of road. Such a condition of things is exceptional in the Western States, where very little traffic usually exists before railways have opened up the resources of the country."[25]

South and west of Pueblo, also, lay a real industrial potential in the Cucharas river coal fields, the prospectus continued. The Denver and Rio Grande had already obtained enough land in that vicinity to secure what amounted to a monopoly. In the heart of the region about 12,000 acres of townsite land were set aside, ready for occupancy, to be sold by the new Southern Colorado Coal and Town Company. "The towns of Trinidad and Cucharas will be no mere villages," the literature promised. "Besides having as a foundation the coal mines and iron and other manufactures, they will do the business of Colorado and New Mexico for an extensive area. No other points are available."

A memorandum agreement of June 30, 1875, explained in more precise terms the difficulty the Denver and Rio Grande faced. It frankly admitted that due to financial disorders in the United States and because of failure in negotiations with the French company, there was no hope of extending the road without additional inducements to the investors. Dr. Bell, upon whose shoulders much of the money-

24. Prospectus, Trinidad Extension, in William Jackson Palmer Papers, State Historical Society of Colorado, Denver.

25. William A. Bell, *Progress of the Denver and Rio Grande Railway* (London, March 10, 1877), item 1047, William Blackmore Papers.

raising work had fallen, devised a new scheme which, as before, involved real estate development that could be used to support the railroad. It was revealed that William S. Jackson, one of the narrow gauge's original officers, held in trust, for himself and others, almost 10,000 acres of land in Huerfano and Las Animas counties. Other parties owned between three and five thousand acres in the vicinity. On the usual premise that these lands would benefit greatly by the construction of a railroad to them, Bell proposed the formation of a land company, some of whose shares would be offered to railroad investors as a bonus.[26]

Jackson explained his part of the plan in a prospectus entitled *Trinidad Pool:*

> It was not until the Summer of 1875 that I was able, in connection with other parties owning large tracts of land in the vicinity of those owned by the Pool, to arrange for the development of the property by procuring the extension of the Denver and Rio Grande Railway. This was accomplished by the organization of the Southern Colorado Coal and Town Company, whose capital stock of one million dollars was issued as full paid in exchange for the lands in proportion to their actual cost without interest.

It was further arranged that half of the town company's stock be sold to the promoters of the narrow gauge, who used it as an inducement to capitalists in raising money for the extension of their tracks. As in the earlier case of the Labran field, the road promised to carry coal and coke to Denver and intermediate points for 20 per cent less than that regularly charged.[27]

During the hot summer months of 1875 Palmer worked steadily at the task of promoting his new pool. "So much hangs on it that it makes one's head whirl to think of the possibility of failure, the shadow of which has been hanging over us very close since the French failed and more or less, ever since the panic," he wrote to his wife. And then the blow fell. In July the house of Duncan, Sherman and Company, in which the Rio Grande interests had considerable bank deposits, failed. "Naturally this shakes confidence for a while in every-

26. Memorandum Agreement of June 30, 1875, in Minutes D&RG Stockholders, July 29, 1876, D&RG Archives.

27. William S. Jackson, *Trinidad Pool* (Oct. 20, 1876), Western History Dept., Denver Public Library.

6. Larimer Street, Denver, 1870s.

7. Railroad War in the Royal Gorge, 1879. The scene looks mighty threatening, but few of the warlike Westerners earned any battle citations in the affair.

one and everything," Palmer explained. "It is of no use to speak to people about new business ventures just now." Then he showed his incurable optimism:

> On the other side are certain compensations. I am very glad the French negotiations did not succeed, at least a half a million of the money would today have been in Duncan Sherman's bank and lost or practically so. So I am glad our new Pool did not get along faster here. A large amount of money would have been collected and deposited with Duncan's bank. On the whole these things are undoubtedly ordered for us better than we could arrange them for ourselves.[28]

On into the fall Palmer persisted, laboriously gathering subscriptions. "The Pool gains slow; I communicate with everybody I ever knew," he wrote. In September he explained to the land speculator William Blackmore that progress was steady, and admitted that there was enough money available to reach Cucharas but "[we] are desirous of compassing Trinidad before striking out." Even though the average subscription was small, the General felt that those who had contributed were "strong." He was now very hopeful of reaching Trinidad, where he expected to get "the whole of the New Mexican trade, worth with the travel about $100,000 per annum to us." Better still was the prospect of a rich coal business, "the dead center of our driving wheel."

It was a good time to build, he thought. Everything was cheap. Iron rails were being offered at Kansas City for $52 a ton. Under such conditions the $500,000 already raised probably would put the road to its immediate goal, equipment and all. That accomplished, there should be some dividends. Why, he said, even the Utah Southern and Utah Western roads, whose stock "is all water of course," were earning 12 per cent and they were not nearly so favorably situated as the Denver and Rio Grande.[29]

Palmer could not shake off the lingering fear that the Atchison Road or the Kansas Pacific might interfere with his plans. In 1874 he did not think either line would get to Pueblo for a long time. By late the next year it was obvious he had been wrong about the Atchison's lethargy. It was getting dangerously close to Pueblo. Palmer hurried

28. Fisher, *Builder of the West*, pp. 246–47.
29. Palmer to William Blackmore, Sept. 24, 1875, item 1013, William Blackmore Papers.

to Boston, where he tried to make an agreement between himself and
the other two roads that would eliminate any building competition.
Since his rivals viewed each other as two Kilkenny cats, he saw a chance
"of stepping in between, making peace, and getting the best permanent terms for ourselves, which will include the abandonment of all
the southern country to us."[30]

Neither of the larger companies was ready to abandon any territory
to Colorado's "Baby Road," but both were willing to cooperate with
it in regard to traffic. The Atchison reached Pueblo late in February
1876, at which time it made an agreement with the Rio Grande to
carry through traffic on to Denver. By this means the Atchison could
offer service to the Colorado capital in competition with the Kansas
Pacific road.[31] That September the Rio Grande made a two-year contract with both rivals, promising to divide all competitive earnings
between them.[32]

Dr. Bell expressed great pleasure over the agreement. Writing early
in 1877, he said that the "trade of Denver with the East has yielded,
during the last three years, more than a million and a half dollars per
annum to the Kansas Pacific Road, and there is no valid reason why,
for the future, this important and growing trade should not be shared
on an equal footing by the new and more southerly route, of which
the Rio Grande Road forms a link of 120 miles." He thought the
arrangement made with the Atchison and Kansas Pacific "as regards
the division of receipts in the through traffic are very favorable to
this line, for each mile of the 120 miles is to be considered equivalent
to a mile and a half as against one mile of the other roads, securing
thereby 50 per cent higher charges per mile."[33]

As the Atchison, Topeka, and Santa Fe approached Pueblo early
in 1876, Palmer poked his somnambulant road into action. For nearly
four years he had been able to do little but add the small piece of
track from Labran into Canon City. But the Atchison had now reached
one of southern Colorado's principal cities, and its very name warned
that it intended to tap the New Mexican trade. Before the end of
January, D. C. Dodge could write: "We are now laying track from
Pueblo at the rate of one and a half to two miles per day. Have all

30. Fisher, *Builder of the West*, p. 247.
31. *Colorado Springs Gazette and El Paso County News*, Feb. 12, 1876.
32. *Railroad Gazette* (Oct. 6, 1876), p. 438.
33. Bell, *Progress of the Denver and Rio Grande*.

the materials to complete road to Trinidad, and will be at or near that place by middle of March unless we should have extraordinary bad weather." He predicted that his road would be hauling freight to Trinidad by the first of April and wondered what "the merchants of Santa Fe think or say about shipping to that point?"[34] The interest of those merchants was indicated shortly before Dodge wrote. A Santa Fe paper reported that as business men watched the road approach Trinidad they willingly had bought about $20,000 worth of Denver and Rio Grande bonds.[35]

During the spring months the contracting firm of Moore, Carlile, and Orman worked hard on the extension. By the end of June, tracks had not only reached Cucharas, near Walsenburg, but a branch southwestward, toward the San Juan mining country, was already twenty-five miles long.[36] The decision to build into the mountains is another example of the westward pull exerted upon the main line. Its intent to move south of Trinidad, into New Mexico, was not altered, but the attraction of the mines was irresistible, and ultimately it would change the direction of the entire railroad.

Toward the end of April 1876 the Denver and Rio Grande reached El Moro, and the people of Trinidad experienced much the same disappointment their friends at Pueblo earlier had known. The new company town was located on the Purgatoire River, about five miles from, and in plain view of, Trinidad. As unhappy business interests of the older place watched the railroad's municipal creation mushroom into a thriving trading center, they resolved that if the time ever came when they could strike back at Palmer and his associates for this deed, the retribution would be harsh and unmerciful.

But the General had no time to worry about local annoyances. As before, he was bent upon larger results, and criticisms of his methods amounted only to minor pin pricks. As the Atchison Road threatened to resume its southwesterly course, excitement mounted among the Rio Grande men. In January 1877 A. C. Hunt wrote a long and impassioned letter to Palmer, urging him to hasten construction toward the San Juan country: "I fear your absence from the active field of work dampens your ardour and causes you to lose sight of the over

34. D. C. Dodge to Frank Ford, Jan. 29, 1876, *Weekly New Mexican*, Feb. 15, 1876.

35. *Weekly New Mexican*, quoted by *Colorado Springs Gazette and El Paso County News*, Dec. 11, 1875.

36. *Railroad Gazette* (June 23, 1876), p. 282.

towering importance of the bold push and a strong pull, for the banks of the Rio Grande." Just beyond the end of the road, he said, lay a million well-watered acres, awaiting nothing but the plow. Now was the time to strike.[37]

A few days later Palmer heard from his chief engineer, J. A. Mc-Murtrie. Go south, said the engineer. Take the road around Fisher's peak, southwest to Raton Creek, and then over the "7765 foot mountain pass" of the same name. By following this route at once, the narrow gauge could command all the trade in that country without fear of competition, for to threaten this territory rivals would have to build through 200 miles of barren country.[38]

Palmer tried desperately to comply with both recommendations. During 1876 he had pressed the San Juan construction to the limit. When the Union Contract Company officials declined to go forward without additional assurances of compensation, he made an agreement with them that further encumbered his already sagging financial structure. The Rio Grande promised the contract company $1,500,000 in full paid capital stock, plus $300,000 in first-mortgage 7 per-cent gold bonds, if it would build to La Veta. When that was accomplished, and if the bonds could then be negotiated at 75 per cent of their face value, the contractors agreed to build on to Grayback Gulch and to the upper Rio Grande River, as fast as securities could be negotiated. For the work from La Veta to the big river, the railroad promised to pay $1,132,000 in first-mortgage 7 per-cent gold bonds. To further insure their agreements, Palmer and his associates consented to leaving the new line from Pueblo to El Moro and the proposed Fort Garland division in the hands of the construction company, which was to retain the income from that trackage until May 1, 1878. If, at that time, the railroad could redeem its pledges, it was to receive possession of the newly constructed extensions.[39]

On into the mountains Palmer drove his railroad, up over La Veta pass, up above 9,000 feet, and down into the San Luis Valley toward Fort Garland. But his resources were running out. Payrolls were not being met and his men were in a rebellious mood. The best he could do was to promise to bring up the arrears to within four months and

37. A. C. Hunt to Palmer, Jan. 15, 1877, item 1172, William Blackmore Papers.

38. J. A. McMurtrie to Palmer, Feb. 6, 1877, McMurtrie Letter Book, D&RG Archives.

39. Memorandum Agreement of June 1, 1876, appended to Minutes D&RG Stockholders, Feb. 26, 1877, D&RG Archives.

MAP 3

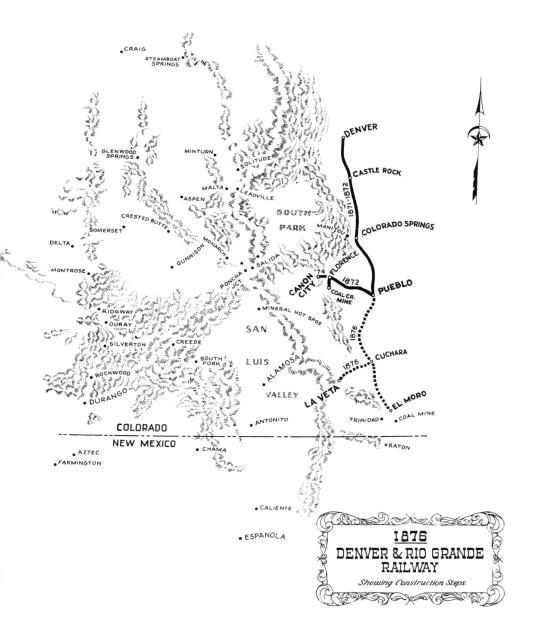

CRAIG
STEAMBOAT SPRINGS

DENVER

CASTLE ROCK

1871-1872

GLENWOOD SPRINGS
MINTURN
SOLITUDE

MALTA
ASPEN
LEADVILLE

SOUTH PARK

COLORADO SPRINGS

CRESTED BUTTE
SOMERSET

MANITOU

DELTA

GUNNISON
MONARCH

MONTROSE

SALIDA
PONCHA JCT.
'74
FLORENCE
1872
CANON CITY
COAL CR. MINE
PUEBLO

MINERAL HOT SPGS.

RIDGWAY
OURAY

SILVERTON
CREEDE

SAN

1876

CUCHARA

SOUTH FORK
LUIS
ALAMOSA

ROCKWOOD

1876
LA VETA

EL MORO
COAL MINE

DURANGO

VALLEY

ANTONITO
TRINIDAD

COLORADO
NEW MEXICO

RATON

AZTEC
FARMINGTON

CHAMA

CALIENTE

ESPANOLA

1876
DENVER & RIO GRANDE RAILWAY
Showing Construction Steps.

try to give them something each month thereafter until conditions improved.[40]

In April 1877 he turned to the bondholders and asked for help. He told them that since the road's inception, interest had been paid regularly on the $19,000 per mile bonded indebtedness up to the year of decision: 1876. The managers had gambled that an extension to Trinidad, accomplished on an issue of bonds at the same rate per mile, would secure the Santa Fe Trail trade as well as that of the San Juan section, "taking away the temptations to other lines to seek it." They had regarded the Atchison Road, by then connected with Pueblo, as a feeder line, bringing trade from the East, and as a market for Trinidad coal all along the unwooded Arkansas Valley for 500 miles. Hoping to take possession of a rich, virgin territory before anyone else could lay claim to it, the Rio Grande people had pushed on to Trinidad.

Now Palmer ruefully admitted that the plan had backfired. The Atchison Road, as it turned out, was not a feeder but a traffic raider. "We regret to announce . . . that during most of last year the Denver and Rio Grande Railway received neither the 'Santa Fe' trade nor the 'San Juan,'" the General confessed. Nor had the coal and coke business developed according to plan. The development of mines, the construction of ovens and other smelting equipment, lagged. Meanwhile, the Atchison, Topeka, and Santa Fe management watched the troubled Rio Grande road and found encouragement in its weakness. Increasingly apprehensive over the shape of things to come, Palmer had thrown his last resources into the San Juan extension, hoping that his westward flight would take him away from the threatened competition. To do it he had appropriated the money intended for interest on the bonds. In the spring of 1877 he confessed his sin to the holders of those investments.

Since there was no money with which to meet current obligations, the railroad management now asked indulgence of the bondholders. The coupons for May 1877 could not be honored. Would the investors be willing to fund those coupons, along with the next two, including those of May 1878? If they would deposit them in trust, the road would issue ten year certificates bearing 7 per cent interest.[41]

40. *Railroad Gazette* (April 20, 1877), p. 182.
41. Notice to the Bondholders, April 30, 1877, in Minutes D&RG Directors, May 3, 1877, D&RGW offices, Denver.

In making the request, Palmer exhibited his usual optimism and unbounded faith in the future. Already, he said, the New Mexican forwarding houses of eastern Colorado were moving to El Moro, a hundred miles closer to their home market. This was valuable traffic. Back in 1874 the Atchison Road had received 10,000 tons of freight when those firms were at Granada, and the Kansas Pacific had profited likewise at Las Animas. By the spring of 1876 the center of wholesale trade had moved westward to La Junta, where the two larger roads, by means of generous rebates, persuaded the merchants to remain for that season. Now to El Moro, a Denver and Rio Grande town, there should come between fourteen and twenty thousand tons of merchandise during the ensuing season.[42] Added to this would be the elusive San Juan trade. The president promised that the extension of the narrow gauge to Alamosa would secure it once and for all.

The bondholders read the arguments and agreed to wait for their interest. Denver papers expressed great pleasure at the decision and assured their readers that the "temporary financial embarrassment" of the pioneer railroad, arising solely from construction outlays and not the falling off of business, had now passed. Taking their cue from Palmer, they explained that unless the road could build its projected extensions, a lot of traffic would be lost. Already the Atchison Road was making itself felt at Pueblo, and even the ox teams beyond El Moro and La Veta were still formidable rivals. By moving westward toward the San Juans, it was expected that between fifty and seventy-five thousand dollars worth of business could be gained each month. To live, the road had to grow.[43]

While Denver urged on the little narrow gauge, hopeful of tapping southern trade, the ancient town of Santa Fe, New Mexico, watched its progress with even more interest. During the spring of 1877 Alexander Hunt and some of his associates visited the latter place, promising that steel rails would touch Fort Garland by July. "We wish he could have told us when it would reach Santa Fe," sighed the editors of the *New Mexican*.[44] Palmer shared that desire. As the road grew, slowly winding through tortuous country, the going became more

42. *The Denver and Rio Grande Railway: Prospectus of the San Juan Trade*, Feb. 1877, item 1179, William Blackmore Papers.
43. *Daily Rocky Mountain News*, July 18, 1877. Denver *News*, quoted by *Colorado Springs Gazette and El Paso County News*, July 21, 1877.
44. *Weekly New Mexican*, April 10, 1877.

difficult, physically and financially. In the original grant of land, set aside as right of way, Congress stipulated that the narrow gauge must reach Santa Fe by June 1877. Obviously, this was now impossible. By request, the legislators set aside that requirement and extended the time to 1882.[45] The whole plan was beginning to falter, and Palmer himself must have wondered if even the extended date would see his road to Santa Fe.

Then other signs of trouble appeared. In the spring of 1877 rumors began to circulate that the road's inability to pay its May interest would result in a request for the appointment of a receiver. By August, rumor became reality. On the tenth of that month Louis H. Meyer, trustee for the bondholders and a representative of interested Dutch investors, filed application in the United States Circuit Court at Denver.[46] It was the desire of those Meyer represented—probably the Dutch, in particular—that the affairs of the railroad company and the construction company be separated. The latter was to return to the railroad the bonds it had received, and if it did not, they would be canceled.

Judge Moses Hallett denied the petition on the ground that the railroad's affairs did not require legal interference. By the time the case appeared in court, the bondholders already had accepted Palmer's proposal to fund the interest coupons. Even the complainant, Meyer, admitted that company matters had been handled in a generally satisfactory manner. There was no evidence of mismanagement and not a hint of dishonesty.[47] Despite all its difficulties, a subsequent report was to show that the road netted over $357,000 in that troublous year of 1877, a figure that, with one exception, was the highest prior to 1880. It was true that for four years the line had failed to pay interest on its bonds and had declared no dividends, but this was at a time when dozens of railroads across the country were in similar straits. The court felt that, under the circumstances, the Denver and Rio Grande management ought to have another chance.

45. *Railroad Gazette* (Dec. 29, 1876), p. 573. *Weekly New Mexican*, Feb. 20, 1877.
46. *Railroad Gazette* (June 15, 1877), p. 273; (Aug. 17, 1877), p. 381.
47. Pueblo *Colorado Chieftain*, Aug. 14, 1877. *Colorado Farmer*, Aug. 16, 1877.

3. *A noisy but bloodless war*

As PALMER TRIUMPHED over his critics in court, made a temporary peace with the bondholders, and launched new plans for the extension of his narrow gauge, he appeared to have parried the most important internal threats to his command of the situation. He had not dismissed the potential danger from rival roads, but economic distress had so tempered their aggressiveness that there was some hope for a peaceful corporate cohabitation among railroads in the mountain West. By the latter part of 1877 Palmer and his associates were almost convinced that their company had a sufficient grasp upon the southern Colorado and New Mexican trade as to make successful competition unlikely. The San Luis Valley was theirs by virtue of an extension across La Veta pass to Fort Garland, and by early 1878 construction toward Alamosa would be under way. Santa Fe merchants watched with mounting interest as two narrow-gauge tendrils reached out like forceps from the North to catch their trade. The nearest, that which now approached Alamosa, was to swing down along the Rio Grande River, while a second, poking its way southward from El Moro toward Raton Pass, promised to cut through northeastern New Mexico along the old Santa Fe trail route. To a casual observer the road that the *Railroad Gazette* called the "longest narrow gauge in the world"—302 miles of it—appeared to be in command.

Actually, the Colorado Company was in serious trouble. It had reached the limit of its financial abilities and was unable to lay practical claim to the numerous extensions it wanted and needed to build. It was unable to conduct a two-front war, should the need arise, and when it headed West to capture the San Juan trade of southwestern Colorado so necessary to its existence, the Raton route had to be set aside for future development. So far as its plans for reaching Santa Fe at an early date were concerned, the delay at Raton proved fatal.

While the Rio Grande floundered, straining every resource to capture as much territory as it could under the circumstances, officials at the Atchison Road hovered about like vultures, waiting for a chance to swoop down upon its weakened rival. Palmer, an expert at playing for high stakes, tried to give the impression that he was dealing from a position of strength and was an equal in the game of grab. His real and only advantage arose from the fact that he held a temporary balance of power between the great Union Pacific–Kansas Pacific combine on one hand, and the oncoming Atchison Road on the other, each of whom sought control of northern Colorado traffic. Referring to the AT&SF, Palmer told David Dodge, "I think it just as well they should understand that we are the only parties now who they can trust to increase their Colorado traffic." His attitude toward Thomas Nickerson, president of the Atchison Company, was friendly but crisp and independent. He discussed freely the possibility of pooling efforts on the part of the larger roads and declined, before he was invited, to

join any such arrangement. Palmer carefully tried to keep aloof from
the pending collision of the larger roads, trying not to offend Nickerson while avoiding any corporate intimacies. He told his general manager, Dodge, that the best course of pursuit was to keep the Atchison
people, the only ones who were likely to build competitively, "comparatively satisfied while our plans are so inchoate."[1]

Toward the end of 1877, relations between the Rio Grande and
the AT&SF became somewhat strained, as representatives of the latter
road began to complain of the treatment they received at the hands
of the narrow-gauge company. When Nickerson himself wrote of the
matter to Palmer, the General was forthright in his answer. He said
it was his understanding that the AT&SF was about to appoint a new
general manager and he hoped that when this was accomplished, such
"a manager might conclude to offer his only western connection the
same price for all trade that it would obtain anywhere else, instead of
relying upon treaties with competitors which they are sure to be brok-
en in time." He pointed out that the Atchison Company was carrying
a very large traffic over Rio Grande tracks but was reciprocating to a
very small degree. So far as any charge of favoritism was concerned,
Palmer pointed out to Nickerson that he had "a pooling contract with
the K.P. under which you are acting. We have to act very discreetly,
surrounded by two such powerful allies & rivals. Although we gather
up & distribute so large a traffic, our share of the results is comparatively small."[2]

The Atchison's new manager was appointed in November 1877.
William B. Strong, forty-two-year-old railroader, was a man of some
twenty years experience, and his rapid rise in the AT&SF organization would soon see him in the president's chair. The selection of an
individual with such an aggressive nature and one of so many ambitions promised early action on the Colorado railroad scene. Shortly
after his appointment, Strong came to Palmer at Colorado Springs,
and in a disarming fashion blandly stated that the Atchison Company
desired only to connect with the Southern Pacific, and even that hope
was faint for the present, because of the enormous amount of money
involved. The new manager then proposed that the Rio Grande and
his line enter into some profitable, noncompetitive arrangement. He

1. Palmer to Dodge, Aug. 20, 1877, enclosing copy of letter from Palmer to Nickerson, same
date. Palmer to Dodge, Aug. 21, 1877. D&RG Archives.
2. Palmer to Thomas Nickerson, Oct. 10, 1877, D&RG Archives.

suggested consolidation, or if that was not agreeable, the leasing of the Denver and Rio Grande by the Atchison Company. Other alternatives included sufficient stock purchase to assure control, or at least an arrangement for exclusive trade with the narrow gauge. Loftily, Palmer demurred, saying that the latter idea was the only one his road would consider and not even that was acceptable at the moment. He seemed to feel that he was in no danger from invasion. "I think Strong appreciates what I told him as to their losing more than they would gain by building to any one of our districts," he confided to D. C. Dodge.

The conversation then drifted to the threat posed by John Evans' South Park and Pacific as it moved steadily toward Leadville and the lucrative trade of that booming mineral center. The men agreed to refuse any of the South Park's freight and to join in controlling the stripling company if it should become dangerous to them. Palmer volunteered the solution. "I remarked the surest & best way of controlling that trade is for us to join in building up to South Arks or Oro (Leadville)," he told Dodge. "Each to put up ½ of the money. He was much interested in this."

Strong agreed to recommend the joint effort up the Arkansas Valley to Leadville, but Palmer, after himself making the suggestion, began to entertain doubts. He was afraid that such a branch might interfere with the Lake City and Gunnison trade. This line of thinking took him to the notion of leasing all Denver and Rio Grande extensions at 30 per cent of the gross earnings. This way no single part of the road would be hurt by the partnership. He knew also that he was running a risk by such a venture. "Even joining on one short Extension would antagonize of course U.P. and K.P. & lose perhaps more than we would gain," he admitted. But if the Atchison people would put up $1,250,000 to help build the extensions, the risk of generating antagonism from Jay Gould's interests was worth while. The upshot of the conversation with Strong was a series of instructions from Palmer to David Dodge to continue negotiations and wait for the Atchison Company to make concrete proposals. "Keep this carefully & confidential or destroy it," he warned his general manager.[3]

While Palmer waited for a definite offer from Strong, he continued to investigate the possibilities of Leadville. The locality had come to

3. Palmer's conversation with Strong is found in a long letter marked "Private" and dated Feb. 1, 1878, file No. 343, D&RG Archives.

national notice in 1860, when the California Gulch gold discoveries were made and "Oro City" had taken its place as one of the foremost placer mining boom towns in the Colorado Rockies. However, within several years the diggings had played out and by 1867 Oro City was nearly deserted. The few miners who stayed on to run their sluice boxes, in hopes of making a living, grumbled continually about the "liquid mud" that clogged their equipment. Two of them, William H. Stevens and Alvinus B. Wood, took some samples of the offending "black mud" to an assay office, where they discovered it contained twenty to forty ounces of silver to the ton. This was in June 1874. They kept their secret well and took advantage of the ignorance of others to stake claims throughout the gulch, telling their employees they were getting just enough lead to make operations pay. By the spring of 1879 their properties had brought them around $200,000.

In the meantime, carbonate of lead ores were being shipped out of the region by an ore buyer named August R. Meyer, the first of which came from the Stevens–Wood mine. In the spring of 1876 some 300 tons of it went to St. Louis for processing. Another shipment, made in the spring of 1877, was of such high content that it caused comment among mining men.[4] Once the word was out, a new rush to the once-abandoned mining camp was on. In September, Palmer took his young chief engineer, John A. McMurtrie, and one of the company directors, Dr. William A. Bell, on an eight-day tour of inspection up the Arkansas and into South Park. They visited Leadville, where Palmer talked with mining men and the doctor bought a clump of dates at a little grocery store operated by the then unknown and unheralded H. A. W. Tabor, who soon would become one of Colorado's silver kings. Palmer returned, quite enthusiastic about transportation possibilities and determined to build into the boom town as soon as possible. He wrote an extremely long letter to his treasurer, Charles B. Lamborn, in which he fully described the freight potential of the area. In addition to the new traffic offered, he pointed out that his company was threatened in this part of Colorado by the Atchison, Topeka, and Santa Fe to the south and by the Denver, South Park, and Pacific to the north. "One line built up the Arkansas Valley should keep both off most effectually," he wrote. For less than a million dol-

4. Don L. Griswold and Jean Harvey Griswold, *The Carbonate Camp Called Leadville* (Denver, 1951), pp. 1–26. See also Charles Merrill Hough, "Leadville, Colorado, 1878 to 1898: A Study in Unionism" (Master's thesis, University of Colorado, 1958).

lars Palmer thought he could build the necessary extension which would thus drive off his enemies, gain new revenue for the Rio Grande, and put the terminus of the new branch within 350 or 400 miles of Salt Lake City, a further extension that he estimated would cost about $3,000,000.[5]

Now, early in 1878, he pursued his interest in the Leadville region. David Dodge, Robert F. Weitbrec, the new treasurer, and Charles B. Lamborn, vice-president, were asked to make further studies of the prospects for a move in that direction. Toward the end of March, Dodge brought in some startling news. Mr. E. Harrison, a mine owner at Leadville, who was then in a position to ship twenty-five tons of ore daily, was on his way East on the invitation of Strong. "They are determined to get his shipments of ore if possible," Dodge warned. "Mr. Strong is getting all the information he can with regard to that section, and, I believe, intends to make a move in that direction." And, added Dodge, the game was getting interesting, for Harrison had told him that if a railroad came into Leadville, the ore traffic out of that place would amount to at least seventy-five tons a day. Harrison himself would promise at least fifty tons a day at a rate not to exceed $10 a ton. "His business alone would almost pay to build the road," Dodge concluded.[6]

Both Weitbrec and Lamborn were enthusiastic about Leadville's freight potential. Weitbrec wrote that the Harrison Reduction Works would make a contract to move as much as 24,000 tons of ore a year from Leadville to Colorado Springs if rail service was available. This, he said, would exceed the New Mexico and San Juan trade combined.[7] Lamborn reported that the Harrison people planned to ship around 100,000 pounds of ore a day during the coming summer, by freight wagon, and they expected to pay $18 a ton to Colorado Springs and Canon City.[8] These were figures that would excite any railroad entrepreneur, and it was just the kind of traffic for which the Rio Grande had been conceived.

While Rio Grande officers contemplated the future of the Leadville

5. Palmer to Charles Lamborn, Sept. 15, 1877, in Carlyle C. Davis, *Olden Times in Colorado* (Los Angeles, 1916), pp. 85–99. *Leadville and Oro,* a confidential pamphlet (New York, 1878), pp. 6–19, D&RG Archives.

6. Dodge to Palmer, March 23, 1878, in *Leadville and Oro.*

7. Weitbrec to Palmer, March 28, 1878, ibid.

8. Charles B. Lamborn to Palmer, April 1, 1878, ibid.

branch trade and watched their main line lying south of that country move westward from Fort Garland toward Alamosa, from which point it was within striking distance of Santa Fe, there was cause for concern from another direction. On February 26, 1878, President Thomas Nickerson of the AT&SF authorized William Strong to go ahead with construction toward Santa Fe. Strong at once directed his chief engineer, A. A. Robinson, to get hold of some men and lay claim to the vital Raton Pass. Robinson promptly boarded a Rio Grande train at Pueblo and headed for El Moro where, late at night, he got a horse and pushed on to the home of "Uncle Dick" Wootton near the Pass. John A. McMurtrie, chief engineer for the Rio Grande, was on the same train and carried the same instructions, but unlike Robinson, he stayed over night at El Moro, unaware of the urgency of the situation. When on the morning of February 29 McMurtrie and his men arrived at the scene of his proposed endeavors, he was greeted by Robinson and a group of transients pressed into service, all busily engaged in what they said was railroad building. The little "armies" of Robinson and McMurtrie, about equal in strength, eyed each other for a while, and after some exchange of threats, the Rio Grande men moved and began to work on an alternative but much less desirable crossing at Chicken Creek. McMurtrie had lost the game by about thirty minutes. To clinch its title to the ground, the Atchison Company asked for, and received, an injunction prohibiting its rival from interfering with construction.[9]

Although Denver papers fretted over the possibility that both the AT&SF and the Rio Grande would build into Leadville, thus giving Pueblo, not Denver, all that trade, there did not seem to be any widespread belief that the Atchison people were so inclined, especially now that they had made their move at Raton Pass. A Pueblo paper stated positively that their proposed line up the Arkansas had been abandoned in favor of continuing the transcontinental line southwest-

9. The story of the seizure of Raton Pass and the subsequent conflict near Canon City has been told in a number of works. For further details see L. L. Waters, *Steel Trails to Santa Fe* (Lawrence, Kan., 1950); Glenn D. Bradley, *The Story of the Santa Fe* (Boston, 1920). James Marshall's *Santa Fe: The Railroad That Built an Empire* (New York, 1945) is a popularized dramatization. Cy Warman in *Story of the Railroad* (New York, 1906), devotes a chapter to the Royal Gorge War. Unpublished sources include: Wilson, "Denver and Rio Grande Project"; Mock, "Railroad Development"; and Logan, "Denver and Rio Grande." See also *Railroad Gazette*, April 26, 1878; Pueblo *Colorado Chieftain*, Feb. 28, March 7, 1878; Colorado Springs *Weekly Gazette*, May 5, 1878.

ward.[10] Outwardly, there seemed to be no emergency over the route to Leadville so far as Palmer was concerned. The Chicago *Railway Review* said that the Rio Grande would complete that branch sooner or later, and certainly not before the mines were more fully developed than at present.[11]

Palmer may have agreed with a Denver paper that the Atchison people were taking advantage of cheap Mexican labor "to play a game of bluff" at Raton, but his chief engineer, McMurtrie, did not believe it. He strongly advised the Rio Grande president either to build across Raton at once or to head south from Alamosa toward New Mexico with all speed. He was convinced that the AT&SF would be across Raton Pass and down to Las Vegas within twelve months.[12] That the Rio Grande was taking no chances on the possibility of a bluff is seen in articles of incorporation that were filed in Denver for the Colorado and New Mexico Railway Company, whose object it was to operate a railroad between El Moro and the New Mexican line, where it would connect with a road to be built across Raton Pass by the Denver and Rio Grande. Among the incorporators were Robert F. Weitbrec, Hanson Risley (general solicitor of the Rio Grande's Land Department), and William W. Borst, the railroad's superintendent.[13] This move of Palmer's came to nothing, for within three weeks he decided to call off the game and concentrate his efforts elsewhere.

The decision to abandon Raton Pass stemmed from Palmer's realization that he could not finance a traffic war with his larger foe, and from the hope that negotiation could be substituted for fighting. There was no sense, as McMurtrie later put it, of pursuing a "cutthroat policy of building two roads into the same country when there was hardly business enough to support one."[14] Another reason for pulling back was the mounting fear that the AT&SF might strike at the Leadville trade by building up the Arkansas, past Canon City. The directness of William Strong's methods was beginning to cause worry in the Palmer camp. On April 14 Weitbrec requested that McMurtrie join him for a trip into that part of the country, but the engineer did not want to go. "I will try to avoid going if possible," he told Palmer, "as

10. *Colorado Chieftain*, March 7, 1878.
11. Chicago *Railway Review*, quoted in Denver *Daily Times*, March 15, 1878.
12. McMurtrie to Palmer, April 14, 1878, McMurtrie Letter Book.
13. The road was incorporated on March 25, 1878 (Denver *Daily Times*, March 26, 1878).
14. McMurtrie to Palmer, April 1, 1881, McMurtrie Letter Book.

all my movements are watched, and should I go I am afraid Atchison will know of it and take it that we mean to move in that direction and to stop us, jump into the Canon and commence work at once. If there could be a small pool raised at once, say $50,000, we could then jump into the canon and I think hold it, although if they were to come in they could trouble us."[15]

McMurtrie's fears were not long in being realized. Two days later, as he began to withdraw his men from their labors along Chicken Creek, A. A. Robinson telegraphed to Strong that this was more than a mere cessation of work. Strong at once replied, telling his engineer to "see to it that we do not 'get left' in occupying the Grand Canyon." Robinson responded by selecting his assistant engineer, W. R. Morley, "as the man most likely not 'to get left' to go to Canon City and look out for the A. T. & S. F. interests."[16] It was a logical choice, for Morley had accompanied H. R. Holbrook of the AT&SF a year earlier when the men made a survey through the Royal Gorge and beyond.[17] He knew the terrain well.

Morley managed to get to Pueblo on a special AT&SF engine, but when he tried to charter one from the Rio Grande to complete the trip to Canon City, he was refused. George S. Van Law, an Atchison Company employee, later related: "We reached Pueblo and boarded the train for Canon City. It wouldn't go. We stayed until the middle of the afternoon and still the conductor held the train. Then wagons were secured to take our party to Canon City. As soon as we were away from the railroad platform the train pulled out."[18] Morley did not wait for his men. He hired a horse and made a trip to Canon City which the Pueblo paper compared to Phil Sheridan's famous Winchester ride during the Civil War. After a frantic dash through the night, one that killed the animal, he arrived at his destination and began to organize a crew with the help of officials from the Canon City and San Juan Railway. This little line, shortly revealed as a subsidiary

15. Ibid., April 14, 1878.

16. Waters, *Steel Trails*, p. 106.

17. The term "Royal Gorge" is usually thought of as being relatively modern, and it is true that it was not generally used at the time of the "War," but the U.S. Supreme Court used it in the case of *Denver and Rio Grande Railway Co. v. C. T. Alling, et al.*, in its October Term, 1878.

18. George S. Van Law "Four Years on Santa Fe Railroad Surveys" (MS, 1931), item 340, D&RG Archives.

of the AT&SF, had been organized in 1877, presumably at the behest of Canon City residents, who not only hated the Rio Grande for its highhandedness in the past, but who also thought the parent road would push rails into Leadville and give the village at the mouth of the Royal Gorge a place in the transportation world. On the morning of April 19 Morley and a host of enthusiastic volunteers from Canon City approached the canyon's entrance and commenced grading operations.

This time the Rio Grande men were on hand with a well-equipped crew of engineers and workmen. McMurtrie was there, along with his assistant, J. R. DeRemer, and two members of the contracting firm of Carlile, Orman, and Crook, an organization that already held a contract to build the road from Alamosa to Santa Fe. A newspaper reporter described the excitement, telling how "McMurtrie and his forces made a rapid march from the depot through the city, chaining the ground from the end of the narrow gauge track to the canon. But by the time his forces arrived on the ground, Morley's party had graded at least one hundred feet of the road." The Pueblo *Colorado Chieftain* was delighted to think that the Rio Grande had again been outfoxed, and it triumphantly titled its story of the contest, "Catching Weasels Asleep, Or How Morley Outflanked McMurtrie."[19] The paper was violently opposed to the Rio Grande and all its stories on the railroad contest were heavily slanted in favor of the Santa Fe. Correspondent B. E. Rockafellow of the *Chieftain,* who was a resident of Canon City and one of the organizers of the Canon City and San Juan Railroad, later said that he wrote the colorful articles "just to tickle the fancy of the public."

Actually, the working parties of both railroads were in the canyon about the same time, at different locations, and while accounts of the affair vary in detail, there is no evidence to show that either group could lay claim to prior occupancy. Both did, of course, and both had their day in court, for the United States Circuit Court for the district of Colorado was to decide in favor of the Canon City and San Juan, while the United States Supreme Court was to state that the Rio Grande was there first.[20]

19. *Colorado Chieftain,* April 20, 1878.

20. *Denver and Rio Grande Railway Co. v. C. T. Alling, et al.,* and *Denver and Rio Grande Railway Co. v. Canon City and San Juan Railway Co.* Cases 811, 812, Oct. Term, U.S. Supreme Court, 1878—item 405, D&RG Archives.

None of the Rio Grande officials ever entertained any doubts that their right to the Arkansas Valley route to Leadville was entirely valid. Palmer had included it in his original certification of incorporation of the railroad; he had ordered it surveyed in 1871 and 1872; again, in 1873, along with Alexander Hunt, he conducted further surveys in the direction of what was yet known as California Gulch; and he had built into Canon City in 1875, showing what he regarded as intent to proceed farther westward. The important thing he neglected to do was to file a plat of the projected line with the General Land Office, in accordance with the act of Congress dated March 3, 1875.[21]

Meanwhile, in 1877, the Atchison Company quietly ordered Holbrook to make the already mentioned survey for the dummy Canon City and San Juan company, following along the line of stakes McMurtrie had set out for Palmer in 1871. McMurtrie later complained that so scrupulously had Holbrook's party adhered to the earlier line that it had "in a number of places . . . taken up my stakes, cut my numbers off and put theirs on."[22] Strong, of the AT&SF, apparently felt that since Palmer had not fully complied with the letter of the law, the route was fair game and he was not going to overlook any opportunities to gain traffic for his company. He would have agreed with one of his employees, who later wrote, "The Denver and Rio Grande scouting engineers put lines of stakes to every part of this mountain region where business was likely to develop. That cocky and resolute —but none too rich—railroad company claimed this territory as its own. It believed in a future life and believed in setting its stakes in the beyond and doing it first."[23] The AT&SF, bound for the West Coast and itself in financial difficulty from time to time, refused to recognize the little upstart narrow gauge whose engineers were so free with their survey stakes. In a game as big as that of transcontinental railroad building, the promise of rich trade from fabulous Leadville

---

21. The law of 1872 did not require the filing of a plat, but the amendment of March 3, 1875, which denied any single company the right solely to occupy the right of way through a canyon or defile, also specified that any road wishing to secure the benefits of the amended law had to file with the register of the land office a profile of the road within 12 months of the location of the route. The core of this law can be found in the *Congressional Record, 3*, P. I (1875), 404, at which time the proposal was being debated. The Rio Grande maintained that its rights dated from 1872.

22. McMurtrie to Robert Weitbrec, April 22, 1878, Robert F. Weitbrec Papers, Notebook 4 (1878), State Historical Society of Colorado Library, Denver.

23. Van Law, "Four Years on Santa Fe."

was too great to ignore, and any barrier to the prize had to be ridden over, roughshod.

The fiction that the Canon City and San Juan Railway was independent and of local origin was short-lived. By the time the AT&SF made ready to invade Leadville, it became abundantly clear who owned the little road with a big name. As late as April 10, 1878, when that company's board of directors met, there was no provision for any construction. It was not until Morley, a virtual stranger, turned up in a state of excited determination, that the Canon City company had any inkling of an immediate building prospect. The president of the small road probably was less acquainted with the situation than Morley, for he did not know how many directors his company had, where his funds came from, or who were the bidders for construction. Several of the road's board members later testified that they held stock, for which they had paid no cash, but other than that they had only the vaguest notion of the corporation's workings or history. For any information the directors and the president had to look to Strong, who was elected to the board on April 10, or to Robinson, who had no connection at all until the day the work commenced.[24] By the morning of April 19 no one in Colorado had any doubts about the parentage of the Canon City and San Juan.

During the first few days of the "railroad war" the greatest excitement prevailed in and around Canon City. According to newspaper reports from Pueblo, the Rio Grande was charged with cutting the Western Union telegraph wire between that place and Canon City to destroy the enemy's means of communication, and of trying to stop the United States mail for the same purpose. Both sides rushed in reinforcements, each trying to buy off the other's men with offers of higher wages. On the morning of Saturday, April 20, engineer De-Remer took a small party of men up the canyon to occupy the Royal Gorge, circled around the Atchison Company's camp at the mouth of that defile, swam the river to the north bank, and laid claim to the vital entrance. The brilliant tactical maneuver was nullified when, that same day, the Canon City company obtained an injunction forbidding the Rio Grande to continue its work in the canyon. Writs

24. Wilson, "Denver and Rio Grande Project," p. 73; Colorado Springs, *Weekly Gazette*, July 27, 1878. Hundreds of pages of testimony can be found in the court records, copies of which are assembled in volumes entitled "D. & R. G. Ry. Co. and Associate Enterprises," Western History Dept., Denver Public Library. See esp. Vols. 3–6.

were served at once on Robert F. Weitbrec, John A. McMurtrie, and others who were holding the disputed territory. Trial was held immediately, after which McMurtrie was put under a $2,000 bond and Weitbrec under a $5,000 bond for violating the injunction.[25] With that the fight shifted to the courts which, McMurtrie bitterly remarked, were probably owned and controlled by the opposition.[26] As a parting shot, said the *Rocky Mountain News,* the Rio Grande men attacked the Atchison workers, drove them from the grade, and threw their tools into the river.[27]

The real question was not so much that of whose construction crews were in the canyon first, but which law of the federal government was applicable. By the act of June 8, 1872, the Rio Grande was granted a general right of way over the public domain, provided that the road should reach Santa Fe within five years. In March 1877, upon application by the management, this period was lengthened to a total of ten years. The Atchison Company's main claim was based on the Right of Way Act of March 3, 1875, passed to protect railroads in general against the monopolization of strategic mountain passes by any one line. Under this law the Canon City and San Juan had surveyed the first twenty miles of its road through the canyon, and the profile was accepted by the Secretary of the Interior on June 22, 1877. Palmer got at the root of the matter when he said, "The question at issue really struck at the foundation upon which the Denver and Rio Grande system of railways rested; and the practical value of the right of way granted it by Congress in 1872 was now put to the test."[28]

The days that followed the initial collision in the canyon saw the Rio Grande forces, barred from that location by injunction, fruitlessly try to locate an alternate route by way of Grape Creek and Texas Creek. The Atchison Company's subsidiary, also, was prevented from working in the narrow defile, and the sheriff's deputies were sent out to see that the court's wishes were obeyed. The Rio Grande, defeated in Judge John W. Henry's court, contended—in somewhat less direct language than McMurtrie had used—that the local courts were biased, and asked to have the case removed to a federal court. Judge Henry

25. *Daily Rocky Mountain News,* April 24, 1878.
26. McMurtrie to Palmer, April 1, 1881, McMurtrie Letter Book.
27. *Daily Rocky Mountain News,* April 24, 1878.
28. *Report of the Board of Directors of the Denver and Rio Grande Railway Company* (1880), p. 7.

refused, remarking that the railroad was already in contempt of his court, but after Robert Weitbrec appeared before him and satisfied the crotchety jurist with regard to the technicalities of the matter, the case was taken before Judge Moses Hallett of the United States Circuit Court. On May 8 Hallett decided that for the time being neither company could continue construction in the canyon. However, until the case was finally decided, the Rio Grande was not restrained from working above that point. Three weeks later, on June 1, Hallett and Judge Dillon, of St. Louis, who was called into the case, issued a ruling. They based their decision upon the act of March 3, 1875, holding that each company had the right to construct a line through the canyon where there was sufficient room, neither to obstruct the other, and since they believed that the Canon City railroad had the prior right, it was given permission to proceed with grading, but it was not to lay any rails until it received permission from the court. It was the intention of the judges to see to it that the Rio Grande be permitted to use the other road's tracks where the defile was too narrow for more than one line.[29]

Upon receiving the May 8 decision, both sides mustered out the larger part of their so-called armies. The AT&SF, in discharging 300 men, offered them $1.50 a day for their services, but since it had promised them $2.00 a day and $3.00 a night for "enlisting," there was a violent reaction to this offer. A. A. Robinson, who was reported as trying to make an escape from Canon City, was cornered in his office by the angry, threatening mob of newly-created veterans. Meanwhile, the locally much-hated Rio Grande made some amends by promptly paying off its men and offering them free transportation to points of hiring.[30] Local papers reported that the turn of events encouraged Rio Grande attorneys, who saw further avenues of legal pursuit in the decision, but Palmer, in writing of it, called the development an "overwhelming defeat." The reason for the president's gloom lay in the fact that the "contest for the Grand Canon was in reality a fight for the gateway, not to Leadville only, but to the far more important, because infinitely larger, mineral fields of the Gunnison country, the Blue and Eagle Rivers and Utah."[31] To be shut out of a major por-

29. Colorado Springs *Weekly Gazette*, June 15, 1878. Two cases were here involved: No. 154, *Denver and Rio Grande Railway Co. v. Ebenezer T. Alling, et al.*, and No. 155, *Canon City and San Juan Railway Co. v. Denver and Rio Grande Railway Co.* They can be found in "D. & R. G. Ry. Co. and Associate Enterprises."

30. *Colorado Chieftain*, May 16, 1878.

31. *Report of the Board of Directors* (1880), pp. 7, 12.

tion of what he regarded as his own domain was discouraging indeed.

The conflict now entered a cold-war stage, with opposing lawyers training their legal guns at each other while the remaining troops engaged in a holding action. D&RG assistant chief engineer, James R. DeRemer, painted "Dead-Line" on a tie and laid it across the grade at the twentieth milepost above Canon City as a warning to the enemy. Four miles farther up, he and his men constructed a stone fortress, and at the thirty-seventh milepost they built another. Years later a Rio Grande employee recalled that arsenals "were maintained by both sides and the siege kept up for months; it was a noisy but bloodless war, most of the warriors using blanks."[32] With the front thus defended, the Rio Grande sought every other means at its disposal to harass the Atchison Company. In June it refused to sell any tickets to the East by way of the AT&SF, trying to cut off that line from Denver. It also tried to block the other road's entrance to Canon City. The Central Colorado Improvement Company, a Rio Grande subsidiary, owned the approaches to that place, and the Atchison people were obliged to condemn under eminent domain to gain access, a process that kept it in court until October 1878.[33]

During the summer of 1878 the Rio Grande pressed its case in the federal courts. In an opinion rendered on August 23, Judge Moses Hallett again stated that both companies were entitled to proceed, with equal rights, under the protection of the court. Neither was to obstruct the other in any manner, but once again the Judge held that where the question of priority appeared, the Canon City and San Juan line had preference because it had complied with the act of March 3, 1875, whereas the Rio Grande had not. Palmer at once appealed the decision to the Supreme Court of the United States, determined to win a clear-cut decision. He warned the Atchison people publicly that he intended to come out on top, and that any work they did on the first twenty miles, or anywhere else between Canon City and Leadville, would be at the risk of later confiscation.

Not content to sit and wait for the high court to make up its mind about the width of the Royal Gorge, Palmer, always the fighter, began further suits against the AT&SF. The origin of this latest litigation stemmed from the fact that the Atchison Company had formed a sec-

32. Mr. and Mrs. James Rose Harvey, "Engineer Walk of the Denver and Rio Grande," *Colorado Magazine*, 24 (1947), 243.

33. Wilson, "Denver and Rio Grande," p. 76. *Railroad Gazette* (June 21, 1878), p. 313.

ond subsidiary, known as the Pueblo and Arkansas Valley Railroad, whose intent it was to build a line between the twentieth milepost and Leadville. The shoe was now on the other foot, for here the Denver and Rio Grande had complied with all the necessary legalities, but the P&AV had this time failed to file its plat with the General Land Office, as required by law. Asserting that there were a number of places on the upper Arkansas canyon wide enough for but one right of way, Palmer threw his crews into the newly contested area on the assumption that he could win any court fight that might arise here. "If this (plan) succeeds the Atchison Company would not be likely to enter the Canon at the Royal Gorge below, because they would not be able to get out *above*," he theorized.[34]

General Palmer, a man of unbounded enthusiasm and never-ending optimism, continued to feel that his organization could do battle successfully with any and all of the major roads who crossed swords with it. In mid-August he wrote from New York to David Dodge, telling his colleague that there was a move afoot, not connected with the major transcontinental companies, "to rid us of our floating debt and to establish such credit for the Co. that we may build independently." He added that "there seems to be so many obstacles, uncertainties, and objections to any alliance that really the risks of independence seem after all to be the least." Earlier in the summer he had said to Dodge that there were rumors of a row between Jay Gould and the bondholders of the Kansas Pacific that would imperil a pledge made by the Union Pacific and Kansas Pacific to aid the Rio Grande. Now, he wrote, if the suit over the Royal Gorge route developed favorably, "I think we can go it alone better than with either of our troublesome partners."[35]

Accordingly, he went ahead. On September 7 Charles F. Woerischoffer and Company, New York financiers, agreed to loan the Rio Grande close to $400,000 to proceed with construction and meet its November bond interest. Part of the price paid was the agreement that the road's board of directors would be enlarged, admitting new

34. The foregoing material, on the Aug. 23 decision and the suit against the P&AV can be found in *Railroad Gazette* (Aug. 30, 1878), p. 429. For a history of the P&AV suit see Brief for the Plaintiff, In the Circuit Court of the United States for the District of Colorado, *Denver and Rio Grande Railway Co. v. Pueblo and Arkansas Valley Railroad Co.*, item 406, D&RG Archives.

35. Palmer to Dodge, June 29, 1878, and Aug. 17, 1878, items 365, 368, D&RG Archives.

members mutually satisfactory to the bankers and to the railroad, and that an executive committee was to be formed, the majority of whose members lived in or about New York and had the power to make policy decisions at intervals between board meetings.[36] The Union Contract Company, builder of so much of the earlier road, at once advertised for bids to grade between Canon City to the mouth of the South Arkansas, right alongside the Atchison Company's branch. At the same time, that rival organization announced that it would build a standard-gauge line into Leadville, under the Pueblo and Arkansas Valley Railroad name.[37]

The resurgence of the Rio Grande was short-lived. The Atchison Company answered the suit against its Pueblo and Arkansas Valley road by merging it with the Canon City and San Juan and setting up headquarters for the new company in Pueblo with a capital stock said to exceed six million dollars. This latest subsidiary announced that it proposed to build at once a whole series of lines, all of which significantly paralleled those of the Rio Grande, not only up the Arkansas Valley but throughout the San Luis and San Juan Valleys, and into the mining country northwest of Denver. It also brought immediate suit against the Rio Grande, alleging that it was interfering with construction of the line above the twentieth milepost on the route to Leadville. Both sides rushed in reinforcements, and again the much-contested right of way was in the headlines, with the erection of new stone forts, patrols of armed men, and threats and counter-threats being reported.[38]

By October, Palmer yielded to the bondholders' insistence that the odds were too great. His organization had tried to continue its expansion in the face of depression and hostility from a major rail line, and now its resources were exhausted to the point of danger. On October 19 Colorado's "Baby Road," as it was affectionately known at home, was put out for adoption. On that day Sebastian B. Schlesinger and James D. Potts, representing the Rio Grande bondholders, signed an agreement with Thomas and Joseph Nickerson of the AT&SF to lease the narrow gauge for a period of thirty years. It had taken the transcontinental line just eight months, after Strong had made his

36. Meeting of the Board of Directors, Oct. 5, 1878, D&RG Archives, D&RGW offices, Denver.
37. *Railroad Gazette* (Sept. 20, 1878), p. 465. Circular No. 44, AT&SF, Sept. 17, 1878, item 377, D&RG Archives.
38. Anderson, *William J. Palmer,* pp. 101, 102.

proposals of January 1878, to force compliance, and now the "Royal Gorge War" appeared to be over. Robert F. Weitbrec, the Rio Grande's treasurer, later explained Palmer's position:

> The money subscribed and paid in had been very largely on the personal solicitation of General Palmer and his associates. The bonds had fallen much below the price paid for them and they were largely held by the original purchasers. There was a moral responsibility which could not and should not be disregarded. If there was any way in which the security of the investment could be increased it was entitled to serious consideration. This was an underlying thought in (the) negotiation.

The immediate hopes of the management were realized, in this regard, for a Denver paper reported that in the matter of a few days after the lease was signed, Denver and Rio Grande stock rose from eight to twenty, and its bonds went up from seventy-four to ninety-four.[39]

The lease provided that the Rio Grande turn over its 337 miles of track, its rolling stock, and its other equipment at a rental that was to begin at 43 per cent of gross receipts, to be scaled down to 37, and finally to 36 per cent. The Atchison Company agreed not to build or to encourage any parallel or competing lines, and any construction beyond Denver and Rio Grande terminal points was to be of a three-foot gauge. The lessee promised that there would be no discrimination in freight or other charges and that rent would be paid by the month. No provisions of the lease could be canceled or modified without the formal written consent of the trustees of the Rio Grande's mortgages. It was finally agreed that all litigation between the roads should cease and that the Rio Grande would be extended to both the San Juan silver mines and to Leadville.[40]

News that the Rio Grande had been leased caused concern in Denver and jubilation in Pueblo. The Denver *Daily Times* twitted one of its rivals for seeming "to regard it as a sort of double-barreled suction tube, whereby Denver is to be transferred in sections to Kan-

39. Robert F. Weitbrec, "A Sketch of the Early History of the Denver & Rio Grande Railroad," *The Trail*, 16 (1924), 6, 7. Denver *Daily Times*, Oct. 22, 1878.

40. Copy of the lease in the Minutes of D&RG Board of Directors, Nov. 5, 1878, D&RG Archives, D&RGW offices, Denver. See also *Railroad Gazette* (Oct. 25, 1878), pp. 520–21, and *Hunt's Merchant's Magazine*, 27 (Oct. 12, 1878), p. 382. The so-called Potts–Schlesinger agreement that preceded the lease can be found in "D. & R. G. Ry. Co. and Associate Enterprises," Vol. 3.

sas City," but the paper admitted that there was "no mistaking the uneasiness of the Gould monopoly under the proposed innovation. It is the wedge which is to split its power over the commerce of the north." Pueblo, on the other hand, thought that the lease was a good thing because it could now come abreast with the capital city and no longer would the metropolitans boast that "Denver is the state." Specifically, the Pueblo *Chieftain* saw the new development as a form of emancipation from the "bullheadedness and blindness" of Rio Grande management, which had tried to throttle the AT&SF and, incidentally, Pueblo, by charging ruinous rates on through traffic as a means of retaliation against its rival.[41] Actually, as a leading railroad journal pointed out, there was not much prospect that great benefits would accrue to the public no matter in whose hands the management lay, for Rio Grande rates were high and probably would remain so under the new arrangement. It was the only way anyone could make any money over a line whose traffic was so light. Moreover, for a railroad so cheaply built, its debt of about $20,000 a mile was high, and in order to pay even the interest, rather high transportation rates were necessary.[42]

While the agreement to lease generally was regarded as the end of warfare between the two lines, it was merely an armistice. Palmer, who bitterly opposed the bondholders' desire to consolidate with, or lease to, the AT&SF, did everything in his power to delay the day when the agreement became effective. At the time of the lease negotiations, the Atchison Company's President Nickerson had tried to get Palmer to drop the litigation over the right of way above the twentieth milepost, promising to take over the contracts and to help the Rio Grande out of its obligations as much as possible, but he got nowhere. Palmer was afraid that if he acceded to this demand he would prejudice the case pending in the courts and a favorable decision here was his last, feeble hope. Nickerson bitterly responded to this conduct, saying, "I did not think that after making peace we should still have war," but Palmer was not moved by the complaint.[43]

December 1, 1878, the day set for the transfer to the AT&SF, came and passed, with the road still undelivered. On the 4th, Palmer wrote a personal letter to Dodge, in which he talked of the "arrogant demand

41. Denver *Daily Times*, Oct. 22, 1878. *Colorado Chieftain*, Oct. 24, Nov. 7, 1878.
42. *Railroad Gazette* (Oct. 25, 1878), p. 516.
43. Wilson, "Denver and Rio Grande," p. 91.

of possession before complying with the plain terms" on the part of Strong and Nickerson. "I have declined, of course, point blank & expressed amazement at the demand," he reassured his general manager. Nickerson also had delayed on the question of the railroad's valuation and the matter of an umpire, giving Palmer the impression, at one point in the negotiations, that the Atchison Company was about to throw up the whole proposition. But as Palmer pointed out, Boston financiers had continued to buy Rio Grande bonds until they had, at the time of writing, about half of the mainline bonds, which convinced him that there would be no backing down now. He guessed that Nickerson had counted "on our yielding to their demand of possession, and offer to deposit security," but he insisted hotly that if "they were to put up Boston itself now, it would not avail. The actual provision of the papers must be carried out or they lose the lease." It angered him that the Atchison people were "insolent & arbitrary and more so at Boston recently," and concluded that things now were "in a thoroughly antagonistic shape."[44]

Deeply angered and completely distrustful of Nickerson, Palmer tried every means at his disposal to delay the actual transfer. But the tide was against him. On November 29, at a general meeting of the stockholders in Colorado Springs, he warned that the terms of the lease might not be fulfilled, only to be answered by a vote of ratification for the agreement. The president, however, was directed to give possession when he saw fit, a bit of leeway he quickly used by charging that the AT&SF had not paid for tools, ties, and other materials on the line, as agreed. Alexander C. Hunt, his representative, was even accused of deliberately neglecting to make the necessary inventory with the hope that enough snow would fall to make such a check impracticable. Again the bondholders stepped in, unwilling to see their plans sabotaged, and made a compromise arrangement whereby the Atchison Company would put up $150,000 as a guarantee that the materials would be paid for. The lessee agreed, provided that the transfer was made no later than December 14.[45] Palmer had played his last card; there was no further avenue of delay open to him. Shortly, he and Strong met at Colorado Springs, where the necessary deposit was made, and the General reluctantly turned over his baby road to the enemy. He telegraphed instructions to his subordinates that at

44. Palmer to Dodge, Dec. 4, 1878, item 396, D&RG Archives.
45. Wilson, p. 93. Colorado Springs *Weekly Gazette*, Dec. 7, 1878.

midnight the Atchison people would take command. It was Friday, December 13.

The transfer took place quietly. Denver merchants were gloomy, some of them feeling that their city would now be caught in between the cross-fire of a bigger railroad battle between the Union Pacific and Kansas Pacific on one side, and the Atchison, Topeka, and Santa Fe on the other, causing them to suffer. The more optimistic took refuge in the thought that perhaps such a war of transportation interests would result in cut-throat competition and a resultant lowering of rates. Pueblo was happy, convinced that *its* railroad—the AT&SF—was now "master of the situation" and that all manner of good things would result in that city. The *Chieftain* reported that when the appointed time came that midnight, the change was effected peacefully, and that while a "good deal of 'chaff' was indulged in by the employees of the Atchison, Topeka and Santa Fe at the expense of the Denver and Rio Grande brethren . . . everyone was good natured over it."[46]

The joviality did not penetrate the country very far north of Pueblo. Five days after the new management took over, Denver learned that rates between that point and Colorado Springs, Pueblo, and Canon City had been raised variously from twenty-five to sixty cents a hundred-weight. The gloom of the capital city merchants deepened. D. C. Dodge, retained as general manager of the Rio Grande portion of the line by the Atchison Company, complained that on the very first day the lessees had violated the agreement, and he continued to make such charges until he was removed from his position.[47] Palmer watched the developments quietly, waiting for his chance to pounce upon the interlopers and wrest away the prize they had taken. There were two possibilities for him to win: first, that a clear violation of the lease could be shown; secondly, that the suit over the canyon route, still pending, would result favorably to the Rio Grande. If either, preferably both, of these things happened, the doughty young railroad entrepreneur would get another chance at running the narrow-gauge line that had been his brain child only a few years before. Like the good gambler he was, he stayed at the table and awaited the turn of the next card.

46. Denver *Daily Times*, Dec. 14, 17, 23, 1878. *Daily Rocky Mountain News*, Dec. 13, 1878. *Colorado Chieftain*, Dec. 19, 1878.
47. Wilson, p. 94. Denver *Daily Times*, Dec. 19, 1878.

4. *The enemy watch our every movement*

During the winter months of 1878–79 the Colorado air was thick with accusations against the Atchison Road. When it talked of leasing the Denver, South Park, and Pacific, to prevent that small rival from competing in the Leadville trade, Dodge loudly denounced the move as a violation of the Rio Grande agreement. His argument was that since there was no provision for terminating the South Park road at Leadville, it could well proceed to Alamosa, and that would mean paralleling Palmer's route, which was strictly forbidden in the lease.[1] There was, at the same time, a good deal of furor over Atchison rate policies. When it raised freight rates sharply and ordered Rio Grande passenger train conductors not to honor any through tickets along its line via Denver, revenues fell off, and since the rental was based upon income, it meant that there was not enough money for the Rio Grande to meet its interest payments. Newspapers friendly to Palmer made the most of the situation, jeering at the supporters of the rival road who had once talked of the Rio Grande's "robbery rates." The Colorado Springs *Gazette* cited the case of a local merchant who recently had paid more to bring goods from Denver to his city than it cost to ship them from New York to Denver. The result of such discriminatory rates was to force any eastbound traffic to go by way of Pueblo and the AT&SF.

At the same time, coal shipments from El Moro and Canon City to Denver (where they might have reached the Kansas Pacific or Union Pacific) practically ceased. When the Atchison road forced its northern rivals into a pooling agreement by denying them the needed coal, the rebates it earned in the pool were listed as AT&SF earnings and were not divided with the Rio Grande. The effect of the pool and of exorbitant rates upon Palmer's line meant that Rio Grande earnings declined close to a thousand dollars a day, while Atchison profits swelled. Clearly, this was prejudicial to the best interests of the leased line and a violation of the agreement.[2]

In February 1879 the Atchison people tried a maneuver that provoked howls of indignation from Rio Grande supporters. During the legislative session one of the directors of the Pueblo and Arkansas Valley Railroad, an AT&SF subsidiary, attached a rider to a minor bill concerning religious denominations that would empower the majority of the stockholders of any corporation to over-ride decisions of the company's trustees. The Colorado Springs *Weekly Gazette* charged that the amendment was pasted onto the printed bill and that it went

1. *Daily Rocky Mountain News*, Jan. 23, 1879.
2. Colorado Springs *Weekly Gazette*, Jan. 4, 1879. Wilson, "Denver and Rio Grande," p. 97.

through the legislature, unnoticed by the bill's managers in both houses. The newspaper was scandalized to think that a major company would stoop to "a willful falsification of the public records" in an attempt to supersede the wishes of the Rio Grande's trustees. The only explanation, said the editor, was that the AT&SF had given up any hope of winning the pending Royal Gorge suit and sought this means of quashing the proceeding through a vote of the stock it controlled. As further proof of the Atchison Company's desperation, he pointed out that in recent days the trust stock and bonds of the Rio Grande had advanced in price, which "shows that the stock operators have no faith in the success of the Atchison legislative trick."[3]

During the same month the AT&SF tried to pay the treasurer of the Rio Grande, Robert F. Weitbrec, a sum just over $32,000 for the January rental of the road, but it was refused on the ground that the manner in which it was tendered would affect the legal rights of the lessor in the disputed questions between the two companies. Toward the end of March a similar attempt was made, in which about $30,000 to cover the February rent was offered. "I declined to receive it as I did when Wilder [E. Wilder, AT&SF Treasurer] made me tender for Jany on the 28th day of Feby," Weitbrec reported. Palmer's chief engineer, J. A. McMurtrie, was present during the discussion, as a witness.[4]

During the early spring months of 1879 tensions heightened. The Atchison people worked desperately to complete as much of their line as possible on the contested route between Canon City and Leadville, presumably on the assumption that it would strengthen their arguments in court. McMurtrie made a trip up the Arkansas River in February to see what he could learn, and reported to Palmer that the opposition had around a thousand men and a hundred teams at work, grading. He estimated that this phase of the work would be completed by the first of May.[5]

The Colorado Springs Gazette watched the proceedings and noted that the home railroad was pushing its fight in the courts, hopeful of a favorable Supreme Court decision that would save the day. The paper agreed with the Denver Tribune's statement that the "curse

3. Colorado Springs Weekly Gazette, Feb. 15, 22, 1879.
4. Memoranda of Feb. 28 and March 31, in Weitbrec Papers, Notebook No. 5 (1879).
5. McMurtrie to Palmer, Feb. (date illegible), 1879, McMurtrie Letter Book "D."

of railway traffic in Colorado has been the swallowing up of the local roads by the trunk lines," and pointed to the present jeopardy of the Rio Grande as an example of this undesirable trend. "These trunk lines will try to make this entire state simply a suburb of Kansas City, Chicago, or St. Louis," warned the Colorado Springs editor. Even Pueblo, once so enamored by the AT&SF that it regarded that line as a kind of philanthropy, was now beginning to see the light, as its merchants found themselves completely at the mercy of the big road. "From the very nature of things it is disastrous to the business of any state to have its local lines manipulated in the interest of large trunk lines," said the *Gazette,* in arguing that the most desirable situation was one in which home roads were operated by those who lived in the vicinity and had both a knowledge of, and an interest in, the enterprise.[6] It was a thesis that Palmer had followed since the inception of the Rio Grande, and one that its management would pursue in the mid-twentieth century. To carry out such a policy effectively was to be one of the major headaches of the "Baby Road." During the winter of 1878–79 it looked almost impossible.

As long as there was a glimmer of hope, Palmer clung to it, determined somehow to triumph over his powerful adversaries. The big break came in January, when the United States Supreme Court handed down a decision in a suit between the Missouri, Kansas, and Texas Railway Company and the Kansas Pacific Railway Company. The facts in this case closely paralleled the point of argument in the Royal Gorge litigation, and the Rio Grande people now became quite excited about their prospects. "It so clearly showed that the Rio Grande would win that for the first time, the Santa Fe people awoke to the fact that they had been badly advised,'' Robert Weitbrec later recalled. "Thereupon they reinforced their legal staff with the best talent they could find and endeavored to have the Grand Canon suit dismissed on the ground that it was a moot case."[7] Palmer's home town paper jeered at the Atchison Road's efforts, saying that before the mentioned Supreme Court decision it had pressed for a decision on the merits of

6. Colorado Springs *Weekly Gazette,* March 15, 1879.

7. "Mr. R. F. Weitbrec's Contribution," Jan. 1920, a typescript, in Weitbrec Papers. In this case, *Missouri, Kansas, and Texas Railway Co. v. Kansas Pacific Railway Co.* (U.S. Supreme Court Reports: 97 U.S. 491), the court held that "The rights of the contesting corporations to the disputed tracts are determined by the dates of their respective grants, and not by the dates of the location of the routes of their respective roads."

the case, but now it was making every effort to delay the judicial proceedings "until it gains by chicanery what it cannot gain in a court
of law."[8]

As the time of judicial decision approached, friends of the Rio
Grande intensified their verbal campaign against the AT&SF. The
Colorado Springs *Gazette* was particularly vituperative, charging that
the opposition had armed men in the canyon, had broken the terms
of the lease upon innumerable occasions, had charged ruinous freight
rates by means of its new monopoly, had manipulated the market to
cause D&RG bonds to fluctuate, had tried to wear out the physical
equipment of the narrow gauge, and had sought to gain all the advantages of consolidation without incurring any of the liabilities.[9]
Even the Denver *Times,* not always in full sympathy with the Rio
Grande, admitted that under present conditions Denver was caught
in between the major transcontinental groups and that neither could
enter the other's territory without paying a heavy penalty. "Nothing
but the cancellation of existing contracts between the A.T.&S.F. and
the Rio Grande, and the restoration of the latter's independence will
break this condition," said that journal. But, it decided, this was "not
likely to occur."[10]

The Atchison management strenuously objected to charges that it
had broken the lease. It declared that all provisions had been carried
out faithfully and that if the Rio Grande had complaints, the agreement provided for arbitration, but this had not yet been requested.
Moreover, said the AT&SF, it had deposited in excess of the necessary
money in trust to guarantee payment of the materials it acquired, even
though the Rio Grande was withholding the inventory of the apprais-
ers. To charges that the Atchison Company was not paying its rent,
William Strong answered that it was paid the first month, but the
receipt given was not in proper form and since then the Rio Grande
had refused the proffered rental because a "proper" receipt was requested. The money was then deposited in trust, in a Pueblo bank.
Furthermore, argued the company, it made no difference whether or
not Sebastian Schlesinger, who held the lease, delivered it to the
AT&SF, because if the terms were complied with, it was still bind-

8. Colorado Springs *Weekly Gazette,* March 22, 1879.

9. Ibid., March 29, April 5, 12, 19, 1879.

10. Denver *Weekly Times,* March 19, 1879.

ing.[11] Palmer promptly denied all these allegations. Rio Grande officials were determined that the lease should not be delivered. On March
3 his board of directors authorized Dr. William Bell, vice-president
of the Rio Grande, to go east and institute suits against the lessees to
set aside the agreement and to enjoin Schlesinger from delivering it.[12]

Closer to home, in early April, there was considerable excitement
in Denver over rumors that the Rio Grande proposed to take back its
line by force. Although no attempt had yet been made, it was freely
reported that such was Palmer's intention, and as evidence that the
Atchison Company was apprehensive, armed guards were posted at
all trains, shops, and depots, as well as along the route being graded
between Canon City and Leadville. On April 10 a *quo warranto* was
filed against the AT&SF by the attorney general of Colorado on behalf
of the state, the writ being returnable on the 22d. The suit, brought by
the Rio Grande, proposed to inquire into the right of the Atchison
Company to operate leased lines in Colorado, as a corporation existing
only under the laws of Kansas.[13]

On April 21, at the very climax of the renewed struggle, the United
States Supreme Court rendered a decision that reversed the Circuit
Court of Colorado and advanced the opinion that under the Act of
June 8, 1872, the Rio Grande had priority in the Royal Gorge. The
high court, rather than deny the AT&SF any right-of-way privileges,
simply set aside the injunction against the Rio Grande and instructed
the Circuit Court to make legal provision for joint trackage in the
canyon at points where it was too narrow for more than one set of rails.
In other words, Palmer's franchise privileges were recognized, but he
was not given the right of exclusive occupation. Nevertheless, the decision was regarded in Colorado as a great victory for the Rio Grande,
and it occasioned a good deal of joy in that camp. Chase Mellen wrote
that when the news came to Colorado Springs, people there put on a
wild celebration, blowing the steam whistle at the sawmill until the
steam gave out. In Denver the decision "created a sensation," and
there was much speculation as to whether a termination of the lease
would follow. There were some who feared that this would kill the
Rio Grande "deader than a door-nail," because the Atchison Company
would then carry out its earlier threat to parallel all of the narrow-

11. Ibid., April 16, 1879.
12. Minutes D&RG Board of Directors, March 3, 1879, D&RG Archives.
13. *Railroad Gazette* (April 18, 1879), p. 217.

gauge's line.[14] This was of no immediate concern to Palmer. At the moment what he wanted most was to have his railroad back.

While the legal reversal drew attention to such physical problems as the contest in the Royal Gorge, there were financial ramifications that presented some embarrassing complications to the Atchison Company. It had negotiated around a million dollars worth of bonds and a million and a half dollars worth of stock, based upon the supposed right of way. The New York *Tribune* guessed that much of the stock was given away as a means of inducing the sale of bonds, and "question may now arise as to the equitable claim of the bondholders upon the stockholders." The journal thought that "the decision promises to raise a multiplicity of nice points."[15] The court's action must have at least raised some doubts in Boston investment circles, a main source of the Atchison's financial support, as to how well the Colorado situation was in hand. The Boston *Advertiser* openly challenged the decision, alleging that the high court had made a mistake in its ruling, and it hinted broadly that the jurists might see fit to reverse themselves at a later date.[16] Meanwhile, Palmer's attorneys continued their legal attack in the Massachusetts courts, insisting that the lease, which had never been delivered, was not valid, and requesting that it be declared null and void.[17]

Out in Colorado Palmer prepared for more direct action. During the last days of May and in early June he and other Rio Grande officials laid plans to take back the road by force. The railroad's archives contain a number of letters and telegrams indicating a build-up in arms, leaving no doubt that the management was willing to engage in violence if necessary. On May 28 Weitbrec inquired of McMurtrie how many carbines, shotguns, and pistols he had at South Pueblo, and learned that there was available one box of rifles and thirteen pistols. An employee named Engle informed Weitbrec that he had six rifles and six pistols at the El Moro coke ovens and added, "I also have on hand & undistributed six Colts revolvers. At [the] mine we have two

14. Chase Mellen, *Sketches of Pioneer Life and Settlement of the Great West* (New York, 1935), p. 27. Denver *Daily Times*, April 22, 23, 1879. *Denver and Rio Grande Railway Co. v. C. T. Alling, et al.*, and *Denver and Rio Grande Railway Co. v. Canon City and San Juan Railway Co.*, Cases 811 and 812, U.S. Supreme Court (Oct. Term, 1878). Copy in D&RG Archives, item 405. See also *Railroad Gazette* (April 25, 1879), p. 230.

15. New York *Tribune*, May 6, 1879. Colorado Springs *Weekly Gazette*, May 17, 1879.

16. Quoted in *Railroad Gazette* (May 30, 1879), p. 302.

17. Ibid. (April 25, 1879), p. 230.

boxes [of] arms said by the deliverer to contain ten rifles & ten pistols with ammunition." From Walsenburg came word that ten rifles and six forty-five caliber revolvers, belonging to the company, were ready. On June 5 Palmer telegraphed to McMurtrie that additional guns were on their way to Pueblo by wagon. The engineer was told he could expect thirty pistols and twenty carbines with ammunition enough for them and for the twenty-five pistols David Dodge had sent on the day before. The next day McMurtrie flashed back a coded message: "New page flesh affable calibre. No bemoan wad tempest," which, decoded, read: "New pistols forty-four calibre. No ammunition with them." The Rio Grande was on a war footing, with all the secrecy and security measures employed by a military organization. An inventory of June 6, written on the president's own stationery, showed that there were 207 pistols and 259 "guns" (presumably rifles) located along the line at strategic points. The General was ready for action.[18]

Dr. William Bell, Palmer's trusted lieutenant, reported "all ready" on the southern front. On June 8 he wrote from Canon City: "The Silver Cliff contingent duly arrived at Spike buck as also the rifles sent for them to the Coal Banks. We went to the Coal Banks in the morning. The operator has been dealt with as you directed by wire. He succeeded in destroying the dispatches & then cut the wire but was unable to communicate the fact that he had been relieved. He is being watched by two guards. We have proof enough to convict him." With reference to coming moves, the doctor wrote, "We now propose 40 of the miners as deputies here & 28 to start on the train here & be dropped along the line. Others are to go direct to the 3 bridges & enough to remain at the banks to load 10 cars daily. A splendid body of 16 mounted men came in tonight. . . . 4 more come tomorrow. The enemy watch our every movement & send armed men after DeRemer & myself to see what we were about."[19]

There is ample evidence to support Bell's statements that "the enemy" was well aware of an impending clash of arms. Records of the Pueblo and Arkansas Valley Railroad show that from April to June

18. Weitbrec to McMurtrie, May 28, 1879, item 411; Engle to Weitbrec, May 29, 1879, item 412; Anderson to Weitbrec, May 30, 1879, item 413; Palmer to McMurtrie, June 5, 1879, item 418; McMurtrie to Weitbrec, June 6, 1879, item 421; Palmer Inventory of June 6, 1879, item 419—D&RG Archives.

19. Bell to Palmer, June 8, 1879, item 423, D&RG Archives.

8. D&RG Engine 169. This narrow-gauge locomotive was built by the Baldwin Locomotive Works in 1883 and entered service in December. In regular service such engines proved to be fast and efficient, one of them having set a speed record between Antonito and Alamosa, Colorado, covering the 28.6 miles in approximately 30 minutes. This particular engine was still in service in the late 1920s and is shown here as it was exhibited in Denver ready to appear at the New York World's Fair in 1939.

there were a number of expenditures for war supplies. Such items as "Colts Revolvers and Ammunition, $112.30," "Arms and Ammunition in April, 1879, $94.50," and "Payroll for May, W. R. Morley's Gang, $6,018" appear in certified copies later reproduced in court records.[20]

During the first week of June 1879 the situation became extremely tense. The *quo warranto* proceedings, begun earlier at the instance of the Rio Grande, came up for a hearing before Judge Thomas M. Bowen of Colorado's Fourth Judicial District and both sides prepared for a showdown. On the 9th Palmer told David Dodge that there were rumors afloat to the effect that the expected injunction against the Atchison Company had been issued, but that the County Clerk at Alamosa, where the proceedings were being held, could not be located to affix his seal to the document. Palmer said he was inclined to believe both stories because the clerk was known to have been purchased by the opposition. Unfortunately, he continued, the whole state was out of communication with "the South" because the Atchison employees had cut the telegraph wires. "They have chopped down the telegraph poles between Florence & our coal mines," he complained.[21] Rio Grande men were furious at the interruption of communications, and argued that it was up to Governor Frederick W. Pitkin to prevent such stoppages of public information. "We think it best that Denver papers should talk square up to the Governor," one of the Rio Grande lawyers advised D. C. Dodge. "Give it to him right between the eyes. He is a hypocrite, and nothing but fright and plain talking will keep him straight. . . . Call upon him to stop the interference daily practiced with the telegraph and trains by the Atchison minions."[22]

During the communications blackout, lawyers fought it out at Alamosa. The AT&SF management charged that Bowen had, by subterfuge, prevented the case from being transferred to a federal court, and its attorneys launched a violent personal attack upon him outside the courtroom. The Colorado Springs *Gazette* shrilled that attempts were afoot to kidnap Bowen to prevent justice from being carried out, and it intimated darkly that the Atchison people would go to any lengths. Despite tumultuous proceedings that frequently strained the court's decorum, Bowen handed down his opinion on June 10. He ordered

20. Anderson, *William J. Palmer*, p. 105.
21. Palmer to Dodge, June 9, 1879, item 432, D&RG Archives.
22. Theodore F. H. Meyer to Dodge, June 9, 1879, item 425, D&RG Archives.

the Atchison road to cease operating the Rio Grande's lines and to refrain from any interference with its operation by the rightful owners.

The next problem was to get the Atchison road to obey the court. All through the conflict, dating back to April 1878, both sides had tended to ignore such rulings and to hold their positions by force as long as possible, while attorneys appealed such decisions. Now the AT&SF took the case to the United States District Court of Judge Moses Hallett, hoping to overturn what the Pueblo *Chieftain* called "Bowen's Infamy."

Palmer was fearful that Hallett would rule adversely, as he had a year earlier, so he decided to regain control while Judge Bowen's order was still valid. Apparently the General was not alone in his suspicions, for the June 12 *Rocky Mountain News* brazenly stated that the *"News* has no confidence in the honesty and justice of Judge Hallett's intentions." Meanwhile, on the 11th, as the sheriffs of various counties undertook to carry out Bowen's order, excitement mounted all along the line. At 6:30 in the morning Colorado Springs watched its local sheriff do his duty, backed by a dozen deputies and Company B of the First Colorado Cavalry. When the men approached the depot, they found it locked and occupied by an armed force. Unwilling to launch an immediate attack, the sheriff looked around for stray AT&SF employees upon whom he might serve his warrants, and after having found a few, he then returned to the depot where he and his men faced a bristling array of gun muzzles. "I don't want any of your foolishness," he said. "Open that door and come out or I'll break it down." After a few tense moments the door opened and the Atchison troops shamefacedly emerged to be arrested at once. By 9:30 the Colorado Springs passenger depot was back in the hands of the Rio Grande, and shortly after noon, a victory dinner was served to the conquering warriors.

There was more excitement at Pueblo, the stronghold of the AT&SF. There the local sheriff opened negotiations early in the day for the return of the property, but his eloquence was not sufficiently convincing. He was backed by about 150 deputized residents, while the opposition had a force estimated at 400, composed of "roughs from Texas and green countrymen from Kansas," as the *Gazette* put it. By three o'clock the sheriff resolved to use force and headed for the roundhouse, where the main body of enemies was barricaded. Before reaching it, he was obliged to capture the telegraph office used by the opposition as an outpost. This required a rush for the door in which several shots were fired. An imported gunman from Dodge City, named Harry Jenkins, was reported killed in the melee, but the only other casualties came from fist fights and headaches caused by the liberal use of gun stocks.

The much-written-about battle at the roundhouse has nearly as many versions as there were participants. Pueblo and Colorado Springs papers represent the most divergent views, with the deputies being heroes in the eyes of the Colorado Springs *Gazette,* and a drunken, armed mob to the Pueblo *Chieftain.* The AT&SF defenders were led by a Texas tough named Thompson, who cravenly submitted, blubbering for mercy, according to the *Gazette.* The *Chieftain* agreed, with regard to the man's name, but differed in its account of the surrender. According to the Pueblo *Democrat,* the roundhouse forces were commanded by "Mr. Thomas, the city marshal of Dodge City."[23] Cy Warman, in his book *The Story of the Railroad,* has a highly dramatized account of the battle, in which he says the Rio Grande men tried to steal a cannon from the militia to batter down the roundhouse, but found that the Atchison men had already stolen it. In this version the famed Bat Masterson, of Dodge City, was in command of the temporary fortress. L. L. Waters, in his railroad volume, also names the fabled "Bat" as the roundhouse leader.[24] Whatever the leadership, the result was quiet surrender, and Pueblo fell without a fight.

23. Colorado Springs *Weekly Gazette,* June 14, 1879, quoting the Pueblo *Democrat.*

24. Waters, *Steel Trails:* "The roundhouse was held by Bat Masterson and his followers" (p. 123). When he wrote his book, Waters had available Charles F. Carter, *When Railroads Were New* (New York, Henry Holt, 1909), who said on p. 278 that the Santa Fe had recruited "a select band of fighting men at Dodge City, under the command of Bat Masterson." Bradley, in *The Story of the Santa Fe,* said only that "it was rumored" that Masterson was on his way to Pueblo (p. 191). Wilson, in his Rio Grande thesis, accepted as fact that the famous Dodge City sheriff actually participated in the roundhouse fight (p. 107). J. M. Meade, an eye witness to much of the railroad war, but who does not say he was in Pueblo in June 1879, makes no mention of Masterson at all. His work is entitled "D. & R. G. War with Santa Fe" (unpublished MS, Rio Grande Archives). There exists some doubt that Meade was the real author. The MS itself has an added note, attesting to this doubt. Waters, who relied upon it, quotes Joseph Weidel, valuation engineer of the AT&SF and a leading authority on the road's early history, who was convinced that Meade was not the author but thought it was nevertheless an accurate account of the war (see p. 493). General descriptions of the excitement of June 1879 are found also in the Colorado Springs *Weekly Gazette,* June 14, 1879; Pueblo *Colorado Chieftain,* June 10, 1879; *Daily Rocky Mountain News,* June 12, 1879; and Warman, *Story of the Railroad,* p. 153. Some years later Ernest Ingersoll, a writer well known to later 19th-century Americans, and one who was on the scene, referred to the roundhouse fight in a story he wrote for young Americans. He made no mention of Bat being present (*Youth's Companion,* Feb. 9, 1888).

Some violence was reported on other parts of the line. It was rumored that a sheriff's posse had collided with a group of Atchison guards near Cucharas, resulting in one or two casualties in each party, but aside from that, the transfer was made peaceably at such places as Denver, Canon City, Alamosa, and other points. Governor Pitkin got back into the good graces of the home railroad by telling the Atchison people, in answer to their complaint that the writs being served were illegal: "I have no more authority to review the proceedings of the district court than those of the supreme court. My duty is to sustain the officers in enforcing the process of the courts." The *Gazette* purred contentedly: "This put the entire matter right."[25]

Palmer's haste and willingness to risk violence may have appeared to some as precipitous, but this was a game in which the stakes were high, and the General must have felt that even if possession proved not to be nine points of the law, it was a move that provided some opportunities. Three days after the capture of June 11, he sought to insure his gain by turning over the road to a receiver, fearing an unfavorable decision at the hands of Judge Hallett, before whose court the case would soon appear. On June 14 Hanson A. Risley, general solicitor for the Rio Grande and a boyhood friend of Palmer's father-in-law, William P. Mellen, took possession. On the 23rd the expected reverse came when Hallett ordered the road returned to the Atchison Company, and now the Rio Grande pleaded for delay on the ground that the line was in the possession of a receiver. Early in July, Judge Miller, who sat on the case with Hallett, decided that the receivership was properly authorized, the request for it having come from L. H. Meyer, who represented the bondholders. The delaying device was successful. The Denver *Daily Times* twitted the Rio Grande management for alleging that it was solvent one day and then requesting receivership the next, but it admitted that the maneuver had provided a breather, as both railroads prepared for the next legal round.[26]

The respite was brief. By July 14 Judge Miller must have entertained second thoughts in the matter, for he then announced that the move into receivership was a mere subterfuge, employed to avoid com-

25. Colorado Springs *Weekly Gazette,* June 14, 1879. Both the *Gazette* and the Pueblo *Colorado Chieftain* reported fatalities in the Cucharas affair. The *Weekly New Mexican* (June 14, 1879) reported 30 killed and wounded and talked of a "big fight" in the Royal Gorge. The *Daily Rocky Mountain News* (June 13, 1879) set the death toll at 6.

26. *Railroad Gazette* (July 4, 1879), p. 370. Denver *Daily Times,* June 16, 23, July 5, 1879.

pliance with Hallett's request to give up the property. Holding that there were no grounds for a receivership, such as insolvence, he dismissed the receiver, Hanson Risley.

On the following morning, Rio Grande attorneys appeared in court asking that the recent order directing them to return the road to the Atchison Company be set aside. The court refused to hear the plea, explaining that the Rio Grande was in contempt and not in a position to ask anything. Hallett explained that it had been only an act of courtesy that allowed the narrow gauge to appear before him after its lawlessness of recent days. With regard to the question of the rights of each party, under the lease, these questions would be heard only after Palmer's officials restored the road to the AT&SF. Judge Miller concurred and took occasion to lecture the aggressive Rio Grande management. Angrily, he told them that they had resorted to mob law, taking property by the use of armed men. "No judge, no court can sit quietly down and tolerate such abuses of process," he said. "The parties in this case had better retrace those steps at once and put themselves right before the court and the country. This is not a country of violence." A newsman reported that the targets of the tongue-lashing sat in their seats, "apparently as if they had been struck by lightning." By the next noon the Atchison Company was again in possession of the road. The court's wishes complied with, Palmer immediately filed a new suit in the United States Circuit Court, asking for a cancellation of the lease and repossession of the property.[27]

During the legal squabble over possession of the property, both companies were jockeying for position in the matter of carrying out the Supreme Court's decision of April 21. The Rio Grande did not yet have permission to utilize its priority in the Royal Gorge, since the Circuit Court, whose duty it was to make proper provision, had not taken the necessary action. In mid-July, Judge Hallett carried out the higher court's mandate, granting Palmer's company right of way through that defile, but it was his interpretation that this also meant prior right all the way from Canon City to Leadville. Now, he said, if the narrow gauge wanted to pursue its right, it must assume all of the road built by its opponents, at a fair and equitable price. This

27. Denver *Daily Times*, July 14, 15, 16, 1879. *Railroad Gazette* (July 18, 1879), p. 392. *Denver and Rio Grande Railway Co. v. Pueblo and Arkansas Valley Railway*, Case No. 186 in Circuit Court of the U.S. for the District of Colorado, item 471, D&RG Archives.

would necessitate some negotiation between the roads as to the matter of proper compensation, and until the question was settled, the Judge forbade either company to carry on any further construction. As the Denver *Times* said, such a delightful delay was all the opportunity the Denver, South Park, and Pacific needed to reach Leadville before either of its rivals.[28]

During the ensuing weeks of quiet along the route to Leadville, the Atchison Company petitioned the Court for permission to construct a more permanent bridge in the Gorge narrows. The result was the famous "Hanging Bridge," an object of continuing curiosity to rail travelers today and viewed by thousands of automobile tourists from the suspension bridge built years later across the top of the Gorge. The Hanging Bridge was unique in that it did not cross any water, but was hung along V-shaped girders, based on either side of the Arkansas, to conduct trains along the sheer cliffs, which, if blasted out to allow room for a roadbed, would have plugged up the river. It was 175 feet long, was built for less than $12,000, and, with some additional support from below, is still in daily use. Except for this bit of construction, all activity along the "battle front" ceased during the summer of 1879, as the contestants carried on their bitter legal battle.[29]

Before July was out, the Rio Grande again had its request to break the lease before Judge Moses Hallett. After he reviewed the entire case at great length, he announced that while he did not think the Palmer people had much right to any consideration, in view of their unruly conduct, he had to admit there was evidence of violation of the document by the other side. He then decided, on July 24, to put the Rio Grande into the hands of a court-appointed receiver, and named Louis C. Ellsworth to that position. A Colorado Springs paper pointed out that the Judge was obliged to make this move in order to keep a ten million dollar property from being ruined, because the Atchison Company was not only allowing the rented property to deteriorate, but it was, in violation of the lease, paralleling the narrow gauge's line in places and had made surveys indicating a continuance of this practice. The paper was quite annoyed with the Judge for making critical comments about the Baby Road, and it asserted that if Hallett himself had, in the original instance, ruled in favor of the Rio Grande's prior

28. Denver *Daily Times*, July 15, 1879. Wilson, "Denver and Rio Grande," pp. 110, 111.
29. For a good description of the construction of the bridge see Wilson, pp. 112–13.

right to the Royal Gorge, there would have been no subsequent violence.[30]

Obeying Judge Hallett's decision, the AT&SF delivered its leased Rio Grande lines to the newly-appointed receiver in mid-August. While Ellsworth was said to be friendly to the larger railroad, he was given strict orders by the court to manage the narrow gauge independently and to show no special favor to any of the connecting roads. Under these changed conditions the Rio Grande set about resuming construction westward toward the San Juans and southward toward El Paso, as well as to Leadville, a city whose inhabitants were now thoroughly annoyed at the delays caused by the long and bitter legal war for the Royal Gorge. In early September the AT&SF revealed it was about to carry out its earlier threat to invade Denver directly. A. A. Robinson, its chief engineer, was ordered to commence construction at once between Pueblo and the Colorado capital, paralleling the Rio Grande all the way. Thus the war between the companies was continued without abatement, with neither side apparently ready to yield.

Then, as passions soared to new heights, there stepped into the picture one of the most widely talked of men in American railroad history. Jay Gould, that master of financial intrigue, had just succeeded in merging the Union Pacific and Kansas Pacific, and with this stroke put himself in an excellent position to strike a mortal blow at the AT&SF. He now offered to buy, through an exchange of stock, one-half of the Rio Grande's trust certificates, which controlled the stock held in trust for that captive company. On September 8, 1879, an agreement was drawn up between Jay Gould and Russell Sage, on the one hand, and Charles F. Woerischoffer, William J. Palmer, and William Scott, on the other, to buy trust certificates covering 37,791 shares of stock at 22 per cent of their par value. Gould and Sage also agreed to advance $400,000 in cash to help the Rio Grande reduce its debt. Palmer and the others agreed, in return, to make no traffic agreements with the AT&SF or any other road that did not provide equal rights to the Union Pacific and Kansas Pacific, and were guaranteed that in any such arrangement there would be no discrimination against the Rio Grande.[31] Both Gould and Sage became Rio Grande board members. Once Gould had gained a foothold in the Rio Grande's corporate structure, part two of his plot against the Atchison Company

30. Colorado Springs *Weekly Gazette,* July 26, 1879.
31. Copy of Agreement, item 490, D&RG Archives. *Railroad Gazette* (Sept. 26, 1879), p. 516.

was revealed. In a move a Denver paper called "Bulldozing the A. T. & S. F." he announced the organization of a new railroad called the Pueblo and St. Louis, to run down the Arkansas Valley some 340 miles to Great Bend, Kansas, where it would connect with a Gould-built extension. The Colorado portion of the line, about 150 miles in length, would be built by the Rio Grande.[32] One of Gould's biographers called it "a typical Gould master stroke," pointing out that the Atchison people were so busy fighting their way into the Southwest that they had left one of their flanks unguarded, and here he chose to strike. During the fall of 1879 the voting certificates of the Rio Grande, purchased at twenty-two, had soared to seventy-five. Now Gould wanted to terminate the war of duplicate construction going on between the Atchison Road and the Rio Grande to protect his own interests. To accomplish it he used his old weapon: the threat of parallel construction against those who were themselves practicing it. By this move, coupled with the reverses the AT&SF was suffering in the courts, the transcontinental was obliged to think seriously about making peace.[33]

The only other worry Gould had with regard to gaining control of the fabulous Leadville traffic was the Denver, South Park, and Pacific, headed by John Evans. In the fall of 1879 he tried to buy a controlling interest in that road. The attempt was unsuccessful, but by means not clear even to the historian of the little road, he was able to exert enough pressure to get a satisfactory traffic division into Leadville and to keep the South Park road out of the San Juan country. The principal benefit that Evans got out of the deal was the immediate elevation to par of his securities, relieving the financial pressure sufficiently to allow further construction of his road.[34]

During the winter of 1879–80 the AT&SF found itself in increasingly difficult straits. As the dangerous Jay Gould threatened it on the one hand, matters in the legal battle with the Rio Grande became steadily more unfavorable on the other. During October the three-man commission, arranged for by Judge Hallett to study the feasibility of two roads up the Arkansas Valley, made its report. It was recommend-

32. Denver *Daily Times,* Jan. 16, 1879.

33. Julius Grodinsky, *Jay Gould: His Business Career, 1867–1892* (Philadelphia, 1957), pp. 180–81.

34. M. C. Poor, *Denver South Park & Pacific* (Denver, 1949), p. 163. Colorado Springs *Weekly Gazette,* Oct. 4, 1879. Denver *Daily Times,* Oct. 1, 1879.

ed that for a distance of 4.09 miles through the Royal Gorge, the two lines would have to share a single track, but from the twentieth mile-post on to Leadville there was ample room for two tracks. Because of the illness of Hallett, court action on the report was postponed until the last day of the year. Then, as the fateful year 1879 died out, Colorado learned that, in effect, the long and bitter railroad war was over, the home company victorious. Judge Hallett denied allegations by the Atchison Company that under conditions of the lease there was no legal Denver and Rio Grande Railway and that the lease in no way affected that railroad's right of priority in the Royal Gorge. He ordered the entire constructed line west of Canon City delivered to Palmer's company at cost, the amount to be determined by a commissioner. If the AT&SF still wished to build into Leadville, it had to do so on the other side of the river.[35]

By January 1880 the Rio Grande was still under the direction of L. C. Ellsworth, receiver; no court had yet invalidated the lease; the AT&SF had the privilege, if it wished to exercise it, of building into Leadville. To President Thomas Nickerson the situation did not appear to be nearly favorable enough to pursue the struggle. Atchison officials were mildly encouraged when on February 2 the Supreme Court denied a Rio Grande request for a writ of mandamus to force the laggardly Circuit Court of Colorado to execute the high court's decision of April 21, 1879. Since the unfavorable decision promised no more than a temporary delay for the Rio Grande, Nickerson and his directors decided to make the most of the situation at the conference table, salvaging what they could before their position became any worse. Early in February, arrangements were made for a peace parley between the quarreling parties, to be held at Boston. From it emerged the so-called "Treaty of Boston" or Tripartite Agreement, whereby the opposing camps settled for a compromise that was to finally end the long and expensive struggle.

The first stipulation in the treaty provided for cancellation of the lease with the return of all Rio Grande stock held in trust. The receivership of the narrow gauge was to be terminated and all litigation stopped, with each company settling its own costs. For surrendering the already-constructed portion of railroad between Canon City and Leadville, the AT&SF received $1,400,000 plus interest for labor and

35. Denver *Daily Times,* Dec. 31, 1879. *Railroad Gazette* (Jan. 9, 1880), p. 23.

materials expended, and an additional award of $400,000.[36] In return for vacating the Royal Gorge route, the Atchison Company required the Rio Grande to abandon the building of its proposed Pueblo and St. Louis line and to go no farther into New Mexico than a point about half-way between Conejos and Santa Fe. The larger road then promised not to build into Denver, Leadville, the San Juan country, or any point west of the Denver and Rio Grande's established lines, provided it received one-half the Rio Grande business in southwestern Colorado and one-fourth of that from Denver. There were also reciprocal arrangements regarding traffic of the Union Pacific over the Denver, South Park, and Pacific tracks near Leadville. The agreement, to last for ten years, thus made an effective physical division of the country over which the two roads had fought so bitterly.[37]

The "war," like all wars, had generated so much heat that it was not easily brought to an abrupt and immediate halt. Shortly after the decision to negotiate, made on February 2, Rio Grande engineers got word from New York that they might proceed toward Leadville. Contracts were let for completing the necessary grading and bridging, but actual construction was delayed until the managerial diplomats could settle upon some of the smaller details. Chief engineer McMurtrie of the Rio Grande charged that due to "considerable stubbornness on the part of the Officers on the other side, the road and material was not turned over to us until about April 5, 1880, at which time track laying commenced where the A. T. and S. Fe were stopped." The precise time of delivery was midnight, April 4, and although there had been no previous announcement of the event, Palmer's home town of Colorado Springs put on a celebration that was long remembered. In the light of blazing bonfires and above the roar of repeated cannon salutes, townsmen yelled themselves hoarse. The railroad's engines, train cars, and even the town itself were decorated with the brightest bunting. Between prolonged screams of locomotive whistles, visitors tried to discover what national holiday was being observed, but their questions were lost in the delirious confusion.

36. The commissioners who studied the matter, using the records of A. A. Robinson, chief engineer for the AT&SF, estimated that the road had cost only $566,216.35. See Anderson, *William J. Palmer*, p. 113.

37. Indenture dated March 27, 1880, signed by Thomas Nickerson, managing director of the P&AV, and by William J. Palmer, president of the D&RG, in William Jackson Palmer Papers, Division of State Archives and Public Records, Denver. *Railroad Gazette* (Feb. 6, 1880), p. 83. Wilson, "Denver and Rio Grande," p. 118.

Out of the celebration came a story that no doubt made the rounds in Colorado Springs for a long time. A young man, described by the local press as "just out from the states," had, earlier that evening, asked some of the livery stable hands about the Wild West. They gravely assured him that from time to time the "red devils" would descend upon the city, killing men, women, and children, and when such an event occurred, it was impossible to halt the bloodshed. When the guns began to boom shortly after midnight, and sleepy-eyed residents tumbled out of their beds to join the celebrants, the stranger quickly concluded that the city was under attack by Indians. He dashed out into the cold spring night, leaving his boots and trousers behind, and prepared to do his bit in a final, heroic defense of the city against the red marauders. When he finally discovered the reason for the turmoil, he returned to his bed, shivering only from the cold night air, "the happiest man in town."[38]

The deliverance of the Rio Grande did not cause any excitement in neighboring cities. In Denver it was almost unnoticed. "There was no formality about the transfer, it having been so quietly accomplished, that but few of the men were aware of the change of management," said one capital city paper. The Pueblo *Chieftain* glumly remarked that the event was "no special occasion for jubilee" among friends of the Rio Grande, and that if any celebration was in order it should be over the fact that southern Colorado was now free of railroad strife and the way to Leadville was at last clear.[39]

The conflict covered two years, almost to a day, and was both a highly significant and extremely expensive affair for the Rio Grande. Back in April 1878, when the trouble began, Palmer had been trying desperately to extend his line to Santa Fe, a point he had to reach by 1882 in order to comply with the specifications under which Congress had granted a right of way. Almost twenty-four months were lost, seventeen of which saw the line either under lease or in the hands of a receiver, as the narrow gauge fought for its very existence. During that time the whole destiny of the road had changed. The original goal, El Paso, had disappeared in the shuffle of papers at a Boston conference table, as had most of New Mexico itself. Not only the Rio Grande's drive to the south, but any hope of extending eastward down

38. Colorado Springs *Weekly Gazette,* April 10, 1880.
39. Denver *Daily Times,* April 5, 1880. *Colorado Chieftain,* April 8, 1880.

the Arkansas Valley, was blocked, leaving it no place to go but west, into the mountains and perhaps to Salt Lake City.

The great prize, Leadville, was a glittering but transitory thing, and for that key to the great mountain treasure chest Palmer's road paid a very high price. For two decades following 1880, Colorado's mines produced annually never less than twenty-one million dollars worth of various minerals, and by 1900 the yearly figure stood at fifty million, lending validity to the correctness of the General's course. In those years the Denver and Rio Grande took advantage of every opportunity to tap sources of mineral wealth, following each new strike with the avidity of any hard-rock miner. Palmer knew that the flow of precious metals would not sustain itself forever, and that a more diverse basis of revenue would have to be developed, but for the moment traffic to and from the mines was sufficient to justify construction. The immediate objective was to exploit the territory he had marked off as his, to get the road built, and to ward off any other hopeful interlopers.

MAP 4

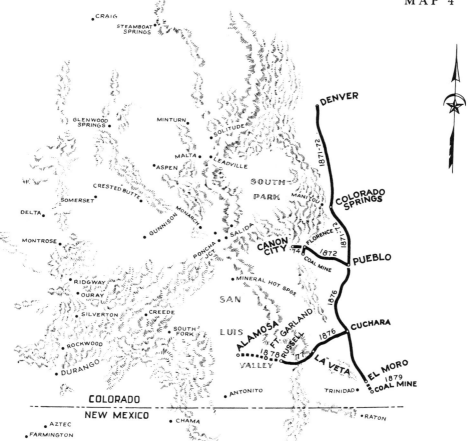

- CRAIG
- STEAMBOAT SPRINGS
- GLENWOOD SPRINGS
- MINTURN
- SOLITUDE
- MALTA
- ASPEN
- LEADVILLE
- SOUTH PARK
- DENVER
- MANITOU
- COLORADO SPRINGS
- CRESTED BUTTE
- SOMERSET
- MONARCH
- DELTA
- GUNNISON
- SALIDA
- CANON CITY
- FLORENCE
- COAL MINE
- PUEBLO
- MONTROSE
- PONCHA JCT.
- MINERAL HOT SPGS.
- RIDGWAY
- OURAY
- SAN LUIS
- ALAMOSA
- FT. GARLAND
- RUSSELL
- CUCHARA
- SILVERTON
- CREEDE
- SOUTH FORK
- VALLEY
- LA VETA
- EL MORO
- COAL MINE
- ROCKWOOD
- DURANGO
- ANTONITO
- TRINIDAD
- COLORADO
- NEW MEXICO
- AZTEC
- CHAMA
- RATON
- FARMINGTON
- CALIENTE
- ESPANOLA

1871-72
1871-72
1872
1876
1876
1876
1878
77
1879

1878-1879
DENVER & RIO GRANDE
RAILWAY
Showing Construction Steps.

5. *In search of undiscovered realms*

THE RIO GRANDE'S westward thrust began in 1876 with the commencement of work on the Fort Garland division. At that time the shift in direction signified no change in the original plan to reach El Paso; it was merely one of several alternative approaches to New Mexico. Moving out of Cucharas, in the direction of La Veta Pass, construction crews headed for the San Luis Valley and Fort

Garland. Palmer intended to push his road in a westerly direction until he reached the site of present Alamosa, before swinging south toward Santa Fe and Albuquerque. Among the plans of the road's projectors was a proposed extension westward from Antonito into the mining regions of the San Juan mountains, a line that was to become much more important in the light of later developments; but at the time it was conceived as only a feeder to the main route.

By July 1876 La Veta Pass was approached and a town company established below it, as had been the custom at other points along the line. Within a few months a thriving community of over a thousand souls was doing a rushing business with the country that lay beyond the railroad. Between fifty and a hundred wagons left the place each day for Fort Garland and other points west. In November contracts were let for the next piece of road to Fort Garland, and a large number of men started to cut out a tortuous path across the mountains. After slow and expensive progress, tracklaying was completed to Garland City, near the fort, in the summer of 1877.[1]

During the fall and winter months of 1877–78 the work was halted as the company paused for breath, trying to raise more money and to make final plans for the plunge into New Mexico. In February the firm of Carlile, Orman, and Crook was given a contract to build the projected thirty miles to Alamosa, on the upper Rio Grande. Most of the country into Alamosa was level, offering so few engineering problems that the work was finished by the end of June 1878. Once the famed river was reached, the narrow gauge had earned its title. By that time the fight for the Royal Gorge, east of the mountains, was in full swing, and for the next two years Palmer's company was so engaged in a fight for its life that further progress to the south was severely hampered.

In the spring of 1878, however, there was still great enthusiasm among the Palmer associates for continuing construction from Alamosa to the vicinity of Santa Fe, particularly after the AT&SF had snatched from them the alternate route over Raton Pass. On June 1 Charles B. Lamborn, associated with the Denver and Rio Grande since the beginning, met with some of Santa Fe's principal men and property owners, explaining that the railroad intended to start south from Alamosa very soon and its management would like to serve that

1. Anderson, *General William J. Palmer*, pp. 77–78. Report of the chief engineer, April 1, 1881, *Annual Report of the D&RG* (1880), p. 31.

city if sufficient inducement were offered. A week later a public meeting was held at which a committee, headed by General Edward Hatch,
was instructed to learn more about the kind of inducements the Rio
Grande wanted. An answer was not long in coming. On the 11th,
Hatch and his committeemen were told that the railroad would enter
Santa Fe for a donation of $200,000, half in cash, half in bonds; a grant
of land for a depot site; and a free right of way through Santa Fe county
to the depot. A vote was taken and the proposal was unanimously rejected. To keep the door open, the committee then agreed to recommend an election to determine whether the taxpayers would approve
such a contribution, but only on the condition that tracks enter the
city by July 1879.

Within a few days Lamborn again met with the committee. After
discussing the original proposition, its rejection, and the suggested
bond issue, he explained that Santa Fe did not lie on the direct southerly route of the narrow gauge and that to deviate from it would involve additional mileage and some serious physical difficulties. He
could not promise that an affirmative vote on the bond issue would
bring in the road, for the maximum amount authorized for consideration was less than $100,000. Should the voters agree to that sum, it
would interest the railroad sufficiently to make surveys, after which
the two parties could negotiate further. Rather sharply, Lamborn
told his listeners that the matter at hand in no way affected the Rio
Grande's decision to pass through New Mexico, for that had already
been determined. If Santa Fe wanted to be on the line, fine; it was
merely a matter of self-interest. If it did not, the railroad would have
to make other arrangements.

This "take it or leave it" attitude deeply angered the townsmen.
In an editorial entitled "The Railroad Question," the local newspaper
defied Lamborn and his company, warning that "the short-sighted
policy of this road in building up small terminal towns in the interest
of and for the pecuniary benefit of their road, as opposed to the in-
calculable loss of prestige and popularity with the business community, bears its own fruit." The editor could well point to cities like
Trinidad and Canon City, where the company had held the same gun
to civic heads, engendering deep hatreds. Even as he wrote, the people
of both these towns were doing all they could to help the AT&SF in
its fight against the Rio Grande.

Santa Fe now had a choice: it could yield and pay what amounted to a ransom, or it could refuse and watch a new town, built by the railroad, sprout up near it, just as Trinidad recently had witnessed the birth of El Moro. The newspaper warned that the price of acquiescence was high: "Taxation in aid of railroads for temporary advantages gained has left scores of monuments along our great western trunk lines in the shape of miserable, half-deserted and bankrupt towns."[2]

The bond negotiations with Santa Fe were unsuccessful, but the Denver and Rio Grande, good to its word that the matter had no bearing on its larger plans, proceeded. In mid-June, Carlile, Orman, and Crook received a contract to prepare a grade from Alamosa to the general vicinity of Santa Fe, a distance of 145 miles, to be completed within five months. The Alamosa *News* stated confidently that the road would be built without fail, because Jay Gould was putting up half the money, and with that kind of support the remainder would quickly be subscribed.[3] As the year 1878 came to a close, it appeared that such optimism was merited. By then the grade between Alamosa and Antonito (near the New Mexican border) had been finished and Palmer had approved the route on to Tres Piedras, in Taos County, New Mexico, sixty-four miles farther south. Then things came to a halt. The winter was so severe that normal operations were impossible, but more significantly, the Rio Grande's war with the Atchison, Topeka, and Santa Fe had reached such proportions that there were no resources available for construction.[4]

The Supreme Court decision of April 21, 1879, favorable to the Denver and Rio Grande, gave that road a tremendous boost. Although the road was then under lease to the AT&SF, and the decision did nothing to alter this situation, the high court's ruling that the narrow gauge had a prior right through the Royal Gorge caused a flurry in eastern financial circles. Anticipating an early release from AT&SF thralldom, Palmer now solicited loans amounting to over five million dollars for the purpose of extending his road in three directions: up the Arkansas Valley to Leadville, westward from Alamosa to the San Juan mines, and southward from Alamosa to Albuquerque. Within

2. *Weekly New Mexican,* June 8, 15, 22, July 6, 1878. *Daily Rocky Mountain News,* June 20, 1878.

3. *Weekly New Mexican,* July 6, 1878, quoting the Alamosa *News.*

4. Report of Robert F. Weitbrec, manager of construction, in *Annual Report of the D&RG* (1880), p. 25. Wilson, "Denver and Rio Grande," pp. 129–30.

five days the amount was oversubscribed, and before long he had offers amounting to ten million dollars.[5]

Santa Fe again took hope. In the fall of 1879 activity once more was observed along the southern extension after a year's delay. A Santa Fe paper admitted that when the stoppage occurred, its readers were very discouraged, not only because of the cessation but because they feared that the rapidly growing San Juan mining country would pull any extension in that direction, "perhaps at the expense of a considerable delay in building south." Thoroughly frightened now at the prospect of being left out in the cold, the editor forgot his early warnings about impending municipal bankruptcy through the buying of railroad bonds, and meekly said that "if our town is not on the natural line of the road, it will be well for us to take such measures as are fair and just to have it pass through Santa Fe."[6] Meanwhile, in December 1879, the Rio Grande let contracts for extending the main line to Albuquerque, and tracklaying south of Alamosa was resumed in February. At the end of March, rails reached Antonito over the grade that had been prepared a year earlier.

Just as the residents of Santa Fe made ready to welcome the narrow gauge, whose arrival seemed now almost a certainty, lawyers in faraway Boston tripped a guillotine that decapitated the oncoming railhead. By the "Treaty of Boston," formalized on March 27, 1880, between the Rio Grande and the AT&SF, the former agreed to go no farther south than Espanola for a period of ten years, as part of a general railroad compromise settlement. Since the Rio Grande had already spent considerable sums of money along the route, even south of Espanola, it decided to salvage what it could by building to the agreed terminus as cheaply as possible. Down along the Rio Grande river tracklayers went, laying ties and rails directly on the sod and clinging to the natural contours wherever they could, a type of construction that provided some dramatic grades for the trains that were to traverse the line. When the road reached Espanola, an intervening gap of thirty-four miles faced Palmer's company. It was filled by the incorporation of another narrow gauge, the Texas, Santa Fe, and Northern, in December 1880, but it was not until 1886 that Santa Fe finally realized its long-desired connection with Denver. By that time

5. *Railroad Gazette* (May 23, 1879), pp. 290–91. Colorado Springs *Weekly Gazette,* May 24, 1879. *Weekly New Mexican,* May 31, 1879. Wilson, p. 104.

6. *Weekly New Mexican,* Nov. 1, 1879.

9. Pike's Peak Avenue, 1880s. Colorado Springs, by this time, was beginning to take on the solidly built appearance that gave meaning to its nickname "Little London."

the Denver and Rio Grande had several years since connected with
Salt Lake City, and the extension to Santa Fe was merely an unim-
portant branch line, lost in the commotion of larger railroad considerations.[7]

The "war years" were vital to the Denver and Rio Grande in several respects. While the outcome, as revealed in the terms of the
treaty, barricaded its original route, shifting the road's general direction from south to west, those requirements were not unacceptable
to General Palmer in the light of new and changed conditions. During
the course of the struggle Leadville's potential was demonstrated and,
as Meredith Wilson put it, that mining mecca "was only an ornate
vestibule to a great mineral kingdom beyond."[8] Deeper in the untapped mountain recesses lay other possible Leadvilles awaiting exploitation.

Now that the threat once posed by the AT&SF was warded off and
his own road was left as the prime contender in a gold and silver empire, Palmer lost no time in staking out his transportation claim. The
Denver and Rio Grande, he wrote, was "enabled by the rapid occupation of these mountain inlets to furnish promptly to every mining
camp, whose business under the facilities afforded by railroad carriage
promises to warrant the expenditure, a branch from one of its trunks."
So rich were some of the ore deposits that their haulage would many
times over pay the cost of feeder lines before the mines were exhausted.
Since prospecting and discovery were spreading westward throughout
Colorado in a general way, Palmer found it "wise and profitable to
keep the main stems through all this gold and silver belt extended
well ahead."[9] Thus a program one might term "railroad prospecting"
became the road's principal policy, as its management sought to cash
in on the boom taking place in a territory it had won over a Boston
conference table.

As final terms of the settlement with the AT&SF were being made,
Rio Grande construction forces stood poised, ready to build at once
to the nearest and most valuable goal, Leadville. At midnight, April
4, 1880, the road was returned to Rio Grande management and immediately work was resumed. Since the construction already completed

7. Wilson, p. 131. Ridgway, "Denver and Rio Grande," p. 40. Not until 1895 did the connecting link come into D&RG control.

8. Wilson, p. 124.

9. Report of William J. Palmer, in *Annual Report of the D&RG* (1880), p. 12.

MAP 5

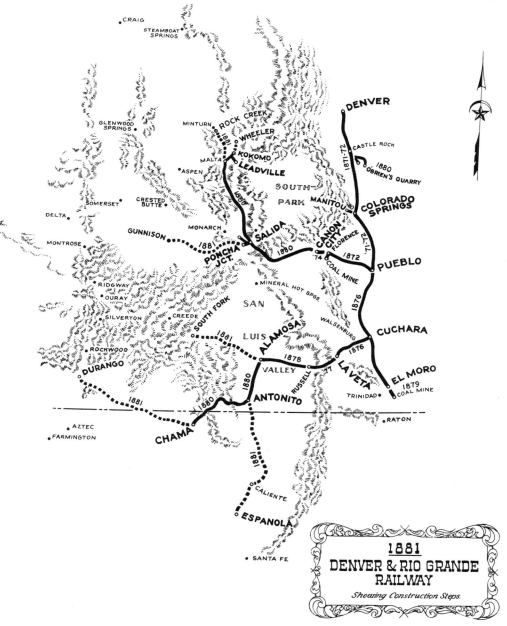

CRAIG
STEAMBOAT SPRINGS

GLENWOOD SPRINGS

DENVER

MINTURN
ROCK CREEK
1881
WHEELER
MALTA
KOKOMO
ASPEN
LEADVILLE

CASTLE ROCK
1871-72
1880
O'BRIEN'S QUARRY

SOUTH PARK
MANITOU
COLORADO SPRINGS

SOMERSET
CRESTED BUTTE
DELTA
MONARCH
GUNNISON
1881
PONCHA JCT.
MONTROSE
1880
SALIDA
1880
CANON CITY
FLORENCE
COAL MINE
'74
1872
'71-72
PUEBLO
1876

RIDGWAY
OURAY
SILVERTON
CREEDE
SOUTH FORK
1881
SAN
MINERAL HOT SPGS.
LUIS
ALAMOSA
1878
VALLEY
RUSSELL '77
WALSENBURG
CUCHARA
1876
LA VETA
EL MORO
1879
COAL MINE
TRINIDAD

ROCKWOOD
DURANGO
1880
1881
ANTONITO
1880
CHAMA

AZTEC
FARMINGTON
RATON

1881
CALIENTE

ESPANOLA

SANTA FE

1881
DENVER & RIO GRANDE
RAILWAY
Showing Construction Steps.

by the Pueblo and Arkansas Valley Railroad, an Atchison Company subsidiary, was, by the terms of the agreement, sold to Palmer's company, completion of the line did not take long. Trains were running into Leadville by August 2, and while that portion of the extension was being finished, crews were at work beyond, across Ten Mile Pass and from Malta over Tennessee Pass, probing for new sources of income.[10] There was a standing joke in Leadville at that time to the effect that if a man on the other side of Mosquito Pass had a wagon load of pumpkins for sale, Palmer would build a branch line across the mountains to reach him.[11]

The recently emancipated narrow gauge intended to tap not only all of Colorado's freight potential, but it set out to re-establish itself as the state's principal conveyor of passengers. In early July 1880 passenger agent F. C. Nims published a full column story in a Denver paper telling readers that the Rio Grande, now over 500 miles in length, was the longest and best equipped railroad in Colorado, as well as being the safest. In ten years not a single life had been lost on the line through accident. This was because every piece of equipment was, as he said, "first class." New Pullman Palace sleepers were used on all night trains, and as General Palmer had once pointed out, such accommodations on a narrow gauge were superior to wide-gauge sleepers, for the berths could hold but one person, lending a kind of privacy not available on those lines where passengers might be expected to share the wider berths. Day trains were equipped with Horton parlor-chair cars, and those passing through the Royal Gorge carried specially built observation cars. All trains, freight and passenger, were equipped with the new Westinghouse air brakes "and all meritorious appliances known to modern skill." It was no wonder, said Nims, that this road was the most popular and most profitable one operating in Colorado.[12]

With Leadville secured at an early date in the new era of railroad peace, the Rio Grande hastened on, anxious to take advantage of a national financial resurgence that made investment money easy and

10. Weitbrec Report, in *Annual Report* (1880), pp. 25, 26.

11. William W. Leeman to Governor O. H. Shoup, Oct. 10, 1921, in Palmer Memorial Clippings, Coburn Library, Colorado College, Colorado Springs. Mr. Leeman, an engineer, claimed credit for Palmer's practice of paying 6 per cent interest on money accrued to any employee who would refrain from collecting his pay for 60 days or longer, as an additional means of financing construction.

12. Denver *Daily Times,* July 8, 1880.

of the enormous traffic from the sharply increased mining activity. Westward from Salida, Alamosa, and Antonito slithered narrow-gauge feelers, probing mountain passes, grasping at the life-giving treasures being wrested from the land by hordes of miners deep in new and unexplored country. The most exciting search was in the San Juan country, tucked away in southwestern Colorado, inaccessible and mysterious. "The railway heard the tales of the prospectors and miners and looked westward . . . toward the new land of promise," wrote a newspaper correspondent who signed himself "Dillenback." "The scene could not have been more alluring. Low, smooth, gently rising hills, covered with grass, and timbered with scattering pines and groves of poplar, extended as far as the eye could reach. . . . They seemed to promise a very Eden for tourists." And there were mountains, "canopied with perpetual clouds; in front were castellated crags, art-like monuments and stupendous precipices. Having allured the railway into their awful fastness, the mountains seemed determined to baffle its further progress." Where was the railroad going, and where would it end, the writer asked? Its destination was as uncertain as the *ultima thule* of the ancients: "It is, apparently, a railway hopelessly gone astray, a sort of knight-errant railway in quest of adventures, a New Columbus, with cars instead of ships, in search of undiscovered realms." It was a railroad with a master prospector at the helm, one that followed the miner and his burro, bound for where they were headed, looking for the same thing, wherever it was. For the moment what more goal was needed?

The San Juan branch, built under the auspices of the Denver and Rio Grande Extension Company, Alexander C. Hunt, president, was constructed in the face of the most complicated problems that ever confronted American engineers. With the flat distances of the high parks left behind, heavy rock-work was encountered in the jagged mountains that guarded the San Juan. From Cumbres Pass to Chama the grade was 4 per cent, the curvature bad, and construction generally of the most expensive nature. At one point, to cover the distance of only a half mile, it was necessary to build two and a half miles of track, trestle, and embankment, one mile of which alone cost $140,000. Nor was this the exception, for to cover the larger distance of thirty-five miles, some sixty-four miles of track had to be laid. Reports of such difficult construction led to the inevitable humorous stories of its problems. On one piece of track, known as the whiplash, the road doubled back upon itself twice, making three parallel tracks in a very short distance. In the lower loop was a section house, and, as a brakeman remarked, if the train did not go too fast, it afforded the section gang time to get pretty well acquainted with the passengers before it passed.[13] Despite the engineering challenge and heavy winter weather, the road had progressed across the divide to Chama by February 1, 1881.

In addition to the physical problem of extremely high passes and tortuous grades, the matter of personnel plagued the railroad. In October 1880 a railroad journal noted that about 2,000 men were at work on the San Juan extension alone, and the company was sending to the front from forty to fifty men a day.[14] Robert Weitbrec, manager of construction, complained that the workmen were getting the highest wages ever paid to railroad laborers in Colorado, but he could not supply the need. Between the fall of 1879 and the spring of 1881, an average of a thousand laborers a month were shipped to the various grading camps on the Rio Grande system from the Denver and Pueblo areas alone. In addition, it had advanced fares to 200 brought in from Canada, 250 from St. Louis, 300 from Chicago, and 1,000 from Kansas, all of whom agreed to refund the advance when they had earned it. "In nearly all cases the men deserted, many went to the mines, a few returned to their homes and the Lord probably knows where the rest are," Weitbrec reported to Palmer. The attempts had cost the road $41,350, of which about $8,000 was recovered. "Any number of worthless fellows are anxious to get a free ride to Colorado," wrote the manager, "and I made up my mind that unless a man could raise enough money to pay his railroad fare and expenses that the chances were he was an undesirable man to have." He tried also to import Negroes from the South. At the time of his report he was in correspondence with a labor contractor in Milan, Italy, but even this project appeared to have little prospect of success. The only real piece of luck Weitbrec had was a successful negotiation with the Mormons, who agreed to send 2,000 laborers, 300 of whom promised to come early in the fall of 1880, bringing along their own teams.[15] But even this venture had its discouragements, for the severe winter weather

13. Durango *Herald*, Aug. 5, 1881.
14. *Railroad Gazette* (Oct. 15, 1880), p. 542. Wilson, "Denver and Rio Grande," p. 134.
15. Weitbrec Report, in *Annual Report* (1880), pp. 27–28. *Railroad Gazette* (Oct. 15, 1880), p. 542.

10. Snowslide Tunnel on Silverton Branch. Frequently, the best way to cope with a snowslide was to tunnel through it. Here is such a tunnel on the Silverton branch, with No. 227 poking its nose out into the daylight.

11. D&RG Train on Big Horn Curve. The winding nature of the narrow-gauge is demonstrated in this view, where the tracks pass a section house three times in their efforts to match a mountain.

12. Tanglefoot Curve, Cumbres Pass, Colorado. Another dramatic example of mountain railroad problems.

produced a number of frozen hands and feet and even death, giving rise to loud complaints from the Mormon boys who had been told that the San Juan climate was mild.

With the coming of spring 1881, Palmer's company drove on, bound for a new town called Durango, which, according to the General, had just "sprung up." It sprang up in the manner of a number of other towns along the line. Dr. William A. Bell, that master of municipal organization, had scouted the country in advance of construction in search of a suitable site for further Denver and Rio Grande land speculation. After failing to come to terms with homesteaders holding land adjacent to Animas City, he made arrangements with several individuals to file claims along the Animas River, a few miles to the south, after which they sold out to the Durango Land and Coal Company. Bruce Hunt, son of railroader Alexander Hunt, was on the scene as early as October 1880, with a stock of goods for sale that he had freighted from the railhead 150 miles to the east. The town's name apparently was suggested by the senior Hunt, who about that time was traveling in the region of Durango, Mexico, where Palmer had railroad interests.

The boosters of Animas City were either men of great confidence or they had not heard of Palmer's technique of building *almost* to an established town and then throttling it, for there seemed to be little fear of that upstart Durango posing any threat. "The Bank of San Juan has issued a circular in which it is stated that a branch office will be opened at the 'new town of Durango on the Rio Animas,' " the Animas City newspaper *Southwest* said on May 1, 1880. "Where the 'new town of Durango' is to be or not to be God and D. and R. G. Railroad only know. If they are in 'cahoots' we ask special dispensation." Neither celestial nor railroad dispensations were handed out; by the end of that year a Durango paper reported that all of "Animas City is coming to Durango as fast as accommodations can be secured." Even the *Southwest* packed up and joined the rush. Some 2500 to 3,000 people crowded into the little box tent town, where saloons, dancehalls, restaurants, and stores at first afforded the only permanent type buildings.[16] The one comfort Animas City got out of Durango's good fortune was the bitter satisfaction of seeing that town's long-planned celebration spoiled when the dignitaries, who were en route to preside over the formalities in early August 1881, were kept away

16. Mary C. Ayres, "The Founding of Durango, Colorado," *Colorado Magazine,* 7 (1930), 85–86. *Railroad Gazette* (Aug. 5, 1881), p. 433. Durango *Herald,* Aug. 5, 1881.

by a washout on the railroad near Navajo. But Durango celebrated anyway, with parades, horse races, a baseball game with Silverton, and a grand hop in the evening. The Governor, who had possessed the foresight to come early, was on hand and said nice things about the benefits of modern railroading.

With Durango reached and the proper honors accorded them, the Denver and Rio Grande workers hurried on toward their goal, Silverton. Tracklaying began in October and continued until the middle of December, when heavy snow brought the construction to a standstill. Work was resumed in January, but progress was slow due to weather conditions, difficult engineering problems, and delays in receiving rails. The railroad's arrival in Silverton was celebrated on the 4th of July, 1882, but it was six more days before tracks were to enter the city, marking the completion of the San Juan division and the extension of the road 495 miles from Denver. The little mining town, incorporated in 1876, had lived a difficult life, always short of supplies and faced by extremely high freight costs. But now, with the entrance of a railway, the dwindling population again grew, and mining activity increased sharply, once more demonstrating the value of efficient and cheaper transportation to a frontier community.[17]

While the management of the Rio Grande satisfied its desire to tap the San Juan mining country of southwestern Colorado, it did not neglect other prospective mineral empires in the mountains. In April 1880, shortly after peace was made with the AT&SF, William A. Bell met with company directors in New York, where an issue of ten million dollars in First Consolidated Bonds was authorized for immediate expansion. About a month later, the stockholders agreed to increase the corporation's capital stock to thirty million, and to advance the road's termini, again indicating that important developments were pending.[18] Within a few days, during May, President Rutherford Hayes signed a special executive order permitting the Rio Grande to build across the Ute Indian Reservation in advance of public settlement, giving further proof that an all-out westward drive was in the making. Later that year a national railroad journal spelled out the narrow gauge's plans, saying it was building in seven direc-

17. Wilson, "Denver and Rio Grande," pp. 135–36. Frank Hall, *History of the State of Colorado, 4* (Chicago, 1895), p. 311.
18. Minutes D&RG Stockholders, May 15, 1880. D&RG Archives, D&RGW offices, Denver. In Nov. 1880 the amount of capital stock was raised to fifty million.

tions, extensions that would add nearly 450 miles of track to the system. One of the mentioned branches was laid off from the mouth of the South Arkansas, below Leadville, westward toward Gunnison, from which point it would soon move rapidly toward Salt Lake City. This particular branch soon became the trunk itself—the main line of the railroad.

There was some urgency about getting to Gunnison at the earliest possible date. According to the tripartite agreement effected at the termination of the railroad war with the AT&SF, the Denver, South Park, and Pacific was to have the right of construction into that mining camp, with joint trackage rights assigned to Palmer's line. So long as this little road remained independent, under the leadership of John Evans, Rio Grande officials felt that they had no real worries. But during 1880 Jay Gould tried to gain control of the DSP&P, a move that Palmer felt would result in Union Pacific control and a circumvention of the agreement. Determined not to find himself again late on the scene, Palmer ordered his engineers to begin grading from South Arkansas (Salida) across Marshall Pass into Gunnison, anxious to stifle any competition. Evans objected, but the Rio Grande lawyers insisted that nothing in the agreement forbade construction of an independent line, and the work proceeded. Palmer did not want to break faith with John Evans, but he did not trust Jay Gould. He regarded the move as absolutely necessary, despite the fact he had agreed that the DSP&P should build the Gunnison line.

The expected railroad race ensued, with the DSP&P officials confident that their early lead would be sufficient to put them into Gunnison first. While the South Park laborers worked carefully, tunneling when necessary and trying to adhere to reasonable grades, the Rio Grande crews hurled their road across Marshall Pass, nearly 11,000 feet above sea level, using steep gradients and sharp curvatures. Time was gained for Palmer when he bought Otto Mears' Marshall Pass toll road for $13,000 and hastened on, leaving the South Park men pecking away at Alpine Tunnel, hopelessly delayed. On August 8, 1881, a Denver and Rio Grande train steamed into Gunnison, signifying a Palmer victory.[19]

Once again the Rio Grande's strenuous efforts to expand and to

19. C. E. Hagie, "Gunnison in Early Days," *Colorado Magazine*, 8 (1931), 126–27. Poor, *Denver South Park & Pacific*, pp. 208–09. Details of the toll-road sale are found in a letter from H. P. Bennet to H. A. Risley, April 27, 1882, item 4307, D&RG Archives.

pre-empt potential traffic sources led to financial difficulties. Not only was the road driving various extensions into remote mining camps, but by the fall of 1881 railroad contractors were hacking away at the wilderness beyond Gunnison, bound for the Utah line. In October, Palmer's London office issued a circular soliciting money to finish the Salt Lake Division and to pay for widening the road between Denver and Pueblo to standard gauge. With the hope of raising at least five million dollars, the company offered investors fifty shares of stock, worth $5,000, and a $1,000 bond for every $5,135 investment of cash. The prospectus, describing details of the plan, told of Colorado's enormous growth and its rise as the nation's leading producer of precious metals.[20]

In a letter to his London agent, A. G. Renshaw, Palmer described in further detail the progress of the railroad. It was now a thousand miles long, he said, reaching nearly all the mining districts of Colorado. At that moment the principal traffic was in coal, about a thousand tons being carried over the line each working day, but he thought the great future lay in precious minerals. In 1870 Colorado had produced only about three million dollars worth, a figure that had risen to twenty-five million by 1880. Production was still on the rise and added to the transportation of agricultural products from Mormon communities once Utah was reached, the future of investments in the mountain railroad looked bright indeed.[21]

The General's optimism was for public consumption only. Within the corporation there were rumblings of discontent and a recognition of the fact that a shortening of financial sails was an absolute necessity. During the hectic months of expansion since the road's release from the Atchison Company, construction had proceeded at a frantic pace on a number of branches. Now, in late 1881, with money running short, some of the projects had to be suspended in favor of others. Palmer called for a reduction of forces on every division, pending the outcome of his most recent solicitations to investors.

In October his general manager, David C. Dodge, acknowledged compliance of the order, but explained that on the Gunnison division it was absolutely necessary to increase the working force temporarily

20. *The Denver and Rio Grande. A Prospectus* (Oct. 26, 1881), Coburn Library, Colorado College, Colorado Springs.

21. Palmer to A. G. Renshaw, Oct. 27, 1881 (printed), in Coburn Library, Colorado College, Colorado Springs.

13. Narrow-Gauge Train on Marshall Pass, 1880s. Note the various levels of track in the distance.

14. Early Mule Team Hauling Freight in the Rockies. The storied mule skinners of early Western wagon-freighting days continued to serve the high-altitude mines and communities inaccessible to rail long after the narrow gauge had reached principal points in the Colorado mountain valleys.

in order to "get the track in safe condition and to keep the rail from getting surface bent." He reported that in various places along the line, track laid on frozen ground had to be replaced as soon as warm weather thawed out the roadbed, and that temporary bridges, built in haste to get trains past, also needed early replacement. "Since we got our road back from the Receiver we have had everything to contend with," he continued. "Our old men were badly demoralized and it was almost impossible to bring them under any kind of discipline and as we were rapidly extending we were obliged to employ a great many new men and many of them were such as drifted out this way from the East having left other roads. . . . Others come with good letters of recommendation and all of them admit they had to learn the business over again when they get to our mountain divisions."[22]

During the winter of 1881–82 Dodge continued to express dissatisfaction with the hasty method of construction. While he acknowledged the necessity for speed, he objected to the fact that in a number of instances contracts had been let and the work begun before the engineers had a chance to locate the line, a practice that resulted in the expenditure of thousands of dollars on work that later was abandoned. Unfortunately, he said, such wasteful practices were still being followed. Weitbrec was about to abandon $200,000 worth of premature construction on the Salt Lake division, executed before making a thorough study of possible routes. He defended the chief engineer, John A. McMurtrie, whom Palmer had criticized, saying the man had merely followed the instructions of Weitbrec, whose judgment was faulty. When the General offered to turn over construction matters to Dodge, the latter declined on the ground that he would not work with Weitbrec, who "has the facility of writing long letters and making out statements about which he knows but little."[23]

Meanwhile, Dodge continued to reduce forces in all departments and attempted to cut the payroll as much as possible. "We do not wish to do anything during the next three or four months that can be avoided or put off," he told the road's general solicitor and land department head in early 1882.[24] The slackening of effort was noticed by a Denver newspaper whose editor asked: "What has become of the

22. Dodge to Palmer, Oct. 22, 1881, D. C. Dodge Letter Book, D&RG Archives.

23. Dodge to Palmer, Dec. 6, 1881, and Feb. 17, 1882, D. C. Dodge Letter Book, D&RG Archives.

24. Dodge to Hanson A. Risley, Jan. 12, 1882, item 4293, D&RG Archives.

Denver and Rio Grande's force of 35,000 men? Four months ago it was stated that this road had more men at work building road than there were in the United States army at that time. . . . The Rio Grande papers say that the entire force of the road is at work in the Black Canon. As this force numbers only 1,000 men, it is a question of some interest to know what became of the other 34,000."[25]

No small part of Palmer's new difficulties stemmed from the machinations of his recent savior, Jay Gould. That accomplished robber baron was determined to establish all of Colorado as one of his transportation domains, an ambition bitterly opposed by the Rio Grande, whose management was just as determined to stay out of his clutches as those of the AT&SF. In the late weeks of 1881, Denver and Rio Grande stock sank noticeably and Gould was openly accused by newspapers of driving down the price so that he could buy control of the line. He had only recently reached that objective with the Denver, South Park, and Pacific, and Palmer was the next victim upon whom he fixed his sights.

Until the annual meeting of the stockholders of the Denver and Rio Grande, held in November 1881, the impression prevailed that Gould had succeeded in buying up stock control, a rumor that died out when Palmer revealed the extent of his own power in the corporation. The reverse did not stop Gould, who reached into his bag of tricks and put on a dazzling display of deception and deceit for his Colorado audience. Following his usual method of wrecking established lines and buying up the remains, rather than building new ones, he tried to undermine Palmer's position by destroying public confidence in the builder of narrow gauges. He seized upon the weakened market conditions, partly brought on by President Garfield's assassination, to spread rumors to the effect that the mines of Leadville were played out and that such other business as the Rio Grande had could not pay the interest on its bonds or dividends on its stock. To this kind of gossip Gould added the charge that there was an overissue of stocks and bonds, that the issues were far above the actual costs of construction, and that somebody was making a large, illegitimate haul out of such proceedings.

Palmer sought desperately to stop the tales, as they spread through eastern papers, and even went so far as to sue the *Wall Street News* for libel. As the General tried to stamp out the brush fires of rumor,

25. Denver *Daily Times*, Nov. 11, 1881.

Gould slipped by his guard and hired spies to work within the very framework of the Denver and Rio Grande. Palmer, who was as tough and competent as any entrepreneur, knew he was in the ring with an eye-gouging, gut-stomping brawler.[26]

All during 1882, as Palmer bent every effort to push his railroad toward the Colorado–Utah line and a connection with the allied Rio Grande Western, he was obliged to carry on a running fight with Gould, who continued to slash at his eastern flank. In May, Dodge admitted to his superior that open warfare with the Gould Union Pacific combine was at hand. The large organization was then giving encouragement to the newly organized Denver and New Orleans road, whose tracks were nearing Pueblo, and, as Dodge put it, "It is very evident we are going to have a fight with the U.P." Dodge foresaw a demoralization of rates between Denver and Pueblo, as well as to Leadville, and knew that "it is going to seriously affect our earnings." One way to retaliate, he said, was to shut off any joint trackage arrangements.[27] His recommendations were followed, and suit was brought against the Union Pacific to recover an alleged $350,000 in rent which that railroad was said to owe for use of Rio Grande track between Nathrop and Leadville. The action was followed by two others, alleging overcharge by the Union Pacific on Rio Grande freight passing over its lines.

At the same time, Palmer stopped the delivery of all freight to the Denver and New Orleans line as a further means of hurting the Union Pacific.[28] John Evans, one of the organizers of the D&NO, had serious complaints about the treatment he had received from the Rio Grande in the running fight it carried on with other lines. He openly accused Palmer's road of controlling the Denver *Tribune* and the Denver *Republican,* both of which were used against his enterprise. He charged the *Tribune* with being a party to "one of the foulest conspiracies in the history of this country. A combination to destroy my reputation in order to defeat the railroad enterprise with which I am connected, and prevent it from becoming a rival of the Denver & Rio Grande Railway."[29]

26. Colorado Springs *Weekly Gazette,* Jan. 14, 1882. *Railroad Gazette* (Dec. 22, 1882), p. 796.

27. Dodge to Palmer, May 16, 1882, D. C. Dodge Letter Book, D&RG Archives.

28. Colorado Springs *Weekly Gazette,* Sept. 30, 1882. *Railroad Gazette* (Oct. 6, 1882), p. 620. E. P. Vining to A. J. Hughes, May 16, 1882, D. C. Dodge Letter Book, D&RG Archives.

29. Denver *Tribune,* Aug. 10, 1881. Denver *Daily Times,* Oct. 14, 1881.

Palmer had one more arrow in his quiver. On May 29, 1882, a subsidiary of the Chicago, Burlington, and Quincy Railroad entered Denver, giving Colorado its fourth rail outlet to the industrial East. It came at the height of the Rio Grande's quarrel with the Union Pacific, and there was considerable speculation to the effect that the mountain railway would now cast its lot with the newcomer. This happy situation, a Utah paper had predicted, would mean that the "Union Pacific will be no longer able to squeeze this territory at its own sweet will and pleasure."[30] Dodge mentioned the development in a letter to Palmer, saying that the Union Pacific's aggressions were sufficient to ease the conscience of the Rio Grande in breaking any previous arrangements with that line. "What they have already done leaves us free to make whatever arrangement we see fit with the C. B. & Q.," he wrote to his chief.[31] The talk of merger, or at least close cooperation, with the CB&Q continued for the next few years, but no through transcontinental trains crossed the Rockies behind Rio Grande engines until well into the twentieth century.

30. *Utah Commercial,* quoted by Denver *Daily Times,* Nov. 11, 1881. See Richard C. Overton, *Burlington West: A Colonization History of the Burlington Railroad* (Cambridge, Mass., 1941), p. 461.
31. Dodge to Palmer, May 16, 1882, D. C. Dodge Letter Book, D&RG Archives.

6. Our army of relief—of rescue

EVENTS OF 1881 and 1882 illustrated some of the major difficulties that lay ahead for the mountain railroad. While Palmer's home-town *Gazette* boasted of the many prosperous cities and towns that blossomed as the rail system spread over Colorado, giving rise to predictions of future prosperity, the General himself spoke of the expansion in enthusiastic terms. He told his stockholders that in 1881

over 380 miles of new track had been added and net earnings had
amounted to more than two and a half million dollars. In just a year
freight haulage had shot up almost 75 per cent and the increase in
passengers carried was 143 per cent. However, 1882 was a different
story. Additions to the road were slightly less than that of the previous
year, giving the line a total of approximately 1,100 miles, but gross
earnings did not keep pace with the increased mileage. The management explained that this was "partly because mining industries have
received a severe check in Colorado by failure of interested parties
to advance new capital, and partly because both passenger and freight
rates were demoralized by competition with rival lines during the
period covering the best traffic months of the year, which reduced
the earnings of your lines to much lower figures than was anticipated."[1]

In the face of mounting obstacles, the Rio Grande pushed on, determined to reach Salt Lake City. As Palmer looked back over a decade
of railway growth in Colorado, he could observe that the territory,
now a state, also had grown very rapidly, and upon this continuous
development he based his future hopes. Between 1870 and 1880, population had increased from 39,000 to 194,000, or 400 per cent; its
metals output from three million dollars to twenty-three, or 800 per
cent; and during the single year 1881 its towns had increased in number from 294 to 369.[2] Surely, reasoned the General, the building program was justified, and if there were temporary difficulties, chargeable
to great outlays of money for construction, the situation would ease
once the management was able to capitalize upon its heavy investment.
The potential was present, and he intended to make the most of it.
"The primary object of the completion of the link of 618 miles between Pueblo and Salt Lake City is to meet the requirements of the
tributary mining districts and the interchange of ores and general
traffic between Colorado and Utah," he wrote early in 1882.

> The agricultural resources of Utah, with the consequent low
> prices prevailing there for such products, and the constantly in-
> creasing demand of the mining districts of Colorado for these
> supplies, must give to the Salt Lake connection a satisfactory east-

1. Colorado Springs *Weekly Gazette,* Jan. 7, 1882. *Annual Report of the D&RG,* 1881 and
1882.

2. A. H. Danforth, "The Colorado Coal and Iron Company," a printed letter–pamphlet
(Feb. 1, 1882), in Coburn Library, Colorado College, Colorado Springs.

bound traffic. The westbound traffic will consist largely of Colorado Coke and Colorado Anthracite, machinery, and other articles made in Colorado, of iron, steel, etc., manufactured there,
also for eastern supplies of all kinds. There is also the special
attraction to the travelling public of the extraordinary scenic
grandeur of the route. The road when completed will make a
new line to the Pacific coast via the Central Pacific Railroad from
Ogden, which will be as short, both in distance and time, as any
existing line between New York and San Francisco.[3]

By the end of August 1882 the road was open beyond Gunnison,
through the Black Canyon, to Cimarron. The last mile through the
Black Canyon was said to have cost more than the entire construction
through the Royal Gorge, and it took more than a year to build.[4] In
September the next twenty-two-mile section was finished to Montrose,
and the Gunnison *News–Democrat* cheered on the workers, saying
"westward the star of empire takes it way, and so does the D. and R.
G." Delta was reached in October, only eighty-seven miles from the
Utah line, and before Christmas, tracklayers covered that distance,
putting the road 462 miles beyond Denver. The General proudly
reported that the rails were made in Colorado by another child of
the Rio Grande, the Colorado Coal and Iron Company. In the final
lunge toward Utah, Palmer had more than 1,000 men and 175 teams
at work, grading and laying track on this section alone.

During the time the westward drive was on, Rio Grande officials
were busy in Utah, making plans to commence construction eastward
from Salt Lake City to meet the oncoming Colorado crews. Early in
December 1880 Dr. William Bell had quietly organized the Sevier Valley Railway Company with the announced purpose of building south
from Ogden as far as the northern boundary of Arizona. From this
route another road would move eastward over Salina Pass, across
Castle Valley to the Green River, and from there to Colorado's western boundary. In the summer of 1881 the Sevier Valley Railway and
the Salt Lake and Park City Railway were absorbed by a new line
called the Denver and Rio Grande Western Railway Company, popu-
larly known as "the Western." Toward the end of the year the Western acquired two more small roads: the Bingham Canyon and Camp

3. Palmer Report, in *Annual Report of the D&RG*, 1881.
4. George A. Roote, "Gunnison in the Early 'Eighties," *Colorado Magazine, 9* (1932), 208.

Floyd, and the Wasatch and Jordan Valley Railroad. Within another six months the Utah and Pleasant Valley Railway Company was added to the collection.

The little railroads that the Western acquired in Utah were primarily mining roads. The Bingham Canyon and Camp Floyd together with the Wasatch and Jordan Valley Railway totaled less than thirty-five miles in length. Together they formed a line running from the Little Cottonwood mining district, through the Salt Lake Valley, to the Bingham mining district on the west. The Utah and Pleasant Valley ran southeasterly from Springville over the Wasatch range. It had been begun in 1878 by Milan Packard, an old-time Montana freighter. Many of his railroad workers received part of their pay in merchandise, and since they often asked for calico, the standard cotton material used for clothing at the time, the short narrow-gauge was called the "Calico Line."[5]

A Salt Lake City newspaper explained the reason for incorporating the Western in Utah:

> The railroad law in force in this territory makes it necessary that the incorporaters of any railroad to be run within the limits of Utah, two thirds shall be actual residents of this territory. Now the Denver and Rio Grande is a private corporation, and did not get its charter from Congress, as did the C.P. and U.P., and for that reason it is forced to comply with the provisions enacted by the legislatures of the several territories and states through which the road intends to run. For this reason the Denver and Rio Grande people induced some friends in this city to organize a company as required by the laws of Utah to secure the right of way for its line through this territory.[6]

There was no doubt that the Rio Grande Western was another of Palmer's projects. In May 1881 the company offered its stockholders the option of taking stocks and bonds in the new corporation at 6 per cent interest plus a bonus of $500 worth of stock for every $1,000 bond taken at par. Stockholders also had the option of taking one $1,000 bond in exchange for each thirty shares of Denver and Rio Grande

5. Hannah M. Mendenhall, "The Calico Road," in *Heart Throbs of the West,* 2 (Salt Lake City, 1940), 28.

6. Salt Lake *Herald,* May 14, 1881.

stock they owned.[7] Both Palmer and Dr. Bell were on the board of directors, and D. C. Dodge, general manager of the Rio Grande, headed the new company.

During August 1882 matters became even clearer when the Denver and Rio Grande leased the Western for a period of thirty years, guaranteeing to pay the leased line 40 per cent of the gross receipts from its trackage and to pay all operating and maintenance expenses. The agreement involved approximately 300 miles of track running from Salt Lake City to the Colorado boundary, plus other service lines in Utah, or a total that was to be no less than 469 miles. Actual management was placed in the hands of a superintendent who was given sole power to operate all services, to establish and enforce rules, and to employ and discharge subordinate officers. With the consummation of this arrangement, it became obvious that the whole Denver and Rio Grande axis had shifted to an east–west position. Rich silver strikes in the mountains of Colorado and a war with the Santa Fe railroad had thrown it into the arms of Utah. El Paso watched with disappointment as the world's longest narrow-gauge swung into a position paralleling that of the major transcontinentals.[8]

As early as March 1881, residents of Salt Lake City were alerted to the possibility of increased railroad activity in their region. A local newspaper published a rumor that the Rio Grande interests had bought the Utah and Pleasant Valley with the idea of connecting Utah and Colorado. The rumor was properly denied, since the sale had not yet been made. However, the Mormons knew that something was afoot because a good deal of real estate was changing hands in the city. Thirty acres of land were reported purchased for the future site of a Rio Grande depot in Salt Lake City. Eastward, at Salina Pass, 300 men were busily grading and laying track. Utah businessmen guessed that they would soon enjoy a railroad boom.[9]

Within a few months direct benefits of the Rio Grande's expansion began to be felt in Utah. Reports from Provo related that all available laborers were being put to work, grading, laying track, and even

7. *Railroad Gazette* (1881), p. 270. For details of the organization of July 21, 1881, see *Proofs of the Organization of the Denver and Rio Grande Western Railway Company* (Salt Lake City, 1881), in Coburn Library, Colorado College, Colorado Springs.

8. *Annual Report of the D&RG* (1882), p. 9. Agreement between the Rio Grande Western Railway Co. and the D&RG, 1882, item 873 in D&RG Archives.

9. Salt Lake *Daily Herald,* March 27, 1881, clipping in Journal History, L.D.S. Church Library, Salt Lake City.

boarding up the sides of flat cars for hauling coal. Farmers along the line used the opportunity for "putting their teams and boys to remunerative employment." Better yet, the promptness with which the Western paid its employees and the liberal prices offered for rights of way made a very favorable impression upon the Mormon community.[10]

Utah was delighted. The Salt Lake City *Herald* said the narrow gauge was by no means narrow track in its plans: "The Denver and Rio Grande is one of the most enterprising, largest, best managed and most active railway corporations in the world. Its managers and chief stockholders are among the oldest, and most thorough-going, as well as wealthiest people in the world." To prove his point, the editor explained that nearly 33,000 men were at work, digging through cuts, putting in bridges, laying rails, and driving spikes on the railroad's various extensions. The number of paid employees exceeded that of of the entire United States Army. This corps of workmen was laying track or planning new routes in twenty-seven different directions. Happily, said the journal, Utah was a part of this great project and it was well, for if Utah would need anything in the next five years, it was railroads. "If the Union Pacific was a blessing to this country, the Denver and Rio Grande will be no less so, in helping to develop resources, and its advent will be hailed with delight."[11]

Almost at once, the Denver and Rio Grande was adopted as a "home" railroad by a good many people in Utah. They were convinced that one of its prime objects in entering southern Utah was to tap the rich iron and coal resources. This would give the users a chance to buy coal mined at home and by local men, "instead of being compelled to keep men at work in another and rival territory, and to burn foreign coal, while we have equally as good an article here." To them, the D&RG meant a boost for home industry and lower coal prices.[12]

The road's construction was watched with great interest and there was continuous talk in the newspapers as to the probable date of connection with Colorado. Newsmen reported that the road had already put new life into parts of Utah. Clear Creek, for example, had become a boom town. Hundreds of tons of coal arrived there every day from

10. Ibid., Oct. 22, Nov. 10, 20, 1881.
11. Ibid., July 27, 1881.
12. Ibid., April 22, Oct. 26, 1881.

15. Salt Lake City, 1870s. Note the two mule cars meeting on the one-track system. At this point the drivers unhitched the mules, taking them to the opposite ends of the cars; then the passengers changed cars and off they went!

Pleasant Valley. So did immense quantities of supplies and freight, shipped from Provo and Salt Lake City. Like the richest mining camps, Clear Creek was a spectacle of overcrowded hotels, of men sleeping on the ground, on flat cars, on depot platforms. Utah was experiencing a railroad bonanza.[13]

Local interest was heightened further as the Rio Grande tracklaying progressed. Farmers and merchants watched with pleasure as the Union Pacific's Utah Central was goaded into action. When it began to move into Pleasant Valley in late 1882, to capture coal outlets, the Rio Grande at once transferred surveyors and graders from other construction and sent them into the endangered area. This delighted Salt Lake City newsmen, who wrote that if such keen rivalry continued, their city would certainly be a great railroad center. To them the Rio Grande was becoming more meaningful every day. "The completion of this new route east will be of vast benefit to Utah in opening up competition in transportation, which will bring a reduction in prices," said the *Tribune*.[14] Soon the Rio Grande would provide an outlet in Colorado to the Burlington and Santa Fe, both of which were barred from the region by the Union Pacific's prohibitive rates. In addition, the Rio Grande would provide an increased local traffic. Correspondent "A.Z." revealed that his trip to the end of the line in November 1882 had given such indications. "I hear that many settlements and towns are springing up between Utah and Colorado and that Denver merchants are already sending their drummers 200 miles westward to catch the new trade," he told Utah readers.[15]

Early in 1882 Palmer told stockholders of the Western that their company then owned or controlled over one hundred miles of finished road in Utah. "All rails and fastenings necessary for the entire line from the Colorado border to Salt Lake City have been bought and paid for. Of these, sufficient to lay one hundred and twenty miles of track have been delivered and are now on hand, chiefly at Salt Lake and Provo." Soon, he said, Denver and Salt Lake City would be connected, and products of Utah and Colorado could be exchanged. Not only were there large quantities of high-quality bituminous coal along the line, but the growing demands of Utah's new industries and the

13. Provo *Territorial Enquirer*, Aug. 26, 1882, in Journal History, L.D.S. Church Library, Salt Lake City.
14. Salt Lake *Daily Tribune*, Oct. 11, 1882.
15. Ibid., Nov. 15, 1882.

mines, whose yield during the previous year exceeded $7,250,000, "give excellent promise of a good local business." Local traffic, plus that done with the east, promised to yield enough money from the outset to cover the bonded indebtedness.[16]

Excitement rose to a new high in the spring of 1883, as the east and west termini of the road neared each other. "The benefits of this new outlet for Utah will be very soon perceived," said the leading Mormon newspaper. "Leaving out all considerations of the competition which it may promote for the passenger and carrying trade to and from the East, there will be new fields opened for local enterprise. Between Salt Lake and Denver supplies will be needed by the settlers in new places, and our farmers and gardeners will find a market for their produce all the way to the Colorado centre."[17] A rival Salt Lake City newspaper said "amen" to this sentiment and revealed its warm feelings toward Palmer's newest project with the remark that "it behooves our citizens and members of the Council to see that a road which will bring our city the traffic and interchange of people be treated in no illiberal spirit."[18]

Western Colorado shared Utah's sense of anticipation. Grand Junction, isolated in the mountain fastness, talked of nothing but a connection "with the outside world," and thrilled to Palmer's words when he predicted that at least one-half of the passenger travel and a large share of the freight monopolized by the Union Pacific would seek out this new and more direct transcontinental route. The town's newspaper referred to the tracklaying crews who made their approach as "our army of relief—of rescue." Soon there would come smoking and snorting locomotives, escorting long trains of cars into the city, and on them would be "thousands of people to populate our beautiful valley, and all the conveniences and comforts that are enjoyed by the people of older cities of our State." The only person who would be adversely affected was the lone horseback rider who twice a week rode out of Grand Junction, bearing letters at a price of from ten to twenty-five cents each.

The initial impact of the railroad turned Grand Junction into a noisy boom town, whose nocturnal uproars must have made the founding fathers wonder about the benefits of civilization. "It was not so

16. Report to D&RG Stockholders, Feb. 1, 1882, item 5721, D&RG Archives.
17. Salt Lake City *Deseret Evening News,* March 28, 1883.
18. Salt Lake *Daily Herald,* June 13, 1882.

bad during the day," wrote a pioneer merchant, "but when darkness
came you could see the big tent–saloons illuminated, hear the music
and knew there was light, warmth, entertainment and liquid refresh-
ments to be had." He admitted that no one was forced to frequent
such places, but he took the view that construction workers found
it more enjoyable than lying around a dreary campfire on cold nights,
cursing the weather and each other. At least, he thought, the hospi-
tality of a saloon provided a "saving on profanity [that] would set a
fellow up a few notches in St. Peter's record by eluding the discomforts
of campfire life." Some of the town's other newcomers offered diver-
sions that wouldn't look well in the record. Colorado Avenue had a
large number of sporting houses where the railroad workers roistered
into the small hours of the morning. The town's newspaper editor
complained about the brawls that took place, saying the "moral effect
of such affairs are terrible upon the community, and so long as such
houses are licensed and allowed to run openly, just so long will they
be a detriment to the town." His colleague, from neighboring Gunnison, clucked that Grand Junction was "fast coming to the front as a
bold, bad town."[19]

As it was with other towns, the construction workers and their
after-hours companions departed as the railhead moved on, leaving
behind a community of businessmen who settled down to trade with
the incoming flow of agrarians. On March 30, 1883, construction
crews of the Western met those of the Denver and Rio Grande a few
miles west of Green River, Utah, where the traditional last spike was
driven, formalizing the joining of the rails. Commercial men of Utah
and Colorado rated it as next in importance to the completion of the
Pacific Railroad in 1869, when similar ceremonies took place at Prom-
ontory, Utah. Now the people of Salt Lake City could go to Denver
and to points east by an alternate route. The distance to Colorado's
capital, via the Rio Grande, was 735 miles, a trip that could be made in
thirty-five hours.[20]

Additional service meant more than added convenience. The completion of the new line, said a small western paper, meant Utah's emancipation from "the throes of a monopoly." The editor agreed with a
Rio Grande official who said, "One day the Union Pacific and the

19. Walker D. Wyman, "Grand Junction's First Year, 1882," *Colorado Magazine*, *13* (1936),
127–37.
20. Bear Lake *Democrat*, April 21, 1883, in Journal History, L.D.S. Church Library, Salt Lake
City.

MAP 6

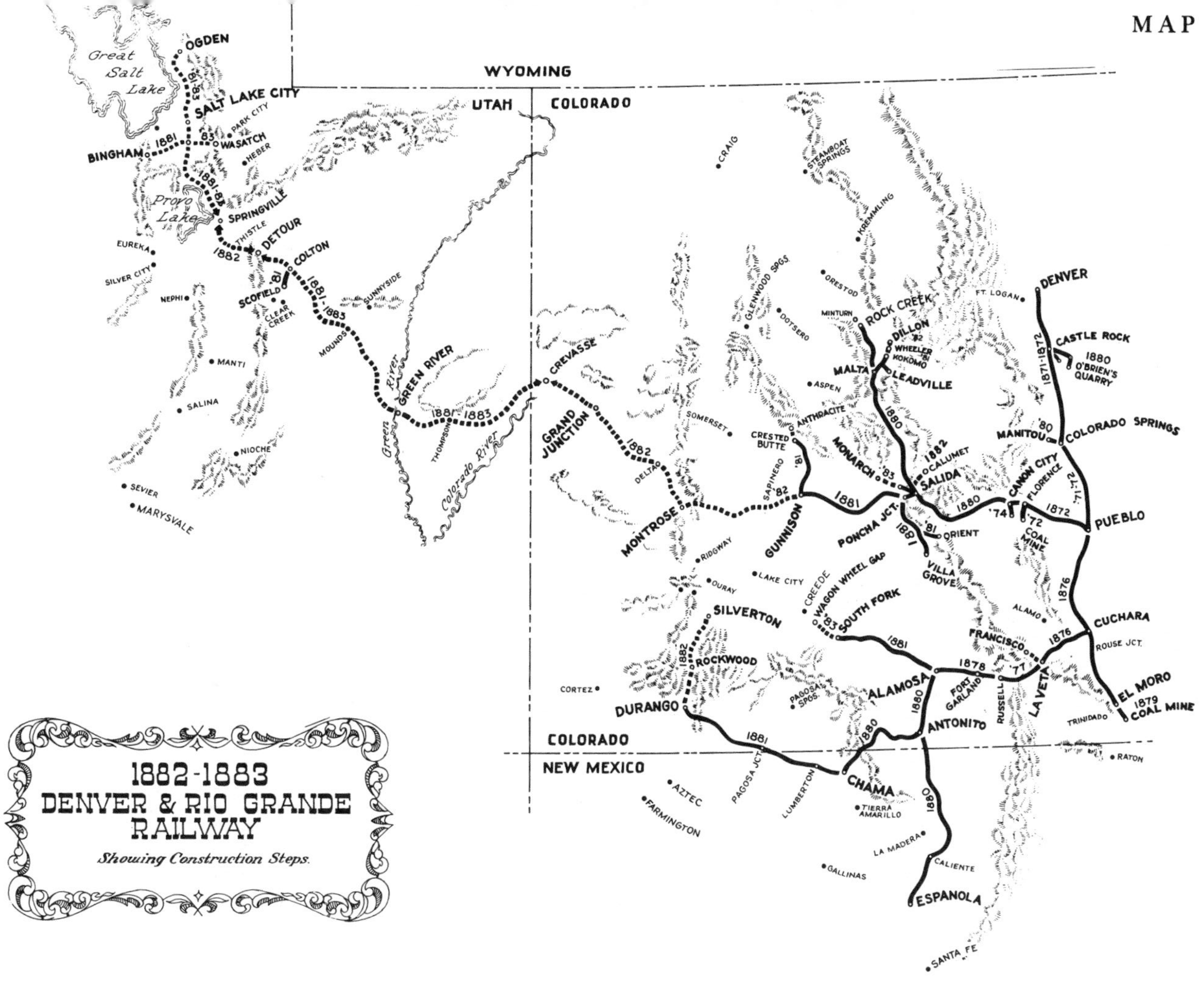

1882-1883
DENVER & RIO GRANDE RAILWAY

Showing Construction Steps.

WYOMING

UTAH
COLORADO

COLORADO
NEW MEXICO

Great Salt Lake

OGDEN
SALT LAKE CITY
1881-83
BINGHAM 1881
EUREKA
SILVER CITY
PARK CITY
WASATCH
HEBER
SPRINGVILLE
DETOUR
COLTON 1881-1883
SCOFIELD 1882
THISTLE
MORONI
MANTI
NEPHI
SALINA
SEVER
MARYSVALE
NIOCHE
Utah Lake

GREEN RIVER
THOMPSONS 1883
Green River
Colorado River
GRAND JUNCTION 1882
GREASY CREEK
DELTA 1882
MONTROSE 1882
CIMARRON
SOMERSET
CRAIG
STEAMBOAT SPGS.
YAMPA
GLENWOOD SPGS.
NEWCASTLE
DOTSERO
CRESTED BUTTE
GUNNISON 1881-82
SAPINERO
LAKE CITY
OURAY
RIDGWAY
SILVERTON
ROCKWOOD 1882
DURANGO
CORTEZ
AZTEC
FARMINGTON

RED CLIFF
MINTURN
CRESTO
ASPEN
LEADVILLE 1880
MALTA
ROCK CREEK
DILLON
WHEELER
RHONDO
LOGAN
DENVER 1871-1872
CASTLE ROCK 1880
O'BRIEN'S QUARRY
COLORADO SPRINGS
MANITOU 1880
CITY 71-72
FLORENCE 1872
CAÑON 71-72
COAL MINE
PUEBLO
FLORENT
VILLA GROVE
SALIDA 1880
MONARCH '83
CALUMET
MARSHALL
PONCHA JCT.
SOUTH FORK 1881
WAGON WHEEL GAP
CREEDE
ALAMOSA 1880
FRANCISCO 1878
FORT GARLAND 1878
ANTONITO 1880
SILVERTON 1881
CHAMA 1880
TIERRA AMARILLA
PAGOSA JCT. 1881
LUMBERTON
GALLINAS
LA MADERA
CALIENTE
ESPANOLA 1880
SANTA FE
CUCHARA 1876
LA VETA 1877
RUSSELL
ALAMO
ROUSE JCT.
EL MORO 1879 COAL MINE
TRINIDAD
RATON
COAL MINE 1876
1878
1876
1880

Central Pacific people are like two chums in a bed, the next day they are like two cats hanging over a clothesline." The newspaper concluded that when two companies are so engaged, other companies are liable to step in to take advantage of the quarreling. He was certain that the frequent ruptures between the two larger lines was really the prime mover that brought the Rio Grande westward to Salt Lake City. [21]

Certainly, other lines watched with jealousy as the Union Pacific and Central Pacific controlled through traffic by the original transcontinental route. But the Central Pacific, a partner in this monopoly, felt no concern at the appearance of the Rio Grande. Rather, it saw an opportunity to threaten its quarrelsome mate. The new mountain railroad, soon to be standard gauged, provided a link between the Central Pacific and roads east of the Rockies, such as the Burlington and Santa Fe lines. With it, they could hold a gun to the head of the Union Pacific. In the latter part of 1881 these four roads entered into an agreement to this end. The Central Pacific agreed to make a traffic division with the Rio Grande on eastbound business, and it was promised similar favors on westbound traffic from Palmer's road.[22]

Utah showed little sympathy for the Union Pacific. For years it had been in a position to act as capriciously as it chose. Now, with the completion of the Rio Grande, the older road displayed its resentment. In May 1883 Provo businessmen learned that the Utah Central, a Union Pacific subsidiary, would charge them the same rate to ship south of Provo that Salt Lake City had to pay. "In other words," said their newspaper, "it is the purpose of the Utah Central and the Union Pacific to discriminate unfairly against this city and in the interests of Salt Lake merchants." Overnight Provo became an all-out Denver and Rio Grande town. "Now is the time for the D. and R. G. Co. to do something and that very speedily," said the *Territorial Enquirer*. "They will find lots of warm friends and allies in the south who only await an opportunity to let the U.P. monopoly understand that they have not forgotten their oppressive treatment in the past."[23] At once businessmen in Payson and Spanish Fork called meetings, asking the Rio Grande to offer them service. They talked of grain and other

21. Ibid., April 28, 1883.
22. Ibid.
23. *Territorial Enquirer*, May 8, 1883, in Journal History, L.D.S. Church Library, Salt Lake City.

produce from their fields, and of the necessity for a connection with
Colorado markets. More than that, "the farmers and business men are
naturally very desirous of having the facilities given them for making
through shipments directly east without being under the necessity of
looking to Salt Lake alone for a market, or to the U.P. railway alone
for transportation east."[24]

The Union Pacific's undisguised resentment of the interloper became apparent as Rio Grande tracks neared Ogden in May 1883. The
depot site, upon which the Rio Grande intended to make a connection
with the Central Pacific, was owned jointly by the Union Pacific and
Central Pacific. The two larger lines had an agreement that no other
road might approach this preserve without the consent of both parties. The Union Pacific now objected, and secured a temporary injunction that barred the newcomer's entrance. Rio Grande workmen,
veterans of the great Santa Fe war, had been threatened before. Once
again they took matters into their own hands. On Saturday night, May
12, 1883, during a heavy rainstorm, they nailed together sections of
rails, fishplates, and ties. Then, hoisting the units on their shoulders,
they carried them forward into enemy territory. When about 200
feet of track had been laid, the plot was discovered and Union Pacific
men rushed to their posts. A switch engine was at once dispatched to
the battleground, where a heavy chain was attached to the oncoming
tracks. Steam was applied and away went part of the Rio Grande
railroad. All during the remainder of the night, Union Pacific cars
were kept running across the contested ground to prevent further
penetrations.

The Rio Grande got around legal and physical barriers by laying
a third rail along the Central Pacific's standard-gauge track and entering the depot grounds on that company's tracks. The Union Pacific
then tried to freeze out its rival by reducing rates between Ogden
and Salt Lake City. "Baby roads and giant corporations engross the
public mind now," said the Ogden correspondent of the Salt Lake
Daily Tribune, as he described the bitter rivalry. The Rio Grande,
always willing to fight, now offered free train rides between the two
Utah cities. Immediately, a rumor was spread to the effect that the
Union Pacific would not only meet this challenge but would give a
cash bonus to anyone patronizing its branch, the Utah Central.[25]

24. Ibid., May 25, 1883.
25. Salt Lake *Daily Tribune*, May 15, 18, 20, 1883.

16. Mule Car, Salt Lake City, 1883. Mule cars were introduced in Sale Lake City in 1872. This one is bound for the Rio Grande depot.

17. Provo, Utah, 1880s. One of the thriving Mormon communities on the Rio Grande system.

During the preceding year, as the Rio Grande neared completion, Salt Lake City journalists had talked about the grumbling of older railroads when new ones entered such places as Omaha and Denver. They anticipated a similar situation for Salt Lake City, and one of them wrote, "Speed the time, for the people are able to stand that sort of thing right well."[26] The people of Utah were entirely familiar with the Union Pacific's power, and as they watched other roads battling it in the Denver region, there was rejoicing over the probable benefits of competition. "All Northern Colorado is under the sole rule of the Union Pacific," wrote a correspondent to the *Tribune*. "It owns all the railroads and all the railroads that are possible. Where it can't run a broad gauge it runs a narrow gauge, and builds and builds aimlessly save to forestall others. It owns the coal, the quarries, everything, but the soil. It is a pity the people couldn't find it to their advantage to move out of such a country and let the boss thief of the world do its own farming as well as hauling."[27]

Rio Grande men encouraged that kind of talk. One of them, unidentified, told a Salt Lake City newspaper reporter that Union Pacific earnings for September 1883 had fallen off sharply and that the road had laid the blame at the door of the Burlington and Missouri, whose tracks recently had entered Denver. Not so, said the Rio Grande informant; the real reason was the completion of Palmer's road into Salt Lake City. He estimated that this triumph would cost the Union Pacific around four million dollars a year, and the opening of the Northern Pacific would cost a like amount. Admittedly, with the Rio Grande forming a link between the Burlington and the Atchison lines east of the Rockies, and with the Central Pacific on the west side, the Rio Grande appeared to provide the necessary connection for those roads to fight the Union Pacific to a standstill. At least this was the anticipation, the hope. Had the Rio Grande actually helped Utah? Yes, said the Rio Grande spokesman. When his road entered Utah, coke was selling for around $20 a ton, a figure that shortly dropped to $10. This permitted a large number of low grade mines to reopen, having been idle because of the high cost of coke.

26. Ibid., Aug. 24, 1882.

27. Ibid., Sept. 30, 1882. The correspondent signed himself "O.J.H." This probably is Ovando J. Hollister, a well-known Coloradan, who was then working for the federal government in Salt Lake City. He was a great admirer of Palmer and openly prejudiced in favor of the General.

His road also claimed to have reduced the rates for shipping lead eastward as much as 66 per cent, not to mention the reduction of rates
on staples and sleeping-car fares.[28]

As the new road went into operation, it was editorially welcomed to
Salt Lake City. In a serious and well-balanced appraisal the *Tribune*
editor said, "We do not hail the Denver & Rio Grande expecting that
it will revolutionize business or religion here; we expect nothing more
from its management except that the owners will try to make money
out of the road, and that they have already discovered that generous
management is more profitable than a too severe one." He saw the
railroad correctly when he spoke of it as "a new outlet for Utah to the
whole East; as a means of opening up a large and valuable new country; as a new artery of commerce."[29]

Denver papers viewed the development in a different light. To
them the Rio Grande was a knight in shining armor, come to save the
Mormons from Union Pacific perfidy. "It is well known that the
Union Pacific has never been very popular with the Mormons," said
the Denver *Times*. It was with these people, not the Utah gentiles,
that the Rio Grande would trade. Already, by its generous contracts
given them, the Rio Grande had gained the favor of the Mormons,
"who naturally looked to it as an ally against the Union Pacific and the
Gentiles." It was the *Times'* opinion that had it not been for the
Mormon friendship, the Rio Grande perhaps never would have been
built to Utah. The Salt Lake City *Tribune* called this piece of journal-
ism "trash." On the contrary, the Union Pacific had been suspected
even of favoring the Utah Mormons rather than the gentiles. Of
course, the Rio Grande would do business with the gentiles. It was
built largely to tap mineral resources, and at least two-thirds of Utah's
business fell into that category. In Utah mining was substantially
gentile in character.[30]

This editorial rebuke did nothing to dim the enthusiasm in Colorado. Admittedly, Denver's connection with the Utah capital was a
rather circuitous one, 735 miles in length, but this did not dissuade
Rocky Mountain businessmen from the belief that the Rio Grande
had "blossomed out into a trunk line, and one of the most important
in the country." Continuing the attack upon the Union Pacific, whose

28. Ibid., Nov. 24, 1883.
29. Ibid., March 29, 1883.
30. Ibid., April 18, 1883.

management had dared bypass Colorado during the '60s, a Denver paper announced that the Rio Grande's latest move was "hailed as a God-send to the railway ridden people of Utah." Bitterly it charged the Union Pacific with having drained every region it ever tapped, including Utah, whose people "have known no greater curse excepting only and always polygamy."[31] Denver boosters appeared to be convinced that a narrow-gauge savior had delivered Salt Lake City from a transportation ogre and that the Colorado capital would be the chief beneficiary of this deed of economic valor.

If Palmer's company aspired to the position of a Mormon pet, it was to be disappointed. While these people openly welcomed any and all new roads, they were not entertaining any ideas of permanent economic preference. As a matter of fact, the Rio Grande's first official operational act was criticized. It had announced its initial run for April 8, which, as it happened, was the Sabbath. On that day there appeared in a Salt Lake paper a complaint against this violation of the Lord's day. Even before this, a Provo paper had charged it with having little regard for its employees. But even if working conditions were undesirable, the Rio Grande was guilty of committing a more serious offense: it was not hiring enough Mormons. The Colorado railroad was charged with the capricious firing of Mormon workers by superintendents who replaced them with imported favorites.[32]

During the fall of 1883 there were further complaints of Mormon boys returning to Utah from Colorado, after having been discharged by the railroad because of their religion. The aggrieved men quoted their former boss as saying that the Rio Grande intended to fire every damned Mormon on the road. The *Territorial Enquirer* took the stories at face value and promptly advised its readers to boycott the Rio Grande. Suddenly the Utah Central returned to favor. The *Enquirer's* editor pointed to it as an example of a Mormon-run road, and said that where it had one accident, the Rio Grande had scores of them.[33] Obviously, it was safer to ride with the faithful.

From out at Castle Valley came more charges against the Rio Grande. A correspondent told the Mormon *Deseret News* that the narrow gauge had appropriated lumber and other private property

31. Denver *Republican*, March 31, May 1, 1883.

32. *Territorial Enquirer*, May 25, 1883, in Journal History, L.D.S. Church Library, Salt Lake City.

33. Ibid., Nov. 9, 1883.

for its own use and had refused to pay for it. The railroad also was said to have run down stock, and instead of receiving compensation, the owners were told they ought to be sued for being so neglectful. Worse yet, the railroad discriminated heavily against Utah in favor of Colorado. "We have also got papers to show where they charged us $62.00 for a car of freight 46 miles, while at the same time they were bringing cars of lumber from Montrose for $50.00," said the complainant.[34]

Another user, signing himself "Biz.," indicated that the brief honeymoon was over. Utah people, he said, were not blind to the benefits conferred by the Rio Grande, but despite all kinds of promising talk, its appearance had not changed the transportation picture very much. "We all know that when the D. and R. G. got through here it would open up a market for our produce in Colorado," he explained in hurt puzzlement, "but in this we have not realized quite what we expected. They have thus far [1884] brought produce from the east for a mere song, and charged at the same time the most extortionate express and freight rates, with few exceptions. . . . We find today that we are blocked out from all trade with the near towns of Colorado, from the fact that the rates are against us."[35]

Thus the Mormons discovered that so far as railroads were concerned, there were no chosen people. Coloradans could have told them that if freight rates were discriminatory, it was not the first time Palmer's railroad had imposed such conditions. He and his associates subscribed to the current principle of charging all that the traffic would bear and the idea that good sports come in last. The Rio Grande was built to exploit mining country, a type of trade that Palmer had described back in 1871 as being highly lucrative. That policy was to be pursued for a number of years to come.

The Rio Grande's penetration into Utah had supplied a good deal of excitement for the Mormons, but as the drama came to a close and the denouement was revealed, some of them must have been irritated at their own economic naïveté. The story of the coming of the railroad to any Western community was an old one: high hopes followed by high rates. There remained, of course, the lingering hope that despite such initial disappointments, a natural rivalry sooner or later would manifest itself between the Union Pacific and the latest interloper.

34. *Deseret News*, Feb. 16, 1884.

35. *Territorial Enquirer*, Feb. 19, 1884, in Journal History, L.D.S. Church Library, Salt Lake City.

Rio Grande management took advantage of the general optimism that prevailed throughout Colorado. Now that the "Baby Road" undertook to find a place among the major roads, its general offices were moved from Colorado Springs to Denver, where several of the larger lines met. Provision was made for meetings of the board of trustees outside of Colorado, when necessary, in recognition of the Rio Grande's increased status among carriers.[36] With great pride, Denver papers quoted the Wall Street *Daily News* when it predicted that the sharp advance in Rio Grande stocks and bonds meant serious competition for the Union Pacific. The New York paper innocently believed that the Rio Grande could, by a threat of a rate war, force its opponent to turn over 50 per cent of its through traffic.[37] One look at the narrow gauge's dog-leg shape, its lengthy, cheaply built road, and its badly extended financial condition ought to have indicated the odds against success in any such contest so far as Denver was concerned. The distance between Kansas City and Ogden, by way of Pueblo (via the AT&SF), approximated that of the Union Pacific route, but even this did not lend any assurance that the Rio Grande could engage in a rate war.

The question of the narrow gauge's ability to compete with its powerful rival to the north was purely academic. From its beginning, Palmer had pushed the Denver and Rio Grande construction to the limit, never letting up long enough to allow an accumulation of profits, ever fearful that rivals would enter the field and pre-empt the territory. The road had been confronted with one financial crisis after another, and its backers were tired of constant requests for a deferral of interest payment on the one hand, and for new funds on the other. In 1881 the management promised to pay a 6 per cent dividend, but due to the demands made by new construction it begged off. At the same time, Palmer had proposed that the Rio Grande Western, intended from its inception as a subsidiary, be leased to the Denver and Rio Grande, a scheme that became operative in May 1883. The lease, and Palmer's continuous policy of expansion, coupled with suspended dividend payments, produced irritations among the bondholders that resulted in a bitter internal quarrel. It reached such violent proportions that the road's very survival was threatened. Under these circumstances the Union Pacific had little to worry about from its upstart mountain competitor.

36. Minutes of D&RG Stockholders, April 13, 1883, D&RG Archives.
37. Denver *Republican,* May 14, 1883, quoting the Wall Street *Daily News.*

7. *God Almighty and Frederick Lovejoy*

THE TREMENDOUS EFFORT to reach Salt Lake City placed an enormous strain upon the resources of the Denver and Rio Grande. Earlier it had pledged itself not to enlarge its heavy floating debt, but in order to complete new construction, the board of directors agreed to increase the stock issue from $29,160,000 to $33,000,000 on the theory that it would allow the 1300 mile road, including the Salt

Lake extension, to be completed. By early 1883, about the time the connection was being made between the Rio Grande and the Western, matters had reached a climax. The railroad then announced that it could not pay the annual dividend, yet its management simultaneously revealed that a new debt had been incurred through a lease of the Western's trackage by the Denver and Rio Grande. It was too much for some of the directors, who all along had held that the expansion was going much too fast.

The rumblings of discontent against Palmer came out into the open during the summer of 1883. In July the *Railroad Gazette* reported that the road's directors had asked Palmer to devote full time to company matters or to resign his position as president. Their reference was to his interests in the Colorado Coal and Iron Company (now called the Colorado Fuel and Iron Corporation) as well as the Mexican National Railway, but it did not touch the heart of the problem.[1] At a stormy meeting of the board of trustees, held in late January, William Bell, Lyman K. Bass, Hanson A. Risley, and J. W. Gilluly—all loyal Palmer men—had resigned. Significantly, each of the new trustees represented outside, non-Colorado interests. Louis H. Meyer was a trustee for the bondholders, but he was also a director of the Pittsburg, Fort Wayne, and Chicago Railroad. William L. Scott was a director of the Union Pacific, A. J. Cassatt was a vice-president of the Pennsylvania Railroad, and Peter Geddes belonged to the Chicago, Burlington, and Quincy road.[2] Although the latter appointee served less than three months, the composition of the board was increasingly anti-Palmer. That fact became apparent when a special committee, appointed to study the road's salary scale and headed by William L. Scott and Henry Sprague, made a report that not only condemned the present management but hinted broadly that Palmer was guilty of mismanagement.[3] David C. Dodge, general manager for the road, heatedly protested the committee's recommendation for wage cuts, arguing that, by comparison with other lines, the employees were sadly underpaid. The trustees ignored him.

The complaints of the board went much deeper than disagreements

1. *Railroad Gazette,* July 20, 1883, p. 486.
2. Wilson, "Denver and Rio Grande," pp. 157–58. Minutes of D&RG Board of Trustees, Jan. 29, 30, 1883, D&RG Archives.
3. *Annual Report of the Board of Trustees of the Denver and Rio Grande Railway Company, 1883,* p. 16.

over wages. From the outset, Palmer had been obliged to fight for control of his territory and of that which he hoped to command, to protect the line's business. It amounted to building "back fires" against the oncoming competitors and it was extremely expensive. For example, in the fall of 1883 engineer John A. McMurtrie submitted an inventory of uncompleted work whose cost was well over a million dollars. The projects included a line out of the Platte Canyon as a shortcut to Leadville and the Gunnison country. It was here that a collision occurred with the Union Pacific's South Park line, one that sent the litigants into Judge Moses Hallett's court. Another extension along the Blue River proposed to make connection in Wyoming with the Union Pacific before that road could enter the Colorado mountains from the north. More than $300,000 was spent on grading only to have the project abandoned. The Grand River extension, also, was begun as a means of warding off the Union Pacific. Another line was proposed in the Chama River country to discourage the AT&SF or the Santa Fe Northern and to preserve for the D&RG the Silverton territory. This would have cost well over a million and a half dollars. The Lake Fork branch, built to beat out the South Park company, was finished in 1889, but at great expense.

These were defensive tactics, held by Palmer to be essential to the road's existence, but they exerted a tremendous drain upon the company's resources and were hard for eastern investors to visualize. Once the grading was finished, there could be no monetary return until more millions were spent for construction and equipment. Faced by such a prospect and the continued deferral of any dividends, it is no wonder that those who were putting up the money had, from time to time, displayed some mental reservations about the freewheeling tactics of General Palmer. If they were somewhat more timid than he, their attitudes are understandable, for theirs was an era of economic fluctuations, financial panics, and general unrest.[4]

During the period of quarreling over policy, Palmer was re-elected president of the Rio Grande Western. Confident that he was in firm control of that line, he struck back at his critics on the Denver and Rio Grande's board. When protests over wage and salary cuts availed him nothing, he resigned his presidency on August 9. Later, in a court case involving the lease between the two railroads, Palmer re-

4. For a good discussion of McMurtrie's inventory see Wilson, "Denver and Rio Grande," pp. 162–64.

called the circumstances of his resignation and said that the Rio Grande had come into the hands of men whose interests were "purely wild and speculative." He singled out William L. Scott as the ringleader of those who had led the board in its improvidence. To Palmer the direction of a railroad's operations from a distance of more than 2,000 miles, by a group of men who had never seen, much less understood it, was sufficient explanation as to why the corporation was on the verge of bankruptcy.[5]

Whatever the merits of General Palmer's arguments, he chose a good time to resign. The prosperity of the years 1880–82 was dwindling, and the circumstances that had stimulated the final burst of construction activity were fading away. The management had no choice but to plunge ahead, much as Palmer had done on repeated occasions, hopeful that the situation would improve. At the annual meeting of the stockholders, held on October 8, 1883, a general mortgage of $50,000,000 was authorized, over half of which was to be used "to provide for present needs."[6] To make matters worse, the Union Pacific again threatened to invade Rio Grande territory by extending its subsidiary, the Denver and South Park, in the direction of the Blue River country and on into the San Juan area. A Denver paper called the intruder "a sort of carpetbagger" and warned its readers that the Union Pacific Company would unhesitatingly sacrifice Colorado to build up its own territory in the Northwest, while destroying the little narrow gauge whose presence had done so much for the centennial state.[7] Even more ominous than the threat of invasion was the Union Pacific's effort to starve out the smaller road. When the D&RG reached Ogden, the older road at once dropped its freight rates between the Missouri River and Utah until the figure, once $3.00 a hundred, fell to twenty-five cents. Formation of the Utah Traffic Association, or pool, did not resolve the matter, for the Union Pacific refused to join, much to the joy of Utah merchants and the undisguised displeasure of those in Colorado. Torn from within and threatened by outside competition, the Denver and Rio Grande found itself once again in serious straits.

The unenviable task of directing the railroad's destiny fell to Frederick Lovejoy, of Philadelphia, who was elected president on Septem-

5. Salt Lake *Tribune*, June 20, 1884.
6. *Railroad Gazette* (Oct. 12, 1883), p. 681.
7. Denver *Republican*, Sept. 21, 1883.

ber 26. Behind him lay thirty years of experience with Adams Express Company, but ahead were enough managerial hazards to raise doubts in any experienced executive's mind. Out of self-confidence or ignorance of the situation, he boldly promised a thorough inspection of the Colorado railroad, after which sufficient repairs and reorganization would follow to make the Rio Grande equal to any road in the country. While he could not more specifically define his policy, he said that it would be one of "vigorous progress" and that he would leave no stone unturned to make the road justify all the hopes of his backers.[8]

Lovejoy's policies were not long in creating an uproar in Colorado. In January 1884 he struck out at the Colorado Coal and Iron Company of Pueblo, headed by General Palmer, by sharply raising freight rates. There was an immediate charge of discrimination on the ground that the freight rate on a keg of nails between Kansas City and Salt Lake City was $1.59, while the rate from Pueblo to Salt Lake City was advanced from eleven cents to $1.48. Colorado's only iron manufacturer felt that home industry was being severely penalized and that such a policy would be detrimental to the whole state.

When the CC&I turned to the Denver and New Orleans Railroad, the Denver and Rio Grande refused to haul its products to Utah for shipment to California points. This presented a real problem to the coal and iron company because, as a child of the D&RG, it had used that line almost exclusively, much to the irritation of the Union Pacific, whose managers boycotted it. None of the Pueblo-made products was permitted in "Union Pacific country." As one of the foundry's representatives complained, "we have been debarred from supplying even the towns in Colorado on the lines of the U.P. from our works."[9] Within a matter of days after Lovejoy issued his restrictive order, the industrial company claimed it had lost $30,000 in orders because of the discrimination against it.

The fight between the Colorado Coal and Iron Company and the Rio Grande Railway revealed the high degree of loyalty of Palmer's long-time friends among railroad employees, and resulted in considerable annoyance to Lovejoy. From the general manager, David C. Dodge, down to the most obscure gandy dancer, there was a sneering resentment toward this "foreigner" who had assumed the General's

8. Ibid., Sept. 27, 1883.
9. Denver *Tribune*, Feb. 28, 1884.

position. At the time of the election, Dodge openly expressed the opinion to Colorado newsmen that "President Lovejoy can't do as much (as Palmer) because he is an Eastern man, and has not the sympathy with the road that General Palmer necessarily had. He will represent to a great extent Eastern interests."[10] Dodge's undisguised animosity to his new superior was even more apparent over the trouble with CC&I. When the press asked him for an interpretation of the matter, he suggested that Lovejoy was trying to squeeze the Pueblo concern. "I have no hesitancy in telling you," he volunteered, "that I think his actions are suicidal so far as the Denver & Rio Grande road is concerned, and also very injurious to the interests of Colorado. The accounts of the road show that during the month of December the money paid on the freight of the Colorado Coal and Iron Company amounted to 26 per cent of the receipts of the whole road. If Mr. Lovejoy can afford to fight such a patron as that, well and good. I don't believe he can."[11]

Open warfare erupted when Lovejoy appointed Robert E. Ricker to succeed R. B. Cable as general superintendent of the Rio Grande Western.[12] Palmer at once objected, telling Dodge that this was an express violation of the lease terms under which Dodge was to direct the management of the leased property. The bad blood existing between Palmer and Lovejoy was revealed by the General's closing sentence in his letter to Dodge: "As a practical question this order will force the issue between the two companies to a hearing or to an open rupture."[13] Even before receiving Palmer's letter, Dodge had notified Ricker that Lovejoy's order violated the lease, and until the Rio Grande Western assented to the new appointment, Ricker was prohibited from participating in the management of that line.[14] Ricker responded by demanding of W. H. Bancroft, superintendent of the "Utah Division" (Rio Grande Western), that he make all requisitions for supplies and send in all payrolls to his office for examination and certification.[15]

Bancroft refused, saying that he was obliged to obey General Man-

10. Denver *Republican*, Oct. 6, 1883.
11. Denver *Evening Times*, March 13, 1884. Denver *Tribune*, March 14, 1884.
12. *Annual Report of the D. & R. G. Western Railway* (to Dec. 31, 1883), p. 30.
13. Palmer to Dodge, March 6, 1884, item 1193, D&RG Archives.
14. Dodge to R. E. Ricker, March 7, 1884, D. C. Dodge Letter Book.
15. Ricker to W. H. Bancroft, March 13, 1884, item 1195, D&RG Archives.

ager Dodge. He then wrote to Dodge, telling him that he would obey no orders but his and that without doubt it would result in Lovejoy sending someone to Salt Lake City who would obey. With reference to the president's demand of obedience, Bancroft admitted "there is a great deal of speculation and excitement among the men as to the result of this order from Mr. Lovejoy."[16]

Both sides prepared for legal battle. At a special meeting of the Denver and Rio Grande board of directors on March 26, it was resolved that since Lovejoy had given orders that President Palmer of the Rio Grande Western had advised Dodge to ignore, there was no recourse but to employ counsel to protect the D&RG.[17] The Rio Grande Western camp took similar steps. Dodge wrote to his railroad's counsel, Lyman K. Bass, who was then in New York, and asked what Palmer proposed to do. Was the General prepared to fight? What were the prospects of a victory?[18] Bass replied that "The fight seems to be forced by the other side. They want the lease of the Western, and yet they don't want to abide by its terms. They want an 'equitable readjustment.' " The attorney was convinced that Palmer's enemies had decided he must be crushed in order to acquire the properties he represented. These motives explained to him why they were willing to circulate lies about the General and to exploit all prejudices against him. Bass suggested that the Western officials wait until the other side realized some of its own weaknesses before talking about any kind of a settlement. Meanwhile, he advised Dodge to hold fast. "I think you are the master of the situation," he said. "The lease makes you the manager. That is a vital condition of the lease. Now Mr. Lovejoy may seek to interfere with your power when he returns, but Mr. Lovejoy is not a formidable adversary. He is hasty, forms his conclusions on half the facts, or no facts at all, and acts ill-advisedly. He has a training that teaches him the art of squeezing and bulldozing, but with no high sense of absolute right and wrong." Bass was unconcerned over Lovejoy's threats not to pay the men. Let him pursue that policy, he told Dodge, and the D&RG would be in receivership in ninety days. Such a development probably would make Dodge, not Lovejoy, the

16. Bancroft to Dodge, April 1, 1884, ibid.

17. Minutes D&RG Board of Directors, March 26, 1884, D&RG Archives. Another action taken by the board at this meeting was the appointment of Edward O. Wolcott, one day to be U.S. Senator from Colorado, as the road's general counsel. His salary was set at $10,000.

18. Dodge to L. K. Bass, March 20, 1884, D. C. Dodge Letter Book, D&RG Archives.

receiver. "That would save both properties. I think this may as well come. The fight has got to be made. We have now the rights, don't yield a point."[19]

While the question of Lovejoy's powers over Rio Grande Western officers was in doubt, no such problem confronted him at Denver. Armed with special permission from the directors to dismiss Dodge or any other subordinate officer, the president prepared to clean house.[20] The intended victim was well aware of this, and toward the end of March he handed in his resignation as General Manager of the Rio Grande. Not to be robbed of an opportunity to inflict injury and humiliation upon a Palmer man, Lovejoy sent a telegram to Dodge over the company telegraph system, telling him he was fired. Instantly, every operator along the line knew that the general manager, out at one of the smaller stations, had been summarily dismissed. But Lovejoy's move backfired. Dodge's return to Denver resembled a triumphal procession homeward of a national hero. At every stop old-time employees gathered around his car, offering to quit, only to be advised that they should stay on. John A. McMurtrie, chief engineer and veteran of the Royal Gorge war, was also discharged, along with B. F. Woodward, telegraphy superintendent.[21] Other Palmer men on the payroll watched nervously and asked each other who was next on the executive guillotine.

Dismissal of high-ranking officers from the company came on the eve of an annual stockholders meeting, and it lent strength to the rumors around Denver that Lovejoy's forces would be reversed at the coming election. Dodge, well-known in his capacity as first vice-president and general manager, represented the Palmer forces, and it was freely predicted that he would unseat the Easterner. There was also talk of Palmer's return to office, but he issued what amounted to a Sherman statement when he said that no consideration could again induce him to accept office. He added that he felt obliged to warn his fellow stockholders and bondholders of the present danger, one that there was yet time to avoid.[22] At the meeting, held in Denver on April 7, Dodge's name was put forward, but he was defeated. Lovejoy and

19. Bass to Dodge, March 27, 1884, item 1198, D&RG Archives.

20. Minutes D&RG Executive Committee of the Board of Directors, March 14, 1884, D&RG Archives.

21. Denver *Tribune,* April 1, 2, 1884. Wilson, "Denver and Rio Grande," p. 167.

22. Denver *Tribune,* March 19, 20, 1884.

Scott were re-elected to the board and a new member, David H. Moffat, was elected to represent local interests. The Lovejoy forces not only carried 258,000 of the 380,000 shares, but they rammed through a resolution censuring Dodge for his "unlawful and unauthorized usurpation of powers."[23]

The action of the stockholders clearly indicated that Palmer's influence on the Denver and Rio Grande was seriously diminished, if not completely destroyed. But the General, who had felt the heat of legal battle before, was not discouraged. His experience during the 1878–80 period, when the AT&SF management appeared to have put him into complete rout, illustrated the virtues of fighting to the bitter end. This time he was in a much stronger position through his unchallenged control of the Rio Grande Western. Obviously, he and Lovejoy were each master of half a railroad, a situation the Chicago *Times* called "one of the most peculiar on record," where "two connecting and practically inseparable lines are thus under the management of two bitterly hostile men, who are doing their utmost to cut each other's throats."[24] If affairs remained stalemated any length of time, a receivership for one or both roads was bound to follow.

The Rio Grande Western managers now dug in, ready to make their stand. On March 3 Lovejoy had issued his General Order No. 2, by which he appointed R. E. Ricker as manager of the Western. A month later, on April 4, Dodge issued his own General Order No. 1, advising all employees on that line that he was in charge and any orders issued by Lovejoy were to be disregarded.[25] Bancroft advised Dodge that the men of the Western were loyal. "I don't think there is a doubt but what I shall be able to hold the fort in case an attempt is made to supersede my orders," he wrote.[26] Cautioning Bancroft to use cipher in all messages, Dodge reassured his superintendent that Lovejoy probably would not make any threatening moves in the immediate future.[27]

Toward the end of April the Western secured an injunction restraining the Denver and Rio Grande from any interference with its

23. Minutes D&RG Stockholders, April 7, 1884, D&RG Archives. Denver *Tribune*, April 8, 1884.

24. Denver *Tribune*, April 14, 1884, quoting the *Times*.

25. Lovejoy's order is quoted in *Annual Report of the R.G.W.* (to Dec. 31, 1883), p. 30; Dodge's order is found in the same document, p. 31.

26. Bancroft to Dodge, April 4, 1884, item 1201, D&RG Archives.

27. Dodge to Bancroft, April 11, 1884, D. C. Dodge Letter Book.

operation and management.[28] Palmer then began a war of nerves by talking about an alliance with the Burlington, a move that would render the Denver and Rio Grande a completely local road unless it wanted to build to Salt Lake City. The Rio Grande Western had the prospect of forming a bridge between the Burlington and itself by means of the recently incorporated Colorado Midland Railroad. Not only would such a move bypass the Denver and Rio Grande, but it would considerably shorten the route between Denver and Salt Lake City, giving the new system all of the Denver–Salt Lake City trade.

While Denver papers fed the rumor, Palmer felt out President C. E. Perkins of the Burlington line. He received no favorable response. With his usual candor and frank objectivity, Perkins explained to the General why he did not intend to enter into any close association. He did not think that the Union Pacific, without provocation, would risk the wrath of other major roads by breaking up the Rio Grande system, and for the same reason he did not want to enter into such a game. "My idea is, as it always has been, that the Denver & Rio Grande property can, and that it should, remain a neutral property, occupying the same mountain region, and feeding the roads to the eastward impartially, in accordance with the general idea which animated you when you undertook the construction of that narrow gauge system." Palmer must have winced slightly at the remarks, for such was a policy he had once clearly enunciated, and it was one that he, now at odds with the Denver and Rio Grande, was trying to violate. Perkins pressed his point: "It is so much for the interest of both the Denver & Rio Grande and the Denver & Rio Grande Western to work together, that you will be obliged, in the end, to find some solution of the present difficulties, whatever they may be." In closing, Perkins clearly implied that he did not want to be used as a means of settling a family dispute in Colorado. Bluntly he told Palmer: "Perhaps the more immediate and direct effect of our going in with you might be to make the Denver & Rio Grande Road more easy for you to deal with in reaching a settlement of your difficulties; but that would hardly be a good reason why the C. B. & Q. should take a hand."[29]

Lovejoy's principal desire was to terminate the lease, after which he could deal with the Western as an independent and isolated road. He recognized the importance of a connection with Salt Lake City,

28. *Railroad Gazette* (April 25, 1884), p. 329. Denver *Tribune*, April 28, 1884.
29. Charles E. Perkins to Palmer, May 5, 1884, item 1216, D&RG Archives.

but he felt that the leased road represented a sufficient burden to carry his own line into bankruptcy. During 1883 the leased line had operated an average of 306 miles, on which it had grossed $805,767, but its expenses had amounted to $802,026, leaving only $3,741, or $12.25 per mile, in net earnings. This figure was $318,566 less than the 40 per cent rental on gross earnings. The leased road's bonds amounted to $6,157,000, on which $369,420 interest was due. To pay the interest alone, the road had to earn $923,550. There was a good prospect that the Western's gross earnings would reach this figure, but its expenses were so high and competition with other lines so fierce that the chance of realizing enough net earnings to make the lease profitable was remote.[30]

Affairs on the main road were in such bad condition that Lovejoy could not afford to risk any more losses. For three years earnings had fallen off and the company's stock sank from 113 to 13. March revenues suffered a catastrophic decline. Net earnings were a mere $17,750 compared to $204,222 for the same month of the preceding year. During the first quarter of 1883 the road had experienced a 73 per cent decline in net earnings. Heavy snows and repeated slides were given as the explanation.[31] Commenting on the Denver and Rio Grande's misfortunes, W. H. Bancroft wrote Dodge that, "I think between God Almighty & Frederick Lovejoy they will bust up the D. & R. G." A Denver paper, stating that the railroad's annual report for 1883 had been "well doctored" to disguise the true state of affairs, suggested that the sooner it was out of speculators' hands and into those of a receiver the better it would be for both the railroad and the state.[32]

Palmer took the lofty but certainly unwarranted position that his successor's brief administration was responsible for all the difficulty. Both he and Dodge told stockholders of the Western that the troubles of their road were attributable to the Denver and Rio Grande for its discriminatory rates, its own maladministration, and the hostility of Frederick Lovejoy. The Western faced other difficulties. Aside from the complexities of organizing a new business, it suffered from washouts and high water that had disrupted traffic for two months, during which time the road was engaged in a disastrous rate war with the Un-

30. *Railroad Gazette* (May 23, 1884), p. 395.
31. Denver *Tribune*, May 14, 1884. *Railroad Gazette* (May 16, 1884), p. 385.
32. Denver *Tribune*, April 28, 1884.

ion Pacific.[33] Unquestionably, both Rio Grande roads were in serious difficulty and only the closest cooperation could save them from disaster. It was extremely unfortunate that each was headed by a strong-willed man determined to crush his opponent regardless of the consequences.

Toward the end of May 1884 the Denver and Rio Grande went to court in an attempt to break the lease. Lovejoy's forces charged that when the document was executed in April 1882, only five directors were present at the Colorado Springs meeting, and that they had not been called together through proper means. Only Hanson Risley, Lyman Bass, David Dodge, Robert Lamborn, and Joseph Gilluly were in attendance, the others not having been notified of the gathering. The management denied that the stockholders had the capacity to ratify the lease agreement at their annual meeting of 1883, that only two-thirds of the stock was represented, and that some 50,000 shares were unrepresented. It was further contended that under Colorado law, no meeting for such a purpose could be held unless each stockholder was given thirty days notice. There were accusations that Palmer had quietly disposed of his holdings in the Denver and Rio Grande after the Western was organized and that since January 1883, Palmer, Dodge, Bass, and Dr. Bell had held less than 300 shares among them. These men, said the Lovejoy camp, then planned the lease with "various unjust, inequitable, oppressive and unfair provisions which were fraudulently procured for the purpose of advancing the interests of the D. & R. G. W. and the Construction Company." Such acts were said to have come to the attention of the Denver and Rio Grande stockholders, and since they regarded the General as hostile to their interests, he was forced to resign. Finally, Colonel Dodge was accused of being an incompetent, unsafe individual, unfit to be manager of the roads, and one whose bad management of the Western resulted in a serious financial loss to the stockholders.[34]

Angered by such bitter accusations, Palmer struck back in defense of his own position. The whole idea of the lease, he said, had been urged upon him by C. F. Woerischoffer, a member of the board of trustees, who was presently the "leading spirit" of the Denver and Rio Grande. The action had been taken to prevent either of the lines fall-

33. *Annual Report of the R.G.W.* (to Dec. 31, 1883), pp. 3-5, 21.

34. Salt Lake *Tribune*, May 22, 1884. Denver *Tribune*, May 26, 1884. *Railroad Gazette* (June 13, 1884), p. 453.

ing into the hands of the Union Pacific or of Jay Gould. He insisted that "without the previous knowledge of friends or enemies, I tendered my resignation. I did this because of waking up to a full appreciation of the real character and intentions of those who had acquired the control of the board, and the danger of allowing myself to be the responsible head, when the power was entirely in the hands of men whose views concerning the railroad business were purely wild and speculative." Again, he singled out the "reckless improvidence" of William L. Scott and several of his codirectors as sufficient reason for leaving.[35] In a report to stockholders of the Western, covering operations for the year 1883, he defended his management of that road, saying that it had not been in operation long enough to show a true picture of its real potential. He thought it would be suicidal for the Denver and Rio Grande to sever the tie between the lines, but if the main road could produce no better results in its managerial attempts, and if it persisted in violating the terms of the lease, he saw no value in continuing the agreement.[36] As far as Lovejoy was concerned, Palmer was scornful of his "recent tendency to sleep with the U.P. people," particularly when there was no need for it. In his opinion the D&RG had only to stick with the CB&Q and the AT&SF to be protected against the Union Pacific.[37]

During June both sides anxiously awaited the outcome of the suits and countersuits pending in court. David Moffat, board member of the Denver and Rio Grande, openly predicted that if the case went against his company, the Western would be abandoned and all D&RG rolling stock and equipment would be withdrawn. Meanwhile, affairs on the D&RG became so serious that it was unable to meet its payrolls. All improvements ceased, and Denver papers loudly complained that the failure to build extensions into promising mining camps was threatening Colorado's economy. Conditions were no better on the Western. Dodge advised Palmer in mid-June that the road in the vicinity of Price River was in an extremely unsafe condition as a result of a work stoppage ordered by Lovejoy the preceding fall. Nor was there much hope of improvement since the D&RG had no money or credit. To make matters worse, Lovejoy now threatened to divide the

35. Denver *Tribune*, June 25, 1884.
36. *Annual Report of the R.G.W.* (to Dec. 31, 1884), pp. 10–11.
37. Palmer to Alfred G. Renshaw (London Agent), June 5, 1884, item 1224, D&RG Archives.

two roads physically if he met defeat in court.[38] At this juncture Palmer handed in his resignation as a director of the Denver and Rio
Grande, with the comment that he had stayed on, after leaving the
presidency, in the hope that he could help protect the property and
to offer his experience in railroading. But now, he said, the reckless-
ness, the folly, and the inexperience of the new management was bearing its full fruit, and he was unwilling to be even nominally responsible for the consequences.[39]

On the 28th of June a legal decision was reached at Salt Lake City.
The preliminary injunction against the Denver and Rio Grande,
issued in April, now was made permanent, and Dodge's continuance
as manager of the Western appeared to be assured. Judge Hunter, of
the United States Circuit Court, sustained the lease and held that even
if it had not been legally ratified, as the plaintiffs charged, the fact that
the lessee took possession of the line confirmed the transaction.[40]
Two days before the decision was handed down, the Western instituted a new suit against the Denver and Rio Grande, requesting payment of moneys owed under the lease. Lovejoy, stung by an unfavorable decision on the validity of the lease and faced by the Western's
legal action to force the payment of debt, was handed another blow
on July 2. On that day the Western filed a petition in Denver asking
for a receiver for the Denver and Rio Grande, alleging that nonpay-
ment of money under the terms of the lease required the action.[41] In
a blind fury Lovejoy struck out at his tormentors. On July 3 he sent
out telegraphic orders to his subordinates to cut the line, and before
the surprised eyes of western Colorado residents, workmen tore up
a mile of Denver and Rio Grande track just east of the state line. The
"Baby Road," of which the mountain folks were so proud, was cut
in half.

Lovejoy's dramatics forced Denver and Rio Grande bondholders
to take action that had long been in the making. Their railroad, deeply
ensnarled in legal actions, suffering severe financial pains as the result
of heavy snow blockades and unable to meet its payrolls, defaulted on
the July bond interest of $600,000. With no mention of the road's

38. Dodge to Palmer, June 14, 1884, item 1225, D&RG Archives.
39. Copy in Minutes D&RG Board of Directors, June 24, 1884, D&RG Archives. *Railroad
Gazette* (June 27, 1884), p. 490. Denver *Tribune*, June 27, 1884.
40. *Railroad Gazette* (July 11, 1884), p. 527. Denver *Tribune*, June 29, 1884.
41. Denver *Republican*, July 3, 1884. Hall, *History of the State of Colorado, 3,* 117.

recent surgery, the bondholders, on July 7, also applied to the United States Circuit Court at Denver for a receivership. On the 9th, Judge Moses Hallett appointed W. S. Jackson, a former treasurer of the road and a Colorado Springs banker, as receiver. His selection generated considerable enthusiasm among employees on the Western, who now felt that their own problems were over. W. H. Bancroft wrote to Dodge, "I don't think we will have any trouble in getting what we want in the future. Good feeling generally exists among the men and people, believing there is no one like the old man."[42] Another of Dodge's friends on the Western was more exuberant. He told the colonel that great excitement took place in the Salt Lake City offices when word of Jackson's appointment was flashed out. Apparently he sent off a highly congratulatory message to Dodge, for he followed it with this explanation: "Well, I am not a drinking man, but we all took champaign [sic] and considerable of it. Perhaps under its influence I sent you the message relating to Mr. Jackson. If there was any impropriety in it, please charge it to the champaign and not to me. . . . I felt as though the D. and R. G. Rwy. had a future, and that its friends could not be crushed out by such an abject apology for a man as that Lovejoy."[43] While Jackson was not Dodge's first choice as a receiver, he told Palmer that this was the only man upon which the anti-Lovejoy forces could agree and that certainly the appointee would do everything that was fair and right to protect the Western's interests.[44] Palmer agreed that the problem of selection had been a "very close game," but remarked that except for the fact that Judge Hallett might regard Jackson "rather one of us," the choice was a good one.[45]

Jackson assumed his new duties on July 12, and within two days he had gained the Court's permission to raise $150,000 to commence paying the employees their overdue wages. By mid-month the break in the track was repaired and work was begun all along the line on damaged bridges and washouts occasioned by recent rains. Shortly, traffic between Denver and Ogden was restored and transcontinental shipments could make their way across the system. Mining camps such as Silverton, in serious jeopardy because of irregular service, took on new life when rail transportation problems were unsnarled.

42. Bancroft to Dodge, July 10, 1884, item 1239, D&RG Archives.
43. George Goss to Dodge, July 9, 1884, item 1238, ibid.
44. Dodge to Palmer, July 13, 1884, D. C. Dodge Letter Book, D&RG Archives.
45. Palmer to Dodge, July 18, 1884, item 1256, D&RG Archives.

During the weeks before the Denver and Rio Grande went into receivership, Palmer and his associates pondered the fate of the Rio Grande Western. Palmer thought that if by September the road could show some promise of earning the necessary $200,000 bond interest due the following March, trouble with the bondholders might be averted. To earn the money, he wanted to operate the line with a minimum of expenses and a maximum of profit. He did not fear the renewal of a rate war with the Union Pacific, for in 1884 that line itself was on the verge of bankruptcy and was in no position to fight.[46] During the spring there was increasing talk about the prospect of receivership for the Western. Lyman Bass, the road's counsel, thought Palmer was the only man who could save anything out of the confusion created by the Denver and Rio Grande's recent management. In commenting upon the state of affairs, he told Palmer that Lovejoy had " more effectually wrecked a valuable property in six months by mere ignorance than a wise knave could have done in a year."[47]

The Western's warfare with its Colorado counterpart resulted in a continuance of the lease, but it did nothing to alleviate the Utah road's mounting financial difficulties. Shortly after Jackson took over the Denver and Rio Grande, the Rio Grande Western made application for receivership at Salt Lake City. W. H. Bancroft, who had been with the D&RG since 1881 and who had many years of railroading experience, was given custody of the road. With the appointment of receivers for both roads and with the lease still in effect, there was a renewed attempt to make the Colorado–Utah narrow-gauge system profitable. Jackson lost no time in making an agreement with the Denver and New Orleans regarding rates between Denver and Pueblo. At the time the D&NO was completed between those points, the Denver and Rio Grande had tried to run it out of business by cutting fares. The warfare had reached a point where both roads were carrying passengers over that 120-mile stretch of road for seventy-five cents a head. This was followed by a gradual increase to $2.50, but it was not enough to be profitable. Jackson and the competing road now agreed upon a figure of $5.00. A Denver paper, noting that Denver and Rio Grande stock had crawled back up to twelve, remarked that "the 'Baby Road' promises to be herself again soon."[48] Dodge, who watched the

46. Ibid.
47. Bass to Palmer, June 25, 1884, item 1229, ibid.
48. *Railroad Gazette* (Aug. 15, 1884), p. 611. Denver *Republican*, Aug. 3, 9, 1884.

larger picture with continued interest, told Palmer that Jackson's stewardship over the property was producing a healthy result. "Already I can see a great change in the feeling among employees as well as the people living along the line," he wrote in August 1884. "They have confidence in the Receiver and the 'don't care' feeling that seemed to control them two months ago is fast disappearing. While I believe the Receiver will find it necessary to make some changes in the officers everything is in much better shape than could have been expected in the short time he has had possession of the property."[49]

The Western showed some improvement, but it continued to be plagued by washouts. Bancroft told Palmer that this problem was serious and that a great many prospective passengers had lost confidence in the line, and to make matters worse, competing lines willingly exaggerated the difficulty in order to capture the traffic. The August 1884 ticket sales were larger than at any time since the road opened, and so great was the desire of tourists to see the country over which the line ran that many of them waited around Salt Lake City as much as ten days in hope of being able to travel the route when repairs were completed.[50] Dodge assured Palmer that $100,000 would put the Western in such condition that similar delays in traffic could be avoided, "which will soon inspire confidence with shippers."[51]

Prospective shippers, however, were not inspired. Lovejoy's track-cutting temper tantrum had cost both lines heavily, and old customers were slow to return. The Burlington, for example, had once sent its transcontinental traffic via the Rio Grande system, but with the rupture in relationships between the two sections of the road, it had transferred its business to the AT&SF. A Denver paper estimated that Lovejoy's "wonderful and masterful stroke" was costing the Denver and Rio Grande around $25,000 a month and the Rio Grande Western about $15,000 a month.[52] In writing to David Dodge, now manager of the Western, Burlington Vice-President T. J. Potter referred to the differences that had arisen between his road and the D&RG, and said that a traffic arrangement between the Burlington and the Santa Fe had developed out of necessity. After Lovejoy's disruption of Rio Grande service, there was no other course for the Burlington. "We

49. Dodge to Palmer, Aug. 30, 1884, D. C. Dodge Letter Book, D&RG Archives.
50. Bancroft to Palmer, Sept. 3, 1884, item 1263, D&RG Archives.
51. Dodge to Palmer, Aug. 30, 1884, D. C. Dodge Letter Book, D&RG Archives.
52. Denver *Tribune–Republican,* Oct. 31, 1884.

either had to do this or quit the transportation of a certain class of California business, and this we did not think desirable." Potter indicated a continued deterioration of relations with the D&RG when he accused that line of further discriminations against his road with Denver merchants.[53]

This loss of business so reduced income that the Denver and Rio Grande defaulted on its November bond interest. In New York the *Commercial and Financial Chronicle* called it inexcusable that the default had occurred without a word of explanation to the bondholders. The journal felt that despite a sharp drop in earnings, there was sufficient money to pay interest on at least the first-mortgage bonds.[54] The road's board of directors agreed, absolutely. In a formal action it passed a resolution to the effect that passing the interest payment was an unwarranted and unjustifiable action on the part of the receiver. It, too, believed that there were enough earnings to cover the payment, and that refusal to do so further embarrassed attempts at reorganization. There were threats of calling for a separate accounting to prove the point.[55]

Foreign bondholders became alarmed at the turn of events. When they noted a 15 per cent drop in November earnings, as compared to the same month of the previous year, they began to talk about foreclosure and reorganization. Earlier in the fall representatives of the English, Scottish, and Dutch bondholders had gone over the property, and even before the November default, there had been talk of reorganizing the roads and consolidating under a single management.[56]

Palmer, never willing to talk about defeat, continued to probe the situation for a solution to his own problems on the Western. Writing from London, he urged upon Dodge the importance of getting the line into such working condition that it would suffer no more costly interruptions. If by March of 1885 the system was operating efficiently and was out of debt, he felt that no court would change the receiver or tolerate foreclosure. This also would reduce the pressure from Denver to join the main road in any complicated reorganization schemes and it would help maintain the Western's independence.[57]

53. T. J. Potter to Dodge, Oct. 27, 1884, item 1265, D&RG Archives.
54. *Railroad Gazette* (Nov. 7, 1884), p. 811, quoting the *Commercial and Financial Chronicle.*
55. Minutes of D&RG Board of Directors, Nov. 5, 1884, D&RG Archives.
56. Denver *Tribune–Republican*, Sept. 29, Nov. 16, 1884. *Railroad Gazette* (Sept. 12, 1884), p. 675.
57. Palmer to Dodge, Nov. 22, 1884, item 1284, D&RG Archives.

Dodge was discouraged over the prospects of getting much inter-change business, particularly that from California, but even without it there remained the possibility of earning enough money to support the road. He estimated that it cost between sixty and sixty-five thousand dollars a month to operate the line, exclusive of the $3800 a month rental on the rolling stock, but such costs would remain about constant whether the road grossed $2500 or $3500 a day.[58] If local trade came up to expectations, there was a good chance that the Western could operate profitably. Considering the delays occasioned by the break in the line, the competitive loss of trade suffered by the establishment of a fast freight line to California over the CB&Q and the AT&SF, and the general stagnation of business across the country, officials of the Western felt that they had made a very good showing during 1884.

Affairs in Denver produced less optimism. The administrative un-frocking of Lovejoy and the return of the Denver and Rio Grande to more friendly hands failed to bear the anticipated fruit. Its management guided by receiver Jackson and by David H. Moffat, who was elected president late in February 1885, was confronted by problems that had accumulated for a long time. By 1884 the entire system, in-cluding the leased lines, measured 1679 miles, compared to 346 four years earlier. While Colorado's growth was great, particularly in 1880 and 1881, it had not kept pace with that of the railroad. The opening of a through line in 1883 provided additional business from the major roads, but the average freight rate declined from 3.62 cents per ton mile in 1881 to 2.77 cents in 1884, making a difference of $1,690,000 in net earnings. Passenger fares, as high as 7.27 cents a mile in 1880, fell to 3.6 cents by 1883, cutting earnings by $620,000. In the face of this, the Union Pacific hauled freight in 1883 for only 1.77 cents a ton mile and passengers for 3.13 cents a mile. During boom years such as 1880 and 1881, when mining men had been willing to pay almost anything for haulage into new and prosperous camps, such charges could be levied, but when the mineral economy leveled off, there were loud demands for rate reductions.

A representative of the foreign bondholders, who spent two months studying matters at Denver during the spring of 1885, thought that more than bad luck explained the Denver and Rio Grande's unhappy

---

58. Dodge to Palmer, Nov. 17, 1884, D. C. Dodge Letter Book, D&RG Archives.

condition. The answer, he said, should be sought in the peculiar way Palmer had managed affairs in favor of other corporations and other individuals, with small regard for the road's actual proprietors. While he had no defense for Lovejoy's conduct, he contended that at least Palmer's successor had not managed the road in behalf of the Colorado Coal and Iron Company or the Rio Grande Western.[59] Aside from his criticisms, the fact remained that as a railroad built to tap mining camps and to live off local traffic, the Rio Grande system was now confronted by the law of diminishing returns. By the mid-'80s, Colorado's bonanza days were nearing an end and a new approach to railroading was demanded. Certainly the main line would have to be broad-gauged to better interchange transcontinental traffic; a number of now unprofitable branches needed pruning; there could be no more expensive internecine warfare; and a much longer administrative view would have to be taken. In many ways the Palmer boom days were over.

While there remained a disposition on the part of Colorado representatives of the road to continue the traditional policy of expansion, eastern and foreign bondholders were very reluctant to increase the size of their investment. English investors were represented in New York by George Coppell, a native of Liverpool, England, who had come to the United States during the Civil War as British Consul at New Orleans. After the war he had gained a wide reputation for his work in rehabilitating bankrupt American railroads. T. H. A. Tromp was the Dutch representative, and the Scottish bondholders were represented by Robert Fleming. The latter group was extremely hesitant to spend any more money for branch lines, having been told by Fleming that they were not making any profit.[60] There was an inclination on the part of some of the bondholders to foreclose the mortgage, but a temporary upturn in business caused them to stay the proceedings.

It is small wonder that the bondholders were discouraged with affairs on the railroad. Hard on the heels of the uproar over Lovejoy's intemperate action and sharply reduced revenues came the road's first major labor disturbance. On May 4, 1885, between four and five hundred Denver shopmen walked off the job, followed by two hundred at Salida and over a hundred at Gunnison. The immediate result was

59. Report of T. H. A. Tromp, in Denver *Tribune–Republican*, July 6, 1885.
60. W. S. Jackson, "The Record vs. Reminiscence," *Denver Westerners Brand Book, 1945,* p. 62.

the discharge of ten men, most of whom belonged to the Knights of
Labor, from the Denver shops. Underlying this grievance was a demand for an increase in wages from $1.50 a day to $1.75. The course of
the strike paralleled that of similar actions across the nation during
these years. Judge Moses Hallett handed out sentences as high as six
months in jail for contempt of court, and the strikers responded with
mass meetings at which the hymnlike "Storm the Fort, Ye Knights of
Labor" was sung with great earnestness. When the Burnham shops
were opened, with scab laborers protected by police officers, typical
mob scenes took place with jeering and spitting at the forces of law
highlighting the proceedings. During late May and throughout the
summer there were a number of attempts to dynamite trains and other
equipment, with the Knights heatedly denying any responsibility for
violence. Management held to its position, letting the news of unsuccessful strikes by the Knights in other parts of the nation, and public
revulsion to dynamiting, do its work. By early November the strike
was dead, although the labor organization issued no formal admission
of defeat.[61]

During this period of strife a reorganization committee, headed by
Coppell, was brought together in New York. By the spring of 1886
the committee proposed a consolidation of the two Rio Grandes, but
Coppell was unable to get the assent of enough of the Western's bondholders to consummate the plan. Palmer, always a difficult opponent,
denied any desire to work against the other road. He held that earnings
of his company had improved sufficiently during the last six months
of 1885 to cover 90 per cent of the bond interest due and that he was
quite optimistic over its future. Obviously he wanted a better price
if a sale were to be made. Earnings on the Western might have been
higher had its management been able to plug some of the leaks in the
system. In mid-1886 Lyman Bass reported to Dodge: "I am . . . advised
that spotters were run over the line of the Western road as against
the passenger conductors last week, and every man on the line was
found to be stealing right and left; but the matter of discharging the
conductors perhaps can be held in abeyance for a few days. These are
the men whom Bancroft has been vouching for in strong terms." Bass
recommended firing the entire force of conductors.[62]

61. Denver *Tribune–Republican*, May 5–12, 17, 19, 20, 22, 23, 25, 27, 29, 30, June 2, 3, 7, 11,
July 17, 19, Aug. 1, Sept. 18, Nov. 4, 1885. *Railroad Gazette*, May 8, 15, June 5, 19, 1885.
62. Bass to Dodge, July 19, 1886, item 1318, D&RG Archives.

The most the Coppell committee could accomplish was an adjust-ment of differences with the Western regarding the lease. In July 1885 the Palmer group had won another legal victory when the court de-cided in favor of the recovery of damages for violation of the agree-ment. A decision in September of that year reaffirmed the legality of the document. In March 1886 it was agreed that the Western would release the Denver and Rio Grande from its bond guarantee obliga-tions, provided the Denver Company surrendered a quantity of rolling stock it was then renting to Palmer's line. Both organizations agreed to refrain from invading the territory of the other and to cooperate fully in the dispatch of through traffic.[63]

Arrangements next were made for a foreclosure and a "friendly sale" of the Denver and Rio Grande, so that the road might be re-organized. On July 12, 1886, by order of the United States Circuit Court and at the request of its bondholders, the Denver and Rio Grande system was sold at public auction. The American and British stock- and bondholders were the purchasers. On July 13 the court con-firmed and approved the sale and on the following day the purchasers took possession. A new company, known as the Denver and Rio Grande *Railroad* was organized, and eighty-eight million dollars in par value securities were issued to retire the sixty-seven million dollars worth of outstanding securities. With the lease agreement dissolved and with William S. Jackson named as its new president, the company once more set out to engage in mountain railroading. On August 1 the Western was released from its receivership and General Palmer resumed control, promising cooperation with his old company, the Denver and Rio Grande. Residents of Utah and Colorado sighed with relief and hoped that the ravages of railroad civil war had not cost their communities too high a price.

63. A Memorandum of Agreement in Minutes D&RG Board of Directors, March 13, 1886, D&RG Archives, *Railroad Gazette* (March 26, 1886), p. 222.

8. You cannot afford not to build

WITH THE APPOINTMENT of William S. Jackson as receiver, and after the receivership, as president, the Denver and Rio Grande was again headed by a Westerner whose understanding of local problems promised an aggressive administration. He had his work laid out for him. During the brief Lovejoy era continuous quarreling and financial contraction had placed the railroad in such a condition of stagnation as to invite competition by more active rivals.

The newest enemy was the Colorado Midland Railroad, organized at Colorado Springs in 1883 by a group of Colorado Springs businessmen, among whom were Homer D. Fisher, a lumberman, and Irving Howbert, a pioneer Colorado banker. The incorporators, who planned to build a road from Colorado Springs to Aspen, were long on grandiose plans but short on money. In the autumn of 1884 there appeared on the scene a Milwaukee banker, who had come West on his doctor's advice. His name was James John Hagerman, and he had an ailment familiar to many of the residents of Colorado Springs: tuberculosis. Before long he began to invest some of the money he had acquired from the iron mines of Michigan's upper peninsula in silver mines at Aspen and coal lands near Glenwood Springs. Fisher and his friends persuaded Hagerman of the feasibility of building a broad-gauge road into the mining camp in which he was interested and soon the "rich, ambitious and restless invalid," as Jackson called him, was president of Colorado's newest railroad.[1] By September 1886 the Midland had thrown a standard-gauge road into Leadville by way of Ute Pass and threatened to invade the boom town of Aspen. Without funds to compete, and deeply concerned over the appearance of the new line, Jackson of the Rio Grande made every effort to neutralize the threat by a proposed series of agreements and compromises. Hagerman eyed the overtures with suspicion and made the unsympathetic remark: "If we will agree to cut our own throats, he will help us do it."

Faced by the necessity for action, Jackson begged George Coppell's reorganization committee for permission to beat the Midland at its own game. The owners of Rio Grande securities must, said the receiver, make effective arrangements to protect the business of the line from encroachment by competing lines. In November 1885 he expressed the conviction that without any question the Rio Grande should build into Aspen. He warned against the old tactics of making a feint in the hope of frightening off rivals. "This action would, in all probability, simply stimulate the movers to more active work,

1. The contest between the Midland and the Denver and Rio Grande is discussed in John J. Lipsey, "J. J. Hagerman, Building of the Colorado Midland," *Denver Westerners Brand Book, 1954*, and Morris Cafky, "The Colorado Midland Story," *Trains, 17* (1957), 17–22. William S. Jackson, son of the receiver, wrote two articles on the subject: "The Record vs. Reminiscence," in the *Denver Westerners Brand Book, 1945*, and "Railroad Conflicts in Colorado in the 'Eighties," *Colorado Magazine*, Vol. 23, 1946. Much of the material used by the younger Jackson may be found on microfilm in the Division of State Archives. See William S. Jackson Correspondence, 1885–86, Division of State Archives and Public Records, Denver.

knowing the Rio Grande is tied up in the Court." He admitted that "the Court is a conservative and careful one [and] it may be difficult to obtain his consent to the issuing of any of the funds of the road for the purpose of holding our ground against aggressors and competition."[2]

During April 1886 Jackson gained the consent of Judge Moses Hallett to make surveys from Red Cliff, then the terminus of the extension over Tennessee Pass, down the Eagle River 'to its junction with the Grand River, and from that point to Glenwood Springs. Aware of the Midland's announced intention to build to Glenwood Springs and from there to the Colorado line, the receiver saw no alternative for his railroad but to occupy the whole valley of the Grand River. As he said to Howard Gilliat, chairman of the Reorganization Committee in London, "You cannot afford not to build. If you do not occupy the Grand Valley with a line of road some other company will, and that too, very speedily." Writing to Coppell, he maintained that even if no other road proposed to enter that territory, it would be wise for the company to stake out a claim and to continue its old policy of warding off rivals by pre-empting any threatened area. "It cannot afford to endure even a thorn in its side without an effort to get rid of it, and certainly, it should be prepared to contest the ground with an enterprise that proposes to invade the territory from which its best income is derived."

By now, Jackson was convinced that the Midland was not bluffing. "From an ordinary business view," he admitted to Coppell, "I would say this building a broad gauge road from Aspen to Leadville was a wild scheme; but when we consider that a private arrangement may now be entered into between the Union Pacific or C. B. & Q. and the Midland Company, it is a dangerous position for the Rio Grande interests." Discounting the fact that the Midland plan was, in the minds of many, a weak one, it was also a well-known fact that the D&RG was without money at hand with which to build. The general belief that it was not governed by a very aggressive policy encouraged even the smallest rivals to build, although their existence might not offer much more than a nuisance value to the older lines.

In addition to the threat of prospective traffic raiding by the Midland, there was a continuing possibility that the Burlington and the

2. W. S. Jackson to George Coppell, Nov. 18, 1885, William S. Jackson Correspondence, 1885–86.

Union Pacific would invade the territory. By May 1886 Jackson admitted frankly that there was "no longer any doubt that the Burlington people are going to build westward from Denver. How soon it may be, of course, I cannot ascertain. Its course apparently is to cross the range directly west of Denver—this being the greatest obstacle it has to encounter—either to continue down the Grand or to cross over to the Yampa and then turn west."[3] A few months later Frank King, field engineer for the D&RG warned that the Union Pacific also was active in the Colorado mountains. In August he telegraphed to the Denver office, in cipher, that "The Union Pacific are surveying along Roaring Fork below Aspen two miles on opposite side from me. Twenty-five Union Pacific graders stopped at Ten Mile House last night; they had a lot of steel, bellows, and a forge. Don't know where they went. Glenwood Springs is full of U.P. engineers and two parties [are] in the canon."[4]

The Union Pacific's projected route ran south from Fort Steele, Wyoming, located 120 miles west of Cheyenne. In September 1886 Charles Francis Adams, Jr., president of that road, inspected Colorado's central mountain area, visiting Gunnison, Idaho Springs, and Leadville. He spent a night in the latter place and was scandalized as he watched the residents at play. "In the evening we saw Leadville by gaslight—an awful spectacle of low vice," he recorded in his diary.[5] The imperfect state of Colorado morality did not, however, cause him to lose his Yankee sense of proportion; there was a penny to be turned out in these wilds and it was of considerable interest to him. Minutes of a Denver and Rio Grande board of directors meeting, held a few weeks later in New York, reveal that the directors took very seriously the intentions of both the Union Pacific and the Burlington to occupy transmontane Colorado, particularly the valley of the Grand (Colorado) River.

Activity by the major roads sent Jackson into a new frenzy of correspondence with the management in New York. In October he told his board of directors that further delay would be extremely harmful and that something should be done at once to protect the field work already finished if the company's rights were to be protected. At the very worst, if the Rio Grande did not propose to use those rights, it

3. Ibid., May 20, 1886, William S. Jackson Correspondence 1885–86.
4. F. P. King to J. C. Wright, Aug. 4, 1886, ibid.
5. Jackson, *Colorado Magazine*, 23, 1, 17.

might be able to exact a price from other roads desiring to build along the routes already surveyed. "We must either assert our ownership and fight for it or quietly abandon it," he argued.[6] "Half-hearted work will not win in this country." He begged Howard Gilliat to urge upon his London colleagues the seriousness of the situation. Although he admitted that "the jig is not up by any means," much valuable time had been lost. Bluntly he stated the case: "All our antagonists are encouraged by the listless, do-nothing policy we have shown, and the people of Colorado are fast coming to the conclusion that the D. & R. G. will allow itself to be flanked out of the strong position it has earned through years of persistent effort."[7]

During the fall of 1886 Jackson continued to fret over his company's lethargy, repeatedly warning the directors of impending competitive construction from the larger systems. The matter of foreclosure, sale, and reorganization of the road had furnished an excuse for delay, but after that was accomplished in mid-July, there seemed to be no hurry among those who controlled the purse strings to follow a more aggressive policy. Jackson, who had been elected president of the new company at a salary of $20,000, kept up the attack, hopeful of putting the wheels in motion before it was too late. Coppell explained that the board was having great difficulty with the London and Amsterdam investors, whose reluctance grew out of the conviction that the disasters of earlier administrations were the result of indiscriminate building of branches and extensions. Fearful of further financial difficulties, they would not agree to more construction. Company officers argued that too much stress could not be laid upon the importance of protecting the property from invasion by other roads. The annual report of 1886 told stockholders that the "railroad situation has become so complex that construction in advance of actual needs is sometimes necessary from a purely strategic point of view. . . . There is danger that more ambitious and more enterprising rivals will, by the construction of other lines, gradually encroach upon the territory that legitimately belongs to your road." These arguments typify the point of view that Jackson and his associates pressed upon Rio Grande board members.

Finally, as winter foreclosed upon the possibility of suitable weather for construction, the board decided to risk the wrath of foreign investors and go ahead with the completion of the system. On October

6. Minutes of D&RG Board of Directors, Nov. 1, 1886, D&RG Archives.
7. Jackson, *Denver Westerners Brand Book, 1945*, p. 74.

18. Aspen, from Hunter's Creek. Once a far-famed mining camp, it is today a ski resort and cultural center, often called the most cosmopolitan small town in America.

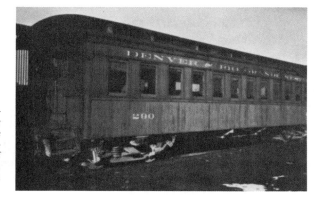

19. Passenger Car of 1880s. Narrow-gauge coach 290 is typical of the many passenger cars placed in service by the D&RG during the eighties. It had a seating capacity of 44 crowded into 38 feet of length and was heated by a coal stove. This car, built by Jackson and Sharp in 1881, was sold in March 1942.

21, 1886, it belatedly agreed that the extension into Aspen was "a pressing necessity, and urgently demanded for the protection of the business of this Company." A week later the gentlemen in New York also approved the construction of an extension from Montrose to the Ouray mining district.

Despite all the disadvantages of lost time, difficult terrain, and heavy weather, Jackson launched his attack upon Aspen. Of all possible extensions, this was the prime target. Stockholders were told of its significance in the company's annual report of 1886:

> Aspen is recognized as second only to Leadville as a mining camp, but its development has been seriously retarded on account of its practical remoteness, due to its separation from the railroad system of Colorado by high ranges of mountains. The heavy cost of wagon transportation has been enough to consume the profit on all except the high grade ore, and, as the wealth of the camp is largely in low grade ores, it is not surprising that the work in most of the mines has been almost suspended, except for the purpose of development, until the advent of the railroad.[8]

Of more immediate importance was the progress of the Midland over sky-high Hagerman Pass toward the valley of the Roaring Fork and into Aspen. The Rio Grande would have to hurry if it hoped to overtake the head start made by that road.

Jackson had prepared the way, but it was to be forty-seven year old David H. Moffat, banker and mining magnate, who would carry out the Rio Grande's latest effort to outdo its rivals. In the spring of 1887 he succeeded the tired and ailing Jackson as president of the road. Moffat had been on the Colorado scene from the early days of its placer mining boom. In 1860 this tall, very thin youth—he weighed about a hundred pounds—started a stationery and book store in Denver, but within a few years he returned to banking, a business he knew better, and became a cashier at the First National Bank. At the bank young Moffat met Jerome B. Chaffee (who was to be one of Colorado's first United States Senators), and together they began to put their money into likely looking mines. Among their investments was the Caribou mine near Boulder, the Breece iron mine at Leadville, the Little Pittsburgh Consolidated (purchased from H. A. W. Tabor), and

8. *Annual Report of the D&RG* (1886), p. 6.

an interest in nearly a hundred others throughout the region. Through his friendship with former Governor John Evans, Moffat became fascinated by the possibilities of railroading in this new and undeveloped country. He was treasurer of the Denver Pacific, and later he associated himself with the Denver and South Park and with the Denver and New Orleans. By the time Moffat took over the presidency of the Rio Grande, he was not only a man of wide financial and investment experience, but one who had taken an active part in the development of Colorado's transportation system.

Beginning at Red Cliff, to which point the Denver and Rio Grande had been built in the fall of 1881, construction crews began to grade and lay narrow-gauge track toward Glenwood Springs. By the end of the summer of 1887 work had progressed so successfully that despite the long delay in getting started, there was a prospect of winning the race. Late on the evening of October 5 the first engine made its way through a newly completed 1300 foot tunnel near Glenwood Springs, and with the last barrier removed, the resort city made its rail connection with the outside world. The next day the town, decked out with streamers, mottoes, and evergreens, demonstrated its appreciation of the new service. From the Hotel Glenwood across the street to Kamm's store hung a large banner carrying the words: "Denver and Rio Grande, Pioneer Railroad of Colorado." Another read: "Glenwood Welcomes the Railroad and Remembers the Stage Coach with Kindness." That evening the welcoming committee spent some $800 it had raised to provide a banquet for President Moffat, Governor Alva Adams, and a number of railroad officials who were on hand for the ceremonies. Fireworks, bonfires, a torchlight parade, and innumerable speeches completed the festivities.[9]

The contest was not yet finished. While crews completed the Glenwood Springs extension, the forty-two mile route up the Roaring Fork to Aspen was a scene of frantic effort. From the direction of Leadville came reports of the Midland's progress. Rio Grande contractors were permitted to raise wages and were given special allowances for extraordinarily difficult sections of construction.[10] Haste was the paramount consideration; suddenly money became secondary.

Upon completion of the job, some 600 tracklayers were treated to

9. Aspen *Daily Times,* Oct. 6, 1887. Interview with Mrs. Perry Malaby, age 92, Aug. 1959. For a brief account of David Moffat's career see *Municipal Facts* (Aug.–Sept. 1923), p. 23.

10. Wilson, "Denver and Rio Grande," p. 182.

MAP 7

CRAIG
STEAMBOAT SPRINGS
DENVER
RIFLE
1889
GLENWOOD SPGS.
1887
MINTURN
ROCK CREEK
FT. LOGAN
1889
DILLON
CASTLE ROCK
1880
O'BRIEN'S QUARRY
1887
MALTA
LEADVILLE
1871-1872
CREVASSE
GRAND JUNCTION
1882
ASPEN
SOUTH PARK
MANITOU
81
COLORADO SPRINGS
SOMERSET
ANTHRACITE
CRESTED BUTTE
83
1880
MONARCH
CALUMET
FLORENCE
ABERDEEN QUARRY
1881
GUNNISON
1881
SALIDA
1872
PUEBLO
MONTROSE
1882
SAPINERO
1882
ABERDEEN JCT.
1889
1881
PONCHA JCT.
VILLA GROVE
ORIENT
CANON CITY
COAL CR. MINE
1880
1887
RIDGWAY
1889
LAKE CITY
WAGON WHEEL GAP
1876
OURAY
CREEDE
SOUTH FORK
SAN
1876
CUCHARA
SILVERTON
1881
LUIS
1882
ALAMOSA
1876
ROCKWOOD
1880
VALLEY
1876
LA VETA
EL MORO
DURANGO
1881
ANTONITO
TRINIDAD
COAL MINE
1879
AZTEC
FARMINGTON
CHAMA
1880
RATON
CALIENTE
ESPANOLA
1882-86
SANTA FE

1889
DENVER & RIO GRANDE
RAILWAY
Showing Construction Steps.

a giant barbecue by the residents of Aspen. The event touched off a celebration that lasted for a week and was highlighted by official ceremonies on November 1. After days of preparation, the city was presented to its visitors for inspection. Thousands of streamers brightened drab buildings, and Chinese lanterns, displayed from windows or suspended across the streets by wires, illuminated the night. The word was out that a special train, bearing President Moffat, Governor Alva Adams, Senator H. M. Teller, and others, was on its way. At six in the evening final preparations were made for a grand parade to begin when the oncoming train signified its approach with a whistle blast. A few minutes before seven, an enthusiastic engineer, aboard a switch engine in the yard, blew three long toots on his engine's whistle and the ceremonies were prematurely under way. Bonfires were lighted on Aspen and Smuggler mountains, and marchers, ready to parade, milled around under the nervous control of the marshals. They waited for nearly an hour and a half. Finally, close to 8:30 P.M., the train puffed into town amidst the shrieks of whistles and the dull roar of blasting powder. From mine entrances high along the hillsides came a shower of colored fire trailing from rockets that streaked across the sky, lighting the way for the celebrants, who marched to meet their visitors. Aspen was deliriously happy.

The effect of the railroad was freely admitted by civic leaders. Its value was well described by the Mayor in his address of welcome: "Before the arrival of the railroad Aspen was . . . inaccessible to or from the outside world. The treasures of our hills and valleys, although almost boundless, could not find a market except at an almost ruinous cost and expense for transportation. Our mines have been practically idle, waiting the coming of the iron horse. . . . We are now entering upon an era of prosperity which will be unprecedented in our history." Newspaper advertisements gave practical meaning to the Mayor's words as merchants announced "Railroad prices—railroad quantities." And the inevitable local poet fixed his message in the lines:

> Then here's to our Aspen, her youth and her age,
> We welcome the railroad, say farewell to the stage;
> And whatever our lot and wherever we be,
> Here's God Bless forever the D. and R. G.[11]

11. Aspen *Daily Times*, Nov. 2, 1887. Robert F. Bartlett, "Aspen: The Mining Community, 1879–1893," *Denver Westerners Brand Book, 1950.*

Not every resident of Aspen raised his cup in toast. Scientific advance over the years has been accompanied by certain sacrifices, and this time it was dairyman Donald McLane who suffered. His cows were so terrified by the blast of the locomotive whistle that they headed for the hills, tail-high and white-eyed. Upon being coaxed back into the valley, they were still so frightened that they were able to give only a dribble of milk, and McLane's customers were put on short rations for a day or so. Before long the herd, along with the rest of the villagers, settled down and took the benefits of civilization in their stride, the moan of the train whistle no longer a novelty in the mountain wilderness.

Three months later, the Colorado Midland arrived at Aspen, bringing the first standard-gauge rails across the high Rockies. However, its effect was felt long before that time. As early as November 4 the Aspen *Daily Times* editor had pointed out that the rate of $4.00 a ton on ore to Leadville and $8.00 a ton to Pueblo or Denver, offered by the Rio Grande, stemmed from the fact that the Midland had already announced that figure. Bluntly, he had told his readers: "The people of Aspen and the state have reason to thank the Midland people for low rates of passenger fare and freight charges as well as they have to thank them for a road to Aspen. It was their movement upon Aspen that made the baby road wake up to protect its interest in this quarter." No one in the Denver and Rio Grande management denied the statement. It was obvious that the Midland's shorter route to Leadville afforded it a chance to haul freight cheaply at a profit, while it was doubtful that the Rio Grande's circuitous route would permit similar gain. But the Baby Road had fought competitive wars before and it would do so again. From the day of Palmer forward, that road never willingly allowed a competitor to move into its domain unchallenged.

The construction race with the Midland exemplified the determination of the Jackson–Moffat administrations to maintain the Denver and Rio Grande as Colorado's leading railroad. From the beginning, in 1871, Palmer had jealously guarded his empire, firm in the belief that if he were to deal effectively with the major roads, he had to have full control of his own territory. The Lovejoy interlude, and the internal bickering that preceded it, had demonstrated that the moment there was a sign of weakness, a new invader would try to wrest away the spoils of transportation warfare. Both Jackson and Moffat understood the necessity of maintaining an aggressive policy. The appearance of the Midland was just another of many attempts to enter the Colorado railroad field, and the challenge was met with the same vigor as shown in the Palmer days. Moffat himself was to one day take on the "baby giant," only to discover, as had the others, that it played a rough game.

Local competitors, such as the Denver, South Park, and Pacific, or J. J. Hagerman's Midland, did not in themselves pose a great threat to the Denver and Rio Grande. But lurking in the background, always ready to move in, were the transcontinentals. Their tendency to absorb local lines and to use their enormous financial resources in rate wars was a serious matter. Already the Union Pacific had taken over the DSP&P. There was a prospect that some other major road would buy up the Midland. Moffat was nervous over the expansionistic tendencies of the big lines, particularly during 1887. Toward the end of that year the AT&SF opened a competing line between Denver and Pueblo, and threw a parallel branch into Canon City, thus breaking the 1880 "Treaty of Boston," by which it had promised to stay out of Rio Grande territory for at least ten years. Early in 1888 the Missouri Pacific reached Pueblo, its westering tendencies causing some nervousness in Colorado railroad circles. At about the same time, the Rock Island announced its intention to enter Colorado Springs from the east. The presence of the standard-gauge Midland, running west from Colorado Springs to the valley of the Grand River, provided grounds for considerable speculation over the Rock Island's plans.

Yet another impatient railroad, the Burlington, had served Denver since 1882. There were increasingly numerous rumors in Colorado papers that this road would like to reach Salt Lake City or Ogden. The continual presence of its surveyors in the mountain country did nothing to quiet such talk. Some of the reports were quite specific. In April 1885 the Aspen *Sun* talked of a proposed Burlington line up South Boulder Creek and on "into Middle Park, tunneling the Continental Divide under James Peak. The tunnel will be 9,000 feet long, the longest west of the Mississippi River." The proposal was not new. Andrew N. Rogers, of Central City, had published a tunnel plan as early as 1867, and it continued to be discussed until one day David H. Moffat undertook the job himself.[12] During 1887 stories of the Bur-

12. Denver *Tribune-Republican*, April 29, 1885, quoting the Aspen *Sun*. See also Edgar Carlisle McMechen, *The Moffat Tunnel of Colorado: An Epic of Empire, 1* (Denver, 1927), 52.

lington's designs upon western Colorado again appeared. A Denver paper commented that the road was interested in the northwestern part of the state, which was "relatively unknown but it is known to contain vast resources of coal and possibly other minerals. Also, there is promise that it will be a rich grazing and agricultural section and the hot springs are possible of tourist exploitation."[13]

By 1887 it became apparent to the Rio Grande management that unless it offered the bigger roads an efficient and easily made interchange, one or more of them would build across Colorado to seek a western outlet from the Salt Lake region. The Rio Grande held an advantage in the fact that except for the Union Pacific, it was the only road offering service between Denver and Ogden. It could connect the AT&SF, the Missouri Pacific, the Rock Island, or the Burlington with the Central Pacific and form a link in a new transcontinental system. Matters came to a head during July when the Union Pacific and the Central Pacific dissolved their eighteen-year-old agreement and the Union Pacific transferred its western business to the Oregon Short Line. This left the Central Pacific with the alternative of building eastward or dividing its business with the Rio Grande system. The great drawback to the latter plan was the Rio Grande's narrow-gauge tracks. Any traffic interchanged had to be unloaded and loaded again, and this operation, executed at both ends of the line, was cumbersome and expensive. To accommodate standard-gauge engines and cars, the road experimented with a third rail, but this was unsatisfactory, for the standard-gauge rail, weighing sixty-five or seventy pounds, stood higher than the thirty- or forty-pound rail used for lighter narrow-gauge rolling stock. When standard-gauge equipment was used on such a system, the cars tilted to one side, causing heavy wear and a high incidence of hotboxes. There was but one answer to the problem: to standard gauge the whole main line.

General Palmer, father of the narrow-gauge system in Colorado and a staunch advocate of it, became convinced that there were no alternatives but to widen the Western's tracks. In the summer of 1887 he talked of the "reckless extent" to which competitive railroad building had been carried on to the east of his system and he expressed the hope that the very number of rivals who threatened to cross the Rockies would serve to hold them all in check and induce them to

13. Denver *Republican*, Sept. 6, 1887.

use the Rio Grande system. "As all these ambitious lines are of stand-ard gauge," he told his stockholders, "and as the Denver & Rio Grande is also contemplating widening the gauge on its Grand River Route in Colorado, the policy of our company should be to widen its gauge in due time so as to receive and carry freely and on equal terms the business of all these rivals—which it can manifestly do more profitably to them than if all or either had to build and maintain independent lines of their own."[14] Here was one place the Rio Grande people agreed with the General, and they determined to keep up with the times by making the necessary changes. In the spring of 1887 Moffat made a trip to New York, where he urged his directors to lay out sufficient capital to widen the company's main-line tracks. Permission was granted, and Moffat at once ordered 21,000 tons of steel rails, twenty-seven locomotives, and a proportionate number of freight and passenger cars at a cost of six million dollars.[15]

The program of expansion and track-widening was as expensive as it was necessary. Before it was well under way, there was evidence that no time should be lost in completing the program. During 1888 the Burlington made arrangements with the Union Pacific for trans-continental freight business, resulting in a considerable decrease of traffic for the Rio Grande system. George Coppell explained to his board that the "ostensible reason for this is the expense incurred in transferring from standard to narrow gauge cars," but to him the move had a deeper meaning. "This forces upon us the question of a Western extension beyond our main line, and it is a subject which will require your earnest attention at no distant day in the view of the many standard-gauge roads which are now connecting with our system." A general demoralization of freight rates that year added to the seriousness of the situation. Moffat reported to his stockholders that in December the average freight earnings per ton mile dropped to 1.87 cents, the lowest in the company's history. The average for the whole year was only 2.19 cents, as compared to 2.39 cents for the preceding year.[16] To make matters even worse, switchmen at Pueblo struck without prior notice, severely hampering freight shipments during September and October.

Meanwhile, concessions had to be made to competitors. John Evans,

14. *Annual Report of the R.G.W.* (for the year ending July 31, 1887), pp. 5, 6.
15. *Railroad Gazette* (June 24, 1887), p. 247. Santa Fe *Daily New Mexican*, June 16, 1887.
16. *Annual Report of the D&RG* (1888), p. 4.

20. Red Cliff, Colorado, 1910. At the head of Eagle River Canyon on the western slope of Tennessee Pass, Red Cliff was a bustling mining and lumbering center of 1,000 people when reached by a D&RG narrow-gauge branch line in 1881. By 1910, after this section had become the double-tracked main line of the road to Grand Junction and the West, its boom days were over.

21. William S. Jackson, about 1903. Like Palmer, Jackson was an aggressive railroader who realized that in the rough and tumble of Colorado's transportation picture it was "build or perish."

futilely trying to make a connection between the Gulf of Mexico and his Denver, Texas, and Gulf Railroad (formerly the Denver and New Orleans), finally united his company with the Denver, Texas, and Fort Worth Railroad, currently building northward through Texas. When this combination threatened to parallel the Denver and Rio Grande tracks between Pueblo and Trinidad, in closing the gap between its two isolated elements, Moffat leased the newcomer trackage rights over that distance for $1500 a mile per year.[17] About the same time, the D&RG agreed to give the Chicago, Rock Island, and Pacific and the Missouri Pacific access to Denver by joint trackage agreements on the Pueblo–Denver run. Such arrangements were not made out of sheer altruism. The D&RG had to choose between cooperation and competition.

While Moffat's company parried the thrusts of major lines from the east, offering them joint trackage agreements to discourage additional building, it plunged ahead in western Colorado, determined to maintain its position of primacy at all costs. In 1887 it added a third rail from Pueblo to Leadville, completed the Aspen narrow-gauge branch, and built the thirty-six mile extension from Montrose to Ouray. The next year another branch, also thirty-six miles long, was undertaken from Sapinero to Lake City and completed in 1889.

Nor was the south neglected. Fearful that some potential source of business might be lost, the railroad sent its chief counsel, Edward O. Wolcott, to Santa Fe to soothe ruffled feathers among the merchants of that neglected city. "We are coming in here to help you build up and develop your wonderful resources in a short time," he promised. "At present our hands are full in Colorado; there we are forced to protect ourselves at once. We now have 400 miles of road under construction and must make haste." But, he said, all that would be accomplished soon, and then "we jump into New Mexico" and soon "Santa Fe will boom as her people never dreamt of. That time is not far off."[18]

Such assurances were typical of those being given to anyone and everyone within reach of the Rio Grande's outstretched rail tentacles. No potential source of traffic exploitation was overlooked, no area of possible invasion by other lines was being neglected. During these months the Denver and Rio Grande maintained a nervous watch over

17. Ibid.
18. Denver *Republican*, Oct. 28, 1887.

northwestern Colorado. Palmer's restiveness posed a constant threat that the Western would entice one of the bigger lines to reach out and join his Utah road. If they chose not to spend that much money, there remained the alternative of connecting with the Midland, whose activity in the Grand River country showed no signs of diminution. To stake at least a verbal claim to the territory, Moffat predicted that the Denver and Rio Grande would build into Salt Lake City. He took the position that the Western, an independent company, had at times embarrassed the operations of his road, and that since both the Burlington and the Missouri Pacific now distributed traffic in Colorado, Utah, and New Mexico, further reliance upon Palmer's road was not advisable. The Denver *Republican* called such talk mere bluff, put forward to frighten the Western into selling out. Any paralleling of the Western's tracks would result in a division of the profits, and there was always the chance that Palmer might win the contest. More significantly, if the Denver and Rio Grande gave up its relationship with the Western, the smaller road would not be isolated, for it stood a chance of connecting with either the Midland or, at some later date, the Burlington.[19]

These facts did not stop Moffat's westward push. During 1888 an organization known as the Rio Grande and Pacific Railroad Company, whose directorate and officers were substantially the same as those of the Denver and Rio Grande, was incorporated for the purpose of building down the Grand River from Glenwood Springs to Rifle Creek, twenty-seven miles. Over a year passed before construction crews went to work. The delay was occasioned by the necessity of gaining permission from the federal government to build across the Ute Indian reservation. Taking advantage of this interval, Moffat made a trip to Europe in an attempt to raise more money. By February 1889 about 600 workers had begun grading and laying standard-gauge track along the Grand River toward Salt Lake City.

During the summer of 1889 there was great mystification in Colorado and Utah over the relations of the Midland and the Denver and Rio Grande railroads. The apparent rivals for northwestern Colorado's traffic "had much to do with each other," as a Denver paper put it. "They have held consultations and have been otherwise intimate. This looks as though the two companies were about to unite." By way

19. Ibid., Jan. 6, 1888.

of warning the paper quoted Section 5, Article XV, of the Colorado constitution, which said that "no railroad corporation, or the lessees or managers thereof, shall consolidate its stock, property or franchises with any other railroad corporation owning or having under its control a parallel or competing line."[20]

Violation of the constitution was avoided by the creation of a new organization known as the Rio Grande Junction Railway Company, owned jointly by the two competitors. Headed by Charles H. Toll, brother-in-law of Edward O. Wolcott of the Denver and Rio Grande, the broad-gauge road was to be built between Rifle and Grand Junction.[21] There was concern among the Palmer people at this unexpected rapprochement. Joseph D. Potts, a director of the Western, expressed his concern over the "apparently joint desire on their part to exclude us." He was puzzled over the new alliance, for, as he said, they "are natural rivals. We are the natural ally of each. Therefore, their position is something of a mystery." Potts warned Palmer that "if they mean to become substantially one, it behooves us to take extra care in any bargain we make with them."[22]

The relationship between the two competing roads was one of necessity, not of friendship. James J. Hagerman, president of the Midland, did not trust or like Moffat, and displayed no hesitation in saying so. In writing to the chairman of his own board, Hagerman said, "Moffat is very ambitious to be considered a big man, but is not half so big as he was when he could wield the Rio Grande club to reward his friends and punish his enemies as he pleased. . . . I do not suppose there are 500 shares of Rio Grande stock owned in Colorado, but to hear the officers here talk, you would suppose they owned it all." However, Hagerman did not underestimate the influence of the rival company. He called it the most powerful in the state: "It can make or unmake many localities. . . . Disorder, power to play tricks, to slaughter rates, to reward friends and punish enemies is what they want."[23]

Denver and Rio Grande managers understood that their partnership with the Midland was a dangerous one, but it seemed a better

20. Ibid., June 5, 1889.

21. Jackson, *Denver Westerners Brand Book, 1945*, p. 77.

22. Joseph D. Potts to Palmer, July 8, 1889, item 1624, D&RG Archives.

23. James John Hagerman to S. S. Sands, Sept. 15, 1889, in John J. Lipsey, "How Hagerman Sold the Colorado Midland in 1890," *Denver Westerners Brand Book, 1956*, p. 271.

MAP 8

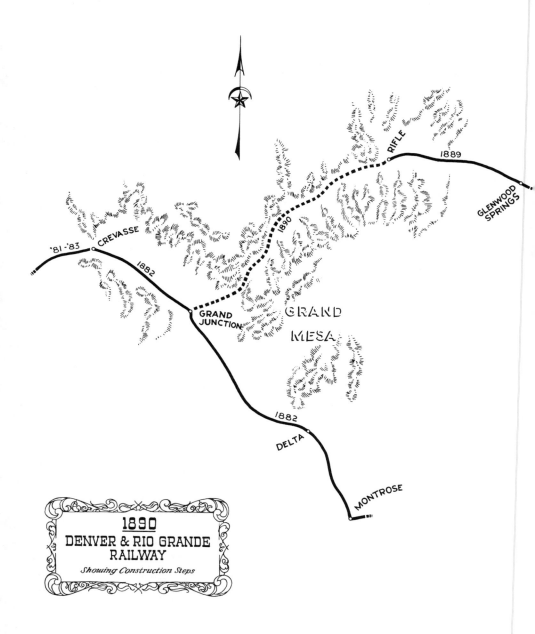

RIFLE

1889

GLENWOOD
SPRINGS

'81-'83   CREVASSE

1882   1890

GRAND
JUNCTION

GRAND

MESA

1882

DELTA

MONTROSE

1890
DENVER & RIO GRANDE
RAILWAY
Showing Construction Steps

solution to the problem than to allow the building of a competitive line. That Palmer and Potts need not have been worried over the alliance was revealed in January 1890, when it was publicly stated that upon completion of the link between Rifle and Grand Junction, the Missouri Pacific and the Rock Island would run through trains from Pueblo and Colorado Springs to Salt Lake City over the Midland, the Rio Grande Junction, and the Rio Grande Western Railway.[24] Moffat was aware of the potential competition. He was troubled by the fact that his broad-gauging program was not yet completed, and if the Rio Grande Junction line was finished too quickly, he would not be able to take the same advantage of it as the Midland. From his standpoint, it was important that the two projects be completed about the same time. As work on the connecting road slowed down, Hagerman was furious. "There is no good reason why the Junction road was not completed by the middle of June," he wrote.

> The delay has been caused solely by the determination of the Rio Grande officials in Colorado not to allow the road to be completed until they can complete their broad-gauge connection with it. They seem determined that the Midland shall not have the advantage of a standard gauge connection to the West until they are ready to share it. The construction has been delayed by every pretext, and every reason but the right one given for it, and the agreement in regard to it violated in letter and spirit.[25]

Before the Junction line was opened for business, affairs took an entirely new turn. In September, Hagerman's road was sold to the AT&SF company, beating out the Rio Grande people who wanted it. Hagerman was delighted, not only because the sale returned to him at a profit all the money he had invested, but because it prevented the Rio Grande from maintaining control of western Colorado. "It enables me, with one grand whack, to get even with the Moffat–Wolcott–Cheesman combination, and pay them and their followers back for all the sneers, belittlement and other dirt they have heaped on me for the last four years," he wrote to one of his associates. In a defensive tone he added, "A fellow would be more than human not to feel this. The Denver & Rio Grande [people] were cock-sure of gobbling up the

24. *Railroad Gazette* (Jan. 17, 1890), p. 49.
25. Lipsey, *Denver Westerners Brand Book, 1956*, p. 284.

Midland, and gave it out publicly that the trade was about to be closed. . . . Coppell, Chairman of the D. & R. G. board, went to London to arrange the money part of it, but we closed with the Santa Fe the day before his arrival. To say that the D. & R. G. crowd in Denver are crazy with rage, chagrin [and] disappointment is putting it mildly."[26]

There was good reason for discouragement at Denver. Not only had the Santa Fe broken its treaty by moving into Denver from Pueblo, but now it was reaching out toward Salt Lake City. There were rumors around Colorado Springs that the Santa Fe also had purchased Palmer's Western.[27] If true, it would be a disastrous blow to the Denver and Rio Grande. The actual developments, and even the rumors, dimmed the brightness of Moffat's achievements. The broad-gauging program, the completion of a tunnel at Tennessee Pass, and other improvements aimed at accommodating transcontinental traffic—all very expensive—appeared to have been in vain.

There was newspaper talk about a possible countering alliance between the Rock Island and the D&RG to build an "airline" straight west from Denver to Salt Lake City. Surveyors were in the field, early in 1891, marking off a route to Golden and Georgetown and beyond, in search of a short-cut through the mountains. Moffat had little to say about his plans. As he tried to find a solution to his new problems, he was confronted by a welter of rumors to the effect that the D&RG was having trouble with the Missouri Pacific and that it was about to be sold to the Burlington or even to the Santa Fe. Added difficulty came when snow blockades isolated Durango and Silverton, cutting off valuable traffic and generating considerable complaint from shippers in those cities.

In the face of these adversities, Moffat was resolved to forge ahead and combat all rivals, regardless of their size. He and his general manager, Sylvester T. Smith, redoubled their efforts to put the line into a competitive position by straightening the road and easing the grades. Moffat was particularly anxious to build directly west from Denver, eliminating the long, circuitous route down to Pueblo, up the Arkansas River, and across Marshall Pass to Gunnison, Montrose, and Grand Junction. The idea may not have been his, but he was one of its chief adherents. Denver papers had for some time lamented the

26. Hagerman to William Lidderdale, Sept. 24, 1890, in Lipsey, *Brand Book, 1956*, p. 281.
27. Colorado Springs *Weekly Gazette*, Oct. 4, 1890.

fact that there was "no Northern Colorado D&RG."[28] As early as 1861 Lieutenant Edward L. Berthoud, accompanied by the famed scout Jim Bridger, had located a pass named after the lieutenant at the head of Clear Creek, but no railroad was inclined to attempt to breach it. Part of the reluctance came from a survey made during the following year by engineer Francis M. Case, who pronounced it unfeasible because of its steep grades, the necessity of a tunnel near the top, and the long season of deep snows.[29] Until David Moffat appeared on the scene, Case's judgment stood, even though during the intervening years the Denver and Rio Grande itself had built over more difficult terrain. It was Moffat's determination to put Denver on a direct, mainline route that was his undoing, both with the D&RG management and subsequently as an independent railroader. During the late '80s he was responsible for the expenditure of some $200,000 of Rio Grande money for surveys in the neighborhood of James Peak.[30]

In August 1891 there was another of the recurring crises in the Rio Grande management. It arose from an old cause: passing a dividend to use net earnings for improvements. Once again the foreign bondholders, chiefly the English and Dutch, issued loud complaints about the manner in which the road was being managed. At a March meeting of the board's executive committee it was recommended that only the most pressing expenditures be allowed. The committee reported that considering the amounts of money spent upon the road during the past four or five years it ought to be in excellent shape and "until the earnings are further developed, and the necessity is shown for a better road bed, stations and appointments than are now possessed by the Company, it is not proper that the Stockholders should be called to make further sacrifices."[31] This increasingly critical attitude toward the Denver management so angered Moffat that on August 25 he resigned as president. In a press interview he explained that the directors in New York wanted to follow a policy he thought injurious to the road. Moreover, they had strenuous objections to Sylvester Smith, the general manager, who was accused of extravagance. When George Coppell questioned Smith on the advisability of a proposed extension into the mining camp of Creede where Moffat

28. For examples see Denver *Republican*, Feb. 22, 1888, and Oct. 4, 1891.
29. McMechen, *Moffat Tunnel*, *1*, 30–33.
30. Jackson, *Denver Westerners Brand Book, 1945*, pp. 87–88.
31. Minutes D&RG Executive Committee, March 12, 1891, D&RG Archives.

had heavy investments, a heated argument developed. Smith's language became "rather emphatic," and Coppell told him no D&RG man could speak to him in that manner. Even hotter words followed, after which Smith explained to reporters, "I am now relieved of the duties of general manager, and I suppose the conversation we had hurried things somewhat." He deeply resented the fact that Coppell had sent out Stephen Little as auditor to investigate the disposition of road funds. Smith referred to Little "as a detective in the guise of an expert accountant [sent] to make out a case against me, and nearly succeeded in making the board believe that I was a thief and ought to be in the penitentiary."

Coppell's version, as told to reporters and later denied, was that there had been growing dissatisfaction with the road's management. He admitted that the property was in excellent condition and superbly equipped, but added, "for all of that, we would like to have a dividend once in a while." He made a significant admission when he said, "There is no sort of doubt but that the recent management ran the road more in the interests of Colorado, but especially of Denver, than those of the stockholders."[32] Here he touched the key issue between the investors and the management from its beginning well into the twentieth century.

There was no doubt that Moffat's successor would be an outsider. Coppell made that perfectly clear when he said, "If we select a Denver man we would have but a repetition of the same old policy, with only the old result. If we took a man from any other Colorado city the new man would perhaps only differ from the Denver management in the points of unloading the advantages." When the position went to Edward T. Jeffery of Chicago, a close friend of the Santa Fe's president, Allan Manvel, rumors of an impending purchase by that railroad blanketed Colorado. After these stories died out, others appeared, to the effect that Jeffery surely would succeed Manvel as head of the AT&SF. None of the gossip had any foundation in fact and the Rio Grande's new president, forty-eight years old when he assumed his duties at Denver, remained in that office until 1912. English born, he had come to this country at the age of thirteen to work for the Illinois Central as an office boy. By 1877 he was general superintendent and

32. Denver *Republican*, Sept. 17, 18, 1891. See also the issues of Aug. 13, 26, 27, 30; Sept. 8, 11, 15, 16.

22. David Halliday Moffat. When he arrived in Colorado in 1860, a tall, 20-year-old youth, Moffat weighed slightly over 100 pounds. This view, taken in later years, suggests that he fared well in the new land.

23. Construction near Soldier Summit, Utah, about 1890. The simple equipment dramatizes the problems faced by crews building mountain railroads.

chief engineer, after which he was made general manager. In him the Rio Grande found one of the best-trained railroad men in America.

At the annual stockholders' meeting in October, D. H. Moffat and Walter Cheesman, both Denver men, were dropped from the board of directors and replaced by E. T. Jeffery and Senator E. O. Wolcott. Immediately after his separation from the Denver and Rio Grande, Moffat withdrew the valuable ore shipments from his mines at Leadville and turned them over to the Union Pacific's subsidiary, the Denver and South Park. More worried than pleased by this sudden embarrassment of riches, Union Pacific officials admitted that "Mr. Moffat is giving us his business, but we would like it better if he did not." The reason for this attitude was that the arrangement violated a pooling agreement, whereby the South Park, the Midland, and the D&RG earlier had agreed to divide the Leadville traffic. The Union Pacific was not prepared for warfare with the Midland's new owner, the AT&SF.[33] As soon as it could, the big road resumed a division of the Leadville traffic with the other roads.

Before the Jeffery regime was very many weeks old, Colorado was thoroughly apprised of its policies. After years of unpaid interest, stock assessments, reorganizations, and other frustrations, the investors had insisted upon the appointment of a man who would make the property pay. Jeffery came west from Illinois with this single purpose in mind and he did not propose to deviate from it. Coppell and the board backed him up, refusing to spend any more money on extensions than was absolutely necessary. Denverites were anxious to have the D&RG build a short cut into Leadville, but Coppell himself quashed the plan, saying it would take at least twelve million dollars to build the proposed 126-mile line. He argued that such a cutoff would have to pay $20,000 a mile in earnings and that it would take 70 per cent of that figure to operate it and pay interest. He did not think that there was sufficient population or products along the route, nor would there ever be, to warrant such an expenditure. It angered him to think that already the railroad had spent some $90,000 surveying the route. He regarded it as money thrown away.[34]

Some construction appeared to be so necessary that to even the most tight-fisted of policy makers its neglect would have been tantamount to stupidity, yet the Denver and Rio Grande management refused to

33. Ibid., Nov. 19, 21, 1891.
34. *Railroad Gazette* (Oct. 9, 1891), p. 716.

move. By 1891 the silver town of Creede was booming, and its need for rail transportation was obvious. A few years earlier the D&RG had built a line from Del Norte to Wagon Wheel Gap only to discontinue service in 1889 because of extremely heavy snows and the great expense of putting the track in shape each spring. Creede was nine miles from Wagon Wheel Gap. David Moffat had heavy investments in Creede and could promise considerable traffic, but when he suggested to the Rio Grande people the necessity of a railroad into the mining camp, he was turned down. Dipping into his private fortune, Moffat built the extension himself and sold it to the Rio Grande in March of 1892.

Another example of the Rio Grande's new conservatism was shown in the Cripple Creek mining rush of 1891. Moffat had extensive holdings here also, and when he again suggested that the "Baby Road" build a branch to accommodate the heavy ore traffic, he was refused. The presence of the Midland at Florissant, only sixteen miles from the new district, frightened off the Jeffery–Coppell group. Once more Moffat said, "I'll build it myself," and thus the Florence and Cripple Creek Railroad was born. He beat out the Midland by a full year, and within a short period of time saw his road grossing $120,000 a month. Later it was sold to the Rio Grande for $3,100,000. Meanwhile, the Rio Grande made the weak gesture of establishing a stage and wagon road from Canon City to Cripple Creek.[35]

Except for the completion of the Rio Grande Southern in 1891, there was little railroad activity in western Colorado. That little narrow gauge was built by Otto Mears, the financier and builder of wagon toll roads, who interested himself in railroads. Its main line, 162 miles long, ran from Ridgway, on the Denver and Rio Grande's Ouray branch, south through Placerville and Ilium to the mining camp of Rico, then circled slightly westward and looped back to make another connection with the Rio Grande system at Durango. Although Mears was the road's president, its board of directors included E. T. Jeffery, J. W. Gilluly, and Arthur Coppell of the D&RG, and through first mortgage bond holdings it was controlled by the larger line. Within two years it was in receivership, with Jeffery appointed as receiver.

Despite local criticisms, the Denver and Rio Grande management clung to its policy of financial retrenchment, with the result that dur-

35. McMechen, *Moffat Tunnel, 1,* 76–80. Wilson, "Denver and Rio Grande," pp. 191–92. Denver *Republican,* Jan. 16, 1892; March 19, 1911. Denver *Post,* March 19, 1911.

ing 1892 its floating debt was reduced by $1,200,000, leaving approximately $100,000 in outstanding bills. After paying its fixed charges and operating expenses, the road was able to pay a dividend to the preferred stockholders, an event that was nearly epochal in the company's history. By the end of June 1893 the last dollar of floating debt had been paid and there were no unpaid vouchers, no bills payable, and no loans at the banks. There was not, as the *Wall Street Journal* remarked, a railroad west of the Mississippi River in such an enviable financial situation.[36]

While such progress brought satisfaction to the railroad's investors, it was not accomplished without some complaints from the employees. During October 1892 there was a strike of engineers, firemen, switchmen, brakemen, and conductors on the system west of Salida. The trouble started with an order prohibiting the stoppage of fast trains at Glenwood or Malta so that trainmen could eat. William Gordon, an engineer on fast freight Number 61 westbound, defied the management, vowing that unless such an order was rescinded he would not take his train out of Minturn, and added that he "did not care a damn if he never worked another minute." When Gordon was suspended for thirty days, other employees met at Minturn and threatened to strike if he were not reinstated at once. Their threat was ignored, and on October 15 they refused to operate the trains. With that, the strike spread over both the second and third divisions. Jeffery promptly ordered the men back to work at the risk of losing their jobs, and at the first sign of defiance to his ruling he began firing employees. Coppell, who was in Denver for the annual stockholders' meeting, called it the most reckless and groundless strike that ever occurred. He could not understand the employees' attitude, asserting that the railroad paid the highest wages of any system in the United States operating more than five hundred miles of road, and its equipment, appliances, and track were the best west of the Mississippi River. To the *Railroad Gazette* the walkout was the "story of a flagrant case of high-handed unionism." With public opinion against the strikers, and employees of the first division refusing to join the action, Jeffery was able to talk the dissidents into returning to work.[37] In less than a week from the time the strike began, trains were moving again.

36. Denver *Republican,* Jan. 1, 10, July 10, 1893.
37. Ibid., Oct. 16–19, 23, Nov. 3, 1892. *Railroad Gazette* (Oct. 21, 1892), p. 787; (Nov. 11, 1892), p. 848.

Jeffery's real test came in 1893. For the first six months the prosperity of the preceding year continued, permitting a very favorable report on earnings at the end of the fiscal year on June 30. The financial situation to that time would have been even more favorable except for a short but severe rate war during April and May. It began in mid-April when the Midland reduced passenger fares and the Rio Grande met the challenge. The Midland made another cut, slashing rates to all points out of Denver, except to Grand Junction, to one dollar, and again Jeffery matched the reduction. When the Midland established a twenty-five cent rate on all Colorado points, carrying passengers for approximately a sixteenth of a cent a mile, the Rio Grande refused to go along and began to raise its fares. By now the major roads were involved, and westerners who wanted to attend the World's Fair in Chicago discovered that they could make the round trip for $30 as opposed to the earlier fare of $61.30. This abnormal condition could not prevail for any length of time. Already the Burlington and the Rock Island were apprehensive at the willingness of the Union Pacific and the Santa Fe to continue the fight. At a meeting of the Western Passenger Association, held in Chicago, attempts were made to resolve the difficulties. Although the Santa Fe dropped out of the association, it was generally understood that higher rates had to be restored, and that railroad agreed to go along with the others. By mid-May the controversy appeared to be ending and travelers hurried home, fearful that the holiday was about over. For Denver merchants the war had been a happy circumstance, since people from all over the state had taken advantage of the situation to pay a visit to the capital city. By early June, Colorado rates were practically restored even though there was still sharp competition among the major roads for Chicago-bound traffic.[38]

Hard on the heels of the rate war came the financial panic of 1893. Before the year was out, such giants as the Union Pacific, the Northern Pacific, and the Santa Fe fell. Across the nation, sixty-five railroads went into receivership that year, making a total of 123 lines then under court control. They represented 19 per cent of the country's railroad mileage.[39] Except for one casualty, the Rio Grande Southern, the Rio Grande system successfully weathered the storm. In Colorado the falling price of silver demoralized business communities and had a se-

38. Denver *Republican*, April 15, 29, 30, May 1, 2, 5, 6, 9, 11–13, 16, 17, 23, June 2, 1893.
39. Ibid., Dec. 22, 1893, quoting *Railway Age*.

24. Narrow-Gauge Train No. 8 Departing Grand Junction, Colorado, early 1900s. The railroad's five-span steel bridge over the Grand River was built in 1904.

25. Silverton, Colorado, about 1910. Forty-five miles north of Durango lay the mining and present-day tourist center of Silverton, reached by the Rio Grande in July 1882. With a population of 2153 in 1910, it was the operating headquarters of three little narrow-gauge railroad companies built by the legendary Otto Mears to serve outlying mines annually producing more than two million dollars worth of ore.

26. Durango, Colorado, about 1910. The tower of the Strater Hotel (today redecorated in Gay Nineties motif to please the tourists), together with other substantial brick business-blocks, laid against the backdrop of Smelter Hill in the distance, indicate the importance of this community, then as now, in the economic picture of southwestern Colorado.

rious effect upon railroads, but it was a less glamorous part of the mining industry that helped Jeffery's company through this time of trouble. Its heaviest traffic was in coal and coke, 80 per cent of which was carried outside the state for sale. Increased agricultural production added another string to the railroad's bow, and it lent assistance in absorbing the shock of the silver collapse. Jeffery's retrenchment policy had placed the railroad in the best financial position it had known for years. Road officials admitted that earnings had fallen off seriously and that money was hard to get, but they resolutely maintained that they were in no danger of receivership.

The situation was much the same on the Rio Grande Western in Utah. Its business held up well during the first half of the year, and then slackened considerably. General Palmer was disappointed over the small number of fares sold to Chicago, where the Exposition opening was two months late. By the time many people were ready to make the trip, the panic was making itself felt and they were reluctant to spend money for pleasure trips. In November he wrote: "Four months have now passed of collapsed silver mining and panic, during which, in all this region, including California, even the business which is not dependent upon the silver industry has been paralyzed, as everywhere else in the United States, by the temporary poverty of consumers and the constriction of credit requisite for the moving of crops and the laying in of the usual stocks of goods." Touching upon the mineral industry, he admitted that the "army of prospectors . . . has melted away, and although they produced nothing for shipment and most of their labor was sunk in worthless 'gopher holes,' it is due to them that fresh discoveries of value were from time to time made, while in the role of consumers they were as useful to the mercantile community, farmers and railway, as though they were actually turning out ore from working mines."

Always able to see the sunnier side of things, Palmer regarded the panic as a blessing in disguise. He told his stockholders:

One important compensation for the losses and troubles, whether due to class-legislation, panics, or the oppression of labor tyrants, from which our railways are suffering, is the fact that they are the severest discouragement to the building of new and competing lines, and as the existing roads are ample to handle the traffic of the country for many years, there seems to be a chance that they may be left alone to develop their traffic in a calmer and healthier way for both road and community, than has prevailed while money could be raised so easily for wild projects.[40]

In Denver, Jeffery stuck to his guns, cutting expenses, trying to make ends meet in the face of declining income. In July the Denver and Rio Grande's gross receipts fell about 40 per cent; in August they were off 50 per cent. All the railroad's officers took voluntary salary cuts ranging from 10 to 20 per cent. When wage reductions for other employees were proposed, there were strike threats, but the president, after explaining the company's financial situation, ordered a 10 per-cent reduction and there was no trouble.[41] When George Coppell came to Colorado for the October stockholders' meeting, he praised Jeffery's efforts and expressed the belief that the depression was lifting. Jeffery also felt that better times were not far ahead. "I do not see that we have much to fear now," he said. "That the Sherman [Silver Purchase] act would be repealed we all believed, and the shock that was bound to result was discounted. We suffered weeks ago all the ill that the first blow of repeal could give us." He pointed out that no railroad in the country was in a very prosperous condition at the moment, and added, "We in the mountains are regarded by Eastern railroad men as doing remarkably well under the circumstances."[42]

During the early months of 1894 the effects of the panic began to wear off and the rate of revenue decline slowed. The Denver and Rio Grande, able to meet its fixed charges of $550,000 in January, was complimented by the local press, which said that "the mountain lines of Colorado were the first railroads in the United States to feel the keen edge of the panic. There was no thin edge to the wedge. It went into the butt at the first clip."[43] Meanwhile, the Colorado Midland went under, leaving Jeffery's line about the only major road in Colorado still solvent. There were rumors that the Union Pacific's subsidiary, the Denver, Leadville, and Gunnison (formerly the South Park), was losing so much money that it would be abandoned. By August it, too, was in receivership.

40. *Annual Report of R.G.W.* (1893), pp. 5–22; (1894), p. 12.
41. E. T. Jeffery to J. M. Walker (trainmaster at Pueblo), Sept. 30, Oct. 7, 1893, items 4462, 5578, D&RG Archives.
42. Denver *Republican,* Oct. 16, Nov. 7, 1893.
43. Ibid., Jan. 4, 1894.

The Rio Grande's gradual ascent from the depths of the general depression was marred by widespread railroad strikes during 1894. The Pullman strike of that year spread when Eugene V. Debs of the American Railway Union called out workers of the western lines. By early July almost all freight and passenger service on the D&RG was suspended. Jeffery stated that his road would tie up for six months if necessary, but he would not give in to the firemen who were the principal cause of the stoppage. When Debs ordered switchmen, machinists, and car cleaners off the job, completing the list of employees on strike, Jeffery appealed to Judge Moses Hallett, who responded with the issuance of an injunction prohibiting any interference with interstate commerce. Federal marshals were requested to put the order into effect. On July 9 a regular train left Denver for Salt Lake City and made the run unmolested; aboard it were seventy-five United States marshals. At the same time federal troops were ordered to Grand Junction to break up the strike at that point. The move was completely effective and the labor rebellion was broken. Unlike the management of the Union Pacific, Jeffery agreed to rehire those who had walked out and normal service was resumed.[44] Although he had been obliged to use the mailed fist to gain a settlement, he sent out a circular to all employees, conveying the management's appreciation of employee loyalty during the recent difficulty. There is no record of the response.[45]

By the end of the year the financial picture showed improvement. During the latter part of the summer, Rio Grande preferred stock advanced more rapidly than that of any other railroad company in the country, and the road's earnings reflected a corresponding rise. In August both passenger and freight trains did a business termed "phenomenal" by a Denver paper. It was not enough, however, to allow a favorable annual report. At the end of the year the president was obliged to tell his stockholders that net earnings were off by a million and a half dollars, a decline greater, with one or two exceptions, than that experienced by any other important system in the nation. He made an indirect admission that his retrenchment policy, which certainly had saved the road from receivership, was having its effect upon the road's equipment. "The passenger cars do not present quite so attractive an appearance, upon the average, as in former

44. Ibid., July 4–8, 10, 11, 1894.
45. E. T. Jeffery to employees, Aug. 2, 1894, item 4466, D&RG Archives.

years," he wrote, "but two or three months' work . . . in the paint shop will, when expedient, remove this slight cause for criticism, if such it be."[46] It was the continued neglect of rolling stock that not only made it look shabby but made it hazardous to ride. Such "milking" of the property without sufficient maintenance or improvement was a practice carried on well into the twentieth century.

The board of directors was perfectly happy with Jeffery's management. He was re-elected, along with all the other officers, at a board meeting held in November. George Coppell told Denver reporters that the New York office was particularly gratified over the Rio Grande's progress during the financial depression and that it was due to the guidance of Jeffery, "a competent and conservative manager." Without such policies, said Coppell, the road certainly would have gone into receivership and would have given Colorado "such a black eye as it would not have recovered from in years."[47]

After the troublous years 1893 and 1894, plagued by the effects of a nation-wide depression and the general labor turmoil that accompanied it, Jeffery's administration settled down to a rather humdrum existence. Except for a decrease in net earnings during 1897, due in part to a long and serious miners' strike at Leadville, the road showed a steady profit until after the turn of the century. Semiannual dividend payments of 1 per cent were resumed in 1897, rising to an annual figure of 4 per cent in 1899 and 1900. These results were not spectacular, but Jeffery had proved an old Palmer theorem that a western road, relatively free from competition, could, with careful management, be made to earn a profit. There was no further building of extensions except for tiny spurs to accommodate additional sources of traffic, but even these were entered into with the greatest reluctance. In June 1895 the D&RG bought the Texas, Santa Fe, and Northern, a short connecting line between Espanola and Santa Fe, finally realizing Palmer's earlier scheme of entering the New Mexican capital. It was obtained for a mere $75,000. That the purchase was of no great significance is seen in the complaints of Denver papers to the effect that the twenty-four hour run between Denver and Santa Fe was "discouragingly tedious," and patrons used the D&RG service only as a "dreadful alternative."[48]

46. *Annual Report of the D&RG* (1894), pp. 4–7.
47. Denver *Republican,* Oct. 22, 23, 1894.
48. Ibid., Sept. 26, 1895.

During the '90s there was an increased effort to build up the Rio Grande's tourist trade. Relaxing his grip upon the purse strings, Jeffery permitted the annual expenditure of as much as $60,000 for advertising. In charge of this department was Shadrach K. Hooper, popularly known as "Major Hooper," who produced a considerable number of well-illustrated booklets for distribution. "Gems of the Rockies" appeared in 1889. It consisted of a dozen tinted views, each accompanied by such descriptive poetry as,

> Land of the rills, whose frontlets face the sun,
> Land of the rills, whose crystal waters run
> With rippling laughter and jocund glee
> To join the sunrise and the sunset sea.

There was a heavy demand for "Rhymes of the Rockies," a fifty-page book of poems and pictures. It ran through fourteen editions, or 350,000 copies. "The Opinions of the Judge and the Colonel as to the Vast Resources of Colorado" appeared in 1894. This was a fiction-type piece, depicting a trip over the line of two imaginary travelers. During the next year Hooper produced "The Geography of Colorado," 75,000 of which were printed. Next came "Slopes of the Sangre De Cristo," 130 pages profusely illustrated. Very popular was "A Honeymoon Letter From a Bride to Her Chum Describing the Beauties of Colorado," done in verse. In addition to the pamphlets, Hooper's department bought a considerable amount of newspaper advertising and sent east a number of lecturers carrying stereopticon views of Colorado and Utah. The *Rocky Mountain News* congratulated Hooper, saying that he had promoted immigration to Colorado and had focused the attention of the East upon the state's climate, scenery, and natural resources. "The result is . . . Colorado is and long has been the best advertised of the Rocky Mountain states. The general public, as well as the Rio Grande road, has reaped the benefits of his enterprising foresight."[49]

Business was good in 1898. In addition to the largest excursion trade in the road's history, the movement of both freight and troops during the Spanish-American War accounted for a sharp rise in receipts. The picture was clouded, however, by an increasing number of accidents on the road. They began to occur with increasing frequency during

49. *Rocky Mountain News*, Sept. 8, 1898.

1897 and continued during the next few years. In May 1897 there was a head-on collision near Grand Junction that killed both engineer and fireman, followed within two days by a second collision, this time with a wagon-load of children in Denver, resulting in the death of five youngsters. In September a Rio Grande passenger train collided with a Midland freight near New Castle killing at least twenty-five people, the actual number of dead being unknown due to a fire that broke out after the wreck. Less than a month later a train jumped the track near Salida and plunged into the Arkansas River, killing two passengers. The road's safety record was better in 1898, but in the fall of 1899 there were two fatal collisions that cost a dozen lives between them, followed by a rash of smaller accidents in 1900.

By the turn of the century, opinion was divided over the management of the Denver and Rio Grande. Coloradans regarded Jeffery's conservative policies with some concern as the road's physical growth ceased, its service declined in quality, and slow deterioration of the property was noticed. Denverites constantly complained about the long, meandering route via Pueblo, which took them well over 700 twisting mountain miles to Salt Lake City. After Jeffery took the helm, there was no further talk about an "airline" directly west to the city of the Saints. Eastern investors, however, were happy over the president's ability to make the railroad pay a profit during times of national financial adversity when most of the nation's lines were in serious difficulty. They were interested mainly in returns, and were totally undisturbed by the fact that folk in Colorado did not approve of milking the road to get them. It had been a long time since the word "dividend" had been associated with the D&RG. Passengers and local shippers might criticize the service offered, but from the standpoint of outsiders, particularly eastern financiers, the property looked attractive.

9. The sick man of Wall Street

THE COMING of the twentieth century was a widely heralded event in the United States, one that reflected a new and buoyant optimism over the nation's economic future. Having recently concluded what Secretary of State John Hay called "a splendid little war" with Spain, Americans witnessed a postwar period of prosperity as nerve-tingling as the recent dramatic military events. Under the benevolent reign of William McKinley, businessmen magnified the scope of their operations and Wall Street rolled out capitalizations the size of which staggered the imagination of the man on the street. Prominent among those who hoped to take advantage of the new era were the railroad giants and their close allies, the investment bankers. The key word in their plans was "consolidation," for in the years that lay ahead it was apparent that the nation's business would be more national in scope than ever before.

A glance at a map of the West revealed possibilities for those who had notions of competing with the already-established transcontinentals. All of the mountain states except one were bisected by one of these roads. Between the Union Pacific and the Santa Fe routes lay most of Colorado and a large part of Utah, an empire in itself, served by smaller lines, only one of which connected Denver with Salt Lake City. Ironically, Colorado had the heaviest population, the most varied sources of local traffic, and the best system of local railroads of any of its neighbors. To the west was the great port of San Francisco and all of central California, connected directly to the rest of the nation by the Central Pacific–Union Pacific alliance, whose relationship at times had been quite unhappy. For years several of the larger railroads kept Coloradans in a state of excited anticipation over the prospect of inclusion on an airline route to the Pacific, but nothing had come of it.

About 1900 the anticipation mounted to new heights. A Denver paper best expressed the feeling: "All the railroads between the Missouri and the Pacific are on the eve of impending changes. The controlling spirits of each system are nervously anxious to conceal their own plans and quite as nervously eager to know what are the intentions of rival systems. Beneath the surface maneuvering for position is going on which may prove to be the prelude of a battle of the giants." The editor then described a condition well recognized by mountain residents, for they had become quite accustomed to it. "Each system is as jealous of the movements of the others as the nations of Europe in their efforts to preserve their balance of power. If one builds a branch or buys a stub reaching into the alleged territory of any other the aggrieved road demands formal explanations. Not to give them is to incur the risk of a railroad war."[1]

Northern Colorado was particularly interested in all rumors about

1. Denver *Republican*, Jan. 19, 1900.

prospective invasion by major lines, hopeful that it would mean the location of Denver upon a direct East–West route. The Colorado capital city, located about equidistant between Cheyenne and Pueblo, was obliged to send its traffic over a hundred miles north or south to enter the flow of transcontinental traffic. Its newspapers complained that in the mountains to the west lay the least developed part of the state, a land as large as the state of Pennsylvania and as yet untapped by a trunk line. "Such another opportunity for railroad builders is not to be found anywhere in the United States at this time," said the Denver *Republican*.[2]

Across the mountains, Salt Lake City expressed the same anxiety. Like Denver, it never had been blessed by inclusion on a transcontinental line although it, too, for years had been titillated by rumors of such a happy development. The census figures for 1900 were somewhat disappointing to that municipality, showing a population of 53,551, or an increase of less than 20 per cent. Local boosters had hoped for a rise of at least 30 per cent.[3] It was recognized that one of the greatest stimulants to community growth was the railroad, and while Salt Lake City was happy to be served by both the Union Pacific and the Rio Grande Western, it yearned for a more important place in the transportation picture. The merest hint of impending construction by any of the major lines sent Salt Lake City papers into a flurry of journalistic excitement.

In 1900 there occurred two events that were to have tremendous long-range influences upon western railroading in general and upon the Rio Grande system in particular. Sometime during that year George Gould's Missouri Pacific Company began to buy Denver and Rio Grande stock, and the latter railroad, in turn, commenced heavy purchases of Rio Grande Western holdings. With that move, the young man made his bid to fulfill the transcontinental aspirations so long entertained by his father. Early in August, Collis P. Huntington died at the age of seventy-eight, leaving to his estate 400,000 shares of Southern Pacific stock. Very shortly, Edward H. Harriman and Kuhn, Loeb, and Company went after the Huntington interest in an attempt to obtain control of the Central Pacific, but before they were finished they were obliged to buy the whole Southern Pacific system. By the

2. Jan. 12, 1900.
3. Salt Lake *Tribune,* Sept. 6, 1900.

end of March 1901 the Union Pacific people commanded 750,000 shares, or 38 per cent of the Southern Pacific's outstanding capital stock. It had cost them nearly twenty-four million dollars. While this did not represent majority control, it was sufficient to keep any other single invader from obtaining dominance and it provided a breather until a better grip could be obtained. Shortly, the Harriman interests would possess $102,000,000 worth of the Southern Pacific's total capital stock of $197,000,000, and the financier could say with justification: "We have bought not only a railroad, but an empire."

George Gould made no attempt to enter the bidding, hopeful that Harriman would not close the Central Pacific to him at Ogden. Rather, he "manifested toward Harriman and his banker associates or overlords at this critical juncture a confidence so child-like as to be altogether inexplicable in a son of Jay Gould who had received his business training at his father's hands. His relations with Harriman were friendly at the time, even 'rather intimate.' "[4] This display of faulty field-generalship on the part of young Gould ultimately forced him to build west of Salt Lake City, a necessity that had serious consequences for the Denver and Rio Grande company.

For years the D&RG had tried to buy the Rio Grande Western. In 1889 the two boards of directors each appointed committees to make the necessary arrangements, but they were unable to come to mutually agreeable terms. The Western and the Colorado and Southern then made heavy joint purchases of Midland stock, which road had gone into receivership in the panic of 1893, thus seriously threatening the D&RG, whose managers concluded that there was nothing else to do but to build an independent extension to Salt Lake City and Ogden. Heavy purchases of Colorado and Southern stock by the Western added to their concern.[5] However, after a lengthy period of soul-searching and an opinion by civil engineer Virgil Bogue that to reproduce the Western would cost over fifteen million dollars, this plan was abandoned. Early in 1899 General William Jackson Palmer indicated a willingness to resume negotiations. He and George Foster

4. Ernest Howard, *Wall Street Fifty Years after Erie* (Boston, privately printed, 1923), p. 13. Salt Lake *Tribune*, Nov. 15, 1902. See also George Kennan, *E. H. Harriman, A Biography, 1* (New York, 1922), 239–43.

5. Charles F. Speare, *The Gould Railroad Lines: Their Condition and Their Capacity* (New York, 1908), pp. 35, 36. Salt Lake *Tribune*, June 3, 1900. Minutes of R.G.W. Board of Directors, June 6, 1900. D&RG Archives.

27. D&RG Ticket Office, Denver, 1909. Located at 17th and Stout Streets.

28. Cartoon of George Gould, March 27, 1901. The expansion of the Gould system—connecting the new Western Pacific to the Rio Grande—excited the residents of Utah, who foresaw the establishment of their city on a new transcontinental line.

29. W. P. camp at Wendover, Utah, about 1907. Even before the Western Pacific was completed, excursion trains using D&RG equipment, including diners, were run from Salt Lake City to construction sites in western Utah. The camp shown here stockpiled cross ties to meet the enormous requirements of the new Railroad in this treeless region.

Peabody, a vice-president of the Western, approached financier George Coppell of the D&RG board with a proposal to sell the railroad and its coal property in Utah. President Jeffery of the D&RG went to New York to take part in the negotiations. After a great deal of dickering, Coppell had to admit defeat, explaining to his board that "it was useless to continue the negotiations with Messrs. Palmer and Peabody, as at each conference they advanced the price at which they were willing to sell the common stock of the Rio Grande Western Railway Company and its coal property until they asked sixty ($60) a share for the stock and $6,000,000 for the coal property, an amount which was nearly double that talked of at the first meeting."[6] At that point the board suspended negotiations with General Palmer until the fall of 1900. Owners of the Western maintained a position they had assumed for over a decade: as the road was strategically located and making money, it was therefore valuable property. And, as Peabody remarked to Palmer when discussing the future, "I have no fear of adverse Ry. legislation at Washington while McK. is President." Obviously, he and Palmer could afford to wait it out.

Early in 1901 there were signs of impending change in the Rio Grande management. During January, Jacob H. Schiff of Kuhn, Loeb, and Company was elected to the board of directors. In the next month the influence of George Gould's stock purchases showed itself when, on the 14th, he was elected to board membership and invited to attend meetings of the executive committee.[7] This event followed by only a few days the announcement that Harriman, backed by the same Kuhn, Loeb, and Company, had gained control of Southern Pacific stock. Before George Gould had been on the board ten days, Denver papers were predicting that he would replace Coppell as chairman. On April 19 George Coppell died, and less than a week later Gould succeeded him, as predicted. Thus the scene was set for a Gould–Harriman struggle.

During the time these changes were taking place, negotiations continued for the acquisition of the Western. On February 8, 1901, a contract was made between Spencer Trask and Company, representing the Palmer group, and Kuhn, Loeb, and Company, giving the latter an option extending to March 25 to purchase that railroad and its subsid-

6. Minutes Executive Committee of D&RG Board of Directors, Jan. 26, 30, 1899, D&RG Archives.

7. Minutes D&RG Board of Directors, Feb. 14, 1901, D&RG Archives.

iary, the Utah Fuel Company, for fifteen million dollars.[8] Engineer Virgil Bogue, formerly of the Union Pacific, made a thorough examination of the property prior to actual purchase. The inspection was completed early in March and final papers were drawn up. During the next month directors of the Missouri Pacific authorized an increase of thirty million dollars in capital stock to provide for the purchase, and on May 15, at a special meeting, the Denver and Rio Grande stockholders voted to approve the transaction. Two weeks later Edward Jeffery became president of the Western and George Gould chairman of its board. Among the members of the new board were Jacob H. Schiff, E. H. Harriman, Frank Gould, and Howard Gould.[9] At the beginning of the fiscal year, July 1, the new management took over. The Western did not, however, lose its identity, for while the Denver and Rio Grande had purchased a controlling interest in its common and preferred stock, a similar transfer of bonds and securities was yet to be effected. Formal consolidation of the two roads did not take place until 1908. It was accomplished then as a reorganizational means of enlarging its mortgage to raise more money. Meanwhile, the lines were operated separately, although by the same management.

The transaction marked the end of General Palmer's railroad career. After thirty years of activity in the Mountain West and Mexico, he retired from active business life. He paid recognition to those who had worked with him in a gesture whose magnitude is still talked about. As one of his biographers explains it, he "had an unexpected profit of $1,000,000," which he divided among the employees from the manager down to the last section hand. One Utah passenger agent was said to have received $35,000. The General then returned to Colorado Springs to engage in the many local philanthropies that are so much in evidence there today.[10]

Gould's control of the entire Rio Grande system gave new life to the talk of its extension westward. Such a move had been a subject of

8. Minutes D&RG Executive Committee, March 22, 1901.

9. For details see Minutes R.G.W. Board of Directors, May 23, 1901, item 4532, D&RG Archives. Included there is Statement and Papers Regarding Acquisition by the D&RG Railroad Co. of the Common Stock of the R.G.W. Railway Co. and the Stock of the Utah Fuel Co., Feb.–June 1901, 117 pp. typescript. See also Minutes Special Meeting of R.G.W. Board of Directors, May 29, 1901, D&RG Archives.

10. Fisher, *A Builder of the West*, pp. 303–04. One of Palmer's employees, a mechanic who worked in the railroad shops at Salt Lake City, later became very well known in the automotive world. His name was Walter Chrysler. (Salt Lake *Tribune*, Feb. 21, 1924.)

discussion around Salt Lake City for more than a decade, but Palmer never was able to put the project into motion. In a letter to Dodge written in June 1890, the General had admitted that it was "premature as regards our financial status." Nevertheless, both men had continued to talk about reaching some point in California in the foreseeable future. By 1890 they had made an examination of Beckworth Pass in the Feather River country, and during the next few years they kept the area under constant observation. In December 1892 M. J. Lorraine, a San Francisco civil engineer, wrote to Dodge, offering to make the necessary surveys. He said that until recently he had been running lines for a project called the San Francisco and Great Salt Lake Railway, but the project had fallen through from lack of financial support. After describing the route through Beckworth Pass down the north fork of the Feather River to Oroville and Sacramento, he offered to make a rerun for $10,000 if it were done before timber growth obliterated the earlier work.[11] The panic of 1893 halted all plans for new construction, and by the time its effects were beginning to be shaken off, the idea of selling the Western had taken root in Palmer's mind. There matters stood until the appearance of Jay Gould's eldest son.

By adding the Rio Grande system to his collection of railroads, George Gould got into trouble. It was one of several mistakes that finally led to his downfall and to the consequent verdict of history that he had failed to fill his father's boots. George's entrance into the Utah transportation picture angered Harriman, who, having purchased the Central Pacific, was in a position to close the Ogden Gateway. From the time the Western opened for business in 1883, there had been friction with the Union Pacific over the division of traffic north of Ogden, but in June 1897, after the Oregon Short Line was freed from U.P. control, an arrangement was made to open the Gateway.[12] In 1899 the Union Pacific regained control of the Oregon Short Line, and in the following year it bought the Central Pacific, making it possible to control both westbound and northbound traffic at Ogden. This effectively reserved for the Union Pacific all business

11. Palmer to Dodge, June 4, 1890, item 1673, D&RG Archives. M. J. Lorraine to Dodge, Dec. 31, 1892, item 1754, ibid. For newspaper comment on the subject see the Denver *Republican*, June 15, 1891; April 16, 1892.

12. *Annual Report of the Rio Grande Western Railway* (June 30, 1897), p. 10. Denver *Republican*, Feb. 11, 28, 1900.

from that point to the Pacific Northwest and to California. It also assured the road a lion's share of eastbound business by charging a shipper local rates if he proposed to transfer his product to the Rio Grande at Ogden, or by giving him the advantage of cheaper through rates if he agreed to use Union Pacific facilities east of that point. Bottled up at Ogden, Gould now had no other choice but to build to California, and in so doing he overreached himself.[13]

With the utmost secrecy, Gould began preparations for the westward thrust. He was becoming fearful that this challenge to Harriman would bring down upon his head the severest of retaliations, and it seemed only prudent to screen his own movements. He was particularly anxious to retain traffic interchange arrangements at Ogden as long as possible. His consulting engineer, Virgil Bogue, wholeheartedly concurred with such an approach, for he recalled an earlier day when, after having located another road, he had made the depressing discovery that its route was dotted with mysterious mining claims of decidedly dubious value. The actual work was placed under the supervision of the Rio Grande's president, E. T. Jeffery, who in turn assigned the task of making surveys to his chief engineer, Edward J. Yard. Well aware that he was much too well-known to make an appearance in California, Yard called in his cousin, H. H. Yard, a mining engineer with no railroad experience, and instructed him to make extensive timber land purchases in Plumas County, California, after which he could build a small railroad for the ostensible purpose of carrying his products to market. During 1902 H. H. Yard employed five crews of land surveyors, who, knowing nothing of railroad prob-

---

13. Some 10 years later E. T. Jeffery, reminiscing on the events that led to the Rio Grande's interest in the Western Pacific, described how the Colorado road had become interested in the project. At the outset Gould himself had a 70 per cent interest in the Western Pacific, but as time passed he transferred the interest to the Rio Grande system. As Jeffery explained it: "The idea of Denver and Rio Grande becoming interested in Western Pacific gradually grew upon us. The Ogden gateway was closed to the Denver and Rio Grande Company by interests controlling the Union and Southern Pacific Companies, and although we were fostering the Western Pacific project, we continued our efforts to secure a re-opening of this important gateway through which the Denver and Rio Grande had enjoyed a valuable transcontinental traffic. As time went on the gateway continued closed, and, one might say, virtually sealed, against the Denver and Rio Grande, and so our thoughts turned to the desirability of interesting Denver and Rio Grande in Western Pacific, instead of continuing it as an independent enterprise." Statement of E. T. Jeffery at Board of Directors meeting, June 5, 1913, Minutes of a Meeting of D&RG Board of Directors, D&RG Archives.

30. Washout, near Nathrop, Colorado, August 1903. Washouts cost the D&RG thousands of dollars. Note the three-rail track built to accommodate both narrow- and standard-gauge equipment.

31. President Theodore Roosevelt and party at Hanging Bridge, Royal Gorge, May 8, 1905. From left to right: Major S. K. Hooper, Secretary Loeb, Frank Tyree, A. C. Ridgway, Judge Latta, President Roosevelt, Dr. Alexander Lambert, J. L. McGrew, James Sloan, Jr., J. G. Graves Thompson, William Delany, Philip B. Stewart, John E. Monk, Jackson Elliott. "Skip" is at the President's knee.

lems, produced little information of any value. Following his other instructions, he organized two small logging railroads: the Butte and Plumas Railroad Company, running from Oroville to the Butte–Plumas county line, and the Indian Valley Railroad, covering the route across Plumas County to Fredonia Pass. So far, the secret had been preserved, but as yet there had not been established an accurate and satisfactory railroad route across the mountains.

Yard, the mining engineer, put his professional knowledge and experience to good use. During his time in the Feather River country, he realized that the multitude of old placer mining claims could furnish any opponent with a formidable means of blocking a new railroad. Accordingly, he filed 673 placer mining claims along the proposed right of way. Bogue, who had been the victim of such tactics, may have been responsible for the idea; if not, he certainly approved of its use in this instance. In any case, the North California Mining Company duly made its appearance, and enough work was carried on to satisfy the minimum requirements of federal law.[14]

Concerned by the loss of time, chief engineer Yard of the Denver and Rio Grande resolved to put one of his own civil engineers on the project. Years later, S. J. ("Sam") Norris recalled that in "the early part of February, 1903, I received a telegram from Chief Engineer Yard to meet him in a certain room in the Brown Palace Hotel in Denver; there I met Mr. H. H. Yard. . . . I was told that I was to report to H. H. Yard and under no circumstance was I to communicate with Chief Engineer Yard. That the utmost secrecy was essential. That I was to call at H. H. Yard's San Francisco office looking for work. . . . I was directed never to admit that I had ever done any railroad work. My qualifications for the job was [sic] to have located a canal in Wyoming." Young Norris was advised even to alter his name as a further precaution, and under no circumstances was he to communicate with his family. It was explained to him that if the Harriman interests discovered Gould's intention to extend the lines to the Pacific Coast, the Ogden, New Orleans, and other gateways for the exchange of traffic would be closed and that the Gould railroads could not live under such conditions. "I want you to fix the grade through the Feather River

14. Gilbert H. Kneiss, *Fifty Candles for Western Pacific,* anniversary issue of Western Pacific *Mileposts* (March 1953), p. 6. This is a 40-page short history of the Western Pacific Railway Company, written by one of its officers. Differing slightly in detail is an account by S. J. Norris in the Oroville *Mercury,* May 31, 1957.

Canyon," said E. J. Yard. He told Norris that "the curves bellied out
where they should belly in and they bellied in where they should
belly out and that he needed some one on the work that he could
depend upon." Assuming the name John Norris, the engineer went to
California to take part in the cloak and dagger maneuvers staged by
George Gould, who stood in the background and denied all connection
with the project.[15]

Meanwhile, further complications had arisen. Arthur W. Keddie, for
a long time county surveyor of Plumas County, had gained local fame
by insisting that a 1 per-cent road grade could be built in the Feather
River Canyon. In 1902 he allied himself with a San Franciscan named
Walter J. Bartnett, who was possessed of some railroad experience,
having been interested in the Alameda and San Joaquin Railroad.
This thirty-six mile venture, built to tap some coal mines, had not
lived up to expectations. Bartnett, a promoter of the old school, now
conceived the idea of extending the midget railroad clear to Salt Lake
City by way of Beckworth Pass. On December 1, 1902, the Stockton
and Beckworth Pass Railroad was incorporated. Then Bartnett paid
a call in New York on George Gould, whose reaction was just what
the promoter had expected: "Here is a man working on a similar project; we had better tie him up." On February 6, 1903, the two men
signed an agreement designed to absorb the various earlier corporative
attempts and merge them into a new company. A month later, on
March 3, the Western Pacific Railway Company was organized. As it
happened, a small road by the same name, built in California in 1869,
was then a part of the Southern Pacific system, and that company raised
objections to the use of the name. Bartnett at once threatened mandamus proceedings, and the Southern Pacific decided not to make an
issue of the question. On March 6 the new line was officially incorporated.[16] Gould continued to keep his name out of the proceedings and
flatly denied all connection with the Western Pacific. Not until 1905,
when he made E. T. Jeffery its president, did he "admit paternity."

During the time George Gould was laying his plans to connect
Utah with central California, his attention was drawn to a burst of
railroad activity on another front. In 1900 William A. Clark, Montana
copper magnate and former United States Senator, had bought a

15. S. J. Norris to the author, July 10, 1959.
16. Oroville *Mercury*, May 31, 1957. Kneiss, *Mileposts* (March 1953), pp. 6, 7. *Commercial and Financial Chronicle* (March 21, 1903), p. 655.

small railroad in the Los Angeles area known as the Terminal line and announced that he would extend it to Salt Lake City.[17] Early in 1902 David H. Moffat, the Colorado mining millionaire, announced his intention to build a standard-gauge road named the Denver Northwestern and Pacific west from Denver, shortening the distance to Salt Lake City from 735 miles to 525, there to connect with Senator Clark's line. He thought it could be done for twenty million dollars. James J. Hill and J. Pierpont Morgan, now in control of the Burlington system, watched these developments with a great deal of interest. That road for years had harbored a desire to invade the mountain West, and here was a golden opportunity. The appearance of two small, connecting roads running between Denver and Los Angeles would provide the Burlington with a means of reaching the West Coast by a trackage agreement or perhaps, at some later date, the incorporation of them into its system. In either case the financial hazards of western railroad building would be assumed by other parties. Morgan, in particular, regarded the situation with more than a passing interest, for he and George Gould had come to a parting of the ways. If future developments bore no fruit other than an opportunity to slap down old Jay Gould's eldest son, as well as the young man's friend, John D. Rockefeller, who owned considerable Missouri Pacific stock, there would be gained a measure of satisfaction in the house of Morgan.

The prospect of renewed railroad activity, sponsored by western millionaires and great transportation combines, was highly exciting to both Denver and Salt Lake City. Denver quivered with delighted anticipation at rumors that one of its own, David Moffat, not only would build the airline across northern Colorado but that he promised to provide a great steel plant, rivaling that of Pueblo, in the capital city's environs. The Salt Lake City *Tribune* was awed by the power of such a combination as that of Morgan, Hill, Moffat, and Clark. They were, said the editor, four of the richest men in the world, men "who can gather more capital than Solomon's mines produced gold, and who have pitted themselves against the Harriman–Gould interests.[18] It will be a battle of the giants." And Salt Lake City appeared to be one of the focal points of the coming conflict. Residents

17. A brief picture of Clark's interesting political and economic adventures may be found in James High, "William Andrews Clark, Westerner: An Interpretive Vignette," *Arizona and the West*, 2 (1960), 245–64.

18. Salt Lake *Tribune*, March 28, 30, 1902. *Daily Rocky Mountain News*, April 4, 6, 1902.

of the Mormon community were very much gratified to think that, at last, their city was to become a great railroad center.

Colorado's attention was focused upon David Moffat, referred to by a Denver paper as "our Moses." In the spring of 1902 his was the most newsworthy name in the central Rocky Mountain region. Hardly a day passed during which the progress of his surveyors, his grading crews, or his money-raising activities did not command a prominent place in local newspapers. In May, James J. Hill paid a visit to Denver, ostensibly to inspect Burlington terminals, but of greater interest to the press was his reported friendship with Moffat and the possibility of an alliance. A month later the Denver railroader's name was linked with that of the Rock Island railroad when it was rumored that he had been approached by that company with an offer of financial backing. So excited did Colorado become over this Rocky Mountain Moses who promised to lead his people through the wilderness that his name also became prominent in political talk. It was well recognized that he had no love for Senator Edward Wolcott, who earlier had played a prominent part in Moffat's removal as Denver and Rio Grande president. Should the Denver and Northwestern project be successful, it was rumored that Wolcott would have to guard carefully his political life.[19]

As the railroad drama unfolded, George Gould kept his silence, secretly plotting the construction of a road from Utah to California and piecing together the rest of his transcontinental system to the east. By the spring of 1902 he was negotiating for the Western Maryland to gain an Atlantic Ocean outlet at Baltimore, and was prepared to spend millions to enter Pittsburgh. With that acquisition, his holdings extended westward from Chesapeake Bay to Ogden, Utah. There were growing rumors as to the nature of the next step, but Gould continued to deny them all emphatically. Attempting to throw Harriman off the scent, he openly stated that he would enter California at Los Angeles via Senator Clark's San Pedro, Los Angeles, and Salt Lake. When he visited Salt Lake City in September, he talked more of building up the roads already in his possession than of making any additions to his already large railroad complex. At Pueblo there were questions about his reported interest in the Colorado Fuel and Iron Company, said to have developed over his desire to protect Denver

19. For comments about Moffat in Colorado papers see *Rocky Mountain News*, 1902, esp. March–July.

32. Bridge on Tintic Branch, 1907. The bridge and tunnel show some of the problems of early railroad construction in the Rockies.

33. Billboard in Denver, Advertising Gould System, 1911. In May when this was erected, the Gould administration was exerting every effort to gain public acceptance and patronage for its attempt to break the strangle hold of Edward Harriman's Union Pacific–Southern Pacific empire on sources of traffic along the West Coast of the United States.

34. Marble-Quarry Workers at Marble, Colo., 1908. Still another turn-of-the-century utilization of the natural resources of Colorado's high mountains involved production at the marble quarry south of Carbondale. In this long cutting and finishing mill, Italian artisans worked the pure white stone into final form and polished it by hand. The largest block of marble ever quarried (100 tons) was processed by the workmen in this mill and now occupies an honored place in the nation's capital as the Tomb of the Unknown Soldier. The photo also illustrates the diversity of Colorado-Utah industries and the attempt to replace the earlier gold and silver mining income.

and Rio Grande traffic. He again denied all, saying: "I have not a dollar's worth of interest in the Colorado Fuel and Iron Company." Yet, within weeks, reports of a major battle for control of that company became public knowledge, and before the year was out the Gould forces controlled eight of thirteen seats on the directorate.[20]

It was during the latter period that a rupture in the relations of Gould and Harriman became apparent. Until that time the public supposed that the men were closely allied, and Gould himself apparently tried to continue the relationship as long as possible, for he registered no objections to the seat Harriman held on the Denver and Rio Grande board of directors. In October there were reports of a serious clash between the two men, stemming from Harriman's plans to expand the Southern Pacific into territory claimed by Gould's Missouri Pacific road. A story circulated to the effect that Gould had asked Rockefeller to help ward off this latest threat of invasion.[21] At the same time, Gould and Harriman found themselves at odds over the struggle for CF&I control with one of Harriman's associates, who publicly labeled Gould a traitor for his stand in the quarrel. Meanwhile, accounts from Salt Lake told how Harriman had forced Senator Clark into a minority position on the San Pedro, Los Angeles, and Salt Lake road, and that the Union Pacific would henceforth control the route into Southern California.[22] By 1905 it would be in operation. Here was another blow to George Gould's plans and one that must have strengthened his resolve to build the Western Pacific. Only a few months were to elapse before Gould and Bartnett made the agreement leading to the incorporation of that railroad.

David Moffat found himself in the middle of the railroad magnate Donnybrook being carried on in Colorado. For some time Gould's influence in New York had been brought to bear against him, and now, in late 1902, Harriman declared war upon the Denver railroad promoter. When Moffat learned of the pressure being exerted upon his financial supporters to dissuade them, he was reported to have said, "By God, the road will be built, if I have to go out and drive

20. *Daily Rocky Mountain News,* Sept. 3, Dec. 10, 1902. The Colorado Coal and Iron Co. was merged with the Colorado Fuel Co. in 1892.

21. Ibid., Oct. 9, 1902.

22. See Kennan, *E. H. Harriman, 1,* 346, for details of the Harriman–Clark Agreement of July 9, 1902. Each party had held one-half of the road's capital stock, with joint control over its management.

spikes myself.''[23] Beset by financial road blocks, unexpectedly difficult construction problems, and an unceasing flood of newspaper rumors that kept his organization in a turmoil, Moffat chipped away at the mountain barrier, determined to reach Salt Lake City. In May 1903 the Denver and Rio Grande people demanded that Moffat share with them the survey of a route he had purchased from the Burlington, running from Kremmling to the D&RG tracks near Dotsero. He refused, saying, "That right of way is too valuable to sell, much less to give away. I am not tied to any line, and my interests are for my own road."[24] Angered, and concerned about Moffat's invasion of territory they claimed as theirs, the Denver and Rio Grande managers promptly filled the air with talk about a direct line west of Denver. Such threats were far from disturbing to businessmen of the capital city. As one paper commented, "Denver could hardly ask anything better than this. The Rio Grande would then have its main line reach this city from the north instead of from the south. Denver would be more than ever the center of the system."[25] The "Queen City of the Plains," however, would have to wait another thirty years for such an achievement. At the moment, Gould had his hands full trying to reach the Coast from Salt Lake City and was in no mood to spend any more money on the Denver and Rio Grande system. In any event, Moffat shrugged off the rumors as being part of the diplomatic game, and moved forward. By early 1904 he had seventy-seven miles of road in operation.

Meanwhile, western newspapers watched with growing interest the emergence of the Western Pacific, uncontrollably curious as to its backer or backers. A San Francisco dispatch of May 28, 1903, told of the company's organizational progress and predicted that actual construction toward Salt Lake City would commence very shortly. This story linked Gould's name with the scheme, explaining that his failure to get a fairer division of traffic from the Southern Pacific had forced him to make his own connection with the Denver and Rio Grande at Ogden. Following the pattern set during the preceding months, the rumor was promptly denied. A Salt Lake City paper stated positively that Gould had no part in the project. When New York newsmen put the question to George Gould, he explicitly dis-

23. *Daily Rocky Mountain News,* Dec. 11, 1902.
24. Ibid., May 5, 1903.
25. Denver *Republican,* Oct. 30, 1903.

avowed any direct interest in the new road.[26] Nor was he willing to
share his secret with Harriman, who also made inquiry. Harriman
was said to have become so upset over the continuing mystery that
he shouted at his competitor: "If you build that railroad, I'll kill
you."[27] While young Gould was indeed a very small chip off the old
block, he would fight when cornered, and that was his predicament at
Ogden.

In the early weeks of 1904 the public received a strong indication
of George Gould's decision. On February 4 an official record was
made at the county court house in Salt Lake City of a fifty million
dollar mortgage of the Western Pacific Company. The Bowling Green
Trust Company, in whose favor the mortgage was drawn, was a well-
known Gould concern. George's brother, Edwin, was its president.[28]
Railroad men and financiers at once assumed that here at least was
indirect confirmation of the rumors so long in circulation regarding
Gould's transcontinental desires. Once again, he refused to admit any
connection with the scheme. "I have not put a dollar into the undertaking," he told reporters of the San Francisco *Chronicle,* "nor have
I any intention to do so. I am not interested in the Western Pacific
directly or indirectly, nor are any of the officials of the several roads
with which I am connected interested in the project. Notwithstanding
all that has been or may be said to the contrary, Mr. Harriman and
myself are friends, and the Gould lines are receiving eminently fair
treatment from the Southern Pacific. . . . As long as the Southern Pacific continues to treat our companies fairly, I see no reason for extending our lines to the coast." A leading New York financial journal,
quoting the San Francisco story, was unmoved by the railroader's
vehement protestations. It believed that eventually the Western Pacific would prove to be an extension of Gould's railroads.[29]

Toward the end of April 1905, more than a year later, it was revealed that Blair and Company, William Salomon and Company, and
William A. Read and Company, all of New York, had organized a
syndicate to take over the Western Pacific's bonds. The announced

26. Salt Lake *Tribune,* May 29, Aug. 12, Sept. 11, 1903.

27. Burton J. Hendrick, "The Passing of a Great Railroad Dynasty," *McClure's Magazine,*
38 (1912), 497.

28. Salt Lake *Tribune,* Feb. 6, 1904. *Daily Rocky Mountain News,* Feb. 5, 1904. *Railroad
Gazette* (Feb. 19, 1904), p. 120.

29. *Commercial and Financial Chronicle* (March 19, 1904), p. 1168, quoting San Francisco
Chronicle.

purpose was the construction of a Gould line to parallel the Central Pacific from Ogden to Oakland. A week later George Gould resigned his Union Pacific directorship on the ground that he no longer could serve on a "parallel and competing line." Mortimer L. Schiff already had left the Rio Grande board, and a few months later Harriman followed him.[30] At last the fight was out in the open.

George Gould's fateful decision was a costly one for the Rio Grande system, for upon the battle-scarred back of that railroad was piled the entire financial burden of the new undertaking. No other part of the nation-wide rail system was asked to share even a portion of the load. Three contracts, each of which involved the Rio Grande, spelled out the details of economic thralldom to be endured by that road for the next decade. Contract A provided that the Rio Grande would purchase second-mortgage bonds of the Western Pacific at 75 per cent par value up to the amount of twenty-five million dollars to help complete the new road. Contract C was a traffic agreement for reciprocal routing over the Western Pacific, Rio Grande, and Missouri Pacific tracks. Most remarkable of all was Contract B, whose broad terms literally presented the Western Pacific with a signed, blank check to be honored by the Rio Grande companies. As an absolute protection to the mortgage holders, the Denver and Rio Grande and the Rio Grande Western were to guarantee the interest, semiannually, on an issue of thirty-year 5 per-cent gold bonds. In other words, after all operating expenses and taxes were paid from the Western Pacific's earnings, the Rio Grande was to supply, if necessary, enough additional money to pay the bond interest. It was to be accomplished by the purchase of promissory notes from the Western Pacific. A further stipulation obligated the Rio Grande Western to supply enough funds to help complete the new railroad, should costs run higher than anticipated. In return, the Western Pacific agreed to turn over to the Denver and Rio Grande 100,000 shares of stock valued at ten million dollars and to the Rio Grande Western 150,000 shares valued at fifteen million dollars. When the Western Pacific increased its authorized capital stock to seventy-five million dollars, the two Rio Grandes would get additional blocks of stock in the same amount as before. The whole arrangement was a questionable gamble for Rio Grande stockholders, but since the Missouri Pacific controlled all but 82 of

---

30. Howard, *Wall Street*, pp. 21, 22.

35. The Famous Hanging Bridge in Royal Gorge. Although it originally supported only 3-foot gauge track, an outside third rail was laid to standard gauge in 1890 between Canon City and Leadville. Until 1911, when the inside rail was taken up, both narrow- and standard-gauge freight and passenger trains operated over this scenic route.

the total 175,000 shares of capital stock represented at the ratifying meeting held on June 8, 1905, at Salt Lake City, there was no trouble in gaining approval of the move.[31]

Edward T. Jeffery, president of the Denver and Rio Grande and a close confidant of George Gould, was placed at the head of the Western Pacific. In the fall of 1905 construction contracts were let and the work was begun. Aside from the normal engineering problems, there were a number of other obstacles that had to be surmounted. The San Francisco earthquake and fire of 1906 occasioned delays; the financial panic of 1907 furnished others; and as if these were not sufficient torments, the Southern Pacific added to the confusion when and where it could. The story of Harriman's attempts to make Western Pacific construction as difficult and as expensive as possible included the hiring of its workmen, and after hauling them far away, discharging them; of assessing unreasonable rates for carrying ties into the San Francisco Bay region; and of trying to prevent the establishment of a terminal at Oakland.[32] As construction crews toiled across the barren land, little towns in Nevada became highly excited about their future. Even though the Central Pacific had long served that region, the coming of a new road promised competition and improved service. When Western Pacific tracks reached Elko in December 1908, the local editor boasted: "This service will make Salt Lake City practically a suburb of Elko. A condition Salt Lakers have been anticipating for months." He added that "Elko's prosperity has been

31. Minutes of R.G.W. Stockholders, June 8, 1905, D&RG Archives. *Annual Report of the D&RG,* (1905), pp. 8–11; (1906), p. 8. Salt Lake *Tribune,* June 8, 1905. *Railroad Gazette* (March 16, 1906), p. 252. Into Contract B (Sec. 11) were written these damning words: "The Pacific Company [Western Pacific], with the consent of the Western Company [R.G.W.], does hereby assign to and specifically pledge with the Trustee, all the rights of the Pacific Company under this agreement, to be held by said Trustee in trust for the benefit and security of the holders of said First Mortgage Bonds, as provided in said mortgage, with power to said Trustee at any time, in case the Western Company shall have neglected or refused to fulfill this agreement or any of the covenants therein contained, and whether or not the Pacific Company shall have made default under any of the provisions of said mortgage, to take any and all proceedings at law, or otherwise, either in its own name as Trustee or in conjunction with the Pacific Company, which it may deem requisite or appropriate, for the purpose of compelling the specific performance by the Western Company of each and every of its covenants and obligations herein contained whatsoever the nature of any such covenant or obligation may be." Copy included in Minutes of R.G.W. Board of Directors, June 23, 1905, D&RG Archives.

32. Howard, *Wall Street,* p. 27. Kneiss, *Milepost* (March 1953), p. 10. Elko *Daily Free Press,* Jan. 26, 1906.

phenomenal without the Western Pacific. Now it will be more than phenomenal."[33] These views were typical of towns all along the proposed route.

It was estimated that the road would be finished by 1908 at a cost of about thirty-nine million dollars, but such hopes were badly shattered. Not until August 1910 was it ready for even limited operations, and the construction cost came to a staggering $79,611,410. It was a well-built road, something its projectors could easily afford, for the Rio Grande was footing the bill. The Denver Company had contributed $31,547,000 of the total amount by the time the road was finished, and it would be obliged to scrape up almost that much more before it was able to free itself from the shackles George Gould had fixed upon it.[34]

The Denver and Rio Grande system was a victim of George Gould's weakness for aggression and his tendency to falter at the climax of battles brought on by this characteristic. Not only was the mountain railroad made a pawn in the larger game and saddled with an almost impossible obligation to support the Western Pacific, but it was also subjected to the same treatment accorded to all the Gould western railroads, that of "starving" or appropriating the earnings needed to keep the equipment in proper operating condition. When the major companies of the railroad chain—the Missouri Pacific is one example —managed to pay dividends, it was done by severely pauperizing the subsidiaries, a policy whose blows fell heavily upon the Rio Grande. Describing the results of such neglect, a student of American business declared in 1912: "Thin, used-up rails, rotten ties, inadequate ballast, wheezy locomotives, dirty stations, passenger and freight cars in disrepair—all these things are found so commonly on nearly all of the Gould lines as to be fairly characteristic."[35] General Palmer, now in retirement, lamented the sad state of affairs in a letter to former Burlington president C. E. Perkins. "As to the D. and R. G.—if it has an engine that doesn't leak, I am not aware of it. Pueblo yards, I believe, are filled with some miles of unused cars. [A. E.] Welby, our old Rio Grande Western superintendent, is now general superintendent, as

33. Elko *Daily Free Press*, Dec. 23, 1908.
34. Howard, p. 28. William Charles Odisho, "Salt Lake to Oakland: The Western Pacific Link in the Continental Railroad System" (dissertation, University of California, 1941), p. 71.
35. Hendrick, *McClure's, 38*, 491.

you doubtless know, of the whole system but things are too far run down for him to make much impression."[36]

It did not require the observations of such an experienced railroad man as Palmer to reveal what was happening to the Denver and Rio Grande. Any passenger who was brave enough to buy a ticket on the line could have given eloquent testimony as to its condition, provided he survived the trip. From the time E. T. Jeffery took over its management in 1891, the prime objective of the owners had been to squeeze out every cent possible, while putting an absolute minimum back in improvements. Gould's entrance into the picture merely accentuated the practice old Commodore Vanderbilt used to call "skinning the roads." The result was an increasing number of wrecks, badly deteriorated rolling stock, and the practical abandonment of time schedules. So notorious did the railroad become for running late that upon one occasion, when its management promised to enforce rigidly a new schedule, a Denver paper printed the story with the added editorial comment, "incredible as this statement may appear."

One of the most spectacular accidents in the catalogue of catastrophes occurred in August 1904, when passenger train Number 11 plunged into the flooded waters of Dry Creek near Eden, eight miles north of Pueblo. A flimsy wooden bridge perched upon stone pilings, unattended by trackwalkers, and a sudden downpour that swept it away, cost more than a hundred trusting souls their lives. "Is human life so cheap that on a stretch of track like that from Buttes to Eden where washouts always occur in the season of floods a railway corporation cannot afford to provide a proper system of track inspection?" asked a Pueblo paper. Bitterly, the editor accused the railroad of making the assumption that it was cheaper to settle with the survivors and the relatives of the dead than to spend enough money to prevent such tragedies.[37]

The Eden wreck was still being talked about around Pueblo when another disaster occurred nearby, in the vicinity of Florence. This time two Rio Grande passenger trains collided head-on, killing some thirty-five people and injuring a great many more. Both personnel and equipment came under heavy criticism in this affair. The tele-

36. Palmer to C. E. Perkins, Jan. 4, 1907, copy of an original letter in the office of Charles E. Perkins, Santa Barbara, Calif., item 2696, D&RG Archives.

37. Pueblo *Star-Journal*, Aug. 8, 1904. Denver *Republican*, Aug. 9, 1904. *Railroad Gazette* (Aug. 12, 1904), p. 242.

graph operator, a youngster of eighteen, had fallen asleep so soundly that train Number 3 thundered past him only twelve feet away without disturbing his slumbers, its engineer unaware that the track was not clear. All across Colorado there was an outcry against the Rio Grande's antiquated signal system. The public sense of outrage was further heightened by the fact that the railroad sent the operator home to Kentucky to visit his father, travel-free, where he stayed until after the coroner's jury found him guilty of negligence.[38]

Public sentiment did not appear to affect Denver and Rio Grande management. Accidents continued, and those who were unconcerned about longevity patronized the road. Early in 1909, when two Rio Grande trains collided near Dotsero, killing twenty-three people, the Denver *Post* cried out that such negligence is "worse than criminal carelessness." The engineer of one of the trains blandly accepted full responsibility, and merely explained that he had misread his watch, thus gaining the impression that he had ten minutes to reach Dotsero. Unknowingly, he already had passed that station, a slight inadvertency that apparently stirred no one on the railroad. "We have grown immune to any shock at reading of our constant railroad tragedies," said the Denver *Post*. Quite appropriately, the paper wondered why freight was sent in steel cars, but passengers were obliged to risk their lives in wooden matchboxes on wheels.[39] In another head-on collision that same year, the engineer merely explained, "Oh, it was my fault—my fault altogether. Oh, why did I ever become a trainman. I was never cut out for it." He survived a wreck that killed twelve and injured sixty-two, by jumping when he saw the other train approaching, but he neglected to share his plans with the fireman who was killed a few moments later.[40] No one was immune from the Denver and Rio Grande engineers, who apparently could not see an object across the tracks if it were "big as a house." Demonstration of this fact was seen in the city of Denver one day when some house-movers found the object of their endeavors stuck at a crossing. Around the bend came a D&RG passenger train, and without so much as the blast of a whistle, it tunneled through the wooden structure with what was described as "an awful crash." As boards and bricks settled to earth, the passengers,

38. *Daily Rocky Mountain News*, March 17–22, 27–29, 1906. *Railroad Gazette* (March 23, 1905), pp. 315–16.
39. Denver *Post*, Jan. 16, 17, 19, 24, 25, 1909.
40. Ibid., Aug. 15, 1909.

conscious only of slightly more than the usual tumult attendant to such a ride, were continued on their adventurous, if somewhat hazardous, journey.[41]

Jeffery's management answered the rising tide of protest against the condition of his railroad by cutting the working force and tightening the purse strings. In the spring of 1907, when he released some 500 men, a Denver newspaper explained: "The reason is to reduce expenses and furnish money for dividends." His action was taken in spite of the fact that some 2,000 "bad order" cars awaited repair and twenty-five locomotives were inoperable.[42] The result was inevitable. Two years later it was publicly charged that the Denver and Rio Grande had been, within the recent past, involved in many more serious accidents than all the other railroads of Colorado combined.[43]

Coupled with the policy of allowing equipment to deteriorate, the once fine relationship between management and labor dissolved during the first decade of the new century. In the spring of 1908 the road informed its shopmen that it would abolish the nine-hour day, pay no overtime for Sundays and holidays, and recognize no unions. Complaining that it had taken them twenty-five years to gain what they had, some 2500 workers walked off the job in mid-March. In an era when labor was generally depressed and unionism in disfavor, it would be expected that the press would come to the defense of the corporate world, but in this case the Denver *Post* hurled charges of penny-pinching at the Rio Grande and said that the case of the strikers "merits the fullest measure of public support and public sympathy." The paper accused the railroad of originating the strike and of rendering a disservice to the state of Colorado.[44]

The year 1911 was historic for the Rio Grande in several respects. On March 18 David Moffat, worn out and ruined financially, died in New York City at the age of seventy-three. He had spent fourteen million dollars vainly trying to fulfill his dream of a railroad directly west from Denver. By 1908 the determined builder had managed to get as far as Steamboat Springs, at a cost of $75,000 a mile, only to find himself in a barren and forbidding land west of the divide, where the

41. *Daily Rocky Mountain News,* April 28, 1904.

42. Denver *Post,* Feb. 17, 1907.

43. Ibid., Aug. 14, 1909.

44. See Denver *Post,* April and May, 1908, for stories of the strike's progress. See also Minutes D&RG Board of Directors, March 20, 1908, D&RG Archives.

two great counties of Routt and Grand had less than 10,000 residents.[45] There the project was stalled while its projector vainly tried to raise more money. When he died, his much-beloved project for a tunnel under James Peak had not even been started. Part of his fortune had been dissipated in trying to run his trains over Rollins Pass, nearly 12,000 feet high, through blinding blizzards and impossible snow drifts. The unbuilt tunnel would have solved a good part of these difficulties. Colorado's towering mountains were only a part of his trouble. Both Harriman and Gould had fought the road at every turn, drying up sources of money that might have helped Moffat wherever they could. His death without doubt brought sighs of relief from the Rio Grande owners, who had for over a decade feared his success. His threat was the most serious they had yet encountered.

The second event of significance for the Rio Grande in 1911 was the decision of the board of directors, on June 13, to pass the semi-annual dividend on preferred stock that had been paid regularly since 1901. As Jeffery explained it to the company's stockholders, the board, however reluctantly, had decided to apply the $1,244,495 that would have been used for dividends to the $1,248,125 sum due September 1 in semiannual interest payment on the fifty million dollars worth of Western Pacific first-mortgage bonds. Financial writers of the time felt that this was a further indication of the Rio Grande's sincerity toward its obligation and that it would serve to add internal strength to the line.[46] Actually, it illustrated the growing dilemma of the road, one that by 1914 led to a plea for sufficient alteration in the terms to lighten the intolerable and inequitable burden the Rio Grande was forced to carry.

A third development of great importance to the railroad was the breakup of the Gould empire. Since the panic of 1907, George Gould had been referred to as the "Sick Man of Wall Street," it being apparent even then that his grip was slackening on his vast holdings. It was said of him at that time, "The vacillation, the little halt, the streak of financial meanness came—and then came enmity, open hostility, the closed hand, and the hard-locked treasury. Mr. Gould had committed the unpardonable crime. He had smitten Wall Street in the only place it feels a hurt, the money nerve. It will take many years

45. McMechen, *Moffat Tunnel, 1,* 122, 123. *Rocky Mountain News,* March 19, 1911.
46. *Rocky Mountain News,* June 15, 1911.

to win forgetfulness."[47] But there was no disposition to forgive on the part of the financial world. Relentlessly, the Deutsche Bank of Berlin, the Rockefellers, and Kuhn, Loeb, and Company moved in, and by 1911 their combined forces unseated Gould from the presidency of the Missouri Pacific Railroad. National periodicals watched with interest as the moneylenders chased the heir to old Jay Gould's fortunes from the transportation field. Readers were treated to accounts of the passing of a great railroad dynasty and the beginning of a new era of banker-control management.[48] Closer to home, those interested in the Denver and Rio Grande's fortunes shed no tears over the breakup. Denver's *Rocky Mountain News* said, quite correctly, "The Gould family have been railroad milkers, rather than railroad builders." In the editor's eyes George could not be charged with having been a railroad pirate or financial buccaneer, in the tradition of Jay Gould, but merely an inefficient and rather lazy man. "The king is dead," said the *News*, "May there be no more kings."[49]

News of the king's death was somewhat premature so far as the Rio Grande was concerned. Like an unwanted guest, he was to stay on for a few years while the railroad staggered forward, dragging along the Western Pacific burden, that albatross Gould had hung around its neck in 1905. Until receiverships for both roads came to the rescue, this was to be a condition of bondage, and even after the Western Pacific's subsequent foreclosure and sale, the Rio Grande was to pay what amounted to alimony. The history of Colorado and of all Western states is replete with examples of financial exploitation by outsiders who had enough money to buy a proprietary interest in the land. George Gould merely furnished another, in his own inept way.

47. C. M. Keys, "The Overlords of Railroad Traffic," *The World's Work, 13* (1907), 8442.
48. See Hendrick, *McClure's*, Vol. 38; "Passing of the Gould Regime," *Nation, 92* (1911), 202–03; "Wane of the Gould Dynasty," *Literary Digest, 44* (1912), 561.
49. *Rocky Mountain News*, Feb. 17, 1911.

10. *We will attempt nothing radical*

THE HEAVY HAND that George Gould had laid upon the Denver and Rio Grande, and the consequent deterioration of that road, did not appear to dim the optimism of Denver boosters. With a faith reminiscent of their pioneer forefathers, they dreamed of the day when the Queen City of the Plains would take its rightful place on the nation's railroad map and thrive upon direct, transcontinental traffic. At a time when the Gould rail empire was breaking up, a Denver paper editorialized upon Colorado's great future, remarking that other transportation magnates were at last beginning to see the importance of their state. James J. Hill was said to be negotiating for the Moffat Road, whose sale had been a subject of constant rumor from its inception, and when that happened, the natural result would be to "complete the tunnel, take in the Rio Grande, and build the Dotsero Cut-off." If Hill did not enter the picture, then Harriman would, and if this did not occur, surely Rockefeller would not miss such an opportunity. "Give the proper railroad facilities to a state like this," said the *Rocky Mountain News,* "and no man can set a limit on its growth." To that newspaper the day of great railroad development was just around the corner.[1]

David Moffat's consuming ambition to drill a tunnel beneath James Peak had spread like a contagion in the minds of the Denverites and those living in other northern Colorado communities. The project was described in newspapers of the time as the "open sesame" to local industrial growth, and there was increasing talk about state support of an undertaking whose benefits would be so widespread. It fired the imagination of railroad enthusiasts to contemplate a route so straight that it plunged through granite barriers on its way west. Once across the first major hurdle, Moffat's railroad looped southward before proceeding to Steamboat Springs, and that little jog reached out tantalizingly toward the Rio Grande's station at Dotsero. A connection of the two roads by a short cutoff would provide the Rio Grande with its much-desired northern outlet at Denver. If a joint trackage agreement could be reached with the Denver, Northwestern and Pacific, both roads could use the proposed tunnel. Here was an additional argument for the justification of so expensive a bore.

It irritated Denverites to think that every conceivable obstruction had been placed in Moffat's path. Lashing out at all railroads serving Colorado, the capital city's press accused them of hemming in Denver's commerce and industries with discriminating rates. "Denver begs and pleads in vain," said the state's oldest newspaper. "The only way Denver can fight and break the strangle hold they have upon it is with another road—one that will shoot straight through to the coast, one that will be under obligations to Denver, one that must build up

1. *Rocky Mountain News,* Jan. 24, 1911.

Denver for the freight and other traffic that will make it prosperous."[2]
This plea for the realization of Moffat's dream is evidence of Denver's
growing frustration over the inability or unwillingness of any railroad
company to connect it directly to Salt Lake City. The Denver and
Rio Grande, once fondly regarded as Colorado's own "Baby Road,"
was among the guilty.

The name of George Gould had come to symbolize the impasse in
Colorado railroad affairs because of his running fight with other important figures in the world of finance. The constant antagonism maintained against him on Wall Street was said to account for the depressed
nature of all Gould securities, including those of the Denver and Rio
Grande. His downfall was regarded as a first prerequisite to the entrance of new money in mountain railroad building. Francis A. House,
a financial writer for the *Rocky Mountain News,* predicted that both
the Western Pacific and Rio Grande systems soon would be free of
Gould's control, an event that would clear the way for a new era of
western transportation. Denver expected to be one of the chief bene-
ficiaries of this development.[3]

Proponents of a shorter route to Salt Lake City were to suffer further disappointments. After Moffat's death, William G. Evans, son
of former Governor John Evans, took up the cause, and he, like Moffat,
was to exhaust his own personal fortune trying to extend the Denver,
Northwestern and Pacific. David C. Dodge, for years Palmer's right
hand man, was appointed general manager, and he assumed the task
of directing construction west of Steamboat Springs. Craig, Colorado,
was the farthest point west the tracks ever reached. There the project
died and with it expired the hopes of northwestern Colorado for a
railroad of its own.

The weakening of Gould's influence in Rio Grande circles was
felt early in 1912 when Benjamin F. Bush, president of the Missouri
Pacific system and a representative of the anti-Gould forces on that
road, succeeded E. T. Jeffery as president of the D&RG. Jeffery, an
out-and-out Gould man, retained his presidency of the Western Pacific until the following year and at the same time succeeded George
Gould as chairman of the Rio Grande's board of directors at a salary
of $35,000. The Rockefellers, having substantially increased their

2. Ibid., Nov. 10, 1912.
3. Ibid., Feb. 17, 1911.

holdings in the Missouri Pacific and the Denver and Rio Grande, were making their power felt.[4]

Bush at once made an inspection of the Rio Grande property, after which he told reporters that money was available for improvements and that a program of double-tracking, grade reductions, and the broad-gauging of more narrow-gauge sections could be expected. In April a twenty-five million dollar issue of twenty-year gold bonds was authorized, fifteen million dollars of which were reserved for improvements and protection of the Western Pacific, seven and a half million for Denver and Rio Grande improvements, and the remaining two and a half million "for Western Pacific purposes."[5] A week later the Moffat Road went into receivership.

Those two pieces of news suggested to Coloradans that the balance of local railroad power was once again hung on dead center. Now that the force of the Moffat lever was dissipated, nothing would frighten the Denver and Rio Grande into spending any large amount of money to improve Denver's place in the transportation world. With its monopoly untarnished, the local road could remain in hibernation, giving the public only what it had to give, unworried about the spread of any progressive ideas by more farsighted rivals. Such improvements as it proposed to make were in the nature of betterments along the already-established line. Anticipated traffic from the Western Pacific dictated the long overdue expenditures, not to mention the necessity of removing the road from the category of a public hazard. In commenting upon the safety aspects of its works program, the Denver and Rio Grande management made a belated recommendation that conditions, customs, and practices "that lead to the loss of human life must be abandoned or corrected."[6] In the light of its fatality record, this probably was the understatement of the day. Unfortunately, as the next few years would demonstrate, the program was not entirely successful.

During 1913 the Rio Grande made some attempts to fulfill its promises of physical improvement. In addition to a number of minor

4. Denver *Republican*, Jan. 5, 16, 17, 1912. *Annual Report of the D&RG*, 1912. George Gould's explanation of the change was that it was effected to give "the whole Missouri Pacific system an identical operating management." Minutes D&RG Board of Directors, Jan. 2, 1912, D&RG Archives.

5. Copy of agreement attached to Minutes of D&RG Board of Directors, March 22, 1912, D&RG Archives.

6. Denver *Republican*, July 9, 1912.

projects, a major one was completed at Soldier Summit, Utah. This undertaking lengthened, rather than shortened, the line, but it reduced the grade from 4 to 2 per cent, allowing one engine to haul a freight train over the divide, where formerly it had necessitated three. The job cost two and a half million dollars and proved to be a wise investment in annual savings to the road.[7]

In addition to physical improvements on the Rio Grande, management attempted administrative changes designed to improve operating efficiency. In mid-summer of 1913 the Missouri Pacific, the Rio Grande, and the Western Pacific roads were combined into a single operating unit. The move was not made without complaints from some of those affected by it. Charles H. Schlacks, vice-president of the Western Pacific, resigned, bitterly charging that when he left the Rio Grande, Jeffery had assured him he would be employed in an independent administration. In accepting the resignation, Gould took the opportunity to state that for some time the move had been contemplated as a means of further unifying the Missouri Pacific's railroad interests. Jeffery became chairman of the Western Pacific's board and Benjamin Bush its president.[8] Bush now was president of three railroads: the Missouri Pacific, the Denver and Rio Grande, and the Western Pacific.

Despite attempts at physical and managerial improvement, Gould's western lines faced increasing difficulties. The year 1913 was a poor one for railroads all across the nation, and although western roads generally fared better than those in the East, they had their problems. Bush could find some comfort in the fact that the Union Pacific was ordered to divest itself of $126,000,000 worth of Southern Pacific stock and to dissolve the monopoly Harriman earlier had obtained for it. This, however, provided no immediate benefits for the Denver and Rio Grande or the Western Pacific in their search for more business.

For the moment there was little to do but to get along as well as circumstances permitted. Plagued by inadequate income, by rising interest rates in a tight money market, and by the enormous indebtedness of the Western Pacific, Rio Grande officials saw no other course than that of retrenchment. "In the present difficulty which railroads all over the country meet, we are determined to exercise the greatest cau-

7. Denver *Post*, Nov. 9, 1913. *Annual Reports of the D&RG*, June 30, 1913; June 30, 1914.
8. Minutes D&RG Board of Directors, July 3, 1913, D&RG Archives.

tion," said Bush, trying to cover his troubles with a blanket statement. "For that reason, it is probable that we will attempt nothing radical and will even sacrifice some improvements that we know are gravely needed."[9]

It was an old story, one that the road's patrons had heard many times before. But now the gravity of the situation was greater than ever. The Rio Grande not only had to nurse along the ailing Western Pacific in the hope that the frail infant would somehow survive, but it was confronted by new dangers. The opening of the Panama Canal threatened to reduce seriously transcontinental freight haulage by rail, and that which remained would be subject to division with the Southern Pacific. This, coupled with the financial uncertainty occasioned by the outbreak of the war in Europe during the summer of 1914, made the outlook grave indeed.

Gould's tightening up of the system did nothing to help the Rio Grande. It was in bad shape, thanks to his misuse of it, and before the Gould phase closed, things were to be much worse. In the summer of 1914, at the instance of the bankers who held Rio Grande paper, the famous engineer John F. Stevens was hired to inspect the property so as to ascertain its condition and probable future earning power. In his report, submitted on September 10, Stevens admitted that the standard-gauge sections of the road were in fair shape, but they were almost devoid of modern signal devices. The annual replacement of rails was about half what it should have been, the ballast was inadequate and of poor quality. The only narrow-gauge track that the engineer thought acceptable was that running from Salida over Marshall Pass to Montrose, the rest being safe enough to run trains "at some rate of speed." The latter had received only the scantiest maintenance in the thirty to thirty-five years since they had been constructed. As for rolling stock, Stevens was willing to concede that it was in as good condition as the archaic shops and tools available for repair could keep it. Most of the cars and engines were out of date, the latter generally lacking sufficient power to operate economically on mountain grades. Pointing out that most of the narrow-gauge lines had been built to tap gold and silver camps long since closed, Stevens criticized the Rio Grande for keeping its rates so high that low-grade mining could not be carried on at a profit. By the same token, he said, agricultural com-

9. Denver *Post,* March 19, 1914.

munities would have sprung up had the railroad not been characterized by poor service and high charges. On that subject he grew caustic:
"During 40 years intimate acquaintance with almost every section of
the Great West I have never known a section which has improved so
little after being provided with transportation facilities." He accused
the Rio Grande of lingering along, a quarter of a century behind the
times.[10]

In another, and vital, area the Rio Grande's lackadaisical policies
proved expensive. Its branch line that carried an enormous tonnage of
the Utah Copper Company's ore from the Bingham mines to the Garfield reduction plant was going to ruin. The copper company lived up
to its promise to ship all ore by the Rio Grande until matters grew so
serious that local transportation was threatened. Finally, when shipments became heavier and service continued to decline, the company
demanded improvements, including heavier rails. Obtaining no satisfaction, the corporation built the Bingham and Garfield Railway
to carry twelve million tons of ore annually on its own line.[11]

These were developments that occurred on the Rio Grande long
after the day of Palmer, Jackson, and Moffat. They would have been
unthinkable in a day when Colorado management commanded the
little mountain railroad, but now at a time when it was a pawn in a
larger financial game, operated by remote control, the reputation of
the Baby Road suffered greatly. Ironically, a mere fraction of the
money poured out to build the Western Pacific would have put the
road in condition to take care of the agricultural and industrial development of the Utah-Colorado area it was built to serve.

The magnitude of the difficulty into which Gould had thrown the
Rio Grande by Contract B was long since apparent. In June 1913 the
board of directors finally faced up to it. At a meeting held in New
York on the 5th, Jeffery suggested "the desirability of having consideration given to the financial relationship of Denver and Rio Grande
and Western Pacific, with a view of placing them on a mutually satisfactory and more practicable basis than they are at present." In
short, the Rio Grande had had enough. The board chairman asked
for permission to call in F. W. M. Cutcheon, general counsel of the

10. Stevens' report is quoted by Henry C. Hall, "Denver and Rio Grande Investigation,"
ICC *Reports, 113* (1926), 108–10.
11. Hall, *Reports, 113*, 110, 111.

36. Colorado's well-known Spa, Glenwood Springs, about 1912. Here it is seen from a high point east of town. In the days of steam it served the D&RG both as an important water and coaling station and as a terminal for engines helping eastbound trains over the grades in Glenwood Canyon.

37. Leadville, Colorado, about 1915. Once the second largest city in Colorado, Leadville often was called the "Cloud City" because of its location just below timberline. This view across the city shows not only a portion of one residential area but also the substantial church, school, and business buildings of an earlier prosperity of 40,000 souls first served by D&RG rails in 1880.

Western Pacific, to make a joint study of the problems. The request
was granted.[12]

The increasing influence of the Missouri Pacific's board made itself felt during 1914. On July 7 those gentlemen passed a resolution
to the effect that as owners of about 30 per cent of the Rio Grande's
capital stock, the Missouri company was greatly concerned about the
burden the Rio Grande was carrying. Another interest payment was
due on September 1 and the Western Pacific had no money to con-
tribute toward it. As a matter of fact, the road's net income for 1912,
1913, and 1914 did not add up to enough to pay the interest on first-
mortgage bonds for a single year. The Denver and Rio Grande owned
twenty-five million dollars worth of Western Pacific second-mortgage
bonds and eighteen million dollars worth of floating debt bonds. The
Wall Street Journal commented: "It is apparent therefore that the
W.P. is annually increasing its floating debt with little hope of catching up with this accumulating burden while at the same time this is
annually becoming a more onerous drain on the D. & R. G."[13]

Even worse, the California company's operations for the first half
of 1914 were in the red to the extent of $138,398.94, which sum the
Rio Grande would have to pay in addition to the required $1,250,000
bond interest. Viewing with alarm what appeared to be a continually
deteriorating situation, the Missouri Pacific board passed the following resolution:

> Resolved, that this Board requests its Directors, who are also
> Directors of the Denver and Rio Grande Railroad Company, to
> express to the Board of said Denver Company that in the opinion
> of this Board it would be unwise to pay the September 1st coupon
> of the Western Pacific First Mortgage unless prior to that date the
> Boards of the Denver Company and the Western Pacific Com-
> pany have reached an agreement respecting the re-arranging of
> the financial relations of the two companies and until a plan based
> upon such agreement shall have been promulgated by the Com-
> panies' Bankers.

At an historic meeting of the Rio Grande board of directors, held
in New York City on August 6, 1914, the question of meeting the
September 1 interest payment was thoroughly discussed. Edgar L.

12. Minutes D&RG Board of Directors, June 5, 1913, D&RG Archives.
13. Quoted by Denver *Post*, June 26, 1914.

Marston, a New Yorker who was a member of both boards but had not attended the mentioned Missouri Pacific board meeting, suggested that the payment be made. He said that the Rio Grande had enough money to do it, that there was a good prospect the Western Pacific's earnings would increase, and that Blair and Company, William Salomon and Company, and William A. Read and Company, through whom the Western Pacific bonds had been sold, had promised that they would "use their best endeavors to devise a plan of readjustment of the finances of the Western Pacific Railway Company." Marston was a partner in the banking house of Blair and Company. He warned that default would entail the danger of a mortgage foreclosure and perhaps receivership for both companies. As he said:

> Such receiverships would certainly result in most serious loss to the stockholders of this Company and certain embarrassment and probable loss to holders of other issues of its securities; and possibly would result in the loss of this Company of control of the Western Pacific Railway Company, which, in the opinion of this Board, is of great value to this Company, and therewith the loss of the entire value of the interest in said Company represented by this Company's investment therein, aggregating more than $40,000,000; and also would result in rendering unsaleable and greatly diminishing the value of a large amount—being several millions of dollars—of securities held in the treasury of this Company.

His argument prevailed, and the Rio Grande board, with the exception of young Kingdon Gould, agreed that the September interest should be paid. A resolution was prepared for public release, at the discretion of the chairman, to the effect that the Rio Grande would live up to its obligation, but in it was included the ominous phrase that "if the Denver and Rio Grande is to continue its support of the Western Pacific, some plan of readjustment of Western Pacific finances and the relation of Denver and Rio Grande thereto must be devised." Clearly, the Rio Grande was running out of both money and patience with its relief program west of Salt Lake City.[14]

During the winter of 1914–15 a committee of Rio Grande board members and "the Bankers," as those who had arranged for the sale

14. Minutes D&RG Board of Directors, Aug. 6, 1914, D&RG Archives.

of Western Pacific first-mortgage bonds were called, labored over the problem of working out some kind of compromise more tolerable to the bond guarantors. As March 1, the next due-date, came closer, there were increased attempts to arrive at a solution. The Rio Grande board met sixteen times between February 4 and 26. During these hectic days it was handed for consideration a "Plan of Readjustment of the Financial Affairs of Western Pacific Railway," referred to by board members as the plan of February 1, 1915, prepared by the bankers and marked "confidential." Joel F. Vaile, general counsel for the Rio Grande, criticized the scheme, which was one of reorganization for the Western Pacific, as being too expensive and dangerous for the Rio Grande. To begin with, the Rio Grande was asked to wipe out some $37,500,000 worth of Western Pacific debts, interest not counted. This was money advanced on second-mortgage bonds and a series of notes. Under the proposal, a new Western Pacific company was to be organized, with the Rio Grande being the principal bondholder. As Vaile pointed out, the arrangement permitted the issuance of more bonds in the event that an annual interest of $1,750,000 was not forthcoming, but this would be an expensive palliative indeed. While it would protect the two companies from foreclosure until the maturity of the income bonds in 1935, the accumulated compound interest by then would have increased the principal from thirty to ninety million dollars, and at that date the sum would be an absolute liability. Even to suggest it was ridiculous. Vaile's opinion resulted in a tabling of the reorganization resolution, while further talks were had with the bankers, looking toward some alternative and more reasonable plan.

On February 10 Jeffery met with the bankers' committee and was told that a prime consideration of any readjustment was the Rio Grande's guarantee of both principal and interest of an issue of twenty-five million dollars worth of first-mortgage bonds to be issued by the new Western Pacific Company. They would engage in no further discussions until this condition was met. After that they agreed to discuss the arrangements under which other bond issues would be made. Jeffery talked with the bankers again on Sunday, February 14, but made no headway. The financiers stuck to their original demand with relation to the guarantee of both principal and interest on the new bond issue. At a board meeting of the 17th the directors agreed to that stipulation. On the 22d a revised plan, conceived by a committee made up of Jeffery, Vaile, and Thomas L. Chadbourne, Jr., special counsel, was presented to the board. It incorporated the bond interest and principal guarantee, already approved, but limited the liability of the Rio Grande in additional bond issues. This plan, known as that of February 22, was turned down by the bankers. Rather than close the door on further discussions, they suggested certain modifications, but these were unsatisfactory to the board, whose members unanimously rejected the changes on February 26. One more try was made. The board proposed the issuance of fifteen million dollars in fifty-year 5 per-cent bonds, guaranteed by the Rio Grande as to interest only and the creation of a further issue of thirty-five million dollars, in which the Rio Grande would "join to the extent of pledging its income to the payment of interest." The idea was unacceptable to the bankers.

At a meeting held on the afternoon of February 26, the bankers made their final proposal. The issue of income bonds, to be used for exchange with the old Western Pacific bondholders, was increased to $32,850,000, and an issue of second-mortgage bonds in the amount of twenty million dollars was to be guaranteed as to interest only. When a vote was called for on this proposition, the board assented unanimously, "putting into final form a plan of readjustment of the relation of this Company to the Western Pacific Company," to quote the secretary's phrase. It was understood that the Western Pacific would ask for a receivership, and plans for that were prepared in advance so that action could be filed on the morning of March 2, the day after default occurred. This was to be a "friendly receivership," one that would take place before any other of the railroad's creditors could make a similar application. Accordingly, when the action took place on schedule, Frank Drum, president of the Pacific Gas and Electric Company, and Warren Olney, Jr., general counsel for the Western Pacific, were appointed as custodians of the property.

Unfortunately, there was a last-minute hitch in the plans of the Rio Grande's board of directors, one that occurred too late to alter the course toward receivership. Sometime between February 26 and March 1 the bankers asked for further modifications in the plan. The board balked at this point, creating a stalemate that was never resolved. A majority of the directors did not construe Contract B to hold the Rio Grande liable for the principal on the bonds; the bankers thought otherwise. Here was the main point of difference between the two contending parties in the negotiation. There was some disposition on the part of the board majority to let the matter go into the courts in the hope that their point of view would be sustained. When there was no agreement with the bankers, this was the course followed. To say the least, it was a calculated risk and one that failed.

The Equitable Trust Company of New York, successor to the old Bowling Green Trust Company, was not willing to stand by without taking some measure to protect itself and those it represented. This organization, an affiliate of Kuhn, Loeb, and Company, was headed by Alvin W. Krech. He spearheaded a group called the Protective Committee, or, as it was more commonly known, the Reorganization Committee, made up of the Western Pacific banking syndicate, the Dutch interests, the Standard Oil Company, and a few individuals. Bondholders were now asked to deposit their holdings with the trust company and to receive in exchange certificates of deposit, thus giving the committee power to deal with the Rio Grande in any litigation that arose in the matter of settlement. By December 1915 the committee had formulated a plan of action. It proposed to create two new companies: the Western Pacific Railway Company to operate the property after foreclosure, and the Western Pacific Railroad Corporation, a holding company that would own the railroad by virtue of its ownership of the road's securities. The reorganization plan specifically announced an intention to have the holding company prosecute the Rio Grande for breach of Contract B.[15]

During the spring of 1915, as the Reorganization Committee perfected its own organization, Krech and his associates attempted to get the question of Contract B into New York courts. They were fearful that if the case was heard in California, the Rio Grande, and not the Western Pacific, would be held primarily responsible for the recent default and would therefore itself be put into receivership. This probably would impair the Rio Grande's ability to respond in the coming damage suit, a development that the committee did not want. The Rio Grande management cooperated with Krech, apparently in the belief that it had a strong case, one it wanted settled as quickly as possible. Nor did it want to be thrown in receivership as a result of any California decision. Accordingly, on May 26, 1915, the Equitable Company filed an ancillary bill in the United States Court for the Southern District of New York, and that court appointed as receivers of the Western Pacific the same men earlier appointed at San Francisco. The

15. Odisho, "Salt Lake to Oakland," pp. 86–87.

Equitable then filed in the New York court a suit against both the Western Pacific and the Rio Grande, asking for a construction of the Rio Grande's responsibilities under Contract B. It was understood by both the Rio Grande and the Equitable Company that the latter had no intention of bringing the matter to immediate trial.[16]

On June 3 the receivers themselves petitioned the California court, asking for instructions as to the enforcement of Contract B. In answer to their contention that the liability of the Rio Grande under the agreement should be adjudicated in the California courts and that the road should be made a defendant in the action, Judge Van Fleet issued an order enjoining the trustee (the Equitable Company) from further proceeding in its New York suit. He reserved for his court the right to decide as to the construction and effect of the contract.

Early in March 1916 the trustee entered Van Fleet's court with a form of foreclosure decree and requested that it be entered at once. Upon his refusal, the Equitable appealed to the Circuit Court for the Ninth District. On March 29 the lower court was reversed and foreclosure proceedings went forward. The Circuit Court held that the Rio Grande's agreement to pay the interest on Western Pacific bonds was separate and independent from other covenants in Contract B and was therefore not involved in the foreclosure suit or properly an issue before the district court.[17]

In order to determine how much money the bondholders had coming under the unfulfilled Contract B, it was necessary to fix a price upon the "old" Western Pacific's property. Although the property had cost over seventy-nine million dollars, the majority bondholders now asked for an "upset" or minimum price of fifteen million. If this figure was accepted, the bondholders then would contend for thirty-five million, or the difference between the upset price and the original bond issue of fifty million. Foreclosure proceedings took place in the summer of 1916. The majority bondholders were impatient at any delay, for with each passing day the Western Pacific's income was rising, and its value was increased accordingly, thus militating against the design to drive down the property's price. This unaccountable development on the part of the Western Pacific, that of making money, was explained away as due to abnormal wartime conditions. The Rio Grande people registered no objections to attempts of the bondholders to get

16. Hall, *Reports*, *113*, 117.
17. Ibid., p. 119.

a valuable property for a pittance, and even cooperated with the trustee in his efforts to hasten the sale. The Rio Grande did not interpret Contract B to mean that it was liable for any more than interest, a view that was not shared by the courts when the question came before them a few months later. Thus there were no objections, except from some of the minority bondholders, when an upset price of eighteen million was fixed for the Western Pacific's sale held on July 1. It included the road's property and $2,177,222 in net earnings held by the receivers, making the actual price of the property itself around sixteen million. Immediately after final services were held over the corpse of the defunct Western Pacific, the stockholders, who were the purchasers, chartered the new Western Pacific Railroad Company in the State of California.

During the months that followed the Rio Grande's failure to pay the March 1, 1915, interest, thus setting in motion the foreclosure of the Western Pacific, George Gould had other problems on his hands. Only a few days after the default, Benjamin F. Bush was elected president of the Missouri Pacific–Iron Mountain system and E. T. Jeffery retired from the directorates of these roads. The press interpreted this to mean the beginning of the end of Gould control of the companies. At a meeting on March 9 some 63 per cent of the Missouri stock was voted, a majority being cast by Otto H. Kahn of Kuhn, Loeb, and Company and by Alexander J. Hemphill of the Guarantee Trust Company of New York. When the proxy committee demonstrated its ability to control the election, there was no longer any doubt that Gould had temporarily lost control.[18]

Another blow fell in August 1915, when the Interstate Commerce Commission upheld the Union Pacific's asserted right to close the Ogden Gateway, thus forcing the Rio Grande to surrender its demand for a division of traffic beyond that Utah city. President Bush of the Rio Grande minimized the probable effect of the ruling, saying it would not take away more than fifteen thousand dollars worth of traffic a year.[19] A look at the railroad's twisting, circuitous route and its slow schedules explains why. The Union Pacific covered the distance between Ogden and Omaha nineteen hours faster than the Rio Grande and its connecting lines, and was 400 miles shorter. Few shippers had sufficient affection for the Rio Grande to ship their goods the longer

18. Salt Lake *Tribune,* March 10, 1915.
19. *Rocky Mountain News,* Aug. 12, 13, 1915.

and slower way. The closing of the gateway was not particularly detrimental to the line at that time, but in later years, when the mountain route to Salt Lake City was shortened by 175 miles and the Rio Grande was able to match the Union Pacific competition in running time and service, it became a serious enough matter to keep both railroads in court over a period of years.

In the face of banker pressure, Gould retreated in the fight for control of the Missouri Pacific, but he took his stand in the mountain fastness of Colorado and fought a last-ditch battle to maintain his position on the Rio Grande. Even here he was seriously challenged. At the annual meeting of stockholders, held on October 19, 1915, Gould managed to retain his position on the board of directors. But it was at the sufferance of Kuhn, Loeb, and Company, to whom he had acquiesced in return for financial aid to the ailing Missouri Pacific. When the board next met on November 4, he turned upon those who had him in leash and bared his teeth in a most unexpected manner. B. F. Bush, who had allied himself with Kuhn, Loeb, and Company in the fight for control of the Missouri Pacific, was peremptorily fired as president of the Denver and Rio Grande, after which Gould organized an executive committee made up of members of his own family. Arthur Coppell was temporarily installed in the presidency, over the protests of Bush, E. L. Brown, E. L. Marston, and Finley J. Shepard. The latter was Gould's brother-in-law. A week later Coppell resigned as president in favor of Henry U. Mudge, of Denver. The move further angered Bush, who had recommended his friend Edward L. Brown of the Western Pacific. Mudge, a former president of the Rock Island, was at the time that railroad's receiver.[20] Apparently Kuhn, Loeb, and Company had lost its control of the Rio Grande board; at least it was unable to stamp out at once the belated and unexpected insurrection of George Gould, who held the reins until 1917.

Mudge promised an improvement program similar to that attempted by Bush, the necessity of which was amply demonstrated to the new president when the train bearing him on his initial inspection trip

20. Ibid., Nov. 5, 1915. Howard, *Wall Street,* pp. 80–86. Henry C. Hall of the ICC had this explanation of Gould's "uprising": "Financial difficulties of the Missouri Pacific, which indeed confronted it in March, 1915, when it permitted the New Denver to default under contract B, had led to the passing of its control in August 1915, from the Goulds to the banking house of Kuhn, Loeb and Company. But although the Missouri Pacific had retained its New Denver stock intact, the new interests in control of the Missouri Pacific were unable to obtain majority representation on the New Denver directorate until September, 1917." *Reports, 113,* 82.

THE EVOLUTION OF POWER

ON THE

Denver & Rio Grande Railroad

First Locomotive 1871 Length 30 Ft.

1003

Pacific Type
Passenger Service, 1913
Length 78 Ft.

1212

Mikado Type
Freight Service, 1913
Length 76 Ft.

1075

Mallet Type, Mountain Service, 1913, Used 1913-32.

38. Typical Locomotives Used by D&RG, 1913. Pride of the Railroad near the end of the George Gould administration was the motive power that entered service late in 1913. This photo chart compares the newest passenger, freight, and heavy-duty mountain engines of the time with the Company's first tiny locomotive—the *Montezuma*.

derailed and tipped over on its side, severely shaking up those aboard.[21] The Rio Grande for some years had been able to show a profit, and its officers generally were desirous of keeping the line and its rolling stock in a suitable condition, but the presence of such unwelcome affiliates as the Missouri Pacific and the Western Pacific, both in receivership now, made it impossible for the little line to support the burden assigned it. The policy of drawing off every available cent for use elsewhere so starved the Rio Grande that there was a real prospect of its own extinction. The state of deterioration brought on by the company's role as a sacrificing parent was enough to make any set of managers despair, but more trouble awaited the railroad at the hands of the angry bondholders, who were determined to have their pound of flesh as prescribed under Contract B.

During the latter months of 1916 there was hope among the board members of the Rio Grande that differences between them and the Equitable Company could be settled out of court. The board's special counsel, Thomas L. Chadbourne, Jr., had, in the preceding year, offered the opinion that Contract B did not involve the road as to liability on the bond principal. Meanwhile, in August 1915, the Missouri Pacific had gone into receivership and was being reorganized by Kuhn, Loeb, and Company. These financiers were, of course, interested in the welfare of the Rio Grande since the Missouri Pacific owned 30 per cent of its stock. Paul Cravath of the Kuhn, Loeb legal staff now informed the Rio Grande directors that he did not agree with Chadbourne's opinion and urged the board to seek further opinion before allowing negotiations with the Equitable people to fail. The noted lawyer Elihu Root was retained at a fee of $5,000, to render his opinion. When Root advised that the Rio Grande would be liable for interest on the remaining bond-value debt—that part not satisfied out of proceeds of the foreclosure sale—and for the sinking fund payments provided for in the mortgage, yet another attorney was engaged. The new man, John Milburn, supported Chadbourne's view, i.e. that the Rio Grande would not have to pay interest on Western Pacific bonds after the sale. During this period Rio Grande representatives had a conference with those of the Pacific Holding Company (otherwise known as the Western Pacific Railroad Corporation), in which alternative settlements were discussed. The holding company offered

21. *Rocky Mountain News,* Dec. 17, 1915.

to turn over to the Denver and Rio Grande the old Western Pacific property if it would issue fifty-five million dollars in 5 per-cent bonds to cover the old Western Pacific mortgage. The offer was refused. With that, the Equitable Company pressed its demand for realization of the unpaid bond principal and showed the seriousness of its intent by gaining a restraining order, granted in New York, to prevent that company from "diverting such of the income of the Denver and Rio Grande as ought to be applied to the payment of its indebtedness." This was in January 1917. The United States district court impounded three million dollars of Rio Grande money on deposit in New York. Later that month the order was extended and amended so as not to apply to the railroad's funds deposited elsewhere.

In August 1917 the case against the Rio Grande was heard before Judge Learned Hand of the United States District Court for the Southern District of New York. It was decided without oral argument and without a jury. The decision awarded the plaintiff damages of thirty-eight million odd dollars, or the difference between the upset price of eighteen million and the fifty-million dollar bond issue, plus accumulated interest.[22] The fault was that of the Rio Grande, said Judge Hand, for a "naive unwillingness to keep on paying their debts." Ernest Howard, one of the Rio Grande stockholders who suffered from the decision, wrote a bitter account of the whole affair, in which he suggested rather strongly that Judge Hand was taken in by the blandishments of the Western Pacific's majority bondholders, whose forces were marshaled by Krech. He was astounded that Judge Hand had fallen for the idea that the foreclosure price of eighteen million dollars anywhere near represented the value of the Western Pacific. In Howard's view Judge Charles M. Hough and his associates on the Circuit Court of Appeals bench also were deceived on this point. They sustained the lower court's opinion. When asked about Howard's accusations a great many years later, Judge Hand wrote: "I have absolutely no recollection of the action of the Equitable Trust Company against the Denver & Rio Grande Western [sic] Railroad Company. It was forty years ago, it was while I was a District Judge, and it may well

22. The exact sum was $38,270,343.17. Its component parts were: interest due March 1, 1915, Sept. 1, 1915, and March 1, 1916, totaling $3,750,000; the "interest on the interest," due June 14, 1917, amounting to $401,911.80; the unpaid principal of $32,272,274 and interest on that amount from July 1, 1916, to June 14, 1917, which came to $1,846,150.92. Figures taken from Howard, *Wall Street*, p. 117. The author has drawn heavily upon Howard, chaps. 8–13, for details of the suit against the D&RG.

be true that Hough and I were 'taken in.' All I can say is that, if so, it was probably not the first or last instance of our judicial blindness. . . . Guilty, or not guilty, my mind has been wiped clear of the whole affair."[23] It is understandable that the Judge might have had difficulty in recalling the particulars of a specific case heard forty-two years earlier. But this was no ordinary piece of litigation. The thirty-eight million dollar judgment was more than nine million dollars larger than the fine levied against the Standard Oil Company a few years earlier—an amount that caused a great deal of public talk—but the extent of the Rio Grande's reverses in court went unnoticed in wartime America. Judge Hand's inability to recall the case was not so much a lapse of memory as an indication of how quietly the financial castration had been performed on a small western railroad. Salt Lake City and Denver papers had paid almost no attention to it. The irony of the whole proceeding lay in the fact that the Rio Grande, more than once at the end of its resources, was solvent at the time it refused to carry its unreasonable burden another step, and as a consequence, it did not itself seek protective receivership.

The immediate effect of Judge Hand's decision was a sharp drop in the price of Rio Grande stock. Preferred stock tumbled from about $40 a share to around $20, and common stock sank from $12 to $7.00. The ruling was appealed, and within a few months it came before the United States Circuit Court of Appeals, presided over by Judges Charles M. Hough, Henry W. Rogers, and Julius M. Mayer, with Judge Hough writing the opinion. On January 3, 1918, the lower court's findings were upheld on all points except that of procedure; there was no alleviation of the heavy judgment assessed by Judge Hand.[24] Judge Hough reaffirmed the plaintiff's contention as to the Rio Grande's liability when he said that it had "inflicted the blow proximately causing death" of the Western Pacific. The case was closed. When the United States Supreme Court refused to review the damage suit, the last avenue of appeal was sealed off, concluding one of the nation's most fantastic episodes of railroad wrecking. The Denver and Rio Grande had been through some bizarre experiences in its tumultuous history, but this was, beyond all question, the most expensive. The only benefit it received was, at long last, freedom from

23. Howard, chaps. 13, 14. Judge Learned Hand to the author, Aug. 18, 1959.

24. Howard, chap. 14. See also Ernest Howard, *A New Story of American Railroad Wrecking* (New York, 1918).

the destructive captivity of George Gould, who made his final and belated bow out of the Colorado railroad scene.

The entrepreneurial demise of George Gould did not, however, mean independence for the Rio Grande system. In October 1917 the anti-Gould forces from the Missouri Pacific placed eight men on the D&RG board of directors, as opposed to only three Gouldites. As a consequence, Edward L. Brown of the Missouri Pacific replaced Mudge as the Rio Grande's president, a move that earlier was frustrated by Gould when Henry Mudge succeeded Benjamin Bush. The bankers behind the Missouri Pacific were now in absolute control of Colorado's Baby Road. But the baby was in serious danger of suffocation at the hands of the Equitable Trust Company, in whose favor the New York courts recently had ruled. The Equitable asked for a lien on about three million dollars worth of the Rio Grande's free assets, and insisted that interest charges for January and February, 1918, be met. After the Equitable had succeeded in getting its hands on the three million dollars in the form of Liberty bonds, it brought action in the New York Supreme Court, where on March 13, 1918, it obtained a judgment totaling $5,632,074.28 against the cash, stocks, and bonds held by the Rio Grande. Very shortly, it scored again, this time in a Chicago court, netting another $967,301.37.[25] In June 1918 all the shares of the Utah Fuel Company, a subsidiary of the Rio Grande, went on the public auction block in New York and were purchased by William Salomon for four million dollars. The money went to the Equitable to be applied toward the judgment.

In January 1918, after the Equitable's first attachment of funds, the Rio Grande board realized that the game was up. There would be no relenting until the Equitable had squeezed every cent it could lay its hands on out of the railroad. At a meeting held on the 14th, the question of receivership came up. Gould, Jeffery, and J. Horace Harding, of New York, opposed the idea, but they were voted down. The majority passed a resolution to the effect that the company was without the ability to pay the judgment against it, nor could it pay the interest already matured upon its funded debt. All efforts to persuade the Equitable Company to stay the execution of its judgment had failed. Receivership was the only answer.

The Equitable could have cried out "broken agreement," had it

25. Hall, *Reports, 113,* 130.

chosen to, for both parties had agreed that there would be no receivership without ample notice. But when the financiers began attacking the Rio Grande's free assets, its directors felt that sufficient faith had been broken to justify its actions. The Missouri Pacific management, guided by Kuhn, Loeb, and Company, was fearful of a complete destruction of the Rio Grande and the loss of its interest in that line. These railroad men were afraid that the Equitable people might double-cross them and ask for a receivership first, one that would work to the Equitable's advantage. The answer lay in anticipating the move by a double cross of their own. The Missouri Pacific board members serving on the Rio Grande board turned, therefore, to a relatively minor creditor, the Elliott Frog and Switch Company of East St. Louis, Illinois, to whom the railroad owed only $17,000, and requested it to institute proceedings. The East St. Louis company complied on January 17, 1918. Loud protests at once were heard from the Equitable Company, but the outcries were turned aside by Judge Robert E. Lewis of the district court at Denver. He refused the plaintiff's request for a lien against the Rio Grande and refused to delay the receivership move. Then Lewis called for help, asking Judge Walter H. Sanborn, senior Judge of the United States Circuit Court of Appeals, to take over the entire proceedings.[26]

Judge Sanborn made short shrift of the Equitable's efforts to stop the receivership. On January 25, 1918, he denied that corporation's request for a dismissal of the Frog and Switch Company's suit and appointed Edward L. Brown and Alexander R. Baldwin as receivers. The latter was a vice-president of the Western Pacific Railroad. The Equitable, however, gained Sanborn's permission to intervene in the receivership proceedings so that it might take legal advantage of its right to collect money awarded it by Judges Hand and Hough. When it tried to appropriate what it could, William G. McAdoo, under whose care the major American railroads had been placed in December 1917, temporarily blocked the move. It quickly became apparent that if the railroad did not pay some of its obligations, a complete disintegration might take place. In mid-May 1918 Judge Sanborn ruled, at a special session at Omaha, that receiver Baldwin must sell $1,500,000 in securities, draw $600,000 from the banks, and use the $1,500,000 the government had contributed for its use of the railroad

26. Denver *Post*, Jan. 9, 18, 19, 1918. See also Hall, pp. 130–31, and Minutes Board of Directors D&RG Railroad Co., Jan. 14, 1918, D&RG Archives.

to pay off $3,600,000 in outstanding indebtedness and overdue interest.[27] Baldwin was now "receiver-in-fact," and Brown represented the government as its agent, the joint receivership having been segregated.

The war had a decided effect upon Colorado's "home railroads." The Rio Grande was the beneficiary of federal aid, while the Midland was not. Not only did the government pay the Rio Grande for the use of its facilities, but to the complete surprise of local officials, it made a grant of nearly three million dollars in May 1918 for betterments and equipment. In the following year the United States Railroad Administration fixed the annual guaranteed compensation of the Rio Grande at $8,319,376, agreeing to make up any amount short of that "parity" earnings figure. The Midland, a long-time sufferer of financial malnutrition and inadequate patronage, gave up the ghost, the government administering the final blow by its policy of aiding one road and not the other. The Moffat Road narrowly escaped the same fate. Its receiver had affairs in such a tangle that during January 1918 traffic came to a complete standstill. Denver, aware that its newfound pride and joy was about to die a-borning, went into action. The Civic and Commercial Association, headed by Finlay L. MacFarland, appealed to Washington, arguing that the vast resources in coal and oil shale of northern Colorado were necessary to the war effort, and that nearly 25,000 people were dependent upon the line. Railroad administrators at Washington held back, unwilling to aid the Denver and Salt Lake (as the Moffat Road now was called since its reorganization in 1913) until receiver W. R. Freeman agreed to give them a larger measure of control. As the Denver *Post* heatedly accused Freeman of waterlogging the road and of a secret intent to junk the property, 280 of its unpaid employees struck, tying up all freight traffic. At this point the government took over for the duration.[28]

Meanwhile, the Rio Grande proceeded under federal government sponsorship, its income guaranteed and the payment of interest and tax obligations ordered periodically by the courts. In the spring of 1920 President Wilson signed the Esch-Cummins bill, providing for the return of all government-operated railroads to their owners on March 1. For the Rio Grande this was hardly emancipation day; it was still in receivership.

27. Denver *Post,* Jan. 26, Feb. 2, May 12, 1918.
28. See ibid., March–Aug. 1918.

II. *After murder singing generally follows*

BY THE FALL OF 1920 the Rio Grande, still in receivership, was in such a weakened financial condition that its creditors forced the property onto the auction block. A few months earlier, a short time after the road was released from federal government control, the Equitable Trust Company renewed its campaign to collect the judgment held against the railroad. By a New York court order the financial house gained permission to sell approximately two million dollars worth of the Rio Grande securities it held as collateral. Then it pressed hard for a collection of the remaining portion of the amount due. On September 25 Judge Walter H. Sanborn, acting for Judge Robert E. Lewis of the United States District Court at Denver, signed a decree ordering the sale.[1]

The move caused some long overdue questions to be asked by Coloradans. The *Rocky Mountain News* summed up the matter in an editorial:

> The principal railroad system of Colorado is about to be sold "under the Hammer" on notes given to guarantee the construction of another railroad system, well beyond the boundaries of this state. This does not sound very good. The Colorado railroad system was kept impoverished for years as wet nurse to this other system, and, strange as it may appear nobody in Colorado, that we know of, entered a single protest. We do not know what is to become of the Colorado railroad that is to be disposed of to make good the losses of a foreign road, but we do know that Colorado citizens are coming to the conclusion that if they do not protect themselves nobody else will do it.[2]

The same newspaper, a few days earlier, had pointed out the fact that the sale would wipe out the common and preferred stock of the beleaguered railroad, shares that were then valued at 2 and $3\frac{1}{8}$, respectively. The Missouri Pacific held at the end of 1918 some 98,000 shares of preferred, but its confidence in the Rio Grande's future was so small that the stock had been disposed of at an average of $16 a share. In 1920 the Missouri company tried to sell its Rio Grande common stock, but found a market for only a small part of it. Meanwhile, that railroad reinvested in protected D&RG bonds. Having got out from under, it was now prepared to watch with interest any bankruptcy proceedings that might take place in Denver.[3]

The sale date, set for November 20, sent minority stockholders into a flurry of activity. On November 1 their attorneys commenced arguments before Judge Robert Lewis in Denver, contending for a postponement. A sharp attack was launched against the methods of George

1. Denver *Post*, Sept. 25, 1920.
2. *Rocky Mountain News*, Oct. 10, 1920.
3. Ibid., Oct. 6, 1920. Hall, *Reports*, Vol. 113.

Gould and his associates, who were charged with disrupting the finances of the road and of bringing about the "peculiar conditions" prevailing within the corporation.[4] They asked that the judgment be set aside. Three weeks later, and just three days prior to the time set for the sale, Judges Lewis and Sanborn denied the motion for postponement. Said the court: "This railroad has now been under receivership for almost three years and more than two-thirds of that time it has been operated by the government. Its physical condition has deteriorated both in rolling stock and safety of the road beds and we believe that the order of sale should stand."[5] A final endeavor to postpone proceedings was turned down on November 19. The next day the sale took place in Denver.

The Denver and Rio Grande was sold for five million dollars, the minimum amount acceptable by the court. About a hundred curious spectators were on hand, principally railroad employees, but only one bid was made. J. F. Bowie, representing the new Denver and Rio Grande Western Railroad Company that had been chartered a few days before in the State of Delaware, presided over the obsequies in what the Denver *Post* called the "last act in the drama of the financial wrecking of the Rio Grande." Or as the paper remarked in another instance, "A parent was sold at auction . . . to satisfy the debts of its child."[6] The final services were brief; only forty-nine minutes were required to perform them. When someone inquired of Bowie if any provision had been made to protect the stockholders of the old company, his response was equally perfunctory: "They will get nothing." The bondholders, in effect, paid themselves five million dollars and squeezed out the stockholders who held almost eighty-eight million dollars worth of common and preferred stock. Ten days after the sale, the new company was incorporated in the State of Colorado for fifty million dollars.[7]

The deed was done, but not quite. The court's confirmation of the sale was necessary, and to prevent it the aggrieved stockholders launched a fight that lasted eight months. They struck their first blow

4. Denver *Post*, Nov. 1, 1920. Minutes D&RG Board of Directors, Nov. 4, 1920, D&RG Archives. *Jefferson M. Levy, et al., v. Equitable Trust Co. of New York*, transcript of record, U.S. Circuit Court of Appeals, Eighth District, No. 4763; on appeal from District Court of the U.S. for the District of Colorado, filed Dec. 6, 1920.

5. Denver *Post*, Nov. 17, 1920.

6. Ibid., Nov. 20, 21, 1920.

7. Ibid., Nov. 30, 1920. *Deseret News*, Nov. 20, 1920.

at the receiver, Alexander Baldwin, asking his dismissal on the ground that he had failed to protect the rights of the stockholders "on account of his position as vice-president of the Western Pacific, whose interests are radically hostile to those of the Denver & Rio Grande Railroad company and its stockholders."[8] This demand availed them nothing, but the loud and public outcries of "robbery" moved Judges Lewis and Sanborn to order a postponement of confirmation until March 25, 1921. In commenting upon the stay, counsel Arthur M. Wickwire of the minority stockholders committee took occasion to express his views on the fate of the Rio Grande:

> It has been subjected to the most gigantic, systematic and brazen looting of any railroad property by Wall Street financiers within the past decade, wherein minority stockholders have been robbed of more than $65,000,000. . . . Not satisfied with having inflicted such great loss upon the Denver & Rio Grande, the interlockers proceeded to procure a judgment against the Denver & Rio Grande for $38,000,000 additional, on the allegation that the acts into which they themselves had forced the company constituted a breach of contract.[9]

Wickwire's group, asserting that it had control of 100,000 shares of stock, proposed to buy the road for ten million dollars, or a figure that was double the amount offered by the bondholders. To prove their intentions the court required an advance of $100,000 payable before March 25. Two facts militated against success: they could not produce that much cash, and if they did, the bondholders could raise the bid all the way to thirty-six million without having to produce any money, since they held a judgment the unpaid balance of which came to that amount. The minority stockholders attempted to satisfy the requirement of $100,000 in earnest money by providing a bond of that size, but Judge Lewis refused to accept it. On March 28, 1921, the court confirmed the sale of November 20.

In a last ditch stand Wickwire laid his case before Senator A. B. Cummins, chairman of the Senate Interstate Commerce Committee. He renewed his charges that the directors of the Rio Grande had deliberately caused default upon the interest of first-mortgage bonds, with the result that the foreclosure also wiped out the second mortgage

8. Denver *Post,* Feb. 6, 1921.
9. Ibid., March 6, 1921.

and some thirty million dollars worth of promissory notes held by the Rio Grande. In effect, about fifty-five million dollars were subtracted from the equity of the Rio Grande stockholders. Then the directorate of the Western Pacific, which interlocked with that of the Rio Grande, stood by while the Equitable brought suit to recover another thirty-eight million. "This masterly stroke of high finance permitted the tail to wag the dog," said Wickwire. "For the Rio Grande, instead of being a creditor in the sum of $55,000,000, became a debtor in the sum of $38,000,000."[10]

Continuing the attack, the attorney told newsmen that incorporation of the new Denver and Rio Grande Western Railroad Company in Delaware made it a legal anomaly and a "tramp" corporation. The fugitive, operating under the notoriously lax tax laws of Delaware, was not permitted to own or operate a railroad in that state. In a letter to E. E. Clark, chairman of the Interstate Commerce Commission, Wickwire requested "on behalf of some 6,000 victimized stockholders" that the Commission "make rigid examination into the reasons why the plans and the ultimate purposes of the Western Pacific interests require them to seek to transfer the title of a railroad system located in the Rocky Mountains into a corporation created on the banks of the Delaware River."[11] On July 11, 1921, the Interstate Commerce Commission instituted an investigation of the Western Pacific and the Rio Grande to determine the manner in which business was being done by these railroads.

The pending investigation of the two railroads did not occasion any further delay in transforming the old Rio Grande into a new corporation. On July 27, Judges Lewis and Sanborn authorized the action, and four days later the old company passed out of existence. The new era was inaugurated with a banquet given on July 31 by Alvin W. Krech, chairman of the board of directors and president of the Equitable Trust Company. That evening Krech and his officials dined in Denver's famed Brown Palace, signifying the victory of the financiers. With them was Joseph H. Young, a relative of Brigham and former head of the Norfolk Southern Railway, the first president of the new railroad.

The high hopes for the future reflected in the toasts that evening were to fall far short of realization. The railroad the Western Pacific

10. Ibid., May 17, 1921.
11. Ibid., May 20, 1921.

investors had bought up for small change was in serious need of a thorough and expensive rehabilitation. And the worst was yet to come. During 1921 the road suffered not only financially and so severely that it failed by two million dollars to meet its fixed charges, but the spring washouts that year were the worst old-time employees could remember. In early June the Arkansas River overflowed, inundating Pueblo with a flood of major proportions. A good deal of yard equipment and one whole train were washed into the river. Service was disrupted for days and the expenses mounted to very discouraging proportions. Even worse, cloudbursts hit the line all summer, periodically disrupting traffic at a time of heavy tourist travel.

The deteriorating condition of the railroad's business can be seen in its employment record at this time. Between January 1 and March 1, 1921, the company laid off 1486 men, explaining that a 50 percent decline in traffic necessitated the move.[12] Two weeks later another 565 men were let go at Salt Lake City, leaving only 184 to maintain the shops in that city. Later that spring some of the men were returned to work, as seasonal traffic picked up, but when winter came there were more layoffs. By January 1922 Denver's Burnham shops were being operated by a skeleton force of 250 men, shops that normally used 1,000 workers. Labor's attitude toward the new management was revealed in an open letter, written by J. A. Bodine, chairman of the Federated Shop Crafts of the railroad, to the line's employees. It said, in part: "If the poor misguided employees who remained in the service, as well as those who may enter the service, have to depend on the faith that the D. & R. G. W. R. R. will keep with them then God help them. This railroad has not, and did not keep faith with its former employees with whom they had signed agreements."[13]

With employee morale low and public confidence sinking to even greater depths, the new owners found themselves in serious difficulties. There were few expressions of surprise around Denver when, in the summer of 1922, new foreclosure proceedings were instituted against the company. The Bankers Trust Company of New York and the New York Trust Company, holders of mortgages amounting to more than fifty-two million dollars, forced the action. These were not debts contracted since the creation of the new company but mortgages of the old Denver and Rio Grande, assumed with the purchase of the road

12. Ibid., March 2, 1921.
13. *Rocky Mountain News*, July 20, 1922.

a year earlier. As Henry McAllister, Jr., attorney for the Rio Grande, put it: "About all the purchasers acquired, therefore, was control of the road, as it had been involved in constant litigation since."[14] The New York financial houses asked foreclosure on the ground that interest payments had been defaulted in October 1921 and April 1922.

On July 21 President Joseph H. Young was named receiver by Federal Judges Robert E. Lewis and J. Foster Symes. In vain, Charles A. Boston, attorney for the New York Trust Company, protested the appointment, arguing that it might be prejudicial to the interests of the bondholders to have an official of the road act in that capacity. Not only was this objection ignored, but Judge Lewis had some plans for the railroad that would not be well received by those seeking interest on their bonds:

> It is common knowledge that the road is badly out of repair. When the case came into this court before, at the time of the forming of the Denver & Rio Grande Western railroad out of the old Denver company, the railroad conditions were promising. The Western Pacific company took the road over, but they have done little with it. The present owners have not seen fit to keep it in condition, and when it comes into this court we shall see that it is put in condition and we shall see that done before it is turned back to the owners. Furthermore, it will be the policy of this court that no interest shall be paid on the bonds of the road until it is completely rehabilitated and the public thus safeguarded.[15]

The Rio Grande's crying need for rehabilitation was more than an accepted fact in Colorado: it was reaching scandal proportions. Frustrated shippers, particularly those living in the western part of the state, had only the choicest of unprintable words to describe the road's service. Newspaper editors expressed the sentiments in strong but somewhat less violent language. When a couple of Durango cattlemen drove a beef herd through Aztec en route to New Mexico, where they planned to ship by the Santa Fe, the small Colorado paper gave vent to its feelings about the home railroad. The drivers "had expected

14. Ibid., July 8, 1922. *New York Trust Co. v. Denver and Rio Grande Railroad Co.* Bill of Complaint filed in the U.S. Court of Colorado, July 7, 1922, Receivership Record, Vol. 1, D&RGW railroad offices, Denver.

15. *Rocky Mountain News,* July 22, 1922.

to ship to Denver over the D. & R. G., but as that road is strictly on the bum and can't furnish anything but disappointments they were compelled to drive 185 miles to Gallup." Juan N. Jaquez, a sheepman at Aztec, encountered the same difficulty when he tried to ship 1200 lambs to market. "Juan has peculiar admiration for the incomparable D. & R. G. and its rotten service," said the local editor, who commented that the Rio Grande stock trains "are seldom behind schedule dates more than two months."

The Cortez *Journal* assailed the Rio Grande periodically during the early '20s, as did the Telluride *Journal,* the Creede *Candle,* and the Montrose *Press.* So angered were farmers who tried to ship their products that in December 1922 the Montrose County Farm Bureau got up a resolution asking their legislators to investigate the breakdown in Rio Grande transportation service.[16]

A few days after the road was put into receivership, the court authorized immediate improvements in the amount of $2,100,000. Heavier rails were planned for several hundred miles of the road, the yards in several cities were to be expanded, and more employees were to be hired. Some of the narrow-gauge sections in southwestern Colorado still used thirty-pound rails, no heavier than those of Palmer's earliest days on the railroad. That fall, Young presented a long-range plan of improvement envisaging the expenditure of some twenty-three million dollars during the next three years, to which the Gunnison *Empire* replied: "After murder singing generally follows." About two-thirds of the amount was anticipated in earnings, the remainder to be raised by the sale of receiver's certificates.[17] By June 1923, nearly a year after his appointment as receiver, Young had spent almost eight million dollars on the improvement program.

The now-familiar question, "What's to become of the Rio Grande?" once again faced Coloradans. There were some outsiders who were willing to provide an answer. The Western Pacific, holder of the road's common stock, and the Missouri Pacific, in control of a large amount of the bonds, proposed to adopt the orphan. The suggestion brought a sharp protest from Richard Sutro, chairman of the Protective Committee for the Refunding and Adjustment Bonds, who warned: "The proposed plan, if carried out, will make the Denver system again the pawn of the Missouri Pacific and Western Pacific interests." He elab-

16. Clippings in file 3623, D&RG Archives.
17. *Rocky Mountain News,* Oct. 6, 1922. Gunnison *Empire,* Dec. 7, 1922.

39. Example of Deterioration of Line during World War I and early 1920s. The results of neglect occasioned by the earlier financial fiasco involved in construction of the Western Pacific are quite evident in this view of the D&RG's main line at Shoshone Tunnel 1 in Glenwood Canyon.

40. Soldier Summit, Utah, 1920s. From November 1919 to November 1929, the D&RG operated this large engine terminal and freight yard astride the backbone of the Wasatch Range. From the summit, light engines were dispatched down the hill eastward to Helper or westward to Thistle, to help trains back up. Only a few houses appear in this view; five years later more than 100 cottages had been constructed as employee homes by the railroad.

orated his objections: "Far from eliminating the difficulties of the Denver system, the consummation of such a plan would in effect, in the opinion of the committee of which I am chairman, seriously jeopardize the interest of the refunding and adjustment bondholders who in time might be wiped out by these connecting interests—just as the stockholders were in the past wiped out by those very same interests." It had been demonstrated, he pointed out, that the Rio Grande was quite able to stand on its own as an independent line, that it had developed about 80 per cent of the traffic passing over it, and had given connecting lines about four times the traffic it received from them. There was no reason why it should be a subsidiary of other railroads. "The Rio Grande is the principal railroad system in the State of Colorado. While it was under the control of the Missouri Pacific and Western Pacific, surplus earnings of the Rio Grande were used to further the interests of those connecting lines, and to develop schemes that were primarily designed for their benefit, instead of maintaining the line itself in condition to give service." He strongly condemned the notion of once again putting the Rio Grande in the hands of "foreign" railroads, "whose interests are wholly divergent from the interest of the people of Colorado."[18]

Denver businessmen found themselves in wholehearted agreement with these sentiments. Several factors gave them reason to be concerned about the future of their city's place in the transportation world. In February 1922 the Moffat Road, still in the throes of the most serious kind of financial difficulty, had asked the federal government for a loan exceeding six million dollars and had been refused on the ground that the line was too poor a risk. Only a few months elapsed before the Rio Grande was again in receivership and more or less up for grabs. During this time a bill had passed the state legislature authorizing state assistance in building the tunnel under James Peak that Moffat had dreamed of until his death. On the face of the situation, it seems ironic that the expensive bore was to be made in behalf of a road that ended in the wilderness of western Colorado and was on the verge of financial collapse. There were, however, several possibilities that brightened the picture. The existence of a tunnel would eliminate the major obstacle to winter travel on the Moffat line; Moffat tracks, at one point, passed about forty miles from those of the

18. Denver *Times*, Jan. 18, 1922.

Rio Grande. A cutoff between Orestod on the Moffat line and Dotsero on the D&RG would permit Rio Grande trains, through a joint trackage agreement, to move straight west of Denver, shortening the route to Salt Lake City by 175 miles. For over half a century Denver had wanted a position on one of the main cross-country lines; here was an opportunity to have it.

The tunnel, to be discussed in the following chapter, was the key— or perhaps more appropriately, the keyhole—to Denver's quest. With David Moffat it had been a vision, an ideal, a great railroad plan. Denver had demonstrated its enthusiasm on countless occasions, patting Moffat on the back and saying, in effect, "Go to it; spend your money." But now the promoter was dead, and his transportation brain child was almost ready for the grave. Normally, Denver business interests might have lamented the development over their morning coffee and perhaps have made mild protestations to the effect that "something ought to be done about it."

The development that brought northern Colorado businessmen to their feet, ready for emergency action, was the prospect that their part of the state was about to be eliminated permanently from the transcontinental picture. In accordance with the philosophy behind the Esch-Cummins Transportation Act of 1920, federal rail-experts were recommending the consolidation of smaller lines. The multiplicity of little railroads was believed to be choking the field, overlapping, and generally retarding the development of an efficient railroad system.

The prospect that either the Santa Fe or the Union Pacific might absorb the Rio Grande was extremely alarming to Denver business interests. William G. Evans, son of Colorado business pioneer John Evans and himself prominent in commercial affairs, frequently acted as a spokesman for Denver merchants. A strong proponent of an independent Rio Grande, Evans had for some time condemned outside control of local roads. In January 1921 he told newsmen: "I believe some of the big transcontinental railroads have partitioned Colorado very much as Poland was partitioned by the Allied powers. The big roads do not have to extend and improve their lines to hold their territory, and they prevent private and local enterprises from building needed lines by shutting off their credit in New York." Pointing his finger at eastern financiers, he accused them of manipulating western railroads to suit their own wishes. The most recent example was the

Moffat Tunnel. "Some of the strongest of those New York bankers have been aggressively opposed for many years to the construction of the Moffat Road and tunnel because, if they were built, it would take some considerable lucrative through business away from roads to the north and to the south of Colorado in which they are heavily interested."[19]

Evans agreed with government rail-experts that if the Rio Grande became a part of any major system it ought to be the Burlington, for this would create a strong transcontinental line between the Santa Fe and the Union Pacific, one that would benefit northern and northwestern Colorado. He contended that the "development of Colorado's western mining, agricultural and oil resources depends on establishing a main transcontinental line through the heart of the state."[20]

In March 1923 a statewide committee was formed to fight any proposals aimed at consolidation of the Rio Grande with main lines running either north or south of Colorado. William G. Evans headed the group.[21] The Denver *Times* supported the purposes of the committee in a strongly-worded editorial:

> The economic future of Denver and Colorado is involved in the disposition of the Rio Grande Railroad in the controversy now under way regarding the zoning of transcontinental railroads. An independent Rio Grande system, controlled by local authority, will insure growth and prosperity not only to Denver, but to the state. . . . If the actual and complete independence of the Rio Grande is not preserved, this road and the Denver & Salt Lake [Moffat Road] must at least be grouped with either the Burlington or the Rock Island system. . . . On the other hand, affiliation of the local systems with the Santa Fe, which has also been proposed, would isolate Denver, divert legitimate traffic from this city and practically remove her from transcontinental routing. . . . The history of the Rio Grande and the history of Colorado are largely one and the same. The heyday of the Rio Grande was a period of acknowledged prosperity for the state as a whole. The absorption of the line by the Gould interests marked a period of decline which was accelerated toward receivership by the Western Pa-

19. Denver *Post,* Jan. 30, 1921.
20. Denver *Times,* Aug. 11, 1922.
21. Ibid., March 1, 1923.

cific venture, until today we find the local road a subsidiary in the hands of the Missouri Pacific and the Western Pacific and in the hands of a court appointee. The necessity of recovering authority over the road, which is an integral part of Colorado and her progress, is becoming more and more apparent in order to render it independent in thought and action and in control of its own policy. Outside domination would be done away with and the system would again become a Colorado institution, instead of a railway plaything in the hands of Wall Street interests.[22]

Denver's anxiety for a union between the Rio Grande and the Burlington system was not shared by officials of the latter road. Hale Holden, president of the CB&Q, stated at an Interstate Commerce Commission hearing that he thought some of the other roads were better prepared to rehabilitate the Rio Grande than his company. He recommended combining all western railroads into four great systems, with either the Southern Pacific or the Santa Fe railroad absorbing the Colorado road. William Z. Ripley, Harvard economics professor retained by the Interstate Commerce Commission to study railroad groupings, did not agree with this conclusion. He thought the Burlington, serving Denver from the east, was the logical connection.

To the dismay of Denver's boosters, the Interstate Commerce Commission discarded the professor's plan in favor of the notion of a Santa Fe merger. In mid-April 1923 Colorado Governor William E. Sweet addressed a gathering of 150 Denver businessmen, outlining the impending danger: "Unless this city cares to witness a period of great retrogression it must fight to the last ditch any sinister influence which will run counter to the noble work started by David H. Moffat in 1902. Only by linking up roads running through Colorado with the Burlington will independent competition with the Union Pacific or the Santa Fe route be assured."[23] William Evans, meanwhile, carried the argument to Interstate Commerce Commission hearings held at Denver. He lectured its examiners on Colorado's geography. This, he pointed out, was an interior state, peculiarly situated with respect to physical characteristics and peculiarly dependent upon rail transportation. It had no navigable streams. Its vast extent of 103,000 square miles was bisected by the Continental Divide, whose towering granite walls long

22. Ibid., March 3, 1923.
23. Ibid., April 14, 1923.

had impeded the flow of commerce between East and West. Wagon and automobile roads crossing this barrier were closed for long periods during winter months. Even eastern and western segments of Colorado were subdivided by great river drainages, making commercial intercourse within those regions difficult. To the east there had been settlement and growth, largely because of the existence of railroads; in the western reaches this happy condition had been delayed because of the absence of railroads. "The western part of Colorado requires more railroads built through it to make its resources available and hasten its further settlement," he told the federal officials. "With adequate railroad transportation facilities provided for it, the western portion of Colorado would soon be supporting well, from its own productiveness, a population far larger than the present population of the entire State."

He argued that the proposed consolidation would kill any chances northwestern Colorado had for rail service because it would deflect the established flow of traffic into the state, turning it toward the Santa Fe system. More than that, even such cities as Trinidad, Pueblo, Colorado Springs, and Denver would suffer, for no longer would they benefit from railroad competition, and hence the service "upon which their commerce has been largely built up" would decline. Along with his fellow Denverites, he realized that once the Santa Fe took over there was little prospect that the capital city ever would sit astride a transcontinental system. Such a development had to be prevented at any cost. As a final buttress to his case, Evans contended that absorption by the Santa Fe would constitute a violation of Colorado's constitution. He held that it would violate that provision which prohibited the leasing, one to the other, or the consolidation of parallel or competing lines.[24]

The Denver press became quite emotional about the danger to northern Colorado commercial life. The *Times* warned editorially that "Colorado is in one of the gravest hours of its industrial history." If Interstate Commerce Commission recommendations with respect

24. Ibid., April 17, 1923. William G. Evans, "Railroad Consolidation and the Tunnel," *Municipal Facts* (Aug.–Sept. 1923), pp. 9–11. For some time Evans had been concerned about the power of outside influences over Colorado's railroads. As head of a special committee of the Denver Civic and Commercial Association, he said in Jan. 1919 that it "would be pusillanimous for Colorado people to sit by and leave the determination of its fundamental railroad questions and rate questions to men in Washington, or bankers in New York." Evans to Finlay L. MacFarland, Jan. 13, 1919, in William Evans correspondence, held by John Evans, Denver.

to the Rio Grande were carried out, the editor predicted, "this state will lie stagnant like a Sargasso sea, while the streams of traffic across the continent sweep by to the north and the south. Colorado would pay daily tribute to the Union Pacific on the north and the Santa Fe on the south. . . . Vassalage would never have been more complete. A new Magna Charta would have to be written for Colorado. Now is the time for defense in a cause that is just."[25] James A. Marsh, counsel for the Colorado Committee on Railroad Consolidation, drafted a memorial for presentation to federal officials at Washington, D.C. "We want to make the voice of Colorado's objection to the proposed merging of the D. and R. G. W. and the Santa Fe railroads so strong that it will arouse public sentiment throughout the entire country, echo to the Atlantic coast, and assail the eardrums of the Interstate Commerce Commission at Washington in tones that will admit of no denial," the attorney told reporters.[26] The hue and cry that was raised in Denver and its outlying districts appears to have carried some weight. The Interstate Commerce Commission dropped its sponsorship of the Santa Fe merger.

No sooner was one threat warded off than another materialized to take its place. The Missouri Pacific and the Western Pacific renewed their desire to share ownership of the Rio Grande. In June 1923 Kuhn, Loeb, and Company and the Equitable Trust Company came forward with a plan to finance the project. There was newspaper talk about the prospect that the new owners would build a Dotsero cutoff upon completion of the Moffat Tunnel, thus affording Denver its long-desired short cut to Salt Lake City through a trackage agreement with the Moffat line. Denver interests, however, had no assurance that the cutoff would be built. The Missouri Pacific, its western terminus at Pueblo, might decide otherwise. The boards of directors of both the Missouri Pacific and the Western Pacific and three bondholders' committees approved the purchase idea toward the end of the month.[27]

Again, Colorado businessmen objected. They did not want to see the Rio Grande released from court custody until there was some assurance that the railroad would be put into better shape and that

25. Denver *Times*, April 18, 1923. Testimony of Professor R. D. George, geologist, University of Colorado, James Marsh questioning, ICC hearings at Denver, April 16–20, 1923. Copy in William Evans correspondence.

26. Denver *Times*, May 1, 1923.

27. *Rocky Mountain News*, June 20, 21, 1923.

the interests of the users would be given a greater measure of consideration. In September representatives of five Colorado improvement committees met with Governor William Sweet, urging him to fight the latest reorganization proposal. They argued that the plan did not properly protect the public interest. It had no provisions for the urgently needed improvements; on the contrary, the reorganized company would be so overcapitalized that revenues needed for betterments would be funneled off in interest and dividends. The State of Colorado made the objections formal by filing a protest, through Attorney General Russell W. Fleming, in which the reorganization plan was opposed.

Meanwhile, Judge Symes held a tight rein on the Rio Grande. When Joseph Young resigned as receiver, Symes appointed Thomas H. Beacom to replace him. President Hale Holden of the Burlington made the recommendation. Supporters of the railroad regarded the receivership as a truly protective situation, one that was beneficial to its patrons. Denver's *Rocky Mountain News* editorialized on the subject, asserting that in recent years the railroad's dilapidated condition had hindered Colorado's development. "A receivership for this road, paradoxical as it may seem, has been a Godsend to most of the State," said the editor.[28]

In mid-December 1923 the Interstate Commerce Commission approved the reorganization plan with one dissenting vote. The State of Colorado quickly protested the decision, reiterating the belief that the new company would be so overcapitalized that no money would be available for badly needed improvements. According to the complainants, another receivership was certain to follow such a course as the Western Pacific and the Missouri Pacific had mapped out for the Rio Grande. Governor William Sweet openly called the plan a hoax on the people of Colorado. Contending that the home road would be in first-class condition if the Western Pacific had not bled it white, he urged that interest payment amounting to $1,250,000, due on January 1, be defaulted so that the funds could be used for betterments.[29] Judge Symes, however, did not permit the default and thereby kept the Rio Grande off the auction block for the time being.

In the early months of 1924 the Interstate Commerce Commission agreed to reopen hearings upon the insistence of the State of Colorado

28. Ibid., Oct. 6, 1923.
29. Denver *Times*, Dec. 15, 18, 22, 1923.

that it had the strongest of objections to reorganization plans. At these sessions the prospective buyers made certain modifications in their offer, hopeful that the move would quiet some of the objections. They proposed that interest on the new mortgage bonds be paid at the discretion of the directors, and they agreed to tone down some of the clauses protecting preferred stockholders. In addition, the Western Pacific and Missouri Pacific promised to purchase at least two million dollars worth of the proposed refunding and improvement bond issue, and even an additional million, if it proved necessary to consummation of the reorganization plan. The concessions were not enough for Colorado's attorney general, Wayne Williams, who argued that they did not solve the problem of overcapitalization. "The State of Colorado will stand pat on its original position," he announced.[30]

The Missouri Pacific persisted in its efforts to buy half the Rio Grande's common stock from the Western Pacific and become a joint owner in the Colorado railroad. Colorado's answer was unchanged: such a partnership would result in repetition of the old practice of exploiting the line in behalf of the parent roads. The State's representatives did not veer from their contention that the proposal was unsound, that it was contrary to public interest, and that the Western Pacific holdings sought by the Missouri Pacific were illegally obtained by the Western Pacific.[31] Interstate Commerce Commission members listened politely and then granted the Missouri Pacific permission to make the purchase. Not even the State of Colorado could gain independence for its principal railroad.

The outcry was loud and acrimonious. The *Rocky Mountain News* responded to the decision with an editorial entitled "Throttling the State." The decision, said the journal, "in a nutshell is, that shipper and consumer are to be saddled with a railroad property excessively over-capitalized and which is to be under the joint control of the Missouri Pacific and Western Pacific railroads and used by them as a feeder for their railroads with secondary regard for the needs of the State." Fight the Commission's decision to the very end, was the editor's recommendation, for if this merger came to pass, the territory served by the Rio Grande would pay a very heavy toll. "And it is not to be forgotten that the unfortunate Colorado railroad, under the control of Gould, was bankrupted and rendered unsafe for ordinary

30. *Rocky Mountain News,* March 6, 1924.
31. Ibid., May 14, 1924.

traffic and its resources used to build the Western Pacific which had not a foot of lines within this State. Tragedy and irony run through the seam of the Denver & Rio Grande railroad."[32]

Strenuous efforts were made, on the part of the minority stockholders, to keep the road in receivership until it could be placed on a paying basis. One of these investors asked Judge Symes to establish an upset price of $42,500,000, but the judge denied the request, saying that such a figure would discourage all prospective buyers. In September 1924 the court announced the road's sale and fixed an upset price of $17,935,700. Late in the next month the transaction took place with the reorganization managers, Kuhn, Loeb, and Company and the Equitable Trust Company, purchasing it at the minimum price. The date was October 29.

Within a month Judge Symes confirmed the sale, and on December 20 the Western Pacific and the Missouri Pacific railroads assumed control of the Rio Grande. J. S. Pyeatt of Houston, formerly head of the Gulf Coast Lines, became the new president. In an apparent effort to placate the apprehensions of Coloradans, the new chief executive announced that the road "will be operated as an independent road in the interests of itself rather than its owners." He quickly qualified his statement, saying that while the Missouri Pacific and the Western Pacific railroads each owned one-half of the stock, the interests of the Rio Grande would be the chief interest. This was followed by a neat bit of double talk: "We will, of course, do all we properly can to work together."[33] Those who had observed outside control of the Rio Grande for a quarter of a century entertained no doubts that the interests of the parent roads would receive first consideration. Their Baby Road was still very much a pawn in the larger game.

32. Ibid., June 13, 1924.
33. Ibid., Dec. 20, 1924.

12. We built the Tunnel!

IT WOULD BE DIFFICULT to single out the most critical period of the Rio Grande's history. Since the days of Palmer, crisis had come close to being the normal situation on the road, with peace and prosperity a fleeting ideal never fully realized. But in June 1923 two events occurred that were to be major forces in the railroad's destiny. The impact of these developments, one of which was a negative influence and the other positive, had a decided effect upon the company's subsequent history. It was a time of decision for the railroad, and the mold for the modern Rio Grande was fixed.

In that month of June, New York bankers came forward with a plan to finance the purchase of the road in behalf of the Western Pacific and the Missouri Pacific, a plan that was accepted by Judge J. Foster Symes, and one that was put into operation in 1924 over the loudest of protestations from northern Colorado. Time was to reveal the weaknesses of the decision, and when the railroad came back into the protective custody of Symes over a decade later, he was not to make the same mistake again. In the intervening period the jurist had learned much about railroading in Colorado. The other event that was to play such a vital part in the railroad's future was the unanimous decision handed down by the United States Supreme Court on June 11, upholding the validity of the Moffat Tunnel Act, which had been signed by Governor Oliver H. Shoup on May 12, 1922.[1]

Except for the brief period when David Moffat was president of the Rio Grande, there had been no serious consideration given by that railroad to building straight west of Denver. It was generally agreed by all concerned that the proposal was a worthy ideal and one that would, if carried out, shorten the distance to Salt Lake City. But since the late '80s, the Rio Grande either had been under management that was more interested in dividends than improvements or its financial condition was such that any major expenditures were out of the question.

As mentioned in an earlier chapter, Moffat had spent some $200,000 of Rio Grande money while he was president of that road, to make surveys in the vicinity of James Peak. The roars of protest from the bondholders had not shaken his belief in the desirability of the idea; on the contrary, its possibilities continued to fascinate him for over a decade. By the turn of the twentieth century his ventures in banking and mining had made him a very wealthy man, but he was not content with the mere possession of money. "I am not satisfied to do nothing," he told one of his friends. "I want to be doing something new—I want to be building or developing some enterprise. I get my pleasure that way." The direction this restlessness was to take was revealed in a message he dispatched one day to two of his Denver associates: "I

1. McMechen, *Moffat Tunnel*, *I*, 161–62. *Rocky Mountain News*, May 13, 1922.

have decided to build a steam railroad from Denver to Salt Lake City."[2]

From the day Moffat's road was incorporated in 1902, it had been a threat to the Rio Grande. The explanation of the failure of the new line to reach its destination lies in the forbidding nature of Denver's mountain backdrop, the financial panic of 1907, faintheartedness on the part of some Coloradans who withheld their support when it was most needed, and the knife-wielding George Gould. That the son of Jay Gould should have placed any obstacle at his disposal in Moffat's path is perfectly understandable. His efforts at building the Western Pacific to provide the last link in his transcontinental system were endangered by the prospect of a competing railroad across Colorado, one that other major roads visualized as filling a gap in their own transcontinental aspirations. The young financier was friendly with a group of eastern and Dutch capitalists who were backing Moffat, and when he withdrew his support, the others followed him. By 1907, Moffat had exhausted his personal fortune of nine million dollars. Four years later he was dead.

In the days that followed World War I there had been a growing fear among Denver and northern Colorado business interests that the long-desired airline to Salt Lake City would never become a reality. The Moffat line was stopped at Craig, in western Colorado, and its financial condition was so weak that the prospect of completion was dim. The tremendous operating costs of the company provided little room for hope of profitable operation in the future. The principal obstacle was the tortuous passage over the Continental Divide. Winter storms closed the road for weeks at a time, and even in the summer months the climb "over the hill" was exceedingly expensive. Four engines of the Mallet type were required to pull twenty-two freight cars across, and if only two cars were added to such a train, another engine had to be included. Although the distance from Denver to Tabernash on the western side was only ninety miles, these engines labored from fourteen to sixteen hours to make the run.[3]

The answer was a tunnel. It would reduce the elevation by some 2400 feet, eliminate about twenty-three miles of track in that particular vicinity, offer a maximum grade of 2 per cent, and largely solve the problem of blizzards high above the timberline on Rollins Pass,

2. McMechen, *1*, 105–06.
3. Ibid., pp. 134–35.

41. Havoc Wrought by Pueblo Flood, June 1921.

42. Typical Washout Scene on D&Rg Line, 1920s. The devastating flood of June 3, 1921, when heavy cloudbursts in the mountains to the west of Pueblo sent the Arkansas river on a rampage, obliterated many miles of both Rio Grande and Santa Fe tracks in this area.

11,500 feet above sea level. To gain some notion of savings in operating costs, one has only to consider the Moffat Road authorities' estimate that 41 per cent of the total figure was due to fighting snow blockades, most of which occurred near the Continental Divide.

The idea of tunneling the Colorado Rockies was older than the state itself. From 1867, when surveyor Andrew N. Rogers of Central City proposed a bore through a hogback not far from the site of the present Moffat Tunnel, until the 1920s, the advantages of such a project continued to intrigue railroad builders. The physical problem of drilling a six-mile shaft through granite was not the main deterrent. During the intervening years a number of other projects, more ambitious than this one, were carried out. In Europe the Mount Cenis, the St. Gothard, the Simplon, and the Loetschberg tunnels all were longer. The big stumbling block in Colorado was money. None of the interested railroads or other sources of private capital were willing to risk sufficient funds to carry out the plan. Obviously, it would have been a very long-term investment of questionable wisdom. Even after Moffat had thrown his road out as far as Craig, there was little stimulus. Investors were reluctant to come forward with an enormous amount of money for a tunnel that promised little more than a reduction in operating costs for an incompleted railroad whose earning record was poor.

It was at this point, in 1911, that the search for funds turned toward the public coffers. Representative Gaines M. Allen of Denver placed before his legislative colleagues a bill "to promote and increase the general prosperity of the state by constructing a tunnel under and through the base of James Peak, a spur of the Rocky Mountains, to be used for public and semi-private purposes." Moffat Tunnel historian, Edgar McMechen, maintained that the bill was drawn up and introduced by the Denver legislator upon his own responsibility. It would have died in committee had not William Evans backed it. Evans, one of the original incorporators of the Moffat Road, also controlled the Republican organization in Denver. He saw a chance to solve the financial problem, and he bent all efforts toward pushing the bill through the legislature. Known as the State Tunnel Construction Bill, it provided for an issue of four million dollars in bonds to carry out the proposed work with the stipulation that the Moffat Road either complete its line to Salt Lake City or build a Dotsero cutoff. Evans' influence carried the measure through the legislature without diffi-

culty, but Democratic Governor John F. Shafroth let it lie upon his
desk without taking action within the required thirty day period. Under the provisions of Colorado's constitution, this automatically
placed the matter before the voters.[4]

It came before Colorado's electorate at the general election of 1912.
Denver's *Rocky Mountain News* came out strongly for passage on the
ground that the tunnel was the open sesame to the state's industrial
growth and that its construction was in the public interest. The paper
openly admitted that the Moffat Road would not be operated profitably
without this improvement, one that Wall Street and the nation's railway magnates selfishly opposed. The *News* charged that the other
roads—and presumably the Rio Grande was a leading offender:
"[they] fall far short of doing their duty by Denver and the state. . . .
They discriminate against it with their tolls; they hem in its commerce
and industries with adverse discriminating rates. Denver begs and
pleads in vain. . . . The only way Denver can fight and break the
strangle hold they have upon it is with another road—one that will
shoot straight through to the coast, one that will be under obligations
to Denver, one that must build up Denver for the freight and other
traffic that will make it prosperous."[5] The voters turned down the
proposal by a vote of two to one.

The next attempt to carry out the tunnel project with public funds
involved the city of Denver. The Moffat Road, having gone into receivership in 1912, had been purchased that summer by New York
financier Newman Erb, who came forth with his scheme a few days
after the November election defeat. He asked Denver to vote bonds to
pay for two-thirds of the construction cost, with the understanding
that he and his associates would pay the other third. He agreed to pay
the interest on the bond issue and to leave the tunnel's title in the
hands of the city. Other roads would be permitted to use the tunnel
route for a reasonable rental. At the regular city election, held on
May 20, 1913, the bond issue passed by a majority of around ten thousand. The results were challenged immediately. District Judge George
W. Allen called the action valid, but in the spring of 1914 the Colorado Supreme Court reversed the decision, holding that the lending

4. Ibid., pp. 126–28. See also the obituary of William Evans, *Rocky Mountain News*, Oct. 23,
1924.
5. *Rocky Mountain News*, Nov. 1, 10, 1912.

of credit by the city to a private corporation was unconstitutional.[6] Erb next tried to accomplish the task with private capital, offering to produce half the needed funds if Denver businessmen would supply the rest. The community responded, pledging some two and a half million dollars, but Erb failed to live up to his part of the bargain and the latest plan collapsed.

During the early stages of the Erb regime the Denver and Salt Lake, as it was now called, managed to show a profit, but this was accomplished by starving the line. By 1917 the results of the policy were apparent: rolling stock, roadbed, and equipment were in a deteriorating condition. Its operations in the red and unable to pay bond interest, the line went into receivership for the second time in a period of seven years. There was talk that the Moffat Road would be junked with Denver investors salvaging what they could from the wreckage. During January and February, 1918, the entire railroad was tied up for a period of thirty days, not an ounce of life-giving freight moving over its tracks. The last vestiges of David Moffat's expensive dream were about to be wiped from the transportation slate.

But Denver was not ready to give up; rather, in the tradition of a famous American naval officer, it had just begun to fight. In May 1918 Finlay L. MacFarland and his Civic and Commercial Association launched a campaign, the main tenet of which was the solution of the Denver and Salt Lake's problems by the construction of a tunnel. General Palmer's long-time associate, Colonel David C. Dodge, who had been on the Colorado railroad scene since the early '70s, was the association's chief adviser. William G. Evans was as vocal as ever, preaching his tunnel crusade to all who would listen. Jesse Fleming, who had been chairman of the Moffat Tunnel Commission in 1912, matched the eloquence of Evans and took his place with other Denver leaders in the fight. "The Denver & Salt Lake Railroad is not an ordinary railroad," said Fleming. "A railroad is an ordinary railroad until it reaches the Rocky Mountains. When it reaches the Rocky Mountains it isn't an ordinary railroad in any sense of the word." He argued that for years the government had spent millions on river and harbor improvements, with no expectation of having the money returned, desirous only of opening up the commerce of large areas of country. Now, said Fleming, the terrain through which the Moffat Road attempted

6. Ibid., Nov. 19, 1912; May 22, 1913. Denver *Post,* July 8, 1914.

passage was so difficult and expensive for tunnel construction that the federal government had a responsibility similar to that of a large city in need of river or harbor improvement. Beyond the barrier lay valuable coal and oil shale fields; the nation would benefit from their exploitation.[7]

The effort to induce the federal government to bore a tunnel, in the interest of opening up the country or even for reasons of national defense, met with no success. Federal officials, however, did take over the road for the duration of the war, as they did with other lines, and thus the imminent danger of junking was averted. Governmental purchases of over a million dollars worth of receiver's certificates and the payment of a yearly rental fee further aided the harassed line. By the war's end the Moffat Road was again in full-time operation, the bondholders happy that the deficit drain had been stopped by financial first-aid from Washington. In an effort to take advantage of this temporary assistance, the road's backers again took up the matter of saving the line by surgery in the Rockies. It seemed clear by now that only this expensive but necessary operation could assure the patient its life. The tunnel was a more vital necessity than ever.

Again William Evans played a prominent part in the stubbornly-fought campaign. He reasoned that if those sections of the state not apt to be benefited by the tunnel had fought public aid, they should be offered some incentive to arouse their instincts of material gain. Why not propose something for everyone? In Colorado there were several major divides, separating important drainages, where railroad tunnels would improve the local transportation picture. Here was the place to seek support and to allay some of the suspicions about the acquisitiveness of Denver businessmen.

In the spring of 1919 a bill passed the legislature and was signed by Governor Oliver H. Shoup, creating a State Railroad Commission, one of whose members was William Evans. Although the legislature was willing to create a commission, it would not furnish its own creature with funds, and the new group had to turn to the city of Denver for aid. With $10,000 provided by this source, surveys were made for three tunnels. On March 1, 1920, at a well-attended meeting held in Denver's city auditorium, the new tri-tunnel plan was unveiled. Briefly, it envisaged the construction of the Moffat Tunnel, a second

7. Denver *Post*, May 12, 1918.

43. 3500 Series Mallet Compound Engine. Last of the compound locomotives (high pressure steam from the rear cylinders reused at lower pressure in the large front cylinders) purchased new by the Rio Grande. Built by the American Locomotive Company in 1923, they were assigned to helper service over Soldier Summit. Engine 3500 was the final survivor when dismantled in October 1951.

44. 3600 Series Mallet Freight Locomotive, 1928. Pride of the Rio Grande and truly one of man's most impressive creations when working, these simple articulated locomotives epitomized the progress of the Railroad's program of betterments and additions during the mid-twenties. They were forced into retirement in 1955 and 1956 by newer, faster, more economical diesel-electrics.

tunnel through Monarch Pass (separating the Gunnison and Arkansas River drainages), and a third through Cumbres Pass (between
the Rio Grande and San Juan River drainages). While the latter two
were less ambitious than the first, both of them were in D&RG
country, and neither directly benefited Denver. To finance the grand
plan a bond issue was proposed in the amount of $18,500,000. All
three tunnels would be owned and operated by the State of Colorado.

Once again, the voters were asked to approve the use of state funds
for developing Colorado's transportation facilities, this time in the
form of an amendment to the constitution. Evans, the work horse as
always, led a group of fellow businessmen in a campaign that covered
the state. The Railroad Commission used every penny it could lay its
hands on to finance a small army of speakers who preached the tunnel
gospel in every corner of the state.[8]

Headquarters for the opposition was at Pueblo. "Little Pittsburgh"
was the state's principal municipal rival to Denver, and its business
leaders were much concerned about the advantages to be gained from
the Moffat Tunnel by the capital city. So long as James Peak remained
unpierced, Pueblo and the Royal Gorge would be the major gateway
through the Rockies. Southern Colorado could not be convinced that
it should pay for a bond issue to accomplish what the Maker already
had done at the Royal Gorge, particularly as this proposed man-made
cut threatened to siphon off traffic. Some said this was a selfish, dog-in-
the-manger attitude; others held it to be no more than a natural in-
stinct for community self-preservation. It made for some very hot
arguments.

Denver and northern Colorado received encouragement from
neighboring Utah. Simon Bamberger, Utah's first non-Mormon governor, was a strong advocate of the Moffat Tunnel and of the Denver
and Salt Lake Railroad. Early in 1920 he visited Denver, promising
that if Coloradans would dig the tunnel, Utah would build a railroad
eastward to Craig. The tunnel, he said, was a prerequisite. "We would
not be justified in building our road to Craig, the Moffat Road's western terminal, until the tunnel is completed, or until the work is sufficiently advanced to show us that it will be completed." He believed
that a line from Provo to Craig could be built for fifteen million
dollars, and he was sure Utah interests could raise the money.[9]

8. McMechen, *Moffat Tunnel*, *1*, 136–43.
9. Denver *Post*, Jan. 10, 1920.

The intensity of the campaign heightened. Those behind the Moffat Tunnel project were pleased when organizations other than those representing business interests lent their support. The Farmer's Union —more properly, the Farmers' Educational and Cooperative Union of Colorado—endorsed the plan during the winter of 1920. Men who had no personal stake in the venture lent support. A good example was Charles A. Lory, president of Colorado A. and M. College, who was prominent on the platform at some of the pro-tunnel meetings held that year. At the invitation of Mayor Bailey, as many as a hundred mayors and prominent businessmen from western slope towns came to Denver to take part in the discussions.

Support came from the most impartial observer of all: Colorado's winter. In mid-April, at the height of the discussions, one of the most severe blizzards in recent years turned back trains trying to cross mountain passes. The Moffat line, over Rollins Pass, suffered from storms almost every winter, but this one also stopped all Denver and Rio Grande trains in and out of Denver. Tunnel proponents were quick to point out that these blizzards, whose ferocity isolated thousands of people in western Colorado, could be defeated by sending trains under the passes rather than over them. Winter storms were followed by summer floods. Here was more ammunition for the tunnel men. In August 1920 the Arkansas River erupted and damaged a forty-six-mile stretch of the Denver and Rio Grande line in the neighborhood of the Royal Gorge. Canon City was isolated. Denver clucked knowingly and talked of alternate routes to avoid such transportation stoppages.

But oratory and vagaries of the weather were not enough. On November 2 voters went to the polls where they rejected the tri-tunnel proposition. Denver voted for it, three to one, but the measure lost out by 10,000 votes in statewide returns. Southern Colorado had preserved its monopoly in the Royal Gorge, and such determined men as William Evans were handed another defeat. The reverse disheartened a number of those who favored the big tunnel west of Denver, but the hard core of enthusiasts who had fought so hard for the project showed no indication of giving up. The fight went on.

By 1921 Colorado's transportation picture was exceedingly dark. The postwar business recession struck hard at all aspects of commercial life, drying up sources of railroad revenue. While the Denver and Rio Grande suffered from falling receipts and depressed business con-

45. Model-T Ford Track-Inspection Vehicle, 1920s. The automobile was converted by D&RG shop forces for use by maintenance of way officials.

46. Mack Railbus, 1920s. One solution to the economics of the light passenger traffic branch line was proposed by the Mack Motor Truck Company as long ago as 1926. This railbus, shown in front of the Railroad's machinery department headquarters building at the Burnham shops in Denver, was in service on a trial basis for a short time, but investment by the company in such equipment apparently was not justified.

ditions, as mentioned in the preceding chapter, the Moffat Road stood on the brink of disaster. In April the latter company's operations were at a standstill, its tracks blocked by rock slides and its treasury empty. Faced by losses in gross revenue of about $250,000 a month, the line's receiver, William R. Freeman, admitted, "The road faces the most serious situation it has ever faced. Its very life is at stake." Even when the Moffat Road was running its trains regularly, it could not always show a profit. The company had been a steady loser for twenty years, with deficits running as high as a million dollars a year immediately after the war. The only possible hope was a tunnel, to reduce operating costs and to inspire completion of the line to Utah. At this point the chances of such a development fell into the category of miracles.

The odds against miracles are almost prohibitive. But that unlikely circumstance occurred and it shattered the principal link in the chain of resistance to Denver's dream of a bore through the Rockies. The site of the event was at Pueblo, that stronghold of opposition to northern Colorado's aspirations.

It began raining along the upper Arkansas River on the first of June and residents of the valley were glad, because May had been very dry. On the second day the rain was harder and the river began to rise. Those who lived along its banks became uneasy but not alarmed. This had happened before. But on the third day the clouds dumped their cargoes, and sheets of water fell upon the land that slanted down to the Arkansas, converting it into a giant funnel whose hydraulic force was aimed at Pueblo.

The alarm was flashed along telephone lines, sending the power company's siren into a mournful cry. Firemen, police officers, deputy sheriffs, and volunteers hurried from house to house with words of urgent warning. Some fled, frightened by the reputation a rampaging river had earned over the years. Others, as always, were morbidly curious. They jostled each other along the levees, anxious to see the display. At half-past eight that night the torrent swept aside a breakwater west of the city, and a wall of water cascaded through its streets, carrying a mass of debris with it. The lights went out. Panic-stricken drivers gunned their engines, laid on their horns, and joined the caravan of mad flight for higher ground. Minutes later a mile-wide swath of downtown Pueblo was submerged under twelve feet of water.

Colorado's second city, lying exposed before the treacherous Arkansas River, had experienced a disaster reminiscent of the San Francisco earthquake. Not only was there flood, but fires had broken out, their flames lighting the sky as fire engines stood immobilized in rivers that once were streets. When the watery cover that obscured the city was drawn away, the damage was revealed. Overturned automobiles, dead horses, smashed railway cars perched at crazy angles, crumpled, splintered houses, loose bricks, bare foundations, and unidentified rubble lay mud-caked where neat squares once had generated civic pride. In dollars, the cost was set at sixteen million. A hundred human bodies were recovered, but the precise toll of human life never was determined. No one knew how many migrant workers had been camped along the river banks or how many of them had scrambled to safety.[10]

When Pueblo recovered from the first shock of the calamity and began its rebuilding program, there was an urgent demand that the tragedy never be repeated. With flood control uppermost in their minds, the city's leaders asked Governor Oliver H. Shoup to call a special session of the legislature to consider the establishment of flood conservancy districts. The Governor complied. In April 1922 the lawmakers met and discovered that the nature of their mission was twofold: a Pueblo Flood Conservancy Bill and a Moffat Tunnel Bill were the only measures subject to discussion. Shrewdly, the Denver crowd had traded upon Pueblo's misfortune to gain its own ends. If the steel city wanted insurance, it would have to pay for it.

The package plan offered Pueblo quieted its opposition to the tunnel, and its representatives voted for the measure in the end, but there was stiff opposition from El Paso, Fremont, and other southern Colorado counties. Despite a number of attempts to amend the tunnel bill to death in the House, it passed with only minor modifications. The Senate accepted the measure as it came out of the House, and it was quickly signed by Governor Shoup. The measure provided for an improvement district whose lands could be taxed to finance a bond issue sufficient to carry out the work. At the time, the *Rocky Mountain News* stated flatly that the "amount of the bond will not exceed $6,720,000," a large part of which sum the people of Denver were expected to pay. That growing city, its need of more water already a matter of concern, would benefit from a water diversion project, sending a supply through the tunnel from the other side of the main di-

10. Willis H. Parker, *Pueblo's Flood* (Pueblo, n.d.). McMechen, *Moffat Tunnel, I,* 155–56. Denver *Post,* June 4, 5, 6, 1921.

vide. As with many other projects of this magnitude, original estimates faded under the glare of realities, and the taxpayers were handed a bill of considerably larger proportions. The original bond issue, it turned out, came to $15,470,000, and this was only a beginning. By 1982, when all the debts have been paid off, the project will have cost approximately forty-five million dollars in principal, interest, and administrative expenses.[11]

To clear away any clouds of illegality that might hinder the bond sales, a friendly suit was instituted in July 1922. This brought into play the real opposition, and the court fight was on. In two decisions the Colorado Supreme Court upheld the legislation, and, as mentioned, the matter found its way to the Supreme Court of the United States, where the findings of the lower courts were affirmed.[12]

Denver's desire to have a place upon a direct transcontinental route was about to be realized. Moffat had dreamed of it, and the tunnel was to be named after him, but it was William Evans and his followers who had carried the campaign to a successful conclusion.[13] Now the engineers were called upon to open a way through the granite barrier that had broken Dave Moffat's heart and almost defeated those who took up the fight after his death. With keen anticipation, Denver watched as workmen commenced construction of that keyhole to the West.

Two months after the Supreme Court decision was handed down, the initial cut was made at the West Portal, followed shortly by an incision at the opposing East Portal. By the time snow flew, workers were underground chiseling away at the six miles of mountain that separated them. Expenses mounted as soft rock and water-filled fissures were encountered, but the work progressed steadily. In the summer of 1926, 125 tons of rock dropped from the tunnel roof, killing six men. After futile rescue operations, the clearing of debris, and disrupted schedules, the men went back to the job. Early Saturday morning, February 12, 1927, ten hard-rock miners punched through the last few feet of rock separating the two sections of the tunnel. In a

11. Ernest Morris, "A Glimpse of Moffat Tunnel History," *Colorado Magazine, 4* (1927), 63–66. *Rocky Mountain News,* April 1, 1922. *State of Colorado Year Book 1951–1955,* p. 523. *1960 Report on Bonded Indebtedness of Counties, Municipalities, School Districts, Moffat Tunnel District and State Departments and Colleges in Colorado* (Denver, 1960), p. 4.

12. 262 U.S. 710 (1923). McMechen, *Moffat Tunnel, 1,* 161–62.

13. See editorial, "The Evans Part in It," *Rocky Mountain News,* Feb. 21, 1927.

little more than three years the two shafts had made an almost perfect connection with regard to line and elevation. It represented a classic piece of engineering.[14]

The excited miners paid little attention to the technical aspects of the achievement. Each crew was anxious to achieve the breakthrough, to win the game, so to speak. When a thin rod knocked away the last bit of rock, a West Portal worker, whose crew had accomplished the feat, put his face up to the small hole and shouted: "Who in hell built this tunnel, anyway?" Back came the answer from the other side: "We built the tunnel."

The West Portal boys claimed the honors and received them. They were taken to Denver, where the city folk turned out to welcome them as returning heroes, back from the wars. A holiday spirit prevailed, thousands crowding the downtown streets to get a look at the little squad of hard-rock miners who had triumphed deep in the heart of the Rocky Mountain front. A drum and bugle corps stepped out in front of the automobile caravan and a detachment of soldiers marched along as an honor guard. Roscoe Davis, foreman of the crew, rode in a new Franklin car, described as one of the sensations of the auto show then being held, accompanied by Fay Lanphier, the reigning Miss America. After Miss Lanphier had presented each of the horny-handed miners with an American beauty rose, they dined at the Cosmopolitan Hotel where they were staying in "luxurious suites."[15] On the following day a formal dedication of the tunnel took place. Denver was deliriously happy, so happy it refused to worry about the bill. Another generation could make that matter its concern.

Those connected with the Denver and Rio Grande were unable to share the expressions of unbounded joy that echoed along capital city streets. The Moffat Road, enormously expensive to operate and terminating in western Colorado's wilderness, had posed no threat even in the days of a run-down and inefficient Rio Grande. But the completion of the tunnel, at public expense, drastically altered that picture. Now there was a real prospect that the Denver and Salt Lake would be built into Utah, particularly if plans made by Utah's late governor, Simon Bamberger, were carried out. In the mid-20s, at a time when the Moffat Tunnel was under construction, Bamberger

14. Edward T. Bollinger, in *Rails That Climb: The Story of the Moffat Road* (Santa Fe, 1950), p. 343, mildly criticizes the tunnel engineering.
15. *Rocky Mountain News,* Feb. 18, 1927.

headed a company known as the Salt Lake and Denver Railroad, whose purpose it was to build from Provo to Craig. In July 1925 the Interstate Commerce Commission conducted hearings at Salt Lake City to determine the railroad needs of northwestern Colorado. President J. S. Pyeatt of the Denver and Rio Grande strongly opposed completion of the Moffat line. In a moment of passion he said to the Bamberger people, "The same finger that pointed to the fall of the Colorado Midland will point to your road if it is built." When he regained control of his temper, he apologized and the statement was stricken from the record of the hearings. Mr. Pyeatt, however, left no doubts in the minds of his listeners as to the degree of concern felt by his company. He said that over the past four years the Rio Grande's net earnings ranged from 1.44 per cent to 2.97 per cent, an amount insufficient to meet interest payments on the underlying bonds. He freely admitted that another through connection between Denver and Salt Lake City "would be disastrous."[16]

Once more the Denver and Rio Grande was faced by an aggravating problem. The two fateful events of June 1923—the Supreme Court action in the Moffat Tunnel case and the purchase of the Rio Grande by non-Colorado interests—threatened to eclipse the local railroad in which General Palmer had placed his efforts and his hopes. The road's owners, the Western Pacific and the Missouri Pacific, were willing to spend money on improvements west of Pueblo, but they showed little inclination to sink any funds in a northern Colorado fight. Denver interests, having won the tunnel campaign, surely would push for construction of a Dotsero cutoff to place that city on a direct, coast-to-coast route. An alternative was completion of the Denver and Salt Lake, which then would supply the missing transportation link. It was a time for decisive action among Rio Grande leaders. The question remained, would they measure up to the demands of the situation?

16. *Deseret News,* July 28, 31, 1925.

13. Disaster confronts the Rio Grande

IN OCTOBER 1924, when the Rio Grande was once more undergoing the agonies of foreclosure, a development took place in Denver that was to be of great significance in later years, but in the attendant uproar of legal proceedings prior to sale, it caused no great stir at the time. In that month the Denver and Salt Lake incorporated a subsidiary known as the Denver and Salt Lake Western, to run through Red Canyon from Orestod to the Rio Grande's station at Dotsero. The completion of what became known at the Dotsero Cutoff would give the Moffat Road people about forty additional miles of track, or a total of 166 miles of railroad between Denver and Dotsero. They could demand, and probably get, from the Interstate Commerce Commission a division of rates on Denver to Salt Lake City business, thus cutting sharply into Rio Grande through traffic.[1]

The threat created by the tiny D&SLW again demonstrated the burden imposed upon the Rio Grande by its so-called foreign ownership. While one parent, the Western Pacific, was interested in a new Denver gateway, the other, the Missouri Pacific, was not. The latter company properly regarded the Pueblo gateway as its important entrance to the Rocky Mountain West. When Rio Grande officers argued the advantages of having their railroad build the Dotsero Cutoff rather than leaving it to the Moffat Road, there was little response from the Missouri Pacific. Nor was this member of the partnership ready to spend enough money to buy up the Moffat to eliminate the threat it posed.

Another major railroad, however, was much interested in the Denver gateway. For years the Burlington system had interchanged transcontinental business with the Rio Grande at Denver, but it was forced to take a back seat to both the Rock Island and the Missouri Pacific, whose roads served Colorado Springs and Pueblo. In the spring of 1926 Denver was excited by rumors that the Burlington would make use of the Moffat Tunnel, then under construction, and would send its trains west either by the Denver and Salt Lake (the completion of which was anticipated) or via the proposed Dotsero Cutoff to Salt Lake City. Arthur Curtiss James, a New Yorker who was said to be the world's largest individual owner of railroad stocks, had recently added control of the Western Pacific to his holdings. At the time, James was a heavy investor in Burlington stock. When the rail magnate visited Denver in November 1926, he denied the possibility of any merger involving the Rio Grande or Moffat Road. He advanced the argument that since 90 per cent of the Burlington was owned by the Great Northern and Northern Pacific roads, both of which had outlets to the Pacific Coast, these companies would suffer by the creation of a third through line.[2] Perhaps this was an excuse rather than a reason.

1. *Poor's Railroad Volume* (1935), p. 2127.
2. *Rocky Mountain News,* June 20, Nov. 27, 1926.

At any rate, he was to take an opposite point of view in the next few years.

Denials of Burlington intentions by James did nothing to quiet the speculations of those who sought a place for Denver on a transcontinental system. Not only was the link between the Burlington and the Western Pacific a transportation natural, but there was a management connection between the lines. Thomas M. Schumacher, a member of the directorate of the Hill roads which controlled the Burlington, was also chairman of the executive committees of both the Denver and Rio Grande and the Western Pacific. It was supposed that he was fully aware of the vital interest the Rio Grande had in the Dotsero Cutoff.

When James returned to Denver in March 1927 for a conference with W. R. Freeman, president of the Denver and Salt Lake, rumors flew so thick and fast that Moffat stock shot up twelve points in a week. Freeman denied any plans for a merger: "The Moffat Road is now chiefly Denver-owned and will undoubtedly remain so." His statement carried no denial of a possible alliance, the prospect of which was considerably heightened when Schumacher spoke of the largest budget in Western Pacific history "in anticipation of the completion of the tunnel and the Dotsero cutoff." His statement that "The Western Pacific will be ready to handle transcontinental traffic when the Moffat road opens" was music to Denver ears.[3] It was more like a dirge to the Denver and Rio Grande. Completion of the Moffat Road without the Dotsero Cutoff would mean the end of the Rio Grande in northern Colorado. The existence of the cutoff would modify the danger but not entirely eliminate it. The only solution appeared to be purchase of the incompleted Moffat Road by the Rio Grande, a development that appeared very unlikely.

During 1927 the Burlington loomed large in the plans for a cutoff. In April, C. G. Burnham, executive vice-president of the Burlington, told Denver reporters: "We expect to make operating agreements in regard to the tunnel and cut-off that will give us an excellent efficient route to the coast from Chicago. The agreement we have in mind would cause our consignments to be delivered in Denver to the Denver & Salt Lake railroad, hauled to Salt Lake City through the tunnel and over the cut-off, and from there to the coast by the Western Pacific. This plan would pave the way for effectual competition against

3. Ibid., Feb. 13, March 9, 1927.

other large railroads." Fixing his eye upon Denver's future, he made a further observation which excited local businessmen. "Denver will become to the Burlington what Omaha is to the Union Pacific and El Paso to the Rock Island. This, of course, means equal prosperity for Denver and the Burlington. . . . Denver's position as a railroad trunk center will be brought about by the fact that Burlington lines extend to the Northwest and Southwest by means of the Colorado & Southern, the Fort Worth & Denver, and the Northern Pacific."[4]

As Burnham was speaking, surveyors were busy west of Gore Canyon, staking out a cutoff route. To the *Rocky Mountain News* this was clear evidence that "the Burlington will construct the cut-off and utilize the route for cross-country traffic." However, the identity of those behind the survey was not at all clear. A. G. Smart, assistant superintendent of the Burlington, denied any knowledge of his company's participation. R. Knox Bradford, Rio Grande superintendent of transportation, said his road was not responsible for the activity. A Moffat Road official admitted only that some of that company's surveyors were working in a vicinity adjacent to the proposed construction area.[5] Three months later W. R. Freeman of the Moffat Road said it was "very probable" that a subsidiary of his company would build the extension and that a joint operations agreement with the Rio Grande would follow. The new route to Salt Lake City, he pointed out, would be sixty miles shorter than that of the Union Pacific.[6]

At this point the future of the Dotsero Cutoff became exceedingly clouded. Newsmen were unable to get any information from various company officials as to their intentions. As the *Rocky Mountain News* said, the project was in an "off-again, on-again stage of progression." Freeman would say no more than that there "have been negotiations for several months." Frank A. Peil, assistant to President Pyeatt of the Rio Grande, shrugged off questions with the remark, "I know of no progress." Pyeatt refused to say even that much.[7] Burlington rumors around Denver were almost nonexistent.

The explanation of the delay was simple: stalemate. The two parties interested in the Dotsero Cutoff could not come to terms as to its future use. "Before we go ahead with plans to build the cut-off, we will

4. Ibid., April 1, 1927.
5. Ibid., April 11, 1927.
6. Ibid., June 2, 1927.
7. Ibid., Feb. 28, March 5, 1928.

have to have assurances from the Rio Grande that it will be used for transcontinental traffic by that line," said the Moffat's guiding genius, Gerald Hughes. "Without such assurances, which we do not have at present, construction of the cut-off would simply create an expensive and relatively useless spur line." Hughes again displayed his company's high card when he reminded the Rio Grande that if agreement over the cutoff could not be reached, they would "go ahead with plans to extend our line from Craig to Salt Lake City." He admitted that this move could be made only if satisfactory arrangements were guaranteed for the interchange of transcontinental traffic at Salt Lake City.[8]

When the Interstate Commerce Commission conducted hearings in Denver in September 1928, Rio Grande management drew back the cloak of secrecy and made plain its desires. In what a local paper called the "surprise feature" of the proceedings, the railroad's counsel, Henry McAllister, took a stand of undisguised opposition to construction of the cutoff unless his railroad built it or unless the Rio Grande leased the D&SLW from the Moffat Road. He suggested as alternatives a joint ownership of the cutoff or a trackage agreement from Denver to Dotsero. "Unless some such agreements are made disaster confronts the Rio Grande," he maintained. "I have no doubt of our ability fully to finance the project."[9]

The "or else" threats Hughes had employed were answered by counterthreats. William H. Williams, New Yorker and chairman of the Rio Grande board, said his road was willing to negotiate any reasonable agreement with the Denver and Salt Lake but admitted that "at present we seem to be deadlocked." At this point he pointed the "or else" gun at his adversaries: "We are prepared to finance and construct a short route if negotiations fall through." As the bitterness of the quarrel heightened, Thomas Schumacher made the comment that unless the Rio Grande operated the cutoff, the running time between Denver and the West Coast would not be shortened. It was an extreme statement and a rather hollow argument. He tried to make the point that a three-line system between Denver and San Francisco would occasion so much delay that it would be better to follow the Rio Grande system via Pueblo. "A small link [the D&SLW] has very little to say, except that it has the veto power," he contended. "It has been my experience that small roads use this power." He, too, talked of building

8. Ibid., April 10, 1928.
9. Ibid., Sept. 19, 1928.

"our own short line from Denver west." President Pyeatt agreed that construction of such a road was a possibility and said it could be done for around twenty million dollars. "The Rio Grande has come to the conclusion it cannot make terms with the Denver & Salt Lake unless it is assured of a direct line into Denver," he testified.[10]

The hearings in Denver ended where they had begun: in a deadlock. Elmer Brock, counsel for the Moffat Road, complained about Rio Grande efforts to alter the purpose of the sessions. The only issue, he said, was that of considering the Moffat's application to build the cutoff: "We object to having any conditions attached to a certificate to build with respect to the proposals of the Denver & Rio Grande Western. We believe it is beyond the power of the commission to deal with any conditions. Certainly if conditions are attached, the permit would not be acceptable to us. The Rio Grande has no application pending." In Brock's opinion there was no question as to the feasibility of the project or of his company's ability to finance it. Nor did the Moffat Road want to sell out to the Rio Grande. Gerald Hughes explained why: "We felt that the Missouri Pacific would not enter into the Salt Lake route through the cut-off whole-heartedly and would not throw business to it because of a possible effect on the Missouri Pacific's Pueblo business."[11]

The Denver business community was appalled at the turn of events. For decades its representatives had struggled to make their city a rail gateway to the West, only to be denied their wishes by out-of-state forces. Now it was about to happen again. The tunnel triumph, for which northern Colorado supporters had fought so hard, stood in jeopardy. Without the through traffic sent over the cutoff, the expensive shaft could well turn into a fiasco of disastrous proportions. Angry taxpayers, faced by the prospect of having a white elephant on their hands, loudly protested the railroad Donnybrook that threatened them as innocent bystanders.

The press was extremely bitter. "Now it is given out by the railroad triumvirate of Missouri Pacific, Rio Grande and Western Pacific, that unless all hope of extending the Moffat Road is abandoned, the Dotsero cut-off will not be built, and instead a new tunnel will be constructed to put the people's enterprise out of business," said the *Rocky Mountain News*. The paper issued a call to arms to do battle with

10. Ibid., Sept. 21, 1928.
11. Ibid., Sept. 22, 1928.

those who threatened the community's prosperity. Should "the combination" either take over the Moffat or control it by external pressure, the tunnel would suffer. Surely, said the editor, the Missouri Pacific would do nothing to encourage shipments via the tunnel, and it would do everything possible to prevent completion of the Moffat Road: "The Moffat tunnel is an eyesore to the Missouri Pacific railroad interests and to other interests on Wall Street that resent the manner in which Denver went about building the tunnel as a municipal or public project." The *News* flatly predicted that if "the big three railroad combine" had its way, the tunnel lease would be canceled and the work would stand as a forlorn but useless monument to Denver's dreams.[12]

Disappointment and disillusion led to bickering and petty hatreds. The *News* attacked both the Rio Grande and its co-owner, the Missouri Pacific, with a bitterness not witnessed in Colorado for years, charging that the combine of which the roads were a part was blocking the state's progress. Then it turned editorial guns upon the Moffat Tunnel Commission, Denver municipal authorities, and local agencies supposedly representing commercial interests, accusing them of "doing as they are told." Stung into a fury by the literary lash, Tyson S. Dines, president of the Chamber of Commerce, expressed most emphatically his resentment of the insinuation that his organization was controlled by the railroads. "I will not talk with you or any representatives of a paper that casts such a slur," he told *News* reporters.[13] Denver was decidedly unhappy.

In December 1928 the Denver and Salt Lake filed with the Interstate Commerce Commission a formal application to build the cutoff.[14] Four years had elapsed since the incorporation of the proposed Denver and Salt Lake Western. The prospect of actual construction sharpened Rio Grande protective instincts, and its attorneys at once intervened in the ICC hearings. Since the railroad they represented was of necessity a participant in any traffic over such a cutoff, these representatives demanded a joint trackage agreement acceptable to them. Here was to be the basis for a hard-fought battle between the two Colorado railroads.

12. Ibid., Sept. 22, 25, 1928. On Sept. 21 the *Rocky Mountain News* published a bitterly anti-Rio Grande editorial, "A Tunnel Bluff," hinting that railroad matters were in the public domain and that the Colorado railroad should not go too far.

13. Ibid., Dec. 14, 1928.

14. *Poor's* (1935), p. 2127.

47. William G. Evans. Son of pioneer Colorado rail-roader John Evans and one of the central figures in the fight for the Moffat Tunnel.

48. Dotsero Cutoff Dedication, June 16, 1934.

During the next few months various business interests favoring the project joined in publicizing its importance to Colorado's future. The Denver Chamber of Commerce appointed a special committee to act on all affairs affecting the Moffat Tunnel; the Denver Real Estate Exchange created a study committee; and a number of local service clubs came forward to offer their services. Even the Colorado Pioneers Society took up the Dotsero question in its deliberations.

However, the event that startled even the laggards into frightened activity was the possible closure of the Moffat Tunnel. At the end of January 1929 the Tunnel Commission threatened forfeiture of contract unless the Moffat Road paid up some $200,000 in "back rent." Railroad officials at once commenced a court action to prevent such a move on the ground that the commission was simply trying to alter the contract. The annual tunnel rental amounted to $345,000, which fell far short of covering the interest payments on some $15,500,000 worth of bonds. What alarmed the Denver taxpayers, who were responsible for paying a large percentage of the bond interest, was the prospect that the Moffat Road would discontinue its use of the tunnel and return to the old Corona Pass route. In fact, the railroad set about putting that portion of its roadbed into operating condition, President Freeman stating that he intended to use it. Although the validity of the Moffat Road's contract was sustained by the courts, there remained a general public nervousness as to the future of the cutoff project. An abandonment of the tunnel, for any reason, would put an entirely new complexion on the Dotsero matter.[15]

At the height of the rental controversy the ICC examiner threw more fuel on the fire by entering a report to the effect that it would be in the public interest if the cutoff were constructed under terms that permitted Rio Grande use of it. Armed with this recommendation, and taking advantage of the fact that the Moffat Road could not proceed on the cutoff until it had straightened out its quarrel with the Tunnel Commission, the Rio Grande steadily strengthened its own position in the matter. That railroad now prepared itself to play a tough game with its opponent.

As the contest grew bitter, the Rio Grande came in for an increasing amount of criticism. Colorado's home road, its Baby Road, was becoming the villain of the Dotsero drama. As an adopted child of large and

15. *Rocky Mountain News*, Jan. 31, Feb. 1, June 28, July 31, 1929.

powerful outside corporate interests, it was placed on the side of financial evil, while the Moffat Road, whose origins also had been local, assumed the role of an innocent, victimized company struggling against the one-eyed monster of Wall Street. Dark things were said in Denver about the Rio Grande's dog-in-the-manger attitude regarding the cutoff—its insistence that it should build or at least have a large measure of control over the new creation. Great changes had taken place since *Rocky Mountain News* editor, William Byers, had accepted General Palmer's invitation to ride the new, shiny little narrow-gauge train to Colorado Springs on that autumn excursion of 1871. Byers, who had become a great Rio Grande booster, was gone; so was Palmer. And the railroad's name had become a dirty word in Denver.

As the year 1930 approached, the *News* assailed the railroad with renewed venom. This was the company, said the newspaper, upon which more than half of Colorado was dependent for transportation. Its tracks were the state's commercial arteries, but unfortunately, the system was affected by an old case of arteriosclerosis which threatened to stifle life-giving circulation. Admittedly, some forty-seven million dollars had been poured into a rehabilitation program over the past six years, to repair part of the damage done during years of Gould neglect, but no money was forthcoming to provide for the all-important direct route west of Denver. There was no vision in the management. President Pyeatt's new budget said not a word about the Dotsero Cutoff, the construction of which would chop 175 miles off the long, serpentine, expensive, uphill and downhill way to Salt Lake City. Nor was the railroad the only sufferer from its own inefficiency; the public paid for such waste in excessive freight charges. "The D. & R. G. W. system must be divorced from the Missouri Pacific system," said the *News* editor. "The alliance is unnatural, unreal and contrary to public policy."[16] A deep sense of civic outrage was needed to correct a palpable wrong. The editor was doing all he could to stir it up.

Admittedly the Colorado railroad picture had its flaws, but the attacks upon the Rio Grande were not entirely justified. As the company's annual reports show, a considerable effort at improvement in shop facilities, motive power, and rolling stock was made during the early twenties. It could not be denied that this was just a start, for of the 1,050 miles of main-line trackage between Denver and Ogden, less

16. Ibid., Dec. 17, 1929.

than 300 were ballasted with slag. Some 450 miles had nothing better than cinders or gravel for support, while another 308 miles were laid on bare earth, devoid of any ballast. During the years 1925 through 1931 this condition was largely rectified: the main line between Pueblo and Ogden was rebuilt and equipped with heavier rails, the slag ballast mileage was doubled, and the remainder of the line was supplied with some form of ballast. Like an old reprobate with a bad name around the community, the Rio Grande was trying to reform, and in the process spent millions for these much needed improvements.

Denver's dismay over the local road's apparent lack of interest in it was not always shared by other sections of Colorado. During the late twenties an extensive program of line revision was undertaken along the Royal Gorge route, eliminating sharp curvatures and improving gradients over the entire line between Pueblo and the Grand Junction area. Concrete and steel trestles replaced wooden structures, tunnel clearances were increased, several new terminal and yard facilities were built, and a block signal system 600 miles long was installed between Pueblo and Midvale, Utah. By 1928 a portion of this development, in the Tennessee Pass sector, boasted of the first centralized traffic control system west of the Mississippi River. Even though millions of dollars were spent, it was hard for the average person to visualize the improvement, particularly if one lived in northern Colorado, where the results were not immediately apparent. Residents of the capital city, far from appreciating the efforts of the railroad's "foreign" owners, generally regarded the expenditures as a plot to build up another part of the state at their expense. They asked one another, "What is the Rio Grande doing for *us?*"

The criticism mounted to a shrill crescendo, but Rio Grande officials maintained a tight-lipped silence, absorbing the editorial kicks and curses with the best humor they could muster. Those on the inside knew there was a plan afoot to break the deadlock over Dotsero, and if it proved successful, the way west would be opened to them. During 1929 unidentified buyers began to pick up Moffat Road stock in increasing amounts. By early January 1930, Denver papers began to buzz with speculation over reports that the line was about to change hands, with Arthur Curtiss James as the most likely suspect in the transaction. For two weeks reporters queried every railroad official they could corner and harvested a bumper crop of denials. No one knew anything. On the 22d of the month the Denver *Post* revealed that the Rio

MAP 9

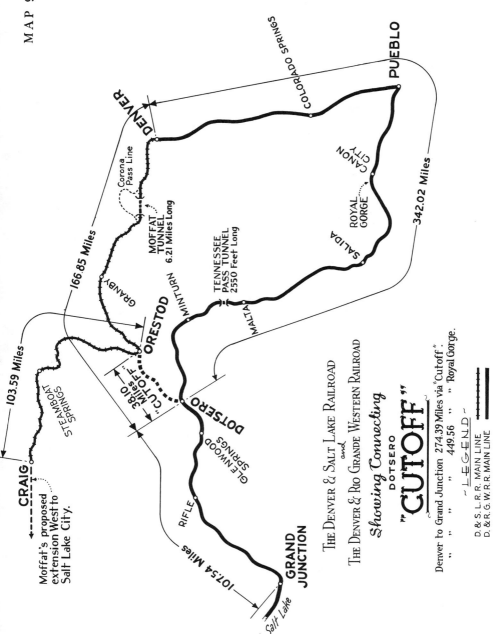

THE DENVER & SALT LAKE RAILROAD
and
THE DENVER & RIO GRANDE WESTERN RAILROAD
Showing Connecting
DOTSERO
"CUTOFF"

Denver to Grand Junction 274.39 Miles via "Cutoff".
" " " " 449.56 " " Royal Gorge.

~LEGEND~

D. & S. L. R. R. MAIN LINE ┄┄┄┄┄
D. & R. G. W. R. R. MAIN LINE ━━━━━

Grande was ready to ask ICC permission to make heavy purchases of Moffat stock. George H. Burr, a New York financier and onetime banker for David Moffat, admitted that he was negotiating for 20,000 shares at a cost of three million dollars. He would not reveal the identity of his clients. The principal sellers were said to be Charles Boettcher and the Virginian, Alexander Berger. Frederick H. Prince, Boston banker, also was reported to be on the verge of selling, a transaction that would give the purchasers control of the Moffat. A day or two later Prince announced the sale of his interests, which, he said, would lead to an early construction of the Dotsero Cutoff.[17]

There was opposition to the stock purchase, Gerald Hughes and Senator L. C. Phipps refusing to sell their holdings, but by February 1 President Pyeatt was able to announce that his road had virtual control of almost 58 per cent of the Moffat's outstanding capital stock. Specifically, the Rio Grande had acquired 21,334 shares and had agreed to purchase 7635 more at $155 each, which would give it 28,969 shares out of a total of 50,000. The purchaser was to discover that this did not constitute control of the Moffat, because 80 per cent of that stock was deposited under a voting trust agreement. Unless it could swing over three of the five trustees, the Rio Grande would have to wait until the termination of the voting agreement in 1937 to take over the reins of power.[18]

Utah interests, long in favor of completing the Moffat Road through northwestern Colorado, had objections to the sale. Residents of the Uintah basin were particularly concerned at the turn of events, a development that threatened to shut them off forever from rail transportation. A delegation met with Utah Governor George H. Dern and asked his aid in forestalling ICC permission for construction of the Dotsero Cutoff. Edwin C. Johnson, Democratic floor leader in the Colorado House of Representatives and a long-time supporter of Craig area interests, reiterated his earlier stand. The Rio Grande should not be permitted to take over the Moffat Road, said the rough-hewn legislator. "They're dangerous. Rio Grande control perhaps would close

17. Denver *Post*, Jan. 7, 8, 16, 22, 1930.

18. Brief on Behalf of the Moffat Tunnel League and Uintah Basin Railroad League, Interveners, ICC Finance Docket 8070, April 28, 1930, copy in Denver and Salt Lake Railway Archives, file 1445C, D&RGW offices, Denver. Testimony of Henry McAllister, in Stenographers' Minutes before the ICC, Dockets 4555 and 8070, "Construction by Denver & Salt Lake Western R.R. Co.," Washington, D.C., June 9, 1932, ibid.

our coal mines. It would take away our livestock business." Much
closer to the real point, he said: "If the Rio Grande takes over the
Moffat we'll be on a sidetrack."[19]

The attitude of the Moffat Tunnel Commission provided another
snag in the proceedings. For several years the commission had sought
means of raising the Moffat Road's rental, but it had not succeeded in
its efforts. A prospective change in renters was seized upon as an opportunity to elevate the figure and thus to relieve the taxpayers who
were making up the difference in bond interest payments. The Rio
Grande had no intention of paying the $845,000 annual rental de-
manded, holding that it should pay only the $345,000 charged the
Denver and Salt Lake it proposed to buy. This stand brought a cry of
outrage from the Moffat Tunnel League, whose representatives accused the Rio Grande of wanting to buy the Denver and Salt Lake
solely "to secure the benefit of operating through the Moffat Tunnel
without paying any rental therefor."

Highly vocal forces from northwestern Colorado and northeastern
Utah allied themselves with the Moffat Tunnel League in opposition
to the Rio Grande. Let the Denver and Salt Lake be joined with the
Burlington, both groups argued. This way, the cutoff, as well as the
Craig extension, would be built. If Pyeatt and his crowd gobbled up
the Moffat, nothing but trouble would follow, for "deep down in its
corporate heart the Rio Grande does not want the Dotsero Cut-off and
only pretends to want the Cut-off because it knows the Cut-off is bound
to be built."[20]

Business groups at Denver and at Salt Lake City took a less dogmatic
stand on the Dotsero question. The Denver Chamber of Commerce
favored acquisition of the Denver and Salt Lake by the Rio Grande,
but only under certain conditions. First, the purchaser should be
bound, positively and definitely, to build the cutoff. Further, it should
guarantee the preservation of interchange and through traffic at both
Craig and Denver. Finally, the Rio Grande should come to some agreement with the Moffat Tunnel Commission over rental rates. Salt Lake
City's Chamber of Commerce and the Utah Manufacturers Association took much the same point of view. Neither of the latter organiza-

19. Denver *Post*, Jan. 24, 27, Feb. 1, 26, March 24, 25, 1930. *Deseret News*, Feb. 1, 1930. Years
later, after World War II and upon Johnson's retirement both as U.S. Senator and Governor
of Colorado, he took a place on the Rio Grande's board of directors.
20. Denver *Post*, April 27, 28, May 4, 1930.

tions was willing to go on record in opposition to the cutoff, but both asked for stipulations protecting the Craig gateway.[21]

Rio Grande attorneys voiced strong objections to such conditions. They were particularly apprehensive about demands that the Craig gateway be left open. What would be the nature of any construction west of Craig, they asked? "Will it be a mere extension to, say, Vernal, or will it extend to Provo or Salt Lake City? Who and how reliable will be its projectors and what will be their motives? What considerations will they give in return for the valuable rights now conferred upon them in absentia and even prenatally?" Making a strong plea before ICC representatives, the attorneys concluded: "We are not aware that any such preposterous demands have ever been submitted to this commission and their refutation must depend upon their inherent folly rather than upon precedent." On May 21 the Interstate Commerce Commission examiner submitted his report favoring the Rio Grande on every point in its petition. It was unwilling, at this time, to recommend the imposition of any restrictions on the ground that such a move was outside the commission's jurisdiction.[22]

The Moffat Tunnel League and the Uintah Basin Railroad League promptly demanded a rehearing on the ground that the situation had been altered. They were referring to the fact that William H. Williams, chairman of the Rio Grande's executive committee, who had offered a great deal of testimony in the case, recently had been ousted. The entrance of the Van Sweringens into the Missouri Pacific counsels had caused the removal. L. W. Baldwin, president of the Missouri Pacific, admitted that his company had, in the past five years, spent thirty-four million dollars on the line between St. Louis and Pueblo. The rumor that the Van Sweringens were picking up stock in the Western Pacific aroused suspicions at Denver that the new order would show little interest in the proposed cutoff. Moffat Road supporters from northwestern Colorado made the most of this street talk. When O. P. Van Sweringen and five of his associates gained seats on the Rio Grande's directorate in June 1930, such speculations appeared to have some foundation.

Although the Rio Grande later came in for increasingly frequent

21. Ibid., April 27, 1930. Copies of resolutions by the Denver Chamber of Commerce, the Salt Lake City Chamber of Commerce, and the Utah Manufacturers Assoc. file 1445C, Denver and Salt Lake Railway Archives.

22. Denver *Post*, April 27, May 21, 1930.

49. Dotsero Cutoff, 1934. Bond station is in the distance.

50. Judge J. Foster Symes. One of the key figures in the building of the new Rio Grande during and after World War II.

accusations of delay over Dotsero, the blame could not be placed at its doorstep in the summer of 1930. The tunnel suit, pending at that time, prevented any decisions about the cutoff, and indeed, it was W. R. Freeman of the Moffat Road who asked the ICC for a six-month extension. In mid-December the commission filed a report, without an order, setting forth its conviction that control of the Denver and Salt Lake by the Rio Grande was in the public interest. This time, however, there were conditions. The purchaser was obliged to buy any minority shares offered within six months of the order date at not less than $155 a share; the Craig gateway was to be left open, subject to change by the commission; the Dotsero Cutoff was to be commenced within six months and finished within two years. When the Rio Grande was prepared to give its unconditional consent to these stipulations, an order would be entered.[23]

The Rio Grande was not yet in a position to accept the conditions, because it had reached no agreement with the Moffat Road over trackage rights on that line or over the proposed cutoff. For reasons already explained, it did not have actual control of the Moffat and it was within the realm of possibility that purchase attempts might fail. In the spring of 1931, after the tunnel lease litigation was settled, the two roads reached an agreement whereby the Denver and Salt Lake granted joint trackage rights between Denver and Orestod. It was further agreed that for $50,000 the Rio Grande could acquire all stock of the little subsidiary, the Denver and Salt Lake Western, and that as a creature of the new owner it should build the cutoff. The Rio Grande was to furnish the necessary funds, estimated at three and a half million dollars. As a protection to the Denver and Salt Lake, memorandum agreements were made between Hughes and Phipps, two members of the minority voting trust, to the effect that the Denver and Salt Lake should be operated as an independent line for its own benefit. There was to be no adverse control exerted by the Rio Grande. Provision was made for purchase of half of the Hughes-Phipps stock any time prior to January 1, 1933, at the $155 price. President Pyeatt announced the decision, in general terms, toward the end of June. Senator Lawrence Phipps confirmed the statement, saying: "A definite understanding has been arrived at that the Dotsero Cut-off is to be built. It will be built promptly and with no delay. There is no question

23. McAllister testimony, June 9, 1932, Stenographers' Minutes before the ICC. Denver *Post*, Dec. 12, 1930.

in my mind that the Interstate Commerce Commission will hand down an order permitting the work to be started under the understanding reached."[24]

In September 1931 the Interstate Commerce Commission promulgated two orders, presumably clearing the way for construction of the long-discussed Dotsero Cutoff. In the first, it authorized the Rio Grande's application to carry out the work, provided it was begun within six months and completed within two years. A second order granted the Rio Grande's request to acquire control of the Denver and Salt Lake through stock ownership, subject to the conditions earlier imposed by the commission. The last legal barrier had been removed. The Rio Grande now was free to buy the 7635 shares it desired and to assume control of the cutoff project. Its problems appeared to have been resolved.

Then new troubles appeared. Henry McAllister later explained the difficulty to the Interstate Commerce Commission: "By the time those orders of September 15th were entered, financial conditions had become greatly depressed, greatly broken and disturbed, and it was apparent that while in June the Rio Grande believed it had its financial arrangements made whereby it could carry out this program . . . the conditions had so vitally changed that the Rio Grande was unable after these September 15th orders were entered to secure that financial assistance."[25] To dramatize his point, the railroad's attorney stated that in June 1931 the road's first consolidated-mortgage 4 percent bonds were selling at approximately ninety. By the following March they had fallen to sixty, a decline that continued until a figure of thirty-seven was reached by June 1932. The nation's greatest depression had dealt the Rio Grande a crippling blow and had apparently foreclosed upon its attempts to open a Denver gateway.

The commission's orders of September 15, 1931, created more problems than they solved. During the time the Rio Grande awaited the decision, it had made an agreement with Kuhn, Loeb, and Company, whereby that financial house was to procure the desired 7635 shares and to hold them until the railroad received ICC permission for their acquisition. When the option expired, the Rio Grande's financial condition was such that it was not ready to comply with all the stipula-

24. Denver *Post*, June 30, 1931.
25. McAllister testimony, March 10, 1932, Stenographers' Minutes before the ICC. See also the testimony of June 9, 1932.

tions the commission had laid down in its orders. Taking the position that the orders were in the nature of permission only, but that if any one of them actually was performed the others would be obligatory, the company sought to delay purchase of the shares. The device used was formation of what was known as the W. M. Corporation, sponsored by the Western Pacific and the Missouri Pacific, and its nomination as the buyer. The Rio Grande then loaned the new corporation $1,237,000 and took a demand note secured by the block of shares. Title to the shares remained with the W. M. Corporation until October 1932, when the Rio Grande canceled the demand note and took over the stock. Meantime, the railroad's counsel argued that it had not accepted the ICC orders and therefore was not obliged to commence construction on the cutoff as directed.[26]

Through a series of extensions the Rio Grande managed to stall off ICC demands to proceed with its plans, arguing that falling income made such a move impossible. Railroad representatives showed that operating income had fallen from $364,430 in March 1931 to $60,069 for the same month in 1932, and for a three months span the figure had dropped from $1,040,000 in 1931 to $185,000 in a comparable period of the next year. Purchase of all minority stock at the $155 price would require approximately $3,182,000, in addition to which the Dotsero Cutoff cost was estimated at three and a half million. Other costs, such as the Rio Grande's share in relining the Moffat Tunnel and joint trackage fees to the Moffat would come to another million. To ask a small railroad to commit itself in the amount of more than eight million dollars at the depth of the depression was to threaten it with bankruptcy, an occurrence that was to take place later under even less stringent conditions.

As the financial picture grew darker during 1932, the Rio Grande was subjected to mounting pressures. The Moffat Tunnel League and the Uintah Basin Railroad League continued their legal drumfire in a stubborn attempt to prevent transfer of the Denver and Salt Lake ownership. Hughes and Phipps, of the Moffat Road, were anxious to see completion of the cutoff, viewing it as the only salvation of their company, and with each passing day their frustrations at delay were increased. Their general counsel, Elmer Brock, charged that the line

26. Minutes D&RGW Executive Committee, Sept. 26, 1931, office of the president, D&RGW, Denver. Letter in Report of Wilbur Newton on Acquisition of Denver and Salt Lake Railway Stock and Income Bonds, ibid.

was losing $2,000 in business every day and would until the connec-
tion was completed. Meanwhile, the Rio Grande had secured exclusive permission to do a job that it now could not afford to perform.
It had lost $110,000 in the last month of 1931, and there was no sign
of improvement in the immediate future. The road was to lose over
$2,500,000 in 1932, and to continue in the red at figures ranging
between two and four million dollars for the next several years. Early
in 1932 the situation was such that President Pyeatt recommended application to the Reconstruction Finance Corporation for emergency
financial relief in the approximate amount of four million dollars.[27]
At the same time, it requested of the ICC a year's postponement on the
Dotsero project, Pyeatt commenting: "We can't borrow any money.
We will have to wait not only until we can borrow money, but until
we can see our way clear to repay what we do borrow. We think the
construction of the cut-off is necessary, but we are not in a position
now to go ahead with it."[28]

Moffat Road stockholders, particularly Hughes and Phipps, were increasingly irritated by the Rio Grande's repeated delays and legal
maneuvering. But Henry McAllister stood by his guns, and Interstate
Commerce Commission hearings at Washington rang with his persua-
sive oratory and cogent arguments. One day in June 1932, while plead-
ing for an extension of time in commencing the cutoff, he provoked
Gerald Hughes into suggesting that the commission was favoring the
Rio Grande. Hughes, in asking for a denial of McAllister's request and
in pressing for immediate action on the project, said that the two railroads had made a private agreement, one to which the commission had
given its approval, and he thought its terms should be carried out.
"All we ask is that you leave private affairs where they are," he requested. In his view there was no reason why the government agency
should intervene on the side of the Rio Grande, and to dramatize his
point, he told a story:

> It is a good deal like the old bear hunter who met the bear on
> the path one day. The old hunter was very profane. But he got
> down on his knees and began to pray, "Oh, Lord, I have been a

27. Minutes D&RGW Board of Directors, Feb. 9, 1932, office of the president, D&RGW,
Denver. Correspondence relating to ICC Docket 8070, in file 1445C, Denver and Salt Lake Railway Archives.

28. Denver *Post*, Feb. 26, 1932.

drunkard; I have been a gambler; I have been wrong; I have broken all of the Commandments. I don't know whether I dare ask you for any favors, but, Oh, Lord, I want you to help me."

And there came no help. So he said, "Oh, Lord, if you can't be for me, don't be for the bear, and if you can't help me, don't help the bear."[29]

As it developed, the commission was somewhat inclined to favor the bear. It did not grant the Rio Grande its request for a nine months delay, but it ruled that the road might have another three months of grace. The roads would resolve their difficulties privately during those months, but this did not lessen the general concern felt about the problem at the time. With great anxiety, railroad men watched the course of events, hoping that somehow the impasse could be resolved.

Nervousness over the dilemma was not confined to Denver railroad circles. The Burlington's interest, apparent since the 1880s, was heightened by completion of the Moffat Tunnel and the prospect of cutoff construction. For three years prior to 1932, that company had tried to develop an interchange on California business with the Union Pacific at Sidney, Nebraska, only to find that the delays encountered had placed the Burlington in a poor competitive position with its big rival. The Denver gateway appeared to be a solution to this problem. It is therefore understandable why rumors of a Union Pacific offer to assume control of the Denver and Salt Lake stirred Burlington executives into action. The latter road's new president, Ralph Budd, and his general counsel, Bruce Scott, hurried to Denver in the early part of 1932 for a conference with Hughes and Freeman.

They found the Moffat men thoroughly annoyed at the Rio Grande's floundering. While Freeman was quite friendly with the Union Pacific, both he and Hughes denied any intention to sell their holdings to an "outside" company. Hughes admitted to Budd that he had an offer of "cash on the barrel head," presumably from the Union Pacific, but he would not sell to any road that might operate the Moffat as a branch line. Hughes, whom Ralph Budd called "the chief policy maker on the Moffat Road," was determined that the little line should serve as a bridge for transcontinental traffic through Denver. "He became convinced that the most logical thing was for the Moffat to be-

29. Stenographers' Minutes before the ICC, June 9, 1932.

come a part of the D. and R. G. W. and that made the Dotsero Cut-off a vital project."[30]

Satisfied that the Union Pacific threat was ephemeral, Budd lent his support to the cutoff campaign. On a visit to Denver in the summer of 1932, he told reporters: "By all means let us have the Dotsero Cut-off as soon as possible. It will add materially to the railroad business of Denver in payrolls and traffic and in connection with the Burlington road will provide the shortest and fastest route from the Pacific Coast to Chicago." He denied any direct financial participation in Dotsero, but admitted that "we are more than sentimentally interested, for it will mean additional business for the Burlington and will vastly help Denver."[31]

To show that he was more than sentimentally interested in the project, Budd turned to his old friend Arthur Curtiss James, who was then in control of the Western Pacific. Budd knew that the Western Pacific had no doubts about its ability to profit from the cutoff, but the Rio Grande's other parent, the Missouri Pacific, was reluctant to threaten its Pueblo gateway by opening a new one at Denver. James was persuaded to lend his efforts toward converting the Missouri Pacific people, which he did by asking that as much consideration be given the cutoff proposal as was being accorded the Rio Grande's more southerly holdings west of Pueblo.[32] The extent to which such pressure from so powerful a man had upon the Missouri Pacific councils is not easily determined; but needless to say, the Rio Grande was in sore need of all the assistance it could find in any quarter.

Whatever the efforts of individual and private sources, they were not enough to solve the financial dilemma into which the Rio Grande had worked itself. James himself had scolded the federal government for its interference in the nation's railroad's affairs, but it was that same government whose funds came to the Rio Grande's rescue through one of its agencies, the Reconstruction Finance Corporation.[33] During July 1932 the interested parties engaged in lengthy conferences, at the suggestion of the ICC, and agreed upon a plan designed to accomplish the desired ends. The settlement, predicated

30. Ralph Budd to author, July 26, Aug. 5, 1960. Budd to Richard C. Overton, April 4, 1949. Richard C. Overton, "What Part Did the Burlington Play in Building the Dotsero Cutoff and Why?" Paper presented before the Mississippi Valley Historical Assoc., Denver, 1959.

31. Denver *Post,* July 14, 1932.

32. Richard C. Overton, "Ralph Budd: Railroad Entrepreneur," *Palimpsest, 36* (1955), 453.

33. See Denver *Post* (Nov. 14, 1931) for James' criticisms.

upon RFC willingness to lend a substantial sum of money, provided for a deposit of Denver and Salt Lake stock. Percy B. Eckhart, a prominent Chicago banker representing a small group of Moffat investors, objected on the ground that the Rio Grande might pick up the large Hughes-Phipps holdings but refuse to buy out the others. To protect these interests, it was agreed, on September 6, that the Rio Grande, within forty days after an ICC order, would deposit as security with the Colorado National Bank of Denver, shares of its Denver and Salt Lake stock equal to the number of minority shares. The Rio Grande then promised to buy out the minority holdings before July 1, 1935, at $155 a share.[34]

On September 12, 1932, the Interstate Commerce Commission recommended that the RFC provide a loan of $3,850,000 to finance the Dotsero project, and within five days approval was forthcoming. Less than two months later, steam shovels were gouging away at Colorado mountain slopes and a little town had sprung up at Dotsero, where only a filling station and a lone house had stood during the long years of negotiation. September 15, 1934, was the target date for completion.

Construction of the connecting link between Dotsero and Orestod (Dotsero spelled backward) was carried out in the same spirit of acrimony that had characterized the project from its original inception. During August 1933, Moffat officials began to complain that the Rio Grande builders were purposely delaying completion until the following summer, when the fruit season would offer that road a heavy and profitable traffic. Until the cutoff was in operation, the Denver and Salt Lake Company was obliged to bear the full burden of tunnel rental. These outcries obliged Jesse Jones, chairman of the RFC, to order an investigation. Late in the year W. W. Sullivan of Jones' organization and two ICC investigators conducted the probe, the results of which were not made public despite the demands of several RFC directors.[35] In the spring of 1934, when he made his annual report to Denver and Salt Lake stockholders, President William Freeman charged that the greatly depressed earnings of the company were due, in part, to the Rio Grande's failure to complete the cutoff "with reasonable diligence." By this time the battles between Freeman and Pyeatt had reached legendary proportions.

34. Supplemental Order, ICC Finance Docket 4555, Sept. 15, 1932, file 1445C, Denver and Salt Lake Railway Archives.
35. Denver *Post*, Aug. 4, Dec. 15, 16, 17, 21, 1933; Jan. 26, 1934.

Formal opening of the short cut by June 16, 1934, some three
months ahead of schedule and for $219,000 less than the estimate of
$3,850,000, did not soothe the Rio Grande's detractors. By mid-May,
Freeman was bombarding the Denver press with the cry: "The cut-off
is completed and trains can be run over it at any time." "The cut-off is
not finished!" Pyeatt maintained. "The physical connection has been
made, but the cut-off will not be finished until the first part of June."

In fact, the last tracks were laid on May 7, but actual union of the
two lines was delayed. "We thought we couldn't wait any longer to
have the cut-off finished," Freeman told the public. "So we laid the
last two hundred feet of track and made the physical connection between the Moffat road and the cut-off." Freeman's enterprise was answered by the chaining of a log, bracketed by four ties, across the track
near Orestod to prevent any trains from running over the new unit.
"I know nothing about any timber being chained on it," was Pyeatt's
charmingly innocent response. "We have taken no action." A glance at
the Denver *Post* lying upon his desk would have revealed a picture of
the man-made log jam.[36] In a day of streamliners, Colorado's railroad
wars went on, Freeman and Pyeatt preserving the tradition.

At the grand opening, verbal wrangling was set aside in favor of
congratulatory speeches and elaborate encomiums. Freeman, fuming
and brooding, sat in one of the Moffat Road cars not far from the
scene of festivities, refusing to participate. President Pyeatt, late to the
function because of delays occasioned by his own employees, listened
at a radio while someone else broadcast his speech. Governor Edwin
Johnson's words also were read for him for the same reason. Ralph
Budd offered for display the Burlington's stainless steel, diesel-powered *Pioneer Zephyr,* and Henry H. Blood, Utah's governor, praised
the ingenuity of engineers who had leveled "the once insurmountable
mountainous barrier between East and West."[37] Out of the confusion
of late trains, missed connections, and the unfamiliarity of Rio Grande
men with Denver and Salt Lake roadbed came the final welding together of the two systems. It had been a long and frustrating day, characteristic of the whole disputatious undertaking, but it signalized a
new era in western transportation.

The celebration, staged on June 16, represented a completion of the

36. Ibid., May 13, 1934.
37. *Deseret News,* June 16, 1934. Denver *Post,* June 16, 1934.

last transcontinental line through the Rockies. Denver had dreamed of it in the 1860s; David Moffat tried to make it come true in the '80s and ever after until his death; the Evans, Hughes, Phipps, and Boettcher families carried forward the crusade after Moffat was gone. The Rio Grande, fighting for its existence as always, entered the campaign belatedly and in a posture of self-defense, but regardless of its motives, it played a major role in bringing about a development so long cherished in northern Colorado.

14. On the river of doubt

IN REVIEWING the events that led to the creation of a new short-line across the mountains to Utah, one is confronted by the inescapable conclusion that General Palmer's brain child was the recipient of no small amount of good fortune. After considerable fumbling, it had not only succeeded in wresting from the Moffat Road the right to build a cutoff long since conceived by that company, but it was handed the means of carrying out the plan by the federal government. During the complicated and acrimonious negotiations that preceded actual construction, the Rio Grande had come up winner in a series of legal actions fought against it by opponents. Time and time again, the patient Interstate Commerce Commission lent a helping hand. The pages of testimony amassed in the hearings conducted by that agency give the impression that Gerald Hughes was more than justified in telling the commissioners his bear story. He was not the only prominent Coloradan whose exasperation with Rio Grande intransigence had found public expression.

Completion of the cutoff did not terminate the era of troubles. In fact, it produced new complications. The owner of the new addition was in a position similar to that of the home builder: the purchase was made and now the property had to be paid for. There was a slight increase in revenue for 1934, "reflecting the effect of short haul mileage via the Dotsero Cut-off," to quote the company's annual report, but the gain was not sufficient to cure the basic ills. The general prosperity of the '20s had contributed little to the railroad's financial health, and now, in the throes of a national business depression, there was real doubt that recent efforts to improve efficiency by means of a cutoff had come in time to avert disaster.

Early in 1934, nearly six months before the cutoff was opened, Rio Grande management once again encountered its traditional dilemma: inability to meet interest obligations. On February 1 interest payment was due on general mortgage bonds whose size now approached the thirty-million-dollar mark. It was rumored around Denver that the Arthur Curtiss James group (Western Pacific) wanted to pay, but that the Van Sweringens (Missouri Pacific) advocated deferral to insure payment on the senior bond interest due in July. Jesse Jones, of the RFC, recommended honoring the February obligation. At a board meeting, held in Cleveland on January 28, it was decided to postpone payment of the $745,000 due on the ground that the law allowed ninety days of grace before proceedings could be brought against the road, and because the move would conserve funds with which to pay taxes due shortly. At another meeting held in late March, the board divided, five to four, on the question, the majority still favoring deferral. The disagreement was resolved by going before the general mortgage bondholders with a proposal that they could avoid default by accepting half a payment and by withholding presentation of their

August 1, 1934, and February 1, 1935, coupons. In other words, the responsibility of keeping the road out of receivership was handed to the bondholders.[1] They had little choice but to approve, as they had done more than once in the past. In April the company met other interest obligations amounting to $660,000, in order to stay out of court. During the summer it also raised $542,000 to pay the first half of the previous year's taxes, much to the relief of twenty-eight counties and more than 300 school districts whose employees faced a cessation of warrant payments. To do this, it was necessary to defer bond interest due on July 1. The burden of taxes and interest, onerous enough in times of prosperity, presented an increasingly serious problem as the depression deepened.

Faced by declining revenue, the obligation of fixed charges, an indebtedness of over $7,500,000 to the RFC, and an enormous mortgage commitment, the Rio Grande wallowed in heavy financial seas. Then came the blow that rocked the corporate structure from stem to stern: a demand to purchase the Moffat Road shares, according to previous agreement. By September 1934 all but 1676 of the 20,530 shares of minority stock were tendered for sale. Of the 18,854 shares offered since July 1, some 15,000 were Hughes-Phipps holdings, held back until completion of the cutoff. The price, $155 a share, was much too high. The stock was worth about $40 a share at the time the decision was made to buy up the Moffat, but the Rio Grande had signified its willingness to pay that much to attract those who were holding the necessary shares. Even now, in 1934, the ICC placed an arbitrary valuation on the Moffat stock of only $77.50 a share for collateral purposes, still maintaining the inflated figure, which had always been well over the market quotation, when discussing the possibility of sale to the Rio Grande. It was old promises, such as this one, that rose to haunt Rio Grande officers at a time when their situation was desperate enough as it was. Over three million dollars, the amount necessary to cover the offerings, appeared to be impossibly large. But if the commitment was not honored, the road stood to lose 20,000 of the 29,000 shares it had purchased and had placed in escrow. July 1, 1935, was the deadline; a solution had to be found before then.[2]

In the autumn months of 1934 the Rio Grande situation was ex-

1. Denver *Post,* Jan. 26, 29, March 23, 27, 1934.
2. Ibid., Sept. 7, 1934.

tremely critical. Earlier in the year there had been talk among the board members of merger or sale in order to relieve financial disaster. By June, Pyeatt was thinking about receivership in view of the fact that $1,230,402.50 interest was due on July 1 and another $745,200 to be paid in August, neither of which sums he could raise. Then came the Moffat stock purchase crisis. In mid-October, Arthur Curtiss James came to Denver, where T. M. Schumacher and Pyeatt met with him to discuss possible solutions to the growing dilemma. "The talk of sales, mergers and consolidations has ceased," James said to reporters. "Who wants to buy a railroad with costs increasing and dividends going down?" All railroads were facing serious problems, he said, such problems as pension plans, cuts in freight rates, cuts in passenger rates, shorter hours, higher pay, and a number of others. It was his gloomy opinion that "the railroad situation is still on the river of doubt."[3]

As the Rio Grande drifted helplessly on that fateful river, there appeared to be but one remaining possibility of succor: assistance from the federal government. Accordingly, the management again turned to the RFC and called for help. It asked for a new loan, in the amount of $3,182,150, with which to purchase the Moffat minority shares. Application was made through its recently-purchased subsidiary, the Denver and Salt Lake Western, on the theory that the little line was organized for the purpose of building the cutoff, that it had no debt except that represented by its stock, and that it was possessed of a better credit rating than the parent. In mid-November the loan application was approved and shortly thereafter the money was available.

The effect of the transaction was to place the Moffat Road under the control of the RFC. As previously mentioned, the agreement to loan the Rio Grande enough money to purchase the 20,530 shares of offered stock included the stipulation that the purchaser must deposit in the Colorado National Bank at Denver an equal number of Moffat shares as collateral. Thus, with 41,060 shares accounted for, plus the 8940 shares it already held as collateral, the RFC controlled all of the Moffat stock. Full voting power of the pledged stock was to be in the hands of the lenders, a condition guaranteed by the promise that Lawrence C. Phipps and Gerald Hughes would resign their directorships when the purchase was made. The Rio Grande then would substitute new voting trustees approved by the RFC, and the new trustees were to

3. Ibid., Oct. 16, 1934.

terminate the voting trust. All officers retained by the Moffat Road
would have to receive governmental approval.[4]

A few days before Christmas 1934, the RFC took over what a Denver
paper called the "first federally owned, controlled and operated railroad in the United States."[5] Not since 1920, when American railroads
were returned to private management after World War I, had the government engaged in such operations in the continental United States.
Even in wartime it did not presume to claim ownership. Technically,
the Moffat line was held in trust until the Rio Grande could pay off
the $10,750,000 it owed the federal agency. That such would be the
case was not anticipated by observers, who saw little hope for the debt-
ridden Rio Grande. The allotted three years, in which it could redeem
its purchase, was not enough time, and "so the present temporary government ownership and control is considered the same as permanent."[6]
While the Moffat Road did not disappear forever into the maw of governmental control, it was to be more than a decade before it was turned
over to its impoverished owner, the Denver and Rio Grande Western.

The passing of the old order on the D&SL was signified by the retirement of "Bill" Freeman as president. The Denver *Post* eulogized
him "as the man whose wizardry as operating executive saved the Moffat Road from the junk pile and turned the 232-mile streak of rust into
a live and vital railroad link which now stands valued, on the basis of
its bonds and stocks, at twenty and one-fourth million dollars." His
connection with the road dated back to 1917, when he and Claude
Boettcher took over as coreceivers. While the road might have been
called "live and vital," its earnings had fallen sharply in the depression
years, much in the manner of other railroads. Its net income was in
excess of $500,000 in 1929, but after that it dropped to less than $5,000
a year during 1933 and 1934.[7]

The search for a man to head the government's newly-acquired
railroad was short. Residents of the mountain West were pleased when
it was announced that Wilson McCarthy, a native of American Fork,
Utah, was the one selected. He was in no sense a railroad man, a fact

4. Copy of ICC Finance Docket 10632, Denver and Salt Lake Western Railroad Company
Reconstruction Loan, file 1445C, Denver and Salt Lake Railway Archives. See also Denver *Post*,
Nov. 21, 1934.
5. Denver *Post*, Feb. 22, 1935.
6. Ibid.
7. Ibid., Dec. 21, 1934. Copy of ICC Finance Docket 10634.

that he was the first to admit, but those who supported his appointment felt that his fine record as a member of the RFC recommended him highly for the position. He had first come to national notice in 1932, when Herbert Hoover appointed him as a Democratic member of that important governmental body. One of the corporation members later revealed that when the name of McCarthy was presented, he had asked, "Who the hell is he?"[8] A year later, when McCarthy resigned to enter private practice in Oakland, California, the questioner knew the answer. The former stockman, lawyer, legislator, and judge proved to be an able representative of his region, and it was with a good deal of misgiving that his colleagues saw him leave. Bankers from all over the nation wrote to him, expressing their appreciation of his outstanding work and their sincere regret at his decision to return to private life. Charles G. Dawes, former vice-president of the United States, then head of the RFC, congratulated the westerner for his part "in the great governmental effort to tide the nation over the most severe economic and financial emergency of its existence" and pointed out that upon "your board was centered the hopes of a desperate people." Dawes admitted that the work had been trying and that collectively and individually, each member "had a hell of a time."[9]

By the fall of 1935 it was clear that the Rio Grande could no longer carry the burden it had assumed. Obligations due by the first of the coming year amounted to more than fifty-eight million dollars, and there were no means of borrowing enough to make the necessary payments. Faced by a staggering $122,000,000 total debt, there was no alternative but that of bankruptcy. Economic distress was no stranger to the road's management; the trouble was chronic. In its sixty-five year history, bankruptcy was a word that had appeared with timetable regularity, and now, having failed to earn the interest on its bonds for five years running, the company was once again headed for the poorhouse. Futile attempts to remain solvent were reflected in the steady deterioration of equipment and roadbeds, as officials desperately sought to meet obligations. That the "Dangerous and Rapidly Grow-

8. Proceedings of the Board of Directors of the Reconstruction Finance Corporation: Farewell to Honorable Wilson McCarthy as a Member of the Board, Sept. 26, 1933, Washington, D.C., Wilson McCarthy Scrapbooks, Vol. 1, D&RGW offices, Denver.

9. Charles G. Dawes to Wilson McCarthy, Aug. 19, 1933, scrapbook in possession of Mrs. Wilson McCarthy, Salt Lake City, Utah.

ing Worse," as it was nicknamed, should now appear in federal court
to plead for assistance caused no great stir in Denver. In fact, its absence might have been cause for comment. The great depression had
struck down mightier railroads than this, and had the little line survived America's deepest economic crisis, it would have been newsworthy indeed.

Not only did the Rio Grande petition the United States District
Court for reorganization under Section 77 of the Federal Bankruptcy
Act, but it also asked that its subsidiary, the Denver and Salt Lake
Western, join it in the proceedings. RFC attorneys protested heatedly
at this inclusion, holding that the little stretch of road between Orestod
and Dotsero, called the Denver and Salt Lake Western, owed it more
than three million dollars, which it had loaned the Denver and Rio
Grande Western to build the Dotsero Cutoff.

Cassius Clay, counsel for the railroad division of the government
agency, argued that merely because his organization held a demand
note against the D&SLW was no proof that it could not meet its obligations. He did not see how it could also seek refuge in bankruptcy.
"The note may not be demanded for ten years," he told the court.
"The company has been able to keep up its interest payments and
can continue to make payments if the Denver and Rio Grande Western
keeps up its lease agreement."

Judge J. Foster Symes, who was to prove himself again and again
to be the Rio Grande's friend, listened to the railroad's counsel, who
contended that the D&SLW had no assets except the new cutoff and,
valuable as that addition was, it was not sufficient collateral to cover
present indebtedness. The court ruled that it could seek the same
shelter as its owners.

The "object of this bankruptcy act is to give relief," ruled Judge
Symes. "Financially embarrassed corporations may come under it without showing insolvency or bankruptcy. To my way of thinking a promissory note payable on demand is a threatening thing when a company
has no means of paying it. Bankers regard companies with much demand paper against them as a bad financial risk." The RFC need not
worry, he added; its rights would be recognized.[10]

The appointment of trustees to manage the Rio Grande next came
before the court. The names of Thomas M. Schumacher, chairman of

10. Denver *Post,* Nov. 19, 1935.

the executive committee of the Western Pacific, and L. W. Baldwin, president of the Missouri Pacific, were suggested. So was that of J. Samuel Pyeatt, president of the Rio Grande. But Judge Symes, a long-time legal figure of Denver, had other ideas. Once before, the Rio Grande had come to his court, petitioning for assistance, and he had then listened to those who suggested outsiders as trustees. And now the road was back again, asking for help. Determined that this would be its last appearance in court, Symes turned to local men. He chose Wilson McCarthy and Henry Swan as cotrustees.

McCarthy, in his short time at the Moffat road, was already eliciting the praise of Denver papers for his excellent management. During 1935 its traffic figures rose sharply as shipments of coal and oil from the company's trade territory increased. The choice of Henry Swan, a highly successful Denver banker, promised bright things for the sad financial condition of the defunct road. It was generally admitted in Denver that the selection of the two men was considered satisfactory by most interested groups, although it was somewhat unexpected.[11]

McCarthy's cotrustee, Henry Swan, was well known in Colorado. As a young Princeton graduate, he had worked with the deputy state engineer in western Colorado surveying irrigation facilities in that area. Later he entered the contracting business, rebuilding parts of the Colorado and Southern Railroad as well as the Denver and Salt Lake line. After his marriage in 1907, Swan turned to selling securities, because it promised a less peripatetic existence, and it was in the financial world that he made his reputation. Like McCarthy, he knew little of railroad management, the problems of rail traffic, or the actual details of a business they now proposed to direct. As the two men faced their task, they took a long look at the bedraggled Rio Grande and studied the circumstances that led it to such a low estate.

A true westerner himself, the crusty McCarthy gathered around him a small group of Denver financiers and legal minds to serve as his advisers in the trying years ahead. Regularly, he turned to John Evans, a leading Coloradan and president of the First National Bank of Denver. Symes also relied heavily upon Evans to assist him in the formation of a workable reorganization plan to support his avowed intention to keep control in the West. Evans, whose family had long been prominent in the development of Colorado, now made his own

11. *Rocky Mountain News,* Nov. 19, 1935.

contribution to the state's history by working tirelessly at the formidable task of reorganization. This mild, sensitive banker, a grandson of one of Colorado's earliest railroad pioneers, time and time again showed that when the chips were down he could be as tough in his own quiet way as the more outspoken onetime cowboy, Wilson McCarthy. Like his father before him, Evans was a firm believer in the independence of the Rio Grande.

Faithful to the court's purpose of freeing the Denver and Rio Grande Western from outside control, John Evans encouraged Symes in his struggle against the persistent efforts of eastern capital to again fix, in connecting carriers, a foreign control upon the line whose past history had been one of bondage. Faced by the immediate necessity of funds to keep the trains moving, McCarthy and Swan appealed to John Evans for financial help. By the early summer of 1936 he had arranged for the purchase by local banks of trustees' certificates amounting to $1,650,000, in order to meet payrolls, honor unpaid current bills, and keep the railroad operating.[12] By this means and by selling $450,000 worth of scrap, a total amount of $2,100,000 was raised. Since the railroad was faced by immediate demands for $1,800,000 to meet these payrolls and current bills, it was just a little better than broke when the money was secured.

Upon the appointment of the trustees, Judge Symes publicly promised to formulate a plan that would insure the road against future bankruptcy, guarantee payment of its obligations, and at the same time restore it to a condition that would permit it to serve its territory properly. From the outset, Symes insisted that the road was a western road, drawing traffic from Colorado and Utah, and that its management should be composed of local businessmen. Toward the end of the period of trusteeship, he clearly expressed the theory upon which he had operated from the start: "The new management should be made up of western men familiar with the problems of customers living in the territory. The control, as in the past, should not be centered in a group of financial institutions in New York City, the officers of which have never willingly ventured west of the Hudson and who set

12. The banks that put up money were: the First National, the International Trust Co., the Denver National, and the Colorado National, all of Denver; the First National and the Exchange National, of Colorado Springs; the First National of Pueblo; and the First National of Salt Lake City.

foot for the first time on their property when invited on an inspection trip by the trustees."[13]

When funds with which the work might be carried on were available, Symes gave trustees McCarthy and Swan the green light. Go ahead, he told them; build up the Rio Grande road. The court would stand behind all reasonable requests. W. W. Sullivan, an examiner of the RFC railroad division, estimated that between fifteen and twenty million dollars would be required to put the Rio Grande and Moffat roads into a condition that would permit them to compete successfully with other carriers. Wilson McCarthy agreed, and announced that he and Henry Swan would spend eighteen million on improvements. Six million would be at once poured into the rebuilding of the physical plant. The road, the roadbed, the right of way, and the rolling stock were to be put in first-class condition.

The program was exactly what Symes wanted. The road had long been neglected, and so stringent were its former economies that the accusation of physical danger to the passengers found some basis in fact. Its reputation was such that when in 1936 Henry Swan invited a banker friend to return east from San Francisco over the line, with the hope of getting a loan from him, the "Dangerous and Rapidly Growing Worse" sobriquet rose up to confound the trustee. Upon asking for Rio Grande routing, the prospective visitor was told by an official of another railroad that it was the most dangerous thing he could do and he was positively risking his life.[14] It was obvious to the court that the first step in restoration of the road was to regain public confidence in it as a common carrier. Symes approved the proposed expenditures. In March 1936 he authorized the trustees to proceed with modernization and granted their first request to spend $1,700,000.[15]

Money to proceed was obtained by the issuance of additional trustees' certificates and with it the trustees began to improve the Rio

13. Quoted in *Investor's Reader* (June 23, 1948), pp. 20–21. Henry Swan praised Symes highly, calling him "the most important factor in the build-up of the railroad and coming out of trusteeship." His "idea was to have a strong railroad, not too heavily burdened with debt, not owned by competitive railroads, but in a physical condition that was strong enough to take care of the handling of the traffic, and that was the first thing he told us when we were appointed." Interview with the author, Aug. 22, 1956.

14. Interview with Henry Swan, Aug. 22, 1956.

15. *Rocky Mountain News*, March 22, 1936.

Grande. Ten thousand tons of heavier rails were purchased at once. Five new passenger coaches and three combination lounge and dining cars—all air-conditioned—were ordered. Ten thousand dollars were spent for mechanical devices to help load automobiles on freight cars, and another $78,000 for creosoting ties.[16]

It was only a beginning. In the spring of 1936 McCarthy promised the people of Colorado, in a speech made at Grand Junction, that in the next few years the Rio Grande would pour millions more into local industry through its purchases of steel, iron, copper, lumber, paint, glass, coal, oil, quarry products, electric energy, and other items. There would be no letup until the once decrepit railroad was in such top condition that it could demand and receive its share of transcontinental traffic. Neither of the trustees was a railroad man, but both took the position that they had a product to sell and they proposed to merchandise transportation just like any other commodity. In order to carry out such a notion, the old shop had to be spruced up, otherwise no new traffic could be enticed. While McCarthy ran the road, Henry Swan went out and laid his case before every financial group known to him, local and otherwise. In a warm letter to McCarthy, Judge Symes made it clear that this was no penny ante game when he remarked, "Henry's got five million more dollars somewhere and as yet I have not been able to drag it down."[17]

Before the trustees had finished, the five million dollars, and more, were "dragged down." Over the objections of five big New York trust companies representing bondholders that held mortgages against the Rio Grande, McCarthy continued his improvement program, spending money, as *Time* put it, "like a drunken gandy dancer."[18] Ralph Wann, one day to be a director of the road, but at that time on the side of the so-called "insurance group," said that his people feared the road was being "gold plated," or overbuilt. Symes, Swan, and McCarthy fought back, insisting upon a complete physical rehabilitation, and, as Wann later confessed, "the position of the Denver crowd was absolutely correct."[19] During 1937 the court was petitioned for permission to spend over eighteen million dollars in that year alone. As

16. Denver *Post*, March 5, 1936.
17. J. Foster Symes to McCarthy, Jan. 28, 1939, Wilson McCarthy Scrapbooks, Vol. 1.
18. *Time*, Feb. 17, 1947.
19. Interview with Ralph Wann, Aug. 6, 1956.

McCarthy explained it, "Our purpose is to improve the Rio Grande consistent with its earning power to a point where it will provide the Intermountain West with a railroad matching the nation's leading carriers."[20] More rails, more freight cars, more shop machinery and tools were wanted. Fifteen new locomotives were required. None had been purchased since 1929. The equipment would be expensive. Go ahead, said Symes; buy it. Late in 1938 the court granted the trustees permission to borrow five million more to retire outstanding trustees' certificates and to proceed with plant improvement.

The move took courage, in the face of economic facts. The same month that Symes indicated his desire to go forward with the reconstruction program, the railroad's annual report was being formulated. It revealed that during 1938 freight revenues decreased nearly 13 per cent, and passenger revenues fell off by 10 per cent. In all departments there were comparable declines.[21] The next year brought little relief. While the downward trend, brought on by a general business recession, halted, no appreciable gains were made. Total revenues were a little more than 7 per cent above those of 1938.[22] McCarthy refused to be discouraged by the cold figures he was obliged to submit in his report. "Business is good," he told reporters. "The outlook for the future is promising and the railroad is getting in line with the trend throughout the nation to have the most modern equipment that can be bought." In a speech at Kansas City he reiterated his optimism to delegates of the American Short Line Railroad Association. "There is real indication that the uptrend is at hand."[23] Certain that they were right, the trustees proceeded, buying four hundred box cars, a hundred automobile cars, and fifty gondola cars.[24]

By January of 1940 McCarthy was talking about a "decided upswing in business conditions which has become prevalent throughout the country and which promises to continue." The road planned to spend three million dollars more during the coming year. As before, Symes approved, and again the eastern insurance companies complained bitterly. They wanted the budget reduced by 25 per cent, cutting out such items as the air-conditioning of passenger coaches,

20. *Rocky Mountain News,* Dec. 12, 1936.
21. *Annual Report of the D&RGW* (1938), p. 5.
22. Ibid. (1939), p. 5.
23. Kansas City *Times,* Oct. 24, 1939.
24. Denver *Post,* June 19, 1939.

the construction of additional signals, and other improvements. Judge Symes listened to their objections and then dismissed them.[25]

By the spring of 1940 the trustees were ready to make the major step of converting to a diesel-powered line. Orders were placed and by the end of the following year the Rio Grande possessed fourteen diesel switch-engines and two small stainless steel diesel-powered passenger trains. The trains were made up of two units, the front car equipped to carry forty-four passengers and baggage, the second containing eight standard sections, two chambrettes, a dinette-observation section, and rest rooms. They were named the *Prospector,* and the cars bore the names of early pioneers of the region. The *David Moffat* and the *John Evans* ran west from Denver, while the *Heber C. Kimball* and the *Brigham Young* made the eastbound run from Salt Lake City. Enthusiastic reporters wrote that the trains, moving along the straightways at more than seventy miles an hour, were "floating, rather, it seemed, than riding the rails." Passengers were protected by a "dead man's button" in the cab that automatically stopped the train within 1500 feet, should the engineer take his foot from it.[26] The enthusiasm with which the trains were put into service was short-lived. Before many trips were made, it was discovered that far from floating along the rails, the underpowered units labored mightily to make the mountain grades. While they proved to be unsuited for use in the Rockies, the small units became popular elsewhere and were the prototype of the modern RDC cars.

Much more successful was the conversion of freight haulage to dieselization. While war emergency passenger-traffic was high, it was freight that accounted for a large percentage of the Rio Grande's income. The coming of diesel-electric locomotives to freight trains marked a great advance in efficiency of operation. On the long mountain grades, steam engines frequently stopped to dump ashes, clean firebeds, and take on coal and water. Diesel locomotives made the pull west of Denver up a steady 2 per cent grade at a uniform speed, eliminating all these stops. Downhill, also, there were great savings. Steam-driven trains were obliged to set and release their brakes every two or three minutes. Heated wheels and other forms of braking trouble de-

25. Salt Lake *Tribune,* Jan. 27, 1940. Denver *Post,* Feb. 6, 1940. *Rocky Mountain News,* Feb. 9, 1940.

26. *Annual Report of the D&RGW* (1941), pp. 6, 8. *Rocky Mountain News,* Nov. 18, 1941. Salt Lake *Tribune,* Nov. 18, 1941.

51. German-built Diesel, 1961. One of three hydraulic locomotives purchased by the Rio Grande in 1961, reported by the manufacturers as the most powerful ever built.

52. Judge Wilson McCarthy. Co-trustee of the D&RGW from November 1935 to April 1947, and president from then until his death on February 12, 1956.

veloped. Stops were made every ten to fifteen miles for periods of a quarter of an hour each to allow cooling. These delays added to the time personnel had to be paid, and they blocked the track for other traffic. Braking by diesel, with the traction motors working against the momentum, eliminated problems familiar to railroaders for over a hundred years.[27]

There were other improvements. As early as 1928 the Rio Grande had introduced Centralized Traffic Control to the West when it installed equipment on part of the line near Tennessee Pass. By means of remote control, single track was utilized and it proved to be about 80 per cent as efficient as double track. The saving in maintenance and repair was tremendous. So successful was the idea that during the war trustees Swan and McCarthy rushed additions, building up the system until by 1947 the Rio Grande ranked fifth in the United States in miles of CTC track.[28]

The introduction of "off-track" maintenance equipment provided another avenue of economy. Formerly a great deal of time was consumed in delays when work trains stopped traffic, but by the use of bulldozers, ditchers, and derricks on caterpillar tracks, repairs were made with a minimum of traffic delay. Actual costs of operation were also much lower. Under the earlier method it had required between forty cents and a dollar to move a yard of earth; now the cost was around five cents. By the end of the trusteeship, the company had purchased $338,400 worth of such equipment, an investment it estimated paid off at least $500,000 annually in savings. Its effectiveness is demonstrated by the fact that in 1945, 71 per cent fewer work-train miles were required than in 1929. Meanwhile the road's track was freed for war traffic, and with a train mile density 58 per cent higher than in 1929, the added utilization was indeed welcome.

Not content with the degree of perfection in their work, McCarthy and Swan provided for the establishment of a company research laboratory. The move elicited considerable criticism from some of the old hands on the line, but when its value was demonstrated beyond question, they agreed that again the trustees were right. The origin of the laboratory came out of a problem as old as railroading: the eternal hotbox. Upon investigation it was found that an inferior type

27. Interview with L. J. Daly, retired D&RGW trainmaster, Aug. 10, 1956.
28. *Investor's Reader*, June 23, 1948. Salt Lake *Tribune*, June 16, 1943.

of oil was being used; the mistake rectified, hotboxes decreased. From there, laboratory scientists proceeded to the investigation of metal stresses, trying to reduce the number of engine side-rod failures and rail breakages. When it was discovered that almost new 112-pound rail developed unexpected kinks, samples were tested in the laboratory, with the result that a different rail was designed. Its thicker web at the top and more steel in the fillet were able to withstand successfully the pounding administered by heavy mountain locomotives. Out of this research came new standards that were adopted by the American Railway Engineering Association in 1946.

By the use of magnaflux, fissures and metal fatigue too minute for the human eye were discovered. The insides of locomotive fireboxes were studied through polarized glass; so were strains put upon model rails. Result: better and more efficient equipment. "Great strides are being made in equipment studies to decrease weight and increase capacity," said Swan in 1943. "High tensile alloys, extremely light yet stronger than heavier metals, are being perfected, and the fields of plastics, electronics and logistics are rapidly being applied to future rail transportation." He and McCarthy were looking toward the post-war years and the problem of competition with all other carriers during normal peacetime traffic conditions.[29] Their willingness to innovate and experiment put them in position to do so.

Part of the program for stronger growth and a more efficient transportation product was pruning. The principal piece of surgery during trusteeship was the elimination of a 125-mile narrow-gauge line running from Antonito, Colorado, to Santa Fe, New Mexico. The change was not effected without complaint. Like marriage, participation in railroad building is sometimes more easily entered into than left. Shippers along the road were not interested in the fact that the branch was losing the Rio Grande around $50,000 a year and needed about $500,000 in improvements if it were to be continued in use. They at once made the familiar appeal to their senators, and "Big Ed" Johnson heard the call. As chairman of the Senate Interstate Commerce Committee, he had more than a usual influence in these matters, and before long the atmosphere was filled with lamentations about the poor little appendage scheduled for amputation. Along with Senators

29. Interview with Henry Swan, Aug. 22, 1956. *Rocky Mountain News,* June 19, 1943; Aug. 10, 1945.

Harry H. Schwartz of Wyoming, Henrik Shipstead of Minnesota, and Dennis Chavez of New Mexico, Johnson charged that the Rio Grande purposely had encouraged motor carriers along the line, while at the same time willfully allowing its own service to deteriorate in order to gain approval of the abandonment. They openly stated that the road let perishable freight rot, by contrived delay, making it almost impossible for ranchers to use its service.[30]

Lamentations, senatorial and otherwise, were of no avail. In 1941 the Interstate Commerce Commission granted permission to discontinue service, and the so-called "Chili"[31] line bowed out. With it went some of the folklore contributed by the narrow-gauge mountain lines of the West. It was said that this was the road on which the conductor, in the caboose, could borrow the engineer's chewing-tobacco plug on one curve and return it on the next, so sharp were the turns. These hairpin curves were reputed to be so tight that the road had to hinge its locomotives in the middle in order to negotiate them. Such tales originated in the tortuous character of the track, as it wound through rough mountain country, dipping deep into valleys and rising high over skyline passes. Built only to satisfy a charter requirement that General Palmer's original road extend to Santa Fe, the branch had long since ceased to be a part of the Rio Grande's general plan, and its abandonment was regarded as a necessary part of the railroad modernization and reorganization.[32]

Meanwhile, other improvements continued to be made on the main line to make it competitive with other transcontinental railroads. Toward the end of the war a new tunnel was constructed at Tennessee Pass, costing a million dollars. While the bore of the shaft is 10,242 feet above sea level, the track alignment was improved and the tunnel's inside dimensions were now large enough for trains to handle any size of load.[33] A few months later the Rio Grande was granted the nation's first permit to install radio communications for end-to-end train communications. Not only did it permit cab to caboose contact

30. *Rocky Mountain News,* June 3, 1941.

31. So called, according to *Time* (Sept. 15, 1941, p. 17), because much of the freight hauled was chili peppers. Old-timers on the Rio Grande have another explanation. Great numbers of Mexican–American migrant workers were carried along the route to places of employment. So standard was their request for food at meal stops that finally the conductors began to shout "Chili" when these roadside eateries were approached.

32. *Business Week* (March 8, 1941), p. 33.

33. Denver *Post,* Nov. 4, 1945.

but train personnel, also, could talk to dispatchers' offices and wayside stations.[34]

Wilson McCarthy was not satisfied with the mere physical improvement of the Rio Grande system. Looking forward to postwar years of keen competition, and demonstrating his belief that the product he had to sell was transportation, he advocated the railroad's entrance into the airline service. In the fall of 1941 he told a group of the Association of American Railroads members that such for some time had been his conviction. He predicted that soon all first class mail would go by air. Noting that in the preceding year airliners had carried three million passengers, he estimated that when the war was over this figure quickly would reach at least twenty million. (It did—by 1951.) Freight also would fly the airways. "It is transportation that we are selling," he told his listeners. "And whether you push a pen, whether you are a brakeman, a conductor or a signalman, the whole purpose of it all is to sell something just as the merchant has to sell his stock before it becomes obsolete and shelf worn and out of date."[35]

In July 1943 the Rio Grande Motorway, Inc., a subsidiary of the D&RGW, formally applied for permission to establish a network of freight and passenger airlines in Colorado and throughout the West. The application stated that at the war's end the railroad company wanted to establish fifteen regular airplane and helicopter lines radiating from Denver. Air, bus, and rail facilities of the line would be so coordinated that passengers might use any or all modes of travel, depending upon their needs or the condition of the weather. Denver papers were extremely pleased over the proposal, and one of them gave high praise to the trustees for their "vision to prepare now for the air-age which is bound to follow the war."[36] The Civil Aeronautics Board was somewhat less enthusiastic; it denied the request. While the Rio Grande did not get a chance to ply the air lanes, the attempt underscored McCarthy and Swan's broad and imaginative approach to problems of modern transportation. Once more, the public was treated to new and bold thinking by these pioneers of modern business frontiers. The fact that their notions of expanding to the clouds did not meet with governmental approval in no way lessened Western enthusiasm for the forward-looking pair of businessmen.

34. *Rocky Mountain News*, Feb. 28, 1946.
35. Denver *Post*, Oct. 3, 1941.
36. *Rocky Mountain News*, July 7, 1943. Denver *Post*, July 7, 1943.

The principal question that must have crossed not only the minds of Judge Symes and the trustees but of all those interested in the Rio Grande was whether the huge amounts of money poured into improvements would pay off. The discouraging years 1938 and 1939 did not provide a rosy picture, but there was no abatement in the management's program of improvement and quest for new traffic. Charles G. Dawes, a long-time banker friend of McCarthy's, was not the only one to foresee the prospect of better times when Hitler's legions marched against Poland in September 1939. In that month he wrote to his friend, saying: "It would seem that the European conflict should stimulate the railroad business decidedly and, I think, business in general." While Dawes expressed a distaste for economic stimulation of this sort, he recognized the impact it would have upon American industry and transportation.[37]

Within three months the Denver *Post* announced that the "Denver & Rio Grande Western Railroad is back on its feet." Rising from what was described as "almost a pile of junk" four years before, the road was said now to be one of the most efficient in the nation.[38] Between 1935 and 1939 over 400 bridges were rebuilt or repaired and 114 were eliminated. More than two million treated ties were inserted, almost four million tie plates installed, and 239 miles of new rail were laid. New sidings now accommodated longer trains, a total of fifteen new and powerful locomotives were in service, while 117 antiquated engines were scrapped.

While the road's rehabilitation was remarkable, revenues were not yet enough improved to let the trustees rest easy. Income from freight rose over 5 per cent that year, while that from passengers declined slightly. The next year showed the first really marked gain when freight revenue jumped more than 21 per cent and returns on passenger transportation increased nearly 17 per cent.[39] McCarthy was extremely hopeful over the turn of events. With a good deal of satisfaction, he announced in October 1941 that the Rio Grande's net income for that month was 69 per cent higher than any month since 1932. Coal led car-loadings for the period, the figure standing at 6965, or an increase of 2331 over the previous October.[40]

37. Charles G. Dawes to McCarthy, Sept. 8, 1939, Wilson McCarthy Scrapbooks, Vol. 1.
38. Denver *Post*, Jan. 21, 1940.
39. *Annual Reports of the D&RGW*, 1940, 1941.
40. Salt Lake *Tribune*, Nov. 28, 1941.

America's entry into the war resulted in a sharp business upturn for all railroads, and the Rio Grande was no exception. The region it served anticipated the coming boom when in 1941 the government located a thirty-million-dollar small-arms ammunition plant in the vicinity of Salt Lake City and another at Denver. Former governor of Utah, Henry H. Blood, revealed McCarthy's interest in the establishments when he wrote, "I shall always remember you as being among those who took hold of the Arms Plant Problem when there seemed little hope of its final realization. You stuck to it until success crowned your efforts. This activity will prove to be a wonderful thing for the state of Utah, and I feel we were right in insisting upon receiving from the government some recognition that would put our state in the front in this undertaking."[41]

Newspapers were quick to notice the effect of the new traffic. They reported that the Rio Grande's net operating income for January 1942 was 161 per cent higher than the same month in the preceding year. By mid-1942 the increase soared to a remarkable 905 per cent. The June figure was higher than that of any month in the road's entire history.[42] By the end of the year Colorado and Utah readers learned that their line was setting new records as war business boomed. Net operating income for 1942 was over seventeen million, as compared to four and a half million for the preceding year. During the year almost five billion net ton-miles were reported, representing a rise of more than 50 per cent. Aside from a new surge in transcontinental traffic, the establishment of local industries largely accounted for the change. Twenty-eight new industries, including several large governmental plants, were located along the line during 1942. Over $5,500,000 of the net revenue were received for moving traffic to and from industries or government plants newly located in the area.[43]

As the war progressed, Rio Grande business made phenomenal increases. Operating revenues, up approximately 29 per cent in 1943, soared to an all-time record of more than seventy million dollars in 1944. The year 1945 climaxed all previous income levels when operating revenues reached close to seventy-five million. The importance of war traffic was clearly demonstrated by the 1946 figures which showed

41. Henry H. Blood to McCarthy, Sept. 4, 1941, Wilson McCarthy Scrapbooks, Vol. 2.
42. *Rocky Mountain News*, Feb. 28, July 28, 1942.
43. *Annual Report of the D&RGW* (1942), p. 8. Denver *Post*, May 18, 1943.

a return of roughly fifty-one million.[44] The sharp drop for that year
was, of course, expected, but in the decade that followed the war's
end even optimists were pleasantly surprised to see operating revenues
climb back to near wartime peaks and finally surpass them.

Even taking into consideration the artificial stimulus of wartime
economy, trustees McCarthy and Swan had produced results that
amazed long-time acquaintances of the Rio Grande railroad. In the
decade between 1935 and 1945 operating revenues jumped from approximately seventeen to seventy million. At the war's end the railroad employed in Utah alone more than 3200 people, and their pay
checks could support a population of nearly 13,000, or about as many
as resided in a place like Logan at that time.[45]

Under the trusteeship, the whole nature of the railroad's service was
changed. During the '30s and '40s the production of coal and metal-
liferous ores in Colorado and Utah steadily declined. If the road were
to survive, it had to find new traffic. The solution lay in developing
"bridge traffic" from other major roads that wanted transcontinental
connections. Back in 1923, traffic originating on the Rio Grande had
amounted to 84 per cent of its total; by 1945 the percentage was only
forty-two.[46] The war, of course, was of major importance. With the
Panama Canal under great pressure by the naval and military arms of
the government, and motor transport severely limited because of short-
ages of gasoline and rubber, railroads came back into their own as carriers. For example, the Southern Pacific's passenger revenue jumped
from 24 million dollars in 1940 to 124 million in 1943. The St. Louis-
San Francisco showed an increase of from three to twenty-three million
in the same period.

The war had another influence. Normally, on the western railroads
eastbound traffic is heaviest. The Pacific campaigns equalized this and
filled the trains headed west. Judge Symes estimated in 1944 that 60
per cent of the inflated earnings of the Rio Grande in the preceding
three or four years had been "due to Government and war business
both freight and passenger."[47] It was during these years that the trus-

44. *Annual Reports of the D&RGW*, 1943, 1944, 1945, 1946.
45. Salt Lake *Tribune*, Oct. 24, 1945.
46. *Railway Age*, April 26, 1947.
47. Memorandum on Confirmation of Plan, in the Matter of the Denver and Rio Grande
Western Railroad Company, Debtor. Memorandum of J. Foster Symes, District Judge, Nov. 1,
1954. In Erskine Myer Papers, D&RGW offices, Denver.

tees demonstrated to the transportation world that their road was not only capable of providing such service, but that it could be done competitively with other lines running through the West. It was a lesson not lost upon rivals, as the Ogden Gateway suits after the war demonstrated.

The very success of the Rio Grande's recovery from financial chaos brought additional difficulties and prolonged the period of trusteeship. From the outset Judge Symes stood, like Horatio at the bridge, and fought off hordes of bondholders and stockholders who struggled to retain the status of their investments. At one time he held at bay fifty attorneys, representing many more than fifty interests, as they clamored for his court to overrule the Interstate Commerce Commission's plan of reorganization. They contended that the RFC was getting all the best of it; that by freezing out common stockholders the Missouri Pacific and the Western Pacific would lose their joint control of the Rio Grande; and that the road should be returned to its original owners because it was not really bankrupt at all. Recent profits tended to support their contention.

The ICC took the position that the Rio Grande ought to merge with the Denver and Salt Lake to form an independent Rocky Mountain system free from outside control. It advocated abolition of the common stock equity, the cutting of fixed interest obligations from around seventy-two to around thirty-seven million dollars, and reduction of the annual interest from nearly six million to less than a million and a half. Refund the RFC loan of almost twelve million, said commission attorneys, and borrow an additional six million. By this means various obligations might be retired and necessary new working capital would be available.

Representatives of the mortgage holders—insurance companies and eastern banks—objected vigorously. They said that the railroad was worth $215,000,000 and that at such a valuation everyone, including common stockholders, should receive more equitable treatment. The ICC viewpoint differed by forty million. Its attorneys argued that the insurance groups had placed a valuation upon the road that was far too high,[48] and that wartime profits were not a true test of the railroad's earning capacity.

By spring of 1941 Judge Symes recognized the impasse that had de-

48. *Business Week* (Aug. 24, 1940), pp. 28–30.

veloped, and handed the case back to the Interstate Commerce Commission for further study. Thus far he had held matters in a firm grip, at one time denying the RFC the right to dispose of collateral put up by the Rio Grande against its loans, and on another occasion voicing strong opposition to the payment of fixed interest charges on the ground that the road could not support such a load. Meanwhile, he continued his fight to free the railroad from outside control. Upon returning the reorganization plan to the commission, he explained his position:

> The Court is of the opinion that the future of this property will be better assured if it is maintained as an independent unit and the control be not sold to any connecting carrier. These carriers are more dependent upon the Rio Grande than it is upon them. Traffic control through stock ownership is artificial and restrictive in nature and tends to limit the value of the public service which the new company can render, as well as weaken the value of its securities, for "Freight traffic gravitates to the fastest schedule as quickly as water seeks its own level."[49]

John Evans, reporting to Judge Symes his recommendations on the reorganization, had used almost identical language. Evans told friends, "if I have made any significant contribution to the railroad, it has been through insistence that complete independence offered the only assurance of future growth and prosperity for the Rio Grande." Early in the trusteeship he convinced Judge Symes that independence was the only sound policy. Throughout the trying years he had strengthened Symes in his determination to achieve Rio Grande liberation from control by any other railroad or combination of railroads.

At one point Evans went to New York at Judge Symes' request to advise the chairman of the insurance group that Judge Symes had become convinced that "the Rio Grande must be independent of any other railroad, for such control can only be restrictive." He vividly recalls the meeting. "What do you or any group out there know about the railroad business?" asked the dictatorial easterner, adding, "That railroad can never stand on its own feet; it must be owned by another railroad or it will have no traffic, and we'll fight to the last ditch to

49. Opinion in the Matter of the Denver and Rio Grande Western Railroad Company, Debtor, March 6, 1941, p. 11. Opinion of J. Foster Symes. In Erskine Myer Papers.

prevent independent operation." With which, Evans countered: "Regardless of how little you feel we know about the railroad business, I fully concur with Judge Symes in his conviction that anything but independence imposes impossible limitations. I feel you are wrong, and that the Rio Grande will emerge from trusteeship free to pursue its own destiny."[50]

Symes struck hard at the practice of milking the company's profits by its former co-owners. In the interest of the public and that of all the creditors, he felt that some provision must be made "that will obviate the basic causes that in the past have brought financial disaster to this property." He pointed at the trouble: the application of earnings to fixed charges not earned, with the resultant deterioration of the equipment and a consequent inability to make net earnings. Avoiding future difficulties would not be hard, "provided the management, like the trustees, has the single purpose of the prosperity of this particular property in mind and does not permit its earnings and traffic to be used and diverted, as in the past, for the benefit of other properties."[51]

In September 1943, after seven years of litigation, Symes approved an ICC plan for reorganization. It was the fourth plan considered since bankruptcy in 1935. There had been considerable argument as to whether the Rio Grande should be consolidated with the Denver and Salt Lake road. The Rio Grande and the D&SL continued to maintain separate offices and offer separate service, despite the Rio Grande's earlier attempts at purchase. As a compromise, it was now provided that the roads could be either consolidated or operated separately. What Symes wanted was the end of trusteeship. "This litigation must be terminated," he announced. "This court is not equipped to run a railroad." The remark must have amused Wilson McCarthy. The Judge had done very well at running it. In fact, at one time he had written to McCarthy, who was absent, saying, "I took over the railroad this morning. Everybody is reporting to me and when you and Henry return I will be very disappointed if you do not find an improvement in everything but the morale. That will probably be all shot to pieces. Reports of first day under my management show all freight and passenger trains on time and no engine failures."[52]

50. Interview with John Evans, Nov. 23, 1956.
51. Symes' Opinion of March 6, 1941, pp. 4, 5.
52. Symes to McCarthy, Jan. 28, 1939, Wilson McCarthy Scrapbooks, Vol. 1.

Symes' desire to get the line out of trusteeship was prompted more by the remarkable recovery of the Rio Grande than by his own modesty. While he was willing to exercise control so long as it was necessary, he felt that the time for independence had been reached. He had complete confidence in McCarthy and Swan, and was entirely pleased by their rehabilitation of the railroad. "When they took it over the railroad was a wreck," he told newspaper reporters. "There were sections of road on which trains could not operate. Today the Denver and Rio Grande Western is doing a splendid job as a transcontinental line doing important war work. The railroad will go back to private ownership in splendid condition with a working force second to none in loyalty and desire to serve the public."[53]

But the road was not promptly released from its governmental custodian. The insurance groups fought on, employing every known legal tactic to exercise control, objecting to every cent spent for improvements. Somewhat impatiently, Symes lectured them for their refusal to face economic facts. The security holders had made a bad investment, he said, "and now look to the bankruptcy court to restore value by some sleight of hand or legerdemain, which either never existed or had been wiped out by mis-management." Admittedly, in any reorganization certain of these investors would suffer. "The procedure is not one designed to recoup losses," the Judge scolded. "No security holder is getting what he thinks he should. All have suffered losses. The plan is not the best imaginable—it is the only one of several that have come before the court with the practically unanimous approval of all interested parties."[54]

On November 29, 1944, the plan of reorganization, already certified by the ICC, was confirmed in the Federal District Court at Denver. Those who opposed it promptly took their case to Judge Walter A. Huxman of the United States Tenth Circuit Court of Appeals, who on May 10, 1945, handed Judge Symes a stunning reverse. Huxman explained his decision: "We think any plan which gives senior bondholders their claims in full by substantially delivering the road to them and gives them surplus cash actually on hand and further enables them to receive in addition the excess war profits which are reasonably sure to come is inherently inequitable and unfair, so long

53. Denver *Post*, Sept. 15, 1943.
54. Symes' Memorandum of Nov. 1, 1944, p. 15, Erskine Myer Papers, D&RGW offices, Denver.

as there are classes of creditors whose claims are not fully satisfied."[55]

The case was now appealed to the United States Supreme Court, which, in early June 1946, rendered its decision. By a vote of six to one, the court upheld the ICC plan, reducing the company's capitalization by more than eighty-eight million dollars, wiping out stockholdings, and satisfying bondholders with amounts ranging from 10 to 100 per cent. It approved the Rio Grande's request for consolidation with the Denver and Salt Lake, as well as the appointment of a five-man committee to carry out the reorganization. This committee was to be headed by John Evans of Denver.[56] Missouri Pacific and Western Pacific attorneys at once filed a petition in Federal District Court, asking that the plan of reorganization be set aside on the grounds that circumstances were altered by a new and unexpected earning power, making the original plan obsolete. Interest rates were down, they argued; the Geneva Steel plant in Utah was now owned by United States Steel and its operations promised much traffic; and finally, national income was up, which in itself altered the former picture.[57]

The bitter rear-guard action being fought by opponents of the ICC reorganization plan annoyed residents of the Rocky Mountain region, and their irritation was publicly reflected by a Denver editor. "Any delay now in putting the Rio Grande reorganization plan into operation is a disservice to the people of Colorado and Utah," he stated editorially.[58] The concern shown was not long lived. In February 1947, by an eight to one decision, the Supreme Court reaffirmed its decision to return the Rio Grande to private ownership. Justice Stanley Reed, who wrote the majority opinion, overruled a stay order issued on November 2, 1946, by the United States Circuit Court at Denver.

Before concluding their tasks as trustees, McCarthy and Swan submitted to Judge Symes an account of improvements on the railroad. Reminding him that at the outset of their task he had instructed them to elevate the condition of the road, the men revealed that they had spent fifty-eight million dollars for additions and betterments, plus almost fifteen million chargeable to operating expenses incident to improvement. In a dozen years the Rio Grande had built or rebuilt

55. Denver *Post*, May 11, 1945. *Rocky Mountain News*, May 11, 1945.
56. Denver *Post*, June 11, 1946.
57. Ibid., Sept. 19, 1946.
58. Ibid., Dec. 20, 1946.

a total of 401 new bridges and had repaired more than that number. More than 1100 miles of rail were replaced, half of which was with new rail. Nearly 500 miles of track were now operated under Centralized Traffic Control.

New equipment characterized the Rio Grande. Ninety-three locomotives, fifty-two of which were diesel, had been purchased since 1935. The road owned nearly 5,000 new freight cars and 500 more were on order. Also on order were stainless steel passenger-cars to fill the Rio Grande's mileage proportion (22.5 per cent) of a new transcontinental train soon to be operated by the Burlington, Rio Grande, and Western Pacific lines between Chicago and San Francisco.

To protect the new trains, and in the interest of economy, other improvements were made. The installation of slide detector fences, the widening of cuts, and the purchase of off-track equipment, meant increased efficiency and more perfectly maintained schedules. Along the route were new and modern depots at nine important cities, improved roundhouse facilities costing a million dollars, and improvements at all principal terminals.[59]

In addition to such tangible additions, the trustees could point to sweeping changes in personnel methods and relations. That indifference no longer characterized Rio Grande attitudes was demonstrated in the care with which new employees were selected, the development of an aggressive, long-range advertising program, and efforts to stimulate local agricultural and industrial development. From a moribund railroad, whose employees frequently gave only the minimum compliance, there had sprung a revitalized business organization staffed by young, imaginative, and alert railroaders. Former attitudes of defensiveness had been supplanted by an *esprit de corps* that was a source of comment throughout the mountain community. There was a time when employees, teased about their "bankrupt hunk of rusty junk" by other railroaders, were reputed to have offered the dubious reply, "Hell, man, we kill more people every year than you carry."[60] Such talk was heard no more. Those who ran the road, from top executive to section hand, were sure that theirs was the best railroad operation

59. Final statement of account of Wilson McCarthy and Henry Swan, Trustees of the property of the D&RGW, and their trusteeship of the Debtors Estate from Nov. 1935 to 12:01 A.M., April 11, 1947. In the District Court of the U.S. for the District of Colorado; in proceedings for the reorganization of a railroad; in the matter of the D&RGW, Debtor No. 8669.

60. *Time*, Feb. 17, 1947.

in the country. This was the fruitful result that Wilson McCarthy and Henry Swan handed over to private management after a dozen years of careful rebuilding and polishing. Characteristically, they refused to take credit for the success, again and again referring to Judge Symes as the man who had saved the home railroad for Colorado and Utah.

For the first time since its founding, the Rio Grande was soundly organized and ready to reap the rewards of independence.

15. *The new Rio Grande*

ON APRIL 11, 1947, the Denver and Rio Grande Western emerged from bankruptcy and a twelve-year period of trusteeship. It was a red-letter day in Denver railroad circles, one that the press quite appropriately hailed as "Independence Day." That morning the reorganization committee, headed by John Evans, held a stockholders meeting at which a new board of directors was elected. To the surprise of no one, Evans became board chairman and Henry Swan the head of its finance committee. Even more appropriately, Wilson McCarthy was selected as the railroad's president.

Immediately the seventeen newly-elected members of the board sat down together and began to lay plans for the future of their organization. They were Westerners. Only Floyd S. Blair, vice-president of the National City Bank of New York, and Harvey J. Gunderson, a member of the Reconstruction Finance Corporation, resided outside the states of Colorado and Utah. That such was the geographic composition of the directory was no accident. All through the period of trusteeship Judge Symes insisted that only when the management was dominated by local, independent men could there be any assurance of avoiding the entanglements that had so persistently plagued the railroad.

This was a condition long desired and long delayed. Years before, General William Jackson Palmer, the road's originator, had told the people of Colorado Springs that his was a policy of "local independence and neutrality between the conflicting east and west lines."[1] Since almost seventy years had elapsed before it came to pass, it was understandable that the management should speak of it with pride. In the release from both trusteeship and outside control, the Rio Grande enjoyed a double emancipation.

The idea of freedom from outside interference came as a pleasant surprise to the mountain folk, who had long since accustomed themselves to the operation of their major business enterprises by "foreigners." The Denver *Post* was happy to announce that the road would be "run by outstanding Colorado and Utah men to best serve the public interest instead of the interests of some other railroad or Wall Street powers."[2] On the morning after the first board meeting there appeared in the Salt Lake City *Deseret News* an advertisement confirming this intent. It announced "The New Rio Grande," and underscored the idea that it was a *"Western* Railroad Operated by Western Men,"* who are "your friends and neighbors, with intimate and sym-

---

1. Colorado Springs *Weekly Gazette,* June 14, 1879.

2. Denver *Post,* April 13, 1947. In informing McCarthy that he would be a member of the new board, John Evans said much the same thing: "You will note that the large majority of the new Directorate will be constituted of Western business executives, citizens of Colorado or Utah, resident along the line of the railroad and familiar with its problems and those of the developing area it serves." Evans to McCarthy, Wilson McCarthy Scrapbooks, Vol. 2.

pathetic understanding of your problems."³ The Salt Lake *Tribune*
editorially endorsed this sentiment on the ground that the Rio Grande
"has long been recognized as an intermountain enterprise" and under
its new, local management, it was bound to prosper.⁴

There was another refreshing aspect to the composition of the reorganized road's first board. One of its members was John E. Gross, re-
gional director of the United States Employment Service, who had
been secretary-treasurer of the Colorado State Federation of Labor
for sixteen years and president of that organization for two years.
"This is believed to be the first time organized labor has been given
representation on the board of an important railroad system," asserted
the Denver *Post*.⁵ It was simply one of the many "firsts" of which the
new management could boast; in the years to follow, local papers were
to be busy reporting others.

For over a decade after the war's end the Rio Grande's course proceeded without change or interruption under the leadership of Wilson
McCarthy. This was to mean that between his time as operating trustee
and as president, the Utah Irishman would guide the road's destiny
for a period of more than twenty years. As the reorganized road's
new head, McCarthy was faced not only with the problem of keeping
his company independent but of piloting it through the dangerous
financial waters that might be encountered in the national transition
from war to peace. The railroad had been, as a Utah paper put it, in
judicial custody for a dozen years, "reporting at intervals like a pa-
rolee," but now it was free.⁶ With that freedom came grave responsibilities that had to be met without the parental protection of the
courts.

McCarthy was perfectly aware of the facts of economic life. He
knew that he and his associates had poured out money for the road's
physical rehabilitation in a manner that rivaled the heyday of New
Deal spending, and that unless national conditions remained favorable, his own brand of pump-priming would result in failure. But
McCarthy was in no position to stop now, or even to slow his pace.
This was a blue-chip game and he had to play it out at the risk of
losing everything he had ventured.

3. *Deseret News*, April 12, 1947.
4. Salt Lake *Tribune*, April 15, 1947.
5. Denver *Post*, April 13, 1947.
6. Salt Lake *Tribune*, April 15, 1947.

During 1947, freight revenues continued to climb, but passenger receipts fell off. Basing his hopes on a record peacetime year for net ton-miles in 1946, McCarthy sought further to improve the road with the hope of regaining the lost passenger traffic.[7] One of his first duties as president was to request of the Interstate Commerce Commission authority to issue over a million and a half dollars in equipment trust certificates.[8] He wanted to continue the expansion program, particularly with regard to passenger equipment. He knew that wartime passenger traffic had been extremely high and unquestionably artificial. Normal conditions would mean a probable drop as well as sharp competition, and he wanted to put the road in a favorable position to compete. That he foresaw difficulties in this respect was reflected in his already mentioned attempt during the war to get government permission to offer air service when peace came, a request that was denied. His fears were realized in 1947, when the company reported a drop of more than four million dollars, or more than 57 per cent, in passenger revenues.

McCarthy was determined to find means of reversing this trend, and in his search he turned to neighboring railroads. For years the Rio Grande had harbored an ambition to serve as an independent link in transcontinental passenger service. In April 1947, just as the road was emerging from trusteeship, the former Utah attorney announced his new plan. Soon, he said, the public would see a streamliner running between Chicago and San Francisco by way of the Rio Grande system. His road was ready to assume its part in the project. Millions of dollars had been poured into track and grade improvement. Now it could come forth as a contributing partner in the larger venture with no apologies for inferior equipment. At the first board meeting on April 11, Chairman Evans reported that contracts had been let to the Budd Manufacturing Company for the construction of fifteen stainless steel passenger-train cars at a cost of $2,040,000. The new train, which became known as the *California Zephyr,* was purchased jointly by the Burlington, the Rio Grande, and the Western Pacific. The six train sets of stainless steel equipment, diesel-powered, would give the three lines an opportunity to compete with other roads serving the trans-Mississippi West. And the new train would dramatize to residents of the Rocky Mountains that the Rio Grande, already connecting with

the Missouri Pacific at Pueblo, the Rock Island in Denver, and the
Southern Pacific at Ogden, was truly a vital transportation bridge for
several major lines.[9]

By early 1948 the Rio Grande's postwar financial picture began to
be revealed. While passenger traffic leveled off substantially below
that of 1946, freight receipts were up nearly 20 per cent. Another
hopeful sign was the fact that in November 1947 the road declared a
$5.00 dividend on preferred stock. This was of almost historic impor-
tance since it broke a thirty-six-year drouth so far as the stockholders
were concerned.[10] Further encouraged by freight income growth, road
officials were hopeful of improvement during the coming year. By
June, McCarthy expressed cautious satisfaction, saying that while
passenger traffic could not rival the war years, when troop movements
were very heavy, or even the postwar year 1946, summer travel was
higher than usual. A slight advance in freight rates also helped, but
in his view the increase was too little.[11]

Unquestionably, the saving feature was the changed nature of the
railroad's freight-traffic picture. A survey showed that in 1948 there
were 1,113 traffic-producing industries along the line, 246 of which
had appeared since 1941. To encourage additional industries, the Rio
Grande Land Company was formed in the spring of 1946. It was a
wholly owned railroad subsidiary, created for the primary purpose of
developing industrial properties in Rio Grande territory. To those
interested the railroad promised warehouse facilities which could be
purchased on a ten-year monthly amortized basis.[12] Most important
of the newcomers was the Geneva Steel plant in Utah, built during
the war by the government at a cost of 191 million dollars and purchased in 1946 by United States Steel for about a quarter of that
amount. During the next year it produced 90,000 tons of steel ingots
per month. By 1949 close to twenty million dollars had been put into
the plant to convert it to peacetime production, giving the mountain
West an industry that breathed new life into the employment and
transportation picture. The first postwar decade of operation wit-

9. *Deseret News*, April 24, 1947. Minutes D&RGW Board of Directors, 1947, in the office
of the president, D&RGW, Denver.

10. New York *Times* (Oct. 28, 1947), p. 35. Denver *Post*, Oct. 27, 1947.

11. *Deseret News*, June 26, 1948.

12. Minutes D&RGW Board of Directors, April 12, 1950, in the office of the president,
D&RGW, Denver.

nessed a steady growth in Geneva. By 1954 there were approximately 7,000 persons employed by what was now known as the Columbia-Geneva Steel Division of United States Steel in Utah. The annual payroll exceeded thirty million dollars and the taxes paid to four Utah counties approached the two million mark.[13]

As early as 1947 the Rio Grande realized an additional four million dollars in revenue from Geneva Steel, a plant that drew other industries to it like a magnet. Clustered around it were companion industries such as the General American Transportation Corporation at Gatex, the Hammond Iron Works at Provo, and the Pacific States Cast Iron Pipe Company at Ironton. Other industries in the area, such as the Chicago Bridge and Iron Company and two large gypsum and plasterboard plants, added to Utah's growing industrial complex. All these additions meant a tremendous revenue boost to the local railroad.[14]

The war's end also brought significant industrial additions to the eastern end of the Rio Grande system. The Colorado Fuel and Iron Corporation, a brain child of General Palmer, had grown steadily since 1872, yet in 1937 it was still a single plant operation at Colorado's "Pittsburgh of the West"—Pueblo. Then came a period of consolidation and growth that saw the acquisition of the California Wire Cloth Corporation, with two plants in California, and in 1945 of the Wickwire Spencer Steel Corporation, with plants in Palmer, Clinton, and Worcester, Massachusetts, and Buffalo, New York. Shortly there followed the inclusion in the company of other plants in Pennsylvania, New Jersey, and Delaware. In 1953 it opened a thirty-million-dollar seamless-tube mill in Colorado, the first of its kind west of the Mississippi.[15] Thus, during the era of McCarthy and because of his active interest in soliciting such new industries as that of United States Steel, the Rio Grande was to witness the growth and development of two major industries ideally located at either end of the railroad. Few executives could have asked for anything more. Added to the industrial traffic was a growing demand for service from agriculture. During the

13. Arthur Baum, "Utah's Big Baby," *Saturday Evening Post*, May 15, 1948. Salt Lake *Tribune*, Jan. 3, 1949; Nov. 8, 1951; Jan. 10, 1954. Press Release by U.S. Steel, Nov. 28, 1955, Utah Historical Society.

14. *Barron's* (June 21, 1948), p. 31. *Investor's Reader* (June 25, 1948), p. 22.

15. Denver *Post*, Oct. 26, 1953. A. M. Riddle, exec. asst. to the president of the Colorado Fuel and Iron Corporation, to the author, Sept. 24, 1957.

53. The Westbound California Zephyr. It is approaching the East Portal of the 6.2-mile Moffat Tunnel under the Continental Divide, 50 miles west of Denver.

'20s the road got very little fruit business, but by the end of World War II it was loading 2500 cars of peaches in two weeks' time during harvest, and upwards of 10,000 cars of produce during the season.[16]

But McCarthy was not content to watch only the growth of his freight business. Falling passenger receipts disturbed him and he was resolved to make every human effort to rectify the situation. Patiently, he waited for the inauguration of the proposed joint-transcontinental service to be offered by the Rio Grande, Western Pacific, and Burlington. By the spring of 1949 the partners formally unveiled their challenge to all other Western roads. On March 19, at San Francisco, the *California Zephyr* was christened with all the fanfare surrounding the initiation of a modern venture. Movie star Eleanor Parker, wielding a bottle of California champagne, performed the christening rites before a group of business and civic leaders that included the president of the Western Pacific, the Mayor of San Francisco, and the state's Lieutenant Governor. Lady passengers on the first eastbound run were presented with corsages of Hawaiian orchids in *Zephyr* colors: gold and silver.[17]

The cooperating roads can thank the Rio Grande and General Motors for contributing an idea that helped to make the *California Zephyr* a famous train and one that was widely copied by competitors. In 1944 Cyrus R. Osborn, a General Motors vice-president (then head of the Electromotive Division), was riding the cab of a Rio Grande diesel freight-locomotive through Glenwood Canyon in the heart of the Rockies. He was so impressed by what he saw through the engine's broad windshields that he remarked to the engineer, "A lot of people would pay $500 for this fireman's seat from Chicago to San Francisco if they knew what they could see from it. . . . Why wouldn't it be possible to build some sort of glass covered room in the roof of a car so passengers could get this kind of a view?" Later that week, at the Hotel Utah in Salt Lake City, Osborn sketched out the first drafts of an upper-deck observatory for passenger cars. Later, after World War II, General Motors engineers used the design to perfect the "Train of Tomorrow," featuring what was to become known as the "Vista Dome." In 1950 the Rio Grande recognized the achievement by erecting a "monument to an idea" near Glenwood Springs. Across the river from the right of way stands a nine-foot-long, 500-pound stainless steel

16. *Investor's Reader* (June 25, 1948), p. 20.
17. *Railway Age* (March 26, 1949), pp. 665–66.

replica Vista Dome car, welded to twin steel rails mounted on a twelve-foot arch of native stone.[18]

To what extent the new train should receive credit for boosting Rio Grande passenger income is hard to fix. In 1948 the railroad showed an additional 5 per cent decline in passenger travel, but in 1949, when the new train was in service, the loss was recovered. That year, in which the *Zephyr* operated only during the last eight months, nearly 120,000 passengers traveled on the streamliner, as compared to about 75,000 a year before on the train it replaced. Two other factors altered the normal pattern of Rio Grande passenger-travel during 1949. A strike on the Missouri Pacific during September and October reduced expected Rio Grande passenger revenues by an estimated $50,000, but events on another road more than made up for the loss. During February the Union Pacific was blockaded by snow in Wyoming, and, as McCarthy later reported, this "contributed substantially to our passenger, mail, and express revenues." The amount was in excess of $200,000.[19]

Rio Grande employees were more than delighted at the chance to offer their tracks as a temporary Union Pacific detour. Aside from the welcome revenue, it helped to combat the notion that the mountain railroad was subject to abnormal stoppage due to slides and heavy snows. A. E. Stoddard, then vice-president of the Union Pacific, acknowledged the favor in a letter to McCarthy at the end of February. "I want you to know of my full appreciation of the wonderful cooperation of your railroad in detouring our trains between Denver and Salt Lake during our recent snow blockade in Wyoming," he wrote. "In addition to the fine spirit of helpfulness, the service rendered was excellent. We had a tough situation to combat, but favorable weather during the past week has enabled us to get pretty well cleaned up and we are operating normally. With best wishes and assuring you of my earnest desire to reciprocate should an occasion arise, I am, Sincerely yours . . ."[20]

All the Rio Grande asked was some "wonderful cooperation" from the Union Pacific. McCarthy could point to a slight upturn in passenger traffic in 1949, but he was obliged to report to the stockholders

18. *Annual Report of the D&RGW*, 1947. Salt Lake *Tribune*, Oct. 1, 1952.
19. *Annual Reports of the D&RGW*, 1948, 1949.
20. A. E. Stoddard to Wilson McCarthy, Feb. 26, 1949, Wilson McCarthy Scrapbooks, Vol. 3.

that due to the postwar economic adjustment, freight receipts had
fallen by nearly 5 per cent. This was much more significant, because
most of the road's income was from freight. One answer to the problem
was to capture some of the traffic outside its own empire, and it was
toward the realm of the Union Pacific that the Rio Grande cast its
eyes.

Several years earlier, McCarthy had revealed to his son a desire to
gain a share of the Pacific Northwest traffic. The thought had lingered,
and now he talked to the Rio Grande's counsel, Henry McAllister.
The lawyer was unenthusiastic, holding that the smaller railroad did
not have a good enough case to merit the effort. He doubted that the
Rio Grande could guarantee any improvement over the Union Pacific service.[21] The president thought otherwise. Since the opening of
the Dotsero Cutoff in 1934, which shortened the Rio Grande's distance
between Denver and Salt Lake City by 175 miles, and as a result of
the many other improvements made, he was convinced that his road
could match anything its rival to the north had to offer. In effect,
Stoddard himself had admitted that in the case of the Union Pacific
traffic diversion during the Wyoming snow blockade, traffic had moved
over the Rio Grande rapidly and efficiently. Convinced he had a case,
McCarthy proceeded. On August 1, 1949, the road filed a complaint
with the Interstate Commerce Commission asking for nondiscrimina-
tory and competitive joint through rates on traffic going to and coming
from northern Utah, southern Idaho, western Montana, eastern Oregon, and Washington. With that move, the fight to open the "Ogden
Gateway" was inaugurated, as little Rio Grande "David" prepared
to take on Union Pacific "Goliath."

Ever since the golden spike ceremonies back in 1869, the Union Pacific had controlled the Ogden outlet to and from the Pacific Northwest. During the ensuing years the little narrow-gauge Rio Grande
that wound through tortuous mountain passes over a long and expensive route offered no problem to the Union Pacific. The larger road
had maintained a working agreement with the Rio Grande, charging
uniform through-rates until 1906, when the Union Pacific gained control of several Oregon lines. After that time, shippers had to pay more
if they wanted to use the Utah-Colorado route. For example, in 1949,
when the case was instituted, an Idaho potato-grower could ship a

21. Interview with Dennis McCarthy, Aug. 7, 1956, at Salt Lake City.

carload by way of the Union Pacific to Denver, and on to Dallas by another road, for $282. But if he chose to send his crop to Ogden and then to Denver by way of the Rio Grande, where another line would take the shipment to Texas, the cost, based on a combination of local rates all the way, rose to $371. In effect, the Rio Grande was barred from participating in Northwest traffic.[22]

At ICC hearings the Rio Grande made open accusations of Union Pacific monopoly and discrimination. Why should the Union Pacific join in through-rates between Portland and St. Louis with other lines, including the Canadian Pacific, which contributed only 368 miles out of a total of 2464 on the run, and still bar the Rio Grande, the complainants asked? What justice was there in denying competitive rights to the Rio Grande, which in 1948 had delivered to the Union Pacific at Denver 361,256 more tons of freight than it had received from its rival, and 607,173 more tons than it had received at Utah exchange points? Why, asked the Rio Grande, should the gateway remain closed when that condition not only prevented Idaho from attaining its desired economic development, but gave those residents inferior, noncompetitive service?[23]

At hearings held in Boise during April 1950, the Union Pacific presented a nine-point defense of its position. Among other arguments, its counsel stated that his road was in no position to act as a "big brother" to the Rio Grande or any other road. Was it fair, he asked, to be required to hand over traffic that originated and frequently terminated on the Union Pacific? In some instances the larger road would lose revenue from a thousand-mile haul in contrast to a haul of a little over a hundred miles from Ogden to Pocatello. Added to this, the distance to certain destinations would be increased up to 200 miles, expensive interchanges would be necessary, and frequently traffic would require a full day longer to reach its destination. To the Union Pacific people this represented inefficient transportation and an economic waste. As a thinly veiled threat, they suggested that if the Rio Grande made a successful invasion of Union Pacific territory, some of the branch lines in the Northwest might have to curtail service and increase rates. Finally, it was charged, this intrusion might reduce

22. *Newsweek* (Aug. 15, 1949), p. 60. *Business Week* (Sept. 10, 1949), p. 30. *Railway Age* (Aug. 6, 1949), p. 62; (Nov. 25, 1950), p. 50.

23. Salt Lake *Tribune,* Dec. 13, 15, 1949.

the efficiency of the entrenched road by lowering its high standards, and even threaten service necessary to national defense.[24]

Back and forth the accusations flew. The Union Pacific resolutely maintained that proceedings had been instituted to establish new through routes. No, said the Rio Grande, the issue was whether the combination of local rates applicable to existing Union Pacific-Rio Grande through routes, from and into exclusive Union Pacific territory, were unreasonable and discriminatory. Back came the Union Pacific representative, asserting that the ICC did not have the power under the original act creating the commission to grant the relief sought by the smaller line. Should it do so, it would "short-haul" the Union Pacific by about a thousand miles without its consent. Besides, he said, there was no substantial public demand or need for the through rates sought. The Rio Grande had merely tried to make it appear so by a "campaign of propaganda, agitation, and accusations against the Union Pacific." In reality, charged the Union Pacific, the complaining railroad would not get more than 10 per cent of the nearly 160,000 annual carloads of freight which the joint through rates would affect, but by enforcing this demand it would have serious repercussions within the U.P. organization.

Rio Grande attorneys had little sympathy for such piteous cries. Shippers and other interested organizations, representing more than 300,000 persons, had signified their belief that the rates sought were both desirable and necessary. "The Union Pacific has assumed that it has a legal and absolute right to its long haul on all traffic that originates or terminates in the closed door territory and that the shippers who favor the complaint of the Rio Grande should be denied access to the markets and the traffic involved at just, reasonable and non-discriminatory rates and should be satisfied with existing combination rates," charged the Rio Grande men. "This claim is without merit since it has long been settled that a shipper is entitled to reasonable and non-discriminatory rates where through rates exist, and that no carrier has a legal or absolute right to the exclusive occupancy of a particular territory or to the traffic which terminates or originates in such territory."[25]

During the summer of 1950 the Utah Public Service Commission entered the picture with an intervening brief, holding that no Utah

24. New York *Times* (April 5, 1950), p. 49.
25. Salt Lake *Tribune*, Aug. 16, 1950.

shipper would be hurt by the establishment of the desired rates and
many would be benefited.[26] In November the ICC received a report
from its chief examiner, Frank Mullen, who had heard the arguments.
He recommended that the Union Pacific be required to open the
door. To him the Denver and Rio Grande route was "not unreason-
ably long or unduly circuitous," and the demand was in the public
interest.[27] Reaction from the opposing camps was immediate. The
Rio Grande was "very much encouraged." Arthur E. Stoddard, now
president of the Union Pacific, held that the report was "in all respects
adverse to the position of the Union Pacific and other defendants."
That road had pioneered rail service into the Northwest and now it
feared it stood to lose fifty million dollars a year through the turn of
events.[28]

Early in 1951 the struggle became bitter. Senator Edwin C. Johnson
of Colorado made a speech over a Denver radio station favoring
through rates. The Union Pacific at once charged that it was "intended
for the purpose of intimidating and coercing the [Interstate Com-
merce] commissioners." "Asinine," replied Johnson. The Union Pacific ought to apologize to the commissioners for suggesting that they
were spineless and cowardly. Nevertheless, said Stoddard's road, this
was just another Rio Grande device to get a favorable decision by deception and the creation of an artificial public interest.[29] Johnson
heatedly denied that McCarthy or any other Rio Grande official had
ever asked him to make a public statement on the subject. When
Denver station KFEL solicited his opinion as to whether shippers
were entitled to through rates via Ogden, he simply stated his belief:
yes.[30] The Rio Grande at once came to Senator Johnson's defense, accusing the opposition of making "completely irresponsible and outrageous" charges against its road and the solon. They were somewhat
vindicated when the Union Pacific was denied its request to reopen the
case so that it could file Johnson's radio address. The ICC called the
petition "not relevant to the issues."[31]

Matters drifted until the summer of 1952, when the ICC ordered a
complete reargument of the case, giving as one reason the appointment

26. Ibid., Aug. 13, 1950.
27. *Railway Age* (Nov. 25, 1950), pp. 50–51.
28. New York *Times* (Nov. 25, 1950), p. 20.
29. Ibid. (Feb. 22, 1951), p. 41.
30. *Railway Age* (March 19, 1951), pp. 74–75.
31. New York *Times* (March 3, 1951), p. 21. *Railway Age* (April 2, 1951), p. 70.

of two new commissioners who needed to hear the facts in order to qualify them for a part in the final decision.[32] Hearings were renewed that October in Washington, D.C. The Rio Grande insisted that it would not gross more than an additional four million dollars in the new arrangement. When the Union Pacific talked about the possibility of curtailing service on its branches should the invasion come off, R. E. Quirk, legal counsel for the Rio Grande, said that road was trying to "put a scare in everyone in Idaho, Wyoming, Oregon, and Washington."[33] After extended arguments, the ICC, on January 26, 1953, ordered the Union Pacific to set up joint freight rates on a group of selected commodities moving through the Ogden Gateway. Rates applied only to livestock, fresh fruits and vegetables, dried beans, frozen poultry, frozen foods, and butter and eggs, moving from the Pacific Northwest, and on granite and marble monuments shipped westward from Vermont and Georgia. The door was opened only a crack, and some of the commissioners said so in a dissent to the ruling.[34] Wilson McCarthy knew he had not won an unqualified victory for his road, but he showed no bitterness. "At least we now have access to those Idaho potatoes," he said, and added that it was a foot in the door, which was "no small potatoes." He guessed that fully 60,000 carloads of potatoes had moved out of Idaho over Union Pacific rails during the preceding year.[35]

That the Denver and Rio Grande was not satisfied with a partial victory was revealed in October 1953, when it asked the federal courts to set aside the commission's January ruling. Its attorneys, in a far less genial mood than its president, charged the ICC order as being "unlawful, arbitrary and capricious," and said it violated the "spirit if not the letter of the federal law." The commission, they said, had ignored the recommendations of its chief examiner in granting the Rio Grande joint rates on only eight classes of commodities moving through the gateway. The result was a continued "closed door" or "restricted territory," which denied farmers in eastern Colorado, Nebraska, Kansas, western Iowa, Minnesota, and the Dakotas from enjoying the joint rates they deserved.[36]

32. New York *Times* (July 30, 1952), p. 40.
33. Salt Lake *Tribune*, Oct. 16, 1952.
34. New York *Times* (Jan. 27, 1953), p. 34.
35. Salt Lake *Tribune*, Jan. 23, 1955.
36. *Deseret News and Telegram*, Oct. 22, 1953.

In the fall of 1954 the Rio Grande received a sharp blow of disappointment when the ruling of a federal court in Omaha reversed the ICC, holding that the commission was without power to open the gateway as widely as it had. The court denied that the commission could enforce joint rates upon shipments that did not require stoppage or transit privileges at points on the Rio Grande.[37] Back to court went the Denver and Rio Grande, again demanding what it regarded as its right to enter Union Pacific territory. A special three judge court at Denver, in January 1955, ordered the whole case reopened, with the statement that "the very thing the Rio Grande seeks is not competitive advantage, but the establishment of just and reasonable through rates and the removal of unjust discrimination which will result in pecuniary profit to the Rio Grande the deprivation of which would prevent the Rio Grande from enjoying increased traffic and increased earnings." Wilson McCarthy applauded this home-town decision with the remark that it "confirms our belief that shippers should have freedom of choice in selecting routes. I am delighted with the decision and we will bend every effort to render the type of service which will attract substantial business to the Rio Grande."[38]

Round one of the fight ended in June 1956 with a Supreme Court decision upholding the earlier ICC ruling. President Stoddard of the Union Pacific tossed in the sponge, and as a national business journal put it, admitted that the Rio Grande management "had played David to his Goliath—and won." Stoddard concluded that it was of no further use to appeal the case.[39] It was a matter of regret in Denver circles that Wilson McCarthy had missed the last minutes of furious legal punching. He had died only a few months before the Supreme Court action. With a foot in the door, the Rio Grande then prepared for the next phase of battle, the objective of which would be the complete opening of the Ogden Gateway. New proceedings would have to be instituted and there were more battles to fight, but deep in his mountain retreat David had just got his second wind.

Meanwhile, as the Rio Grande sought means to expand its traffic from outside origins, a general house-cleaning from within had been taking place. During McCarthy's tenure of almost a decade, the process of pruning dead branches from the main trunk went forward in the

37. *Railway Age* (Nov. 1, 1954), p. 12.
38. Salt Lake *Tribune*, Jan. 14, 1955.
39. *Forbes Business and Finance* (Aug. 1, 1956), pp. 19–20.

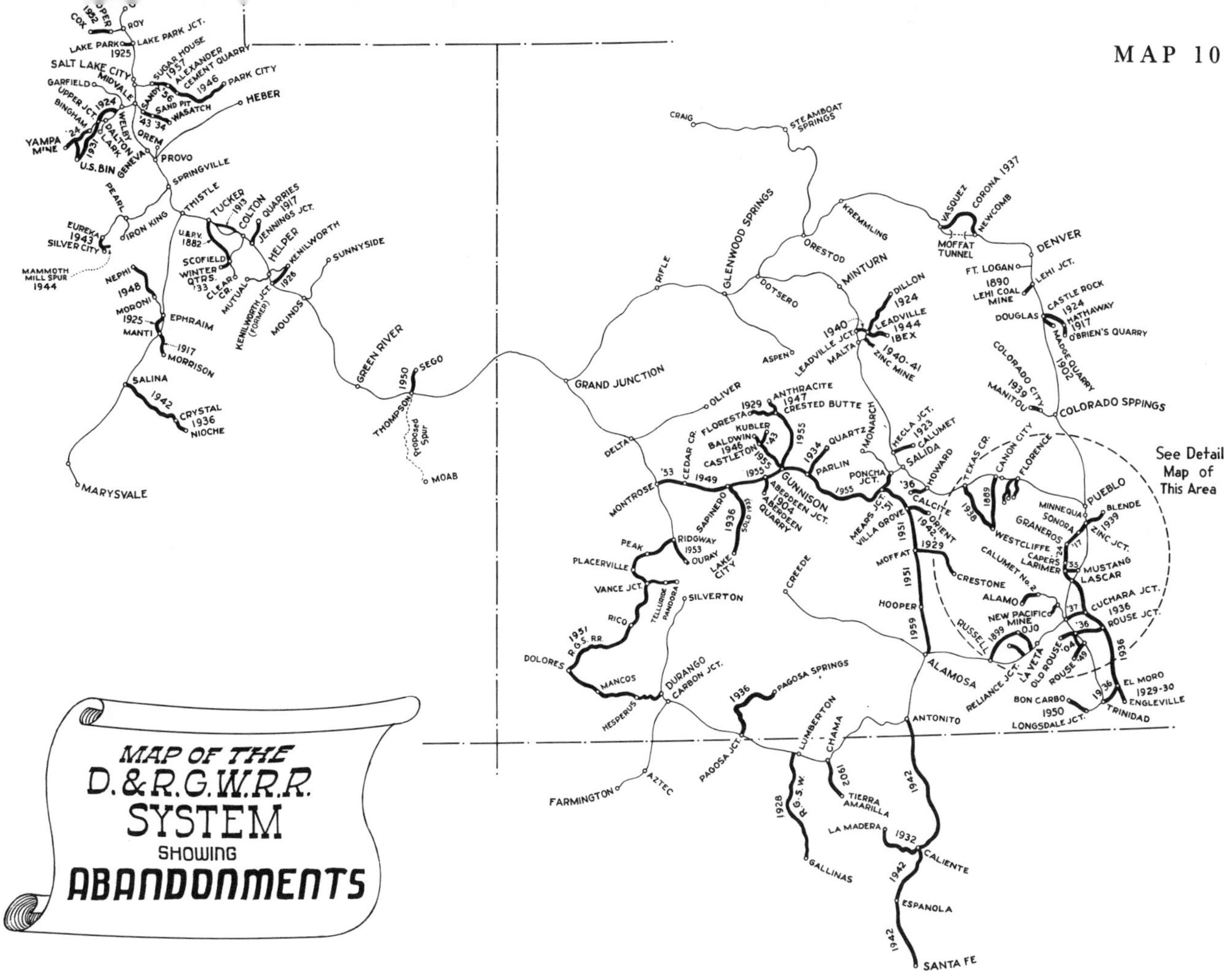

MAP 10

MAP OF THE
D.&R.G.W.R.R.
SYSTEM
SHOWING
ABANDONMENTS

See Detail Map of This Area

MAP 11

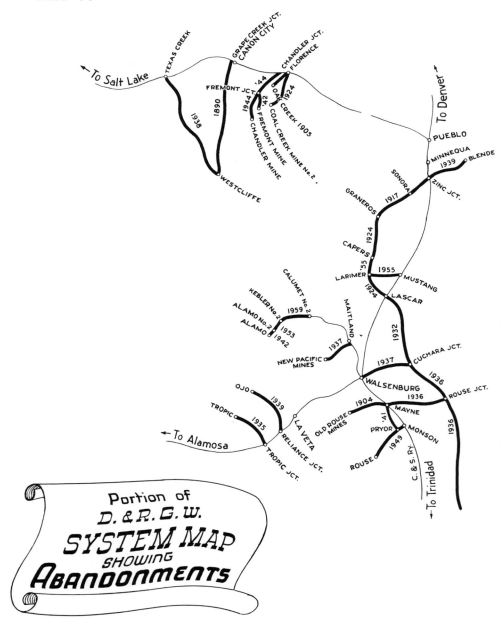

Portion of
D. & R. G. W.
SYSTEM MAP
SHOWING
Abandonments

interest of efficiency. For example, in 1947 the road asked abandonment of a portion of the San Pete Valley branch in Utah, a piece of
track nearly twenty-four miles long. The reasons were typical of those
advanced in the case of other abandonments: a once-profitable traffic
in agricultural products and livestock no longer existed. Costs of operation were falling far behind revenue.[40] About the same time, the
road requested permission to discontinue passenger traffic on the
Marysvale Branch, in Utah. Again, receipts showed a steady decline,
and in this case the post office had failed to renew a special mail contract. There were vociferous objections. As Norman J. Holt, mayor
of Richfield, complained, "We of the community provide the company freight income. . . . We do not think the railroad should be
permitted to deny us this vital service while retaining the cream of
the business. Our convenience is their moral obligation."[41] In both
cases, permission to suspend service was granted.

Colorado portions of the Rio Grande also underwent surgery. In
1948 a twenty-six-mile stretch of narrow-gauge track running from
near Sapinero to Cedar Creek, built in 1882 as part of the original
main line, was abandoned. A sharp 4 per cent grade, expensive to operate, and over which a sheep-hauling business was fading, pointed
only to an economic dead end.[42] Then came a request to end passenger
service on the narrow gauge between Alamosa and Durango. The suspension came in January 1951, amidst loud complaints from the "fan-
ciers of quaint railroads" who hated to see that picturesque remnant
of old-time railroading end.[43]

Narrow-gauge addicts saw their domain diminished by almost 150
additional miles during the next two years. The Rio Grande asked
permission to take up its tracks from Poncha Junction (near Salida)
to Gunnison and Sapinero as well as the Crested Butte and Baldwin
branches. The decision came after the Colorado Fuel and Iron Corporation revealed its intention to dismantle the big coal mine at Crested
Butte. McCarthy explained that all his road had received from the
condemned portion of track for the past few years was a steadily mounting deficit. The Crested Butte operations of the CF&I contributed

40. Minutes D&RGW Board of Directors, Dec. 22, 1947, in the office of the president,
D&RGW, Denver.

41. Salt Lake *Tribune*, March 2, 1947.

42. *Deseret News*, May 27, 1948.

43. *Life* (May 22, 1950), pp. 82–84. New York *Times* (March 4, 1951), p. 23.

two-thirds of what traffic there was; without that freight, the question of continuing service was settled in the negative.

"Passing of this brings a feeling of sadness since it removes the last remaining segment of the original narrow gauge between Denver and Salt Lake City via Marshall Pass," wrote the president. The line had opened for business in 1881 and was perhaps the most glamorous railroad ever built in the West. When it crossed Marshall Pass, nearly 11,000 feet above sea level, it had the distinction of making the highest railroad crossing in North America. But now it was no longer a part of the main line and it had carried no passengers since 1940. From 1950 to 1952, inclusive, this section of road cost the Rio Grande over $500,000 in losses. During the first five months of May 1953, just before closure, only four trains carrying revenue freight went over the pass to Gunnison and back.[44] As the year ended, the railroad made one more amputation. It asked for a discontinuance of passenger service between Salt Lake City and Ogden, on the ground that the operation was losing between seventy and eighty thousand dollars a year on that extension.[45] But as McCarthy pointed out, sentiment had to be sacrificed for economic realities. By the close of 1954 he could report that during the year his road had received about $850,000 in tax credits for the value of nondepreciable property retired.[46]

There were other abandonments, the most important of which was the Rio Grande Southern, built in 1891 to serve the mining industry. Its 172.4 miles of narrow gauge, in receivership since 1929, ceased operations at the end of 1951.[47] This and the others mentioned are indicative of the Rio Grande's pruning policy, aimed at keeping the road in a healthy physical and financial condition and at facing realities. A study of these withered limbs would reveal the great changes effected in the economies of Utah and Colorado, particularly in the latter, during the early years of the twentieth century. The precious metals industry, upon which so much of General Palmer's building was predicated, had just about completed a circle, and if the Rio Grande were to live, it had to look in new directions.

Passenger transportation continued to be one of the perplexing

44. Salt Lake *Tribune*, Aug. 26, 1952. New York *Times* (Oct. 4, 1953), p. 1.
45. Salt Lake *Tribune*, Oct. 2, Dec. 11, 1953.
46. Ibid., Dec. 20, 1954.
47. *Annual Report of the D&RGW*, 1952. *Rocky Mountain News*, Nov. 14, 1951. This total of 172.4 miles includes an extension to Pandora from the end of the Telluride branch.

problems faced by all railroads in the nation. At the close of the war in 1945, gasoline rationing was removed and automobile manufacturers turned from the temporary task of building military equipment to that of replacing the worn-out family car. Railroads and bus lines soon felt the competition, particularly on short runs. The Rio Grande, having operated bus lines for about twenty years, suffered in both departments. Consistent with its policy of dropping those services it did not find profitable, the railroad rather early after the war decided to sell its bus-passenger facilities.

The Rio Grande Motor Way, established in March 1927, included the Western Slope Motor Way and the Rio Grande Motor Way of Utah. The Western Slope Motor Way was purchased after the railroad had failed to prevent the appearance of competitive motor service in western Colorado. It adopted the "if you can't lick 'em, join 'em" position when the independent motor carriers demonstrated their superiority of service and flexibility between the small and more remote communities of rural Colorado. The story was the same in Utah. Rio Grande Motor Way expanded steadily, until by 1947 it was operating a bus transportation system that paralleled nearly all lines of the parent railroad. As well as discouraging further bus competition in its territory, the railroad found its subsidiary a useful argument when it proposed the abandonment of some of its unprofitable branch-line trains. In the face of outcries from various small communities threatened by the loss of service, the Rio Grande was able to contend that the company offered a satisfactory substitute and that it was not leaving these municipalities without public transportation. In 1956 the company calculated that cancellations of passenger or mixed train-service during the preceding three decades were saving it in excess of a million dollars a year.

Early in 1948 the railroad was approached by the Continental Bus System with an offer to purchase its bus operations. The bus company was then building a transcontinental system of its own and the Rio Grande's holdings provided a necessary link between the Middle West and Far West. Since the Rio Grande's branch bus lines were not generally profitable, an offer was entertained. After some negotiations, the bus property and operating rights were sold to Continental for $562,364.10, soon after which the new owners dropped the unprofitable portions of their new purchase. Since the purchase price was over $100,000 in excess of the book value of the tangible and intangible property of the Motor Way, the railroad felt it had made an entirely satisfactory transaction.[48]

Coincidental with the abandonment program was the Rio Grande's acceleration of improvement through research. Late in 1954 the Grand Junction *Daily Sentinel* published a rumor that a uranium-powered locomotive was under construction in the railroad's Denver shops. "The entire project being done under Army and Atomic Energy Commission contract, is locked up in a secrecy tighter than Ft. Knox," said the story. McCarthy denied the reports, saying that Ray McBrian, chief of the road's research department, had been working on the possibility of utilizing atomic energy in running diesel-electric locomotives, but to date no such project had been launched. Rumors die hard and this one was no exception. Salt Lake and Grand Junction papers persisted, telling their readers that there were reports of secret runs being made on the main line.[49]

The Rio Grande made no effort to conceal the fact that it was experimenting with atomic energy, but quite correctly it denied that the progress made was as great as reported. In March 1955 the Atomic Energy Commission signed a contract with the Rio Grande and the Baldwin-Lima-Hamilton Corporation of Philadelphia, which provided for a joint study of atomic-powered railroad locomotives. Ray McBrian had spent portions of the preceding fifteen months working on what he believed to be a revolutionary design for such an engine. The project was not received with complete enthusiasm by the traditionally conservative railroad world, much to the annoyance of Wilson McCarthy. Impatient with the characteristically cautious attitude taken toward the powerful atom, McCarthy brushed aside pictures of horrible atomic-train wrecks painted by other railroad executives and their legal advisers. Largely through his insistence, the Association of American Railroads appointed a special committee to study the application of atomic power to the nation's rail lines.[50]

At the time that the Rio Grande was given governmental permission to proceed with its atomic engine studies, it also asked for consent to test atomic switch-lamps to be developed jointly with the U. S. Radium

48. Minutes D&RGW Board of Directors, April 12, 1950, in the office of the president, D&RGW, Denver. *Rocky Mountain News*, Oct. 14, 1948. *Brief History and Outline of Reasons for Establishing and Maintaining Rio Grande Motor Way, Inc.*, D&RGW offices, Denver.

49. Salt Lake *Tribune*, Dec. 14, 1954, quoting the *Daily Sentinel*.

50. Ibid., Dec. 2, 1956.

Corporation of Morristown, New Jersey. By February 1957 McBrian's laboratory had on display a new lamp that would glow continuously at working brightness and without refueling for at least twelve years. Operating without oil or electricity, its atom-powered rays could be seen far down the track by a locomotive engineer. Outwardly, the lamp looked much like switch-lamps used throughout the nation. Its four glow-disks, about three inches in diameter, were heavily sealed behind a glass that resembled a large watch crystal. The light source came from a phosphor coating, illuminated when exposed to atomic radiation. Krypton-85, a radioactive gas stored behind the glass, provided the power. The gas, chemically inactive, offered no potential danger because it escaped into the air and diluted rapidly were the glass to be broken by accident.

The new switch-lamp offered the railroading business nothing revolutionary in a practical way, since switch-lamps could be operated efficiently by more traditional means, but the new source of power was suggestive of unexplored frontiers in the world of the scientist. McBrian admitted quite candidly that this "light is really a by-product of our atomic locomotive studies." The railroad's research program, broad and unlimited in scope, was aimed at two principal goals: the application of an atomic power unit to the propulsion of locomotives or to stationary power sources such as generating units, and the application of nuclear principles and discoveries to any area of railroad operation where an economy or better operational methods could be achieved. In its probings, McBrian's laboratory was apt to come across any number of applications of nuclear physics, some of which would be useful to his company, others perhaps suggestive of further research in related fields.[51]

The bold and open-minded approach to the Rio Grande's experimentations, thoroughly encouraged by company officers, had long since demonstrated the value of such a program. At its Burnham Shops laboratory, established in 1936 during the trusteeship, the railroad carried on a relentless quest for new methods of saving and prolonging the life of expensive rolling stock. Spectrographic analysis of lubricating oils, to determine the presence of harmful impurities, was one of the early outcomes. In 1952 an electron microscope was purchased to examine more carefully oils, fuels, and gasolines. By utilizing the

51. Denver *Post,* Feb. 17, 1957. Ray McBrian, "Atomic Methods Promise New Horizons in Railroad Research," *Railway Age* (Feb. 25, 1957), pp. 42–44.

new microscope, fuels of the lower price range could be prepared for diesel locomotives with a resultant saving of nearly two cents a gallon.[52] Similarly, the use of a recording densitometer, which revealed with great accuracy the content of metallic particles in lubricating oil, provided sufficient warning to prevent excessive wear failures.[53] In his annual report for 1954 McCarthy stated that lower fuel costs, resulting from the use of this scientific equipment, had saved the road $372,790 during the year.

In the first postwar decade the Rio Grande vindicated those who had placed their faith in its ability to prosper as an independent transportation facility. During the years that followed its Independence Day, the little rebel of the Rockies, freed at last from economic thralldom imposed by outside forces, pursued a course that drew expressions of admiration from the American railroading world. With an operating ratio reduced to what a leading business magazine called a "spectacular 63.1%," and its car loadings reversing a national downward trend that developed in the second half of the 1950s, the mountain railroad was in sound financial condition.[54] Stockholders looked with satisfaction at the 1956 report and noted that the wartime high in operating revenues of seventy-five million dollars was surpassed by more than six million, with a net return of just under $12,200,000. During the war, Judge Symes had explained that the high revenues were "due to Government and war business both freight and passenger." Now, when there was no war, the explanation had to be sought not on the national scene, where the general railroad picture was far from bright, but within the Rocky Mountain Empire itself and from a once-bankrupt railroad that had put its faith in western people and proved a point.

In the record year of 1956 Wilson McCarthy died—at the zenith of his own career and that of the road to which he had dedicated himself. His successor was forty-one-year-old Gale B. "Gus" Aydelott, a youngster among railroad executives but one who had spent twenty years growing up with the modern Rio Grande. The new president belonged to a family of railroaders. His father, James Aydelott, was for many years one of the Burlington's top operating officers, having retired from that line in 1947 as general manager. The younger Aydelott

52. Salt Lake *Tribune*, March 25, 1943. *Annual Report of the D&RGW* (1952), p. 10.
53. *Annual Report* (1953), p. 10.
54. *Forbes* (Sept. 1, 1957), p. 23.

54. G. B. "Gus" Aydelott and Board Chairman John Evans suggest here that mountain railroading is not all headaches.

came to the Rio Grande fresh from the University of Illinois in 1936, a college graduate who showed his willingness to start at the bottom by taking a job that summer as a track-gang laborer. Having worked his way through various jobs as track inspector, engineering assistant, roadmaster, and trainmaster, he emerged as a division superintendent in 1948. In 1954 he was appointed vice-president and general manager, and in August 1955 he became executive vice-president, succeeding Alfred Perlman, who had recently left that post to become head of the New York Central Railroad. Six months later Aydelott reached the top of the Rio Grande's executive structure.[55]

The death of Wilson McCarthy occasioned no significant changes in company policy. John Evans, whose hand never had been far away from the corporate throttle since the period of trusteeship, was chairman of the board, and his presence offered assurances that the transition in the president's office would be accomplished without difficulty. Aydelott, trained in the school of the "New Rio Grande," thoroughly subscribed to the bold approach that had come to characterize the railroad under McCarthy's tutelage. Publicly, he announced that his predecessor's concept of the best way to run a mountain railroad would be strictly adhered to. Privately, he admitted, with a rueful grin, that affairs were in such good shape there was not much to be done except keep the machine oiled and in motion. That this was merely an attitude of humility was to be shown by the crop of fresh ideas that issued from his office before his day of command was very old.

The young executive took over at a very fortuitous time. By 1956 well over a third of the Rio Grande's tonnage was picked up and turned over to connecting roads, whereas during the 1920s the figure amounted to only about 5 per cent of the total. Bridge traffic now accounted for nearly half of all the railroad's revenue. Another factor that contributed to these days of prosperity was the economic growth of the Rocky Mountain area. Included in the industrial expansion were a number of uranium mines and uranium processors, a large percentage of which depended upon the Rio Grande for freight service.[56]

To accommodate new sources of business and to keep the physical property in top operating condition, the new management con-

55. Minutes D&RGW Board of Directors, Aug. 22, 1955, in the office of the president, D&RGW, Denver. Salt Lake *Tribune*, Feb. 28, 1956. *Railway Age* (March 5, 1956), p. 58.
56. Salt Lake *Tribune*, March 30, 1956. *Deseret News and Telegram*, May 28, 1956.

tinued its inherited policy of improvement. During 1957 it set aside $7,250,000 for additional equipment, principally rolling stock, bringing to more than 150 million the total spent on improvements since McCarthy had begun his major rehabilitation program twenty years earlier. With the purchase of ten more heavy-duty diesel-electric locomotives, the road now owned 254 of these units, the last standard-gauge steam engine having been retired on the last day of 1956. During the next few years similar amounts of money were earmarked for further improvements to prepare the railroad for "the increased potential confidently anticipated," as Aydelott expressed it.[57]

On March 21, 1959, the *California Zephyr* celebrated its tenth birthday. This crack streamliner, shared by the Rio Grande with two other railroads, carried over a million and a half passengers, traversed eighteen and a half million miles, and posted a recorded average daily occupancy of 89.4 per cent of capacity in its first decade of operation. Its occupancy history was claimed as a record unexcelled by any other means of transportation.[58] These figures were indeed glad tidings in an era of declining passenger revenues across the nation, but they spoke of only one aspect of the picture. This particular service, with its six sets of equipment that made up the train, was the only passenger-carrying facility in which the Rio Grande participated at a profit, the Durango-Silverton narrow-gauge tourist attraction being the one possible exception. The *Royal Gorge* and the *Prospector,* operating between Denver and Salt Lake City, generally were losers.

It has been said that a little success is a dangerous thing, and in a way the *Zephyr's* performance was a disservice to the Rio Grande. Its achievements lent the impression that, contrary to public talk, passenger service *was* paying and that this railroad was making money from such facilities. When the company approached the State Public Utility Commission for permission to abandon unprofitable passenger service on local runs, the success of passenger business of other parts of the road was bound to pervade the atmosphere of the hearings. At such abandonment requests it was not difficult for residents of the area involved to take the attitude that the railroad had reverted to Commodore Vanderbilt's "public be damned" posture. The company,

57. Denver *Post,* Jan. 13, 1957; Jan. 4, 1959. Salt Lake *Tribune,* Jan. 13, 1957. *Annual Reports of the D&RGW,* 1957–60.

58. *Railway Age* (March 30, 1959), p. 68. *Annual Report of the D&RGW* (1959), p. 26.

however, was obliged to forego the luxury of sentiment and to study the balance sheet instead. From a financial point of view it had some sympathy for a statement once attributed to another great railroader, James J. Hill: "A passenger train, sir, is like the male teat: neither useful nor ornamental."

The Aydelott regime encountered stiff resistance to passenger-service reduction. In 1956 the Rio Grande proposed discontinuance of passenger trains on the old Moffat line on the ground that the Denver-Craig run was losing money. Just as quickly, residents of Middle Park and the Yampa Valley formed a committee and lodged a loud protest. Colorado's Public Utility Commission conducted hearings in January and March, 1957, at which the railroad maintained that the trains were an economic waste. Aydelott asserted that "the people neither use nor want the service they provide, as evidenced by the fact that an average of only nine people per day ride each train, which requires a crew of six railroaders." On December 3 the commission denied the company's petition, holding that the railroad's use of the Moffat Tunnel constituted a subsidy, and the Rio Grande was therefore obliged to operate these trains regardless of patronage or of attendant loss.[59]

Equally frustrating to the Rio Grande's executive officers was an attempt to sell the Durango-Silverton narrow-gauge line. This forty-five-mile piece of road, winding along precipitous ledges above the Animas River, this historic "train to yesterday," had captured the imagination and the hearts of those who knew it. Each summer day nearly 400 tourists clambered aboard the brightly painted cars as an ancient black locomotive breathed steam, gave off spine-tingling sounds of another era, and promised several hours of adventure in the remoteness of Colorado's mountains. Then it slowly clicked its way out of Durango, the whistle moaning a soothing song that did not quite drown out the expletives of those unfortunates who had not thought about reservations and were left behind. To steam-railroad enthusiasts, a passionately dedicated and highly vocal group, the idea of selling this last bit of history down the river was a kind of heresy that would have made Simon Legree blush.

To all romanticists the corporate heart is cold. And few children are convinced when father says, "This is going to hurt me worse than it

59. *Rocky Mountain News*, Sept. 12, 1956. Boulder *Daily Camera*, Jan. 26, 1957. *Railway Age* (Jan. 6, 1958), p. 35. *Annual Report of the D&RGW* (1957), p. 7.

does you." While the notion of selling the Silverton line caused breast-beating among those who loved it, the owners wanted to let it go before excessive slides or the cost of making extensive equipment and track replacements took a large bite out of the company's treasury. In the autumn of 1959 a prospective buyer was found: the Helen Thatcher White Foundation of Colorado. If ICC permission could be gained, the Rio Grande proposed to sell the narrow gauge for $250,000. Since the prospective new owner was a nonprofit corporation, the consummation of such a deal would have meant a sizeable loss of taxes to the counties involved. In the ensuing commotion, pressures, tangible and intangible, were exerted, with the result that the offer to buy was rescinded. To accomplish the original purpose of the White Foundation, namely to continue summer passenger service on that line, a group of western Colorado businessmen organized the Durango-Silverton Railroad, whose announced purpose was that of making a profit. Hearings were conducted at Durango late in 1960 to consider the railroad's request for abandonment. In June 1961, ICC examiner Lester R. Conley submitted a negative recommendation but agreed that the company could suspend operations each year between October 1 and June 1. For the time being, at least, the Silverton would continue its summer operations under Rio Grande management.[60]

During the months that the Rio Grande was making an unsuccessful attempt to divest itself of the Silverton narrow gauge, its attorneys were before the Interstate Commerce Commission examiners with another request. In August 1957 the road filed a petition with the commission, requesting equal status with respect to the solicitation and distribution of Southern Pacific freight traffic passing through Ogden. While this case had no connection with the Ogden Gateway suit, it was similar in that it sought to gain for the Rio Grande additional transcontinental traffic.

By a commission order of February 6, 1923, known as the "Central Pacific Order," the Southern Pacific was obliged to solicit freight traffic preferentially for the Union Pacific on all business moving east or west by way of Ogden. The order was issued at the time the South-

60. Exceptions of Applicant to Recommended Report and Order of Lester R. Conley in the Matter of the Application of the D&RGW to Abandon a Portion of its Narrow-Gauge Line between Durango and Silverton, Colo., Docket FD-20943, D&RGW offices, Denver. *Denver Post*, June 7, 1961. On May 2, 1962, the ICC denied the Rio Grande's application.

ern Pacific was granted permission to assume control of the Central Pacific and it was imposed as a means of preventing the Southern Pacific from discriminating against the Central Pacific Route in favor of its other line through El Paso, Texas. Since the Rio Grande was not in a competitive position in 1923, it offered no objections to the arrangement, but during the intervening years, with the completion of the Moffat Tunnel and the Dotsero Cutoff, and the consequent shortening of its route between Denver and Salt Lake City, the mountain railroad had itself altered the original conditions.

In stating the Rio Grande's position, Aydelott said: "Equality of opportunity for all carriers to participate in the central-northern California traffic route east or west through Ogden is the object of this petition." R. Knox Bradford, Rio Grande vice-president, made his company's argument even more specific with the charge that any requirement causing the Southern Pacific to solicit freight traffic preferentially for the Union Pacific was "unlawful discrimination . . . contrary to the stated national transportation policy and undue prejudice against the Rio Grande." The complainants also objected strongly to a purported agreement entered into between the two larger railroads in 1924, under which the scope of the preferential solicitation arrangement was enlarged and extended beyond the commission's original order.[61]

Hearings were conducted in Salt Lake City in January and again in March, 1960. In mid-September the examiner submitted his recommended supplemental report and order, favoring the Rio Grande. The opposition immediately entered exceptions and the matter then went before the commission for a final ruling from that body.[62]

While Aydelott's legal staff kept itself busy trying to pare down operations that were of doubtful value within the corporate structure and battling for more business from connecting lines, his engineering department continued its program of improvement. In the summer of 1958, at a time when the railroad was feeling the pinch of a nationwide business recession and more than one businessman talked of retrenchment, the Rio Grande announced its intention to build a microwave system for trunk line communications between Ogden, Denver, and

61. Salt Lake *Tribune*, June 18, 1957. *Railway Age* (June 24, 1957), p. 7. See also Finance Docket 2613, Control of Central Pacific by Southern Pacific, ICC *Reports*, 76 (1922–23), 530.
62. *Annual Reports of the D&RGW*, 1957, 1958, 1959, 1960. Denver *Post*, Sept. 22, 1960.

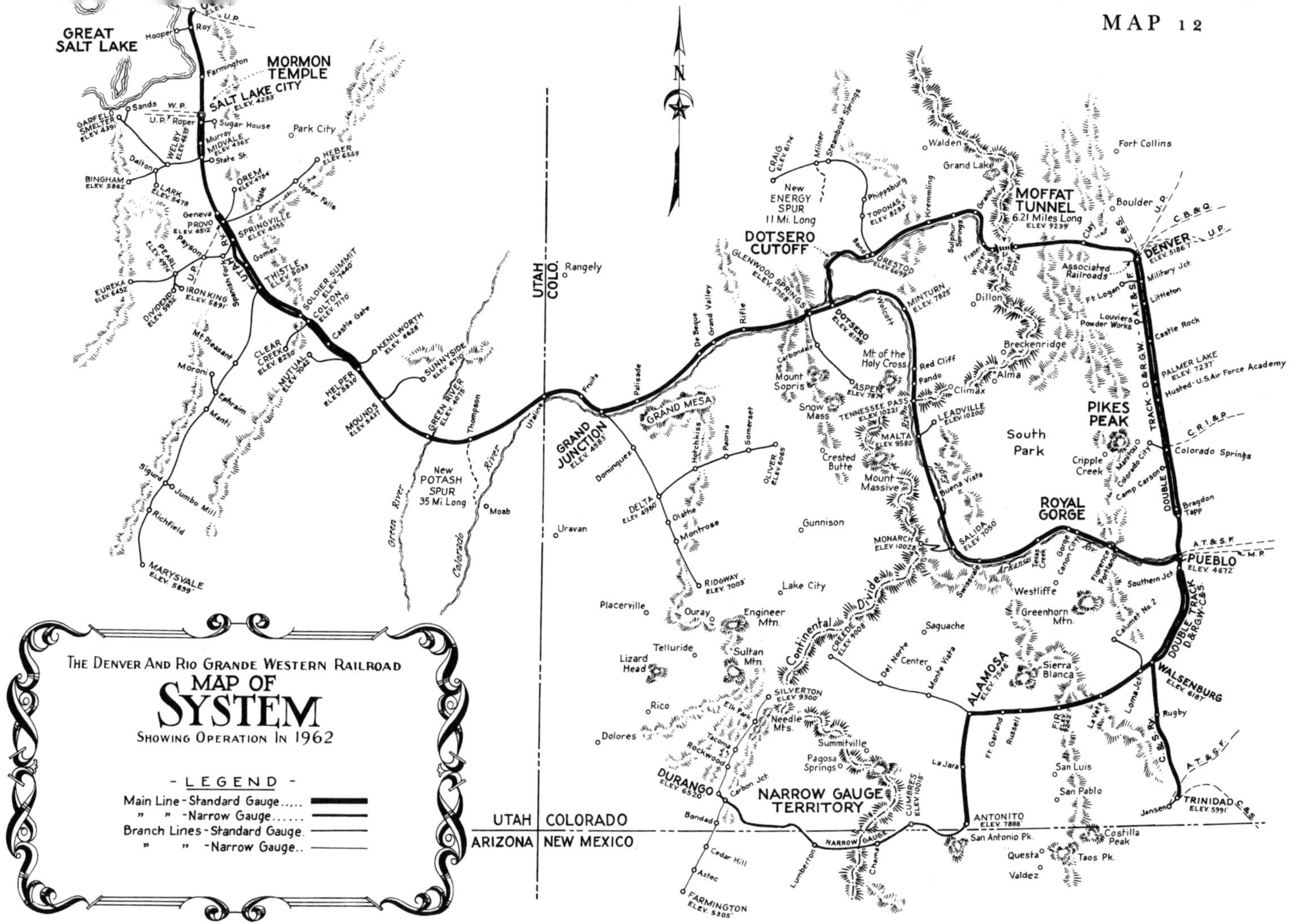

MAP 12

N

UTAH
COLO.

UTAH COLORADO
ARIZONA NEW MEXICO

GREAT
SALT LAKE

MORMON TEMPLE

SALT LAKE CITY ELEV 4230

Fort Collins

Boulder

DENVER ELEV 5161

MOFFAT TUNNEL 6.21 Miles Long ELEV 9239

PIKES PEAK

Colorado Springs

Cripple Creek

ROYAL GORGE

PUEBLO ELEV 4672

DOUBLE TRACK - D.&R.G.W.

WALSENBURG ELEV 6187

TRINIDAD ELEV 5991

ALAMOSA ELEV 7544

ANTONITO ELEV 7888

CUMBRES ELEV 10015

NARROW GAUGE TERRITORY

DURANGO ELEV 6520

FARMINGTON ELEV 5305

Continental Divide

DOTSERO CUTOFF

DOTSERO ELEV 6136

New ENERGY SPUR 11 Mi. Long

CRAIG ELEV 6176

Steamboat Springs

GLENWOOD SPRINGS ELEV 5758

LEADVILLE ELEV 10155

GRAND JUNCTION ELEV 4583

GRAND MESA

DELTA

Gunnison

Lake City

Telluride

Durango

Moab

Rangely

NEW POTASH SPUR 35 Mi. Long

GREEN RIVER ELEV 4055

South Park

Breckenridge

Mt. of the Holy Cross

Mount Massive

Mount Elbert

THE DENVER AND RIO GRANDE WESTERN RAILROAD

MAP OF SYSTEM

SHOWING OPERATION IN 1962

- LEGEND -

Main Line - Standard Gauge	
" - Narrow Gauge	
Branch Lines - Standard Gauge	
" - Narrow Gauge	

Pueblo. Revelation of this plan was made public in the face of local
newspaper talk that the company's gross earnings for the first six
months of the year were down nearly seven million dollars as compared to a like period in the preceding year. Although the picture was
improved by the year's end, the road's operating revenues declined
over eight million dollars during 1958. Unmoved by the recession's
punishment, Aydelott announced a $6,750,000 improvement program.
When this was completed, the railroad would have put 112 million
into additions and betterments in the twelve-year period 1947–59.
Following in the footsteps of McCarthy, he believed in improving his
railroad, not milking it to answer demands of stockholders when the
going was rough.[63]

Operating revenues suffered a further, if smaller, decline in 1959,
but in 1960 they experienced a welcome upturn. During these months
of doubt the Rio Grande went forward with its microwave installation,
a system that was in operation by mid-1961. The new means of communication was given the popular name "Shipper Facts" to provide
the public with a capsule explanation of its function. Now it was possible for full information on any freight car moving across the Rio
Grande system to be transmitted to a point of use within one minute.
By electronic means, a waybill facsimile could be passed from tower
to tower across the Rockies, carrying all the basic information about
a freight car and its contents. A high speed computer could reveal
where a freight car came from, who shipped it, when it was sent on its
way, and where it was going. Such questions as what was in the car,
what was the value of the contents, and who owned the railroad car
were answered almost instantaneously. The once-rumpled waybill,
creasing in the conductor's pocket, now flew through the air to Denver,
Pueblo, Grand Junction, Salt Lake City, and Ogden. A magnetic
memory also kept an inventory of cars on hand at any rail terminal,
providing information as to the commodity, the tonnage, and the destination of each, information that could be printed up at the rate of
150 cars per minute.[64]

In another departure from tradition the Rio Grande ordered three
revolutionary new hydraulic-drive diesel locomotives from West Germany late in 1959 at a cost of around a million dollars. The engines

---

63. *Railway Age* (July 7, 1958), p. 7. Denver *Post*, July 27, 1958; Jan. 4, 1959.
64. Denver *Post*, June 25, 1961.

operated on a principle similar to the fluid drive used in automobiles, the power supply being applied through fluid-activated turbines without the use of electric-traction motors on the drive wheels. The Southern Pacific also ordered three of these 4,000 horsepower units. As David P. Morgan, editor of *Trains* pointed out, "a considerable degree of intestinal fortitude" was required by these railroads "both in a mechanical and political sense." Not only was there some question as to whether the hydraulics would pay off mechanically, but the purchases were made in the face of "buy American" pressure that tended to make foreign purchases unpopular, despite the fact that no American manufacturer had the experience to bid on such units. "Still, self-preservation is the first law of corporations as well as of the jungle," said Morgan, "and the railroads' operating ratios and competitive pressures are far too high for them to ignore technological developments, whether spawned here or abroad."[65] If the engines failed to be a profitable gamble, it would not be the first time the Rio Grande, or any other railroad, had been disappointed in a purchase, but as Morgan had said, competitive pressures in railroading were too great to ignore such opportunities and the old credo of "nothing ventured, nothing gained" still operated.

In autumn of 1960 the Rio Grande passed its ninetieth birthday. During the nine decades since its incorporation that October day in 1870, it had experienced financial growing pains, lived through five receiverships, and fought off the incursions of larger roads which, in one case, had resulted in temporary captivity and, in another, in bankruptcy. It had been mauled in a struggle between local interests and those who lived in such far-off lands as New York, had fluctuated between periods of brilliant leadership and years of executive incompetency, and had felt the caress of prideful words alternated by bitter tongue-lashings from the westerners it served. Whatever its condition, whether that of financial despair or confident prosperity, the heartbeat of the railroad pulsed with the hope of eventual emancipation and independence of corporate action. Since the day of General Palmer, this had been the thought of those who lived with the road, of those who saw the land and its main artery of commerce as reciprocal parts of a growing economy. And on that ninetieth birthday, John Evans, chairman of the board, was telling the Denver papers the never-ending

65. *Trains*, 20 (1960), 5. *Railway Age* (June 20, 1960), p. 14. Denver *Post*, Dec. 20, 1959.

55. A Westbound Manifest Freight Train. On the Moffat Tunnel route near Granby, Rio Grande rails parallel the Colorado river. High peaks of the Continental Divide form an impressive backdrop.

story recounted repeatedly to older generations of journalists—no, the Rio Grande was not up for sale or merger.[66]

The occasion for these denials followed familiar patterns. In a new era of mergers which recalled the days of McKinley, major railroads across the country were strengthening their holdings through the absorption of smaller lines. Reverberations were felt in the West late in 1960 and early in 1961, as the Santa Fe and the Southern Pacific sought to control that illegitimate child of the Rio Grande, the Western Pacific. Since the Rio Grande was heavily dependent upon interchange traffic with both the Southern Pacific and the Western Pacific, its instincts for self-preservation were aroused. Control by the Santa Fe probably would mean a diversion of traffic from Utah through Arizona and New Mexico, a prospect that quickly sent the Rio Grande into the opposing camp. For the same reason the Union Pacific adopted a similar point of view. Aydelott's statement to the press that "the public interest and the Rio Grande's own will be safeguarded better if Southern Pacific wins control of Western Pacific" did not suggest that he approved of such a transcontinental merger. Possession of the Western Pacific by either of the contesting major roads could pose problems for the Rio Grande, but if the sale was inevitable, the Denver company hoped its new owner was one whose attitudes were apt to be the most friendly to connecting lines. Speaking for his own road, Aydelott said: "the Rio Grande wants to remain independent."[67]

As the giants of the transportation world snarled at each other and maneuvered for position in the hunt, smaller railroads grew concerned, for they were the hunted. The Union Pacific watched the contest closely, ever alert to the consequences of the Santa Fe-Southern Pacific struggle, its own destiny jeopardized by the noise of battle beyond the Great Salt Lake. In February 1961 trading in railroad stock grew brisk with an unusual demand for Rio Grande. The Union Pacific, said press rumors, had acquired 500,000 shares of the relatively small but strategically located Rocky Mountain railroad, a figure that was believed to represent around 10 per cent of its total issue. Aydelott's company urged its stockholders to watch such trends and warned against participation in any moves that might lead to outside control of their railroad.

66. Denver *Post*, Oct. 25, 1960. Statement by John Evans to civic and industrial leaders at Salt Lake City, July 17, 1961, copy in the office of the president, D&RGW offices, Denver.

67. Denver *Post*, June 13, 1961. *Rocky Mountain News*, July 21, 1961.

In a sense, history had completed another full circle, and the Rio Grande, Colorado's only east-west main railroad, again stood in the same danger zone that had so concerned General Palmer. Those who were close to the heart of the matter looked back over almost a century, remembered the consequences of putting the "Baby Road" out for adoption, and fervently hoped that the lessons learned in the turbulent years of corporate adolescence would not be lost upon a modern generation.

Bibliography

THE BULK of archival material relating to the Denver and Rio Grande Railroad is located at the office of State Archives and Public Records, Denver. Four 4-drawer filing cabinets contain chronologically arranged documents dating from the road's incorporation. There are some Palmer letters in this collection but almost nothing from the pen of later executive officers. At the railroad's offices, on Stout Street, are filmed copies of much of the above-mentioned material as well as annual reports, minutes of board meetings, miscellaneous papers of the Rio Grande, and the files of the Denver and Salt Lake Railroad. In the footnotes of this work the document cited is always from the State Archives collection unless the holdings at the railroad offices are specifically mentioned.

Palmer's private correspondence is collected in the Palmer papers, State Historical Society of Colorado, Denver, along with the personal papers of William A. Bell, Robert Weitbrec, and William S. Jackson. The State Archives has most of these papers on film. The only McCarthy papers are found in four volumes of McCarthy scrapbooks held at the company offices. They contain principally newspaper cuttings, photographs, telegrams, mementos, and an occasional letter.

INTERVIEWS

Bradford, R. Knox, Sept. 14, 1956.
Mr. Bradford, vice-president, traffic, came to the Rio Grande in August 1923 with T. H. Beacom (operating vice-president of the Rock Island), who succeeded Joseph H. Young as receiver.
Colwell, William O., Aug. 10, 1956.
Treasurer, Denver and Rio Grande Western. Mr. Colwell's railroading experience began on the Rio Grande road in 1924. In 1927 he went to the Denver and Salt Lake, where he worked until the spring of 1947, when that road became part of the Rio Grande.
Daly, L. J., Aug. 10, 1956.
A former trainmaster, retired in 1953, Mr. Daly took his first railroad job with the old Moffat road in May 1903.
Fitzpatrick, John, Sept. 11, 1956.
A member of the Rio Grande's board of directors, Mr. Fitzpatrick was formerly the editor of the Salt Lake *Tribune*.

Grimes, Oliver J., Sept. 13, 1956.
   Mr. Grimes is the retired general traffic manager of the Rio Grande.
Harker, George, Sept. 9, 1956.
   Mr. Harker was a brakeman with the Rio Grande, 1937–50.
Johnson, Edwin C., Aug. 29, 1961.
   At one time a Union Pacific train dispatcher and telegrapher, Mr. Johnson
   moved to Colorado in 1909 to recover from tuberculosis. He homesteaded in
   northwestern Colorado, operated a farmers' cooperative association, served in
   the Colorado Legislature, was elected lieutenant governor and later governor.
   He also represented Colorado in the U.S. Senate and serves as a member of
   the Rio Grande's board of directors.
King, J. E., Aug. 7, 1956.
   A locomotive engineer who went to work for the Rio Grande in July 1906.
McCarthy, Dennis, Aug. 7, 1956.
   Mr. McCarthy, a Salt Lake City attorney, is the son of Wilson McCarthy.
Page, J. D., Aug. 7, 1956.
   A Rio Grande fireman and locomotive engineer since 1935.
Swan, Henry, Aug. 22, 1956.
   A Princeton graduate, Mr. Swan worked as deputy state engineer in western
   Colorado in his early postgraduate days. He then engaged in the contracting
   business, and in 1906 had a part in building a portion of the Moffat road.
   From 1935 to 1947 he was co-trustee with Wilson McCarthy.
Wann, Ralph J., Aug. 6, 1956.
   A long-time Colorado businessman and president of the Royal Gorge suspen-
   sion bridge near Canon City, Mr. Wann served as a member of the Rio
   Grande's board of directors until his death in 1960.

LETTERS, PERSONAL PAPERS, AND MANUSCRIPTS

In the Coburn Library, Colorado College, Colorado Springs

William Jackson Palmer, *Scrapbook*. An important collection of newspaper clippings, correspondence, and articles of various types, in the library's unclassi-
   fied section.
Rio Grande Western, *Western Scrapbook*. A collection of clippings concerning
   the Western, in the library's Colorado Room.

In the Denver Public Library Western History Collection

David C. Dodge Correspondence, 1868–71 (Letter Book).
Nannie O. S. Dodge, "In Memory of Colonel D. C. Dodge." A typescript dated
   1923.

In the Denver and Rio Grande Western offices, Denver

Erskine Meyer Papers.
Arthur Ridgway, "Denver and Rio Grande: Development of Physical Property
   in Chronological Narrative," 1921.

Stenographers' Minutes before the Interstate Commerce Commission, Finance Dockets 4555 and 8070: "Proposed Construction by Denver & Salt Lake Western Railroad Company," March 10, 1932; "Construction by Denver & Salt Lake Western Railroad Company," June 9, 1932.

In the Division of State Archives and Public Records, Denver

David C. Dodge Correspondence, 1879–85 (Letter Book).
James A. McMurtrie Correspondence, 1877–84 (Letter Book).
Robert F. Weitbrec, "A Contribution to the Railroad Building Era in Colorado."
J. M. Meade, "D. & R. G. War with Santa Fe," Item 401, Denver and Rio Grande Archives. A 17-page typescript thought to have been written by a member of the Santa Fe engineering staff. It is not known positively that Meade wrote it; it is possible that Glenn Bradley worked with him in producing it.

In Letters to the Author

Ralph Budd, July 26, 31, and Aug. 5, 1960.
Learned Hand, Aug. 18, Sept. 4, 19, 1959.

In the State Historical Society of Colorado Library, Denver

William Abraham Bell Papers.
N. Z. Cozens Letters, 1870–76.
William S. Jackson Correspondence, 1885–86.
William Jackson Palmer Papers.
Robert F. Weitbrec Papers.

In Miscellaneous Locations

William Blackmore Papers, Museum of New Mexico Library, Santa Fe.
William G. Evans Correspondence, in the possession of John Evans, First National Bank Building, Denver.
Prof. R. D. George, testimony taken before the Interstate Commerce Commission hearing in Denver, April 16–20, 1923. Copy in the William G. Evans Correspondence, in the possession of John Evans.
J. W. Reagan, Report of Resources and Other Data of the San Juan Basin in Colorado, Utah, and New Mexico, by J. W. Reagan of Long Beach, Calif. A carbon of typescript issued by the Durango Exchange, Durango, Colo.

PRINTED SOURCES

Equitable Trust Company of New York v. Western Pacific Railway Company and the Denver and Rio Grande Railway Company (Feb. 21, 1917), 231 *Federal Reporter*, pp. 478–96.
First Report of the State Railroad Commission of Colorado, Denver, Dec. 6, 1919.
Hall, Henry C., "Denver and Rio Grande Investigation," *Interstate Commerce Commission Reports, 113* (1926), 75–160.

Journal History, Salt Lake City, 1830–. A well-kept, indexed collection of newspaper and magazine-article cuttings held by the Library, Historian's Office,
Church of Jesus Christ of Latter Day Saints. By June 1960 it totaled 950 volumes.

Poor's Manual of the Railroads of the United States, 57 vols. New York and
London, 1868–1924; presently: *Poor's Railroad Volume.*

Rio Grande Railroad Reorganization: Principal Consummation Documents. A
collection of documents pertaining to the reorganization of 1947. Denver and
Rio Grande Western offices, Denver.

State of Colorado Year Book, 1951–1955, Denver, State Planning Commission,
1955.

Books

Anderson, George LaVerne, *General William J. Palmer: A Decade of Colorado
Railroad Building, 1870–1880,* Colorado Springs, 1936.

Beadle, J. H., *The Undeveloped West; or, Five Years in the Territories,* Philadelphia, 1873. Beadle was the Western correspondent for the Cincinnati *Commercial.*

Bell, William A., *New Tracks in North America,* London, 1870.

Bollinger, Edward T., *Rails That Climb: The Story of the Moffat Road,* Santa
Fe, N.Mex., 1950.

——— and Bauer, Frederick, *The Moffat Road* (Denver, 1962), contains a good
deal more information and is less "folksy" than Bollinger's earlier work on
this subject.

Bradley, Glenn D., *The Story of the Santa Fe,* Boston, 1920.

Brayer, Herbert O., *William Blackmore: Early Financing of the Denver & Rio
Grande Railway and Ancillary Land Companies, 1871–1878,* Vol. 1 of *Wil-
liam Blackmore: A Case Study in the Economic Development of the West,*
Denver, 1949.

Carlton, A. B., *The Wonderlands of the Wild West with Sketches of the Mormons,* 1891.

Carter, Charles Frederick, *When Railroads Were New,* New York, 1909.

Colborn, Edward F., *A Glimpse of Utah,* Denver, 1906.

Crum, Josie Moore, *The Rio Grande Southern Story,* Durango, Colo., 1957.

Cunningham, Frank, *Big Dan: The Story of a Colorful Railroader,* Salt Lake
City, 1946. A biographical work about Daniel G. Cunningham written by his
nephew. "Big Dan" worked up from machinist to superintendent of shops for
the Rio Grande at Salt Lake City.

Davis, Carlyle Channing, *Olden Times in Colorado,* Los Angeles, 1916.

Donan, Patrick, *Utah; Being a Concise Description of the Vast Resources of a
Wonderful Region,* Denver, 1904.

Farrington, Selwyn Kip, *Railroading from the Head End,* New York, 1943.

——— *Railroading the Modern Way,* New York, 1951.

Fisher, John S., *Builder of the West: The Life of General William Jackson Palmer,* Caldwell, Idaho, 1939. In this biography of Palmer the Rio Grande is treated rather briefly in two chapters.

Galloway, John D., *The First Transcontinental Railroad: Central Pacific, Union Pacific,* New York, 1950.

Gillette, Edward, *Locating the Iron Trail,* Boston, 1925. Gillette, a civil engineer, passed through the Royal Gorge in 1879 on his way to an assignment near Leadville. He and his party were closely watched by the defending Rio Grande forces.

Gilpin, William, *The Cosmopolitan Railway: Compacting and Fusing Together All the World's Continents,* San Francisco, 1890.

Graff, John Franklin, *Graybeard's Colorado,* Philadelphia, 1882. Concerns a trip from Philadelphia to Colorado in 1881–82, with descriptions of the Leadville and Gunnison country.

Grodinsky, Julius, *Jay Gould: His Business Career, 1867–1892,* Philadelphia, 1957.

Hall, Frank, *History of the State of Colorado,* 4 vols. Chicago, 1895.

Hooper, Shadrach K., *The Gold Fields of Colorado,* Denver, 1896.

———— *Rhymes of the Rockies; or What the Poets Have Found to Say of the Beautiful Scenery on the Denver and Rio Grande,* Chicago, 1896.

———— *Camping in the Rockies,* Denver, 1903. "Major" Hooper's publications were puff pieces for the railroad, but they are now of more interest for historical reasons.

Howard, Ernest, *Wall Street Fifty Years After Erie; Being a Comparative Account of the Making and Breaking of the Jay Gould Railroad Fortune,* Boston, 1923. Howard was more than a muckraker. He was an "angry young man" for a very good reason: as a stockholder in the Rio Grande he suffered financial loss in the reorganization that followed the Western Pacific fiasco.

———— *A New Story of American Railroad Wrecking: Denver and Rio Grande, Western Pacific, and the Missouri Pacific's Part in the Affair.* A 60-page booklet published by the author in 1918. It was the basis for the above-mentioned book.

Howbert, Irving, *Memories of a Lifetime in the Pike's Peak Region,* New York, 1925.

Hunt, Louie, *The Silverton Train: A Story of Southwestern Colorado's Narrow Gauges,* Leucadia, Calif., 1955.

Johnson, David F., "The History and Economics of Utah's Railroads," in *Utah: A Centennial History,* Vol. 2, New York, 1949.

Kennan, George, *E. H. Harriman: A Biography,* 2 vols. New York, 1922.

Leckenby, Charles Harmon, *The Tread of Pioneers,* Steamboat Springs, Colo., 1944.

Lyman, Clarence A., *Fertile Lands of Colorado and Northern New Mexico,* Denver, 1909.

Marshall, James, *Santa Fe: The Railroad That Built an Empire,* New York, 1945.

McMechen, Edgar C., *The Moffat Tunnel of Colorado,* 2 vols. Denver, 1927.

Mellen, Chase, *Sketches of Pioneer Life and Settlement of the Great West,* New York, 1935.

Money, Edward, *The Truth About America,* London, 1886.

Ochs, Milton B., *Heart of the Rockies,* Cincinnati, 1890.

Overton, Richard C., *Gulf to Rockies: The Heritage of the Fort Worth and Denver-Colorado and Southern Railways, 1861–1898,* Austin, Tex., 1953.

Palmer, William J. (?), *The Westward March of Emigration in the United States, Considered in its Bearing upon the Near Future of Colorado and New Mexico,* Lancaster, Pa., 1874. A little book, dated Colorado Springs, March 1874, presumably by Palmer.

Parker, Willis H., *Pueblo's Flood,* Pueblo, Colo., n.d.

Peabody, George Foster, *William Jackson Palmer: Pathfinder and Builder,* Saratoga Springs, N.Y., 1931. A privately printed collection of addresses about Palmer.

Perkin, Robert L., *The First Hundred Years: An Informal History of Denver and the Rocky Mountain News,* New York, 1959.

Pratt, Edwin A., *American Railways* (London, 1903), chap. 10.

Riegel, Robert E., *The Story of the Western Railroads,* New York, 1926.

Samuelson, Carleton M., *Support of Public Schools in Colorado by the Denver and Rio Grande Western Railroad,* Denver, 1938.

Spooner, Charles E., *Narrow Gauge Railways,* London, 1871.

Sprague, Marshall, *Newport in the Rockies: The Life and Good Times of Colorado Springs,* Denver, 1961.

Stanton, Irving W., *Sixty Years in Colorado: Reminiscences and Reflections of a Pioneer of 1860,* Denver, 1922.

Tandy, Francis Dashwood, *Colorado Handbook,* Denver, 1899.

Thomas, Frank H., *The Denver and Rio Grande Western Railroad: A Geographic Analysis,* Northwestern University Studies in Geography, 4, Evanston, Ill., 1960.

Turpin, Jeanette, *General William J. Palmer: Founder of Colorado Springs, Builder of the Denver and Rio Grande Railroad,* n.d.

Warman, Cy, *Story of the Railroad,* New York, 1898. Several chapters are concerned with the Rio Grande. Not always reliable.

Waters, Lawrence L., *Steel Trails to Santa Fe,* Lawrence, Kans., 1950.

Whittaker, Milo Lee, *Pathbreakers and Pioneers of the Pueblo Region,* Philadelphia, 1917.

ARTICLES

Ayres, Mary C., "The Founding of Durango, Colorado," *Colorado Magazine,* 7 (1930), 85–94.

Bartlett, Robert F., "Aspen: The Mining Community, 1879–1893," *Westerners Brand Book, 1950* (Denver, 1951), pp. 133–60.

Baum, Arthur W., "Utah's Big Baby," *Saturday Evening Post*, May 15, 1948. The story of Geneva Steel.

Burnett, Robert N., "George Jay Gould," *Cosmopolitan, 35* (1903), 59–61.

Cafky, Morris, "The Colorado Midland Story," *Trains, 17* (1957), 17–22.

Colwell, Raymond, "Lake City," *Westerners Brand Book, 1950* (Denver, 1951), pp. 111–30.

Cunningham, Frank, "David H. Moffat . . . Empire Builder," *Tradition, 4* (1961), 5–13.

"Denver and Rio Grande, The," *Fortune, 40* (1949), 97–105, 210–16.

Ellis, Erl H., "A Broad Gauge Tail on a Narrow Gauge Dog," *Westerners Brand Book, 1954* (Denver, 1955), pp. 157–73. Concerns the broad gauge from Durango, Colo., to Farmington, N.Mex., changed to narrow gauge in 1923.

Ellsworth, Alonzo E., "Early Denver Business," *Westerners Brand Book, 1950* (Denver, 1951), pp. 245–62.

Evans, William G., "Railroad Consolidation and the Tunnel," *Municipal Facts, 6* (1923), 9–11, 21.

"General William J. Palmer, A Builder of the West," *World's Work, 15* (1908), 9899–9903.

Greever, William S., "Railway Development in the Southwest," *New Mexico Historical Review, 32* (1957), 151–203.

Hagie, C. E., "Gunnison in Early Days," *Colorado Magazine, 8* (1931), 121–29.

Harvey, Mrs. James, "The Leadville Ice Palace of 1896," *Colorado Magazine, 17* (1940), 94–101.

Harvey, Mr. and Mrs. James Rose, "The Quarries of Castle Rock Area," *Colorado Magazine, 23* (1946), 114–28.

——— "Engineer Walk of the Denver & Rio Grande," *Colorado Magazine, 24* (1947), 241–49.

Hendrick, Burton J., "The Passing of a Great Railroad Dynasty," *McClure's Magazine, 38* (1912), 483–502.

High, James, "William Andrews Clark, Westerner: An Interpretive Vignette," *Arizona and the West, 2* (1960), 245–64.

Hildreth, P. S., "The Western Pacific," *Railroad Age Gazette, 46* (1909), 563–71.

Howard, William Willard, "A Picturesque American Railway," *Harper's Weekly, 32* (1888), 78–79.

Jackson, William S., "The Record vs. Reminiscence," *Westerners Brand Book, 1945* (Denver, 1946), pp. 59–89. Story of the Rio Grande versus the Colorado Midland written by the son of Receiver William S. Jackson.

Keys, C. M., "The Overlords of Railroad Traffic," *World's Work, 13* (1907), 8437–45.

Lipsey, John J., "J. J. Hagerman, Building of the Colorado Midland," *Westerners Brand Book, 1954* (Denver, 1955), pp. 97–115.

——— "How Hagerman Sold the Midland in 1890," *Westerners Brand Book, 1956* (Denver, 1957), pp. 267–85.

McBrian, Ray, " 'Atomic' Methods Promise New Horizons in Railroad Research," *Railway Age* (Feb. 25, 1957), pp. 42–44.

McMechen, Edgar C., "The Story of the Moffat Tunnel," *Municipal Facts, 6* (1923), 3–8, 21.

Mendenhall, Hannah M., "The Calico Road," in *Heart Throbs of the West,* 2, Salt Lake City, 1940.

Morgan, Nicholas G., "Mormon Colonization in the San Luis Valley," *Colorado Magazine,* 27 (1950), 269–93.

Morris, Ernest, "A Glimpse of Moffat Tunnel History," *Colorado Magazine, 4* (1927), 63–66.

Newcomb, H. T., "The Recent Great Railway Combinations," *Review of Reviews, 24* (1901), 163–74.

Overton, Richard C., "Ralph Budd: Railroad Entrepreneur," *Palimpsest, 36* (1955), 421–84.

Roote, George A., "Gunnison in the Early 'Eighties," *Colorado Magazine, 9* (1932), 202–14.

Sanford, Albert B., "Recollections of a Trip to San Luis Valley in 1877," *Colorado Magazine, 10* (1933), 172–79.

Speare, Charles F., *The Gould Railroad Lines,* New York, 1908. A reprint of a series of articles that ran in the *Evening Mail.*

Walker, J. B., "Sixteen Hundred Miles of Mountain Railways," *Cosmopolitan, 19* (1895), 17–28.

Warman, Cy, "Capturing a Railroad in Colorado," *Denver Republican* (Oct. 4, 1896).

Weitbrec, Robert F., "Sketch of the Early History of the Denver and Rio Grande Railroad," *Trail, 16* (1924), 3–8.

Wyman, Walker D., "Grand Junction's First Year, 1882," *Colorado Magazine, 13* (1936), 127–37.

PAMPHLETS

Barclay, James W., *The Denver and Rio Grande Railway of Colorado* (1876), item 1137, Blackmore Papers, Museum of New Mexico Library, Santa Fe.

Bell, William A., *Progress of the Denver and Rio Grande Railway* (London, March 10, 1877), 3-page pamphlet, item 1047, Blackmore Papers, Museum of New Mexico Library, Santa Fe.

Colorado Coal and Iron Company, The (1882), Coburn Library, Colorado College, Colorado Springs.

Denver and Rio Grande, The: A Prospectus (London, 1881), Coburn Library, Colorado College, Colorado Springs.

Denver and Rio Grande Pamphlets, 1870–1879, Denver Public Library. Six bound volumes of assorted Rio Grande pamphlets.

D. and R. G. Railway of Colorado and New Mexico, The, London, 1871.

Jackson, William S., *Trinidad Pool* (Oct. 20, 1876), Western History Dept., Denver Public Library.

Kneiss, Gilbert H., *Fifty Candles for Western Pacific.* A 40-page pamphlet produced as an anniversary issue of the Western Pacific's publication, *Mileposts,* March 1953.

McCarthy, Wilson, *General Wm. Jackson Palmer (1836–1909) and the D. & R. G. W. Railroad,* Princeton, 1954. Printed for the Newcomen Society in North America.

Pueblo Colony of Southern Colorado, The, Lancaster, Pa., 1874.

There is Gold in Colorado, Denver, n.d. A beginner's handbook of gold mining published by the Rio Grande's Passenger Department.

Train to Yesterday, The, Rahway, N.J., n.d. A pamphlet describing the Durango-Silverton narrow gauge, published by Railroadians of America.

Whitman, Frederic Bennett, *Western Pacific—Its First Forty Years,* New York, 1950. Printed for the Newcomen Society in North America.

Newspapers

Aspen *Daily Times* (Aspen, Colo.).

Boulder *Daily Camera* (Boulder, Colo.).

Colorado Chieftain (Pueblo, Colo.).

Commercial and Financial Chronicle (New York, N.Y.). A weekly newspaper representing industrial interests in the U.S.

Daily Elko Free Press (Elko, Nev.).

Daily New Mexican (Santa Fe, N.Mex.).

Denver *Daily Times* (Denver, Colo.).

Denver *Post* (Denver, Colo.).

Denver *Republican* (Denver, Colo.). Also published as the *Tribune-Republican.*

Denver *Tribune* (Denver, Colo.).

Deseret News (Salt Lake City, Utah). Title changed to *Deseret News and Telegram,* Sept. 1, 1952.

Durango *Herald* (Durango, Colo.).

Durango *Record* (Durango, Colo.).

New York *Times* (New York, N.Y.).

Ogden *Daily Herald* (Ogden, Utah).

Rocky Mountain News (Denver, Colo.).

Routt County Sentinel (Steamboat Springs, Colo.). A Republican weekly, the predecessor of the *Pilot.*

Salt Lake *Daily Herald* (Salt Lake City, Utah).

Salt Lake *Tribune* (Salt Lake City, Utah).

Territorial Enquirer (Provo, Utah).

Weekly Gazette (Colorado Springs, Colo.).

Unpublished Dissertations and Theses

Bridenhagen, Clement, "John Evans: Western Railroad Builder," master's thesis, University of Denver, 1951.

Daniels, James Harold, "A History of the War for the Royal Gorge," master's thesis, University of Denver, 1954.

Hough, Charles Merrill, "Leadville, Colorado, 1878 to 1898: A Study in Unionism," master's thesis, University of Colorado, 1958.

Logan, Paul Stewart, "The History of the Denver and Rio Grande Railway, 1871–1881," master's thesis, University of Colorado, 1931.

Mock, Samuel Donald, "Railroad Development in the Colorado Region to 1880," doctoral dissertation, University of Nebraska, 1938.

Odisho, William Charles, "Salt Lake to Oakland: The Western Pacific Link in the Continental Railroad System," doctoral dissertation, University of California, 1941.

Spence, Clark Christian, "Robert Orchard Old and the British and Colorado Mining Bureau," master's thesis, University of Colorado, 1951.

Wilson, Owen Meredith, "A History of the Denver and Rio Grande Project, 1870–1901," doctoral dissertation, University of California, 1934.

Index

D&RG. *See* Denver and Rio Grande Railway Company

D&RGW. *See* Denver and Rio Grande Western Railroad Company

Denver and Rio Grande Railway (Railroad) Company (D&RG): opening celebration, 1–2, 283; passenger cars, 1–2, 21, 100; engines, 1–2, 21–22; reaches Colorado Springs, 1–2, 18, 20–22; Palmer starts organizing, 5–6, 8–11, 13–14; charter route, 13, 15, 22, 26–27, 59, 61, 75, 316; decision to use narrow gauge, 14–15, 18; incorporation, 15–16, 359; first board of directors, 15; contract with Union Contract Company, 15–16 (*see also* Union Contract Company); Pueblo extension, 15, 22–25, 27, 29; route to Rio Grande, 15, 22, 44, 50, 93; success of first year, 20–21; effect on Colorado, 21, 25, 34–36, 113, 135–37, 144, 150, 153, 176, 187, 221–22, 250–51, 283, 299, 362; Colorado attitude toward, 22 (*see also* Colorado)

extension to Canon City, Labran coal fields, 23, 25–29, 42, 59; effect of *1873* panic on, 29–30, 33; war with AT&SF for Royal Gorge route, 26–27, 29, 53, 55, 57–66, 84, 87–90, 93–94, 98, 117, 134; Royal Gorge suits, 57 n., 58, 60–65, 67, 69, 72–76, 79–80, 82–83; financial operation (*1872–74*), 30, 36–37; Trinidad extension, 31–33, 37–38, 41–43, lack of funds for, 44, 46–47; Santa Fe extension, 31, 47–48, 50, 58, 61, 89, 93–96, 98, 169, 186, discontinued, 315–16; Cucharas extension, 32, 41, 43

fares and freight rates, 33–36, 67, 71, 130, 142, 150, 164, 167; importance of mines to, 32–33, 41, 43, 130, 221; effect of weather on, 33; accidents, 33–34, 100, 129, 187–88, 211–13, 219; San Juan extension, 38, 43–44, 46–47, 66, 85, 93, 101–02, 105; relation to Southern Colorado Coal and Town Company, 38–39, 48; financial difficulties (*1875*), 38–39, 41; traffic agreement with KP and AT&SF, 42, 46; favors El Moro over Trinidad, 43; loss of Raton Pass, 44, 50, 55–56, 93; Fort Garland extension, 44, 50, 92; failure to pay interest on bonds (*1877*), 46–48; Alamosa extension, 47, 55–56; financial operation (*1877*), 48; receivership suit (*1877*), 48; situation (*1877*), 49–50; Gunnison extension, 52, 106, 115, 134, 174, 345–46; Leadville extension, 52–56, 66, 85, 87–88, 90, 95, 98, 100, 134, 169

AT&SF lease of, 52, 65–66, 71–74, 95; stock prices, 66, 86, 110, 131, 142, 147, 185, 235, 240; transfer to AT&SF, 67–69; suit against

AT&SF to revoke lease, 75, 79–80; removed from AT&SF control, 80–82; returned to AT&SF control, 82–83, AT&SF loses control of, 84–85, 88–89; Ellsworth appointed receiver of (*1879*), 84; AT&SF threat to parallel, 85; Jay Gould buys into, 85; to build road for Pueblo and St. Louis, 86; Treaty of Boston, 87–88, 96, 98, 165, 174; change to east-west position, 89–90, 92, 117, 124, 128; "prospecting" policy, 90, 98, 100–01, 107, 114–15, 128, 130, 151, 222, 345; expansion, *1876–78*, 93

returned to Palmer, 98; buys P&AV construction, 100; attempt to regain passenger trade, 100; expansion plans, *1880*, 105–06; seeks investors, 105, 107; cutback (*1881–82*), 107–10; Salt Lake City extension, 107, 111, 114–15, 118, 120–22, 124–26, 132–33, 141–42 (*see also* Denver and Rio Grande Western Railway), direct line to, 231 (*see also* Dotsero Cutoff); Jay Gould's attempts to control, 110–12; rivalry with D&NO, 111, 147; relation to RGW, 111, 116–17; suit against UP, 111; considers merger with CB&Q, 112; financial operation (*1881–82*), 113–14; lease of RGW, 117, 131, 133, 141–43, 147, 153; Utah attitude toward, 117–18 (*see also* Utah); size (*1881*), 118; chance to join transcontinental line, 121, 166; Palmer resignation, 131, 133–35

financial operation (*1882–84*), 131–33, 135, 142–45; non-Coloradans on board of, 133, 137, 139; uncompleted projects, 134; Lovejoy presidency, 135–45, 150, effect on, 146–48, 151, 154, 164; board, Palmer's criticism of, 135, 144; war on CCI, 136–37; employees, support of Palmer, 136–38, fired, 139–40; fight with RGW, 137–40, 147 (*see also* Lovejoy); Jackson receivership (*1884*), 138–40, 145–47, 154; stockholders meeting (*1884*), 139–40; stockholders, attitude toward Palmer, 143; suit to break lease of RGW, 143, 145, 147; relation to CB&Q, AT&SF (*1884*), 144

separation from RGW, 144–46; RGW lease-damage suit against, 145, 153; reconnected to RGW, 146; rate agreement with D&NO, 147; loses CB&Q trade to AT&SF, 148–50; relations with CB&Q, 148–49; default on bond interest (*1884*), 149; foreign investors' role in, 149–53, 155, 158; need for broad-gauge track, 151; strike, *1885*, 151–52; *1892*, 180; *1894*, 185; *1908*, 213; effect of Coppell's committee on, 152–53; sale of (*1886*), 153, 158

Glenwood Springs, Colo.: coal fields near, 155; Midland route to, 155–56; D&RG route to, 156; UP activity at, 157; reaction to arrival of D&RG, 161, 163; RG&P plans to build at, 170; stopping trains at, 180; monument to Vista Dome, 335–36

Golden, Colo., 21, 174

Goldrick, O. J., 2

Goodnight, Charles, 23

Gore Canyon, 277. *See also* Dotsero Cutoff

Gould, Edwin, 206

Gould, Frank, on board of RGW, 195

Gould, George: control of Missouri Pacific Company, 191; ambitions, 191; relations with Harriman, 192, 196–97, 204, 206; elected head of D&RG board, 194; becomes RGW board chairman, 195; control of Rio Grande system, 195–96; interest in WP, 197, 200, 204–06; plans to extend D&RG system to Pacific, 199–200, 205; plans to build transcontinental system, 202, 206; reveals plans for WP, 207; management, effect on D&RG system, 207, 210, 214–15, 221–22, 250, 255–56, 283; lines, condition of, 210; efforts against Moffat, 214; breakup of empire, 214–15, 217–19, 230–31; regains control of D&RG, 231; D&RG freed from, 235–36; opposition to D&RG receivership, 236; effect on D&SL, 259. *See also* Missouri Pacific, Denver and Rio Grande

Gould, Howard, on board of RGW, 195

Gould, Jay, 196, 259; control of UP, 52; row with KP, 64; reaction to AT&SF lease of D&RG, 67; threatens AT&SF by buying into D&RG, 85–86; stops AT&SF-D&RG war, 86; financing of D&RG Santa Fe extension, 95; efforts to control DSP&P, 106; buys control of DSP&P, 110; as threat to D&RG, RGW, 110–12, 143–44; as strategian, 192; dynasty, 215

Gould, Kingdon, 225

Granada, 47

Grand County, Colo., 214

Grand Canyon of the Arkansas. *See* Royal Gorge

Grand Junction, Colo., 181, 284, 358; reaction to D&RG-RGW connection, 121; effect of D&RG on, 121–22; Rio Grande Junction line between Rifle and, 171, 173; D&RG route to, 174; D&RG strike at, 185; collision near *(1897)*, 188

Grand Junction (Colo.) *Daily Sentinel:* quoted, 121–22; cited, 348

Grand River: D&RG extension to, 134, 167; D&RG surveys, 156; CB&Q plan to build

along, 157; Rio Grande and Pacific plans to build at, 170

Grand River Valley: D&RG plan to occupy, 156–57; UP, CB&Q interest in, 157; Midland line to, 165, 170

Grant, Ulysses S., 13

Grape Creek, Colo., 61

Great Bend, Kans., connection to Colorado, 86

Great Northern, owner of CB&Q, 275

Greeley Colony, 18

Greeley (Colo.) *Tribune*, 2

Green River, Utah, 115; D&RG-RGW drives last spike near, 122

Greenhorn Valley, Colo., 32

Greenwood, William H.: interest in D&RG project, 9, 13; drives first spike in D&RG, 18; forms land company, 23

Gross, John E., 330

Guarantee Trust Company, control of MP, 230

Guaymas, 11

Gulf of Mexico, 169

Gunderson, Harvey J., 329

Gunnison, Colo.: D&RG branch to, 52, 115, 134, 174, 345–46; mineral fields, 62; D&RG-DSP&P race for, 106; strike of D&RG at, 151–52; Adams' visit to, 157

Gunnison (Colo.) *Daily Review-Press*, quoted, 122

Gunnison (Colo.) *Empire*, quoted, 246

Gunnison (Colo.) *News-Democrat*, quoted, 115

Hagerman, James John: presidency of Midland, 155, 165; opinion of Moffat, D&RG, 171, 173. *See also* Colorado Midland

Hagerman Pass, Colo., Midland crosses, 160

Hall, Henry C., quoted, 231

Hallett, Judge Moses: decision on D&RG receivership *(1877)*, 48; decision on Royal Gorge case, 58, 62–63, 75–76; decision on D&RG suit to recover lease from AT&SF, 80, 82–85; interpretation of Supreme Court ruling on Royal Gorge, 83–84; order in support of Supreme Court decision on Royal Gorge case, 86–87; decision on UP-D&RG fight for Platte Canyon, 134; appoints W. S. Jackson as D&RG receiver *(1884)*, 146; jails strikers, 151; orders sale of D&RG, 153; D&RG expansion *(1886)*, 156; injunction against D&RG strike, 185

Hammond Iron Works, 333

Hand, Judge Learned, decision on WP-D&RG case, 234–35, 237

Harding, J. Horace, opposition to D&RG receivership, 236

Harriman, Edward H.: control of CP, SP,

Red Cliff, Colo., D&RG extension to, 156, 161
Reed, Stanley, 325
Reiff, Josiah C., forms land company, 23
Renshaw, A. G., 107
RFC. *See* Reconstruction Finance Corporation
RGW. *See* Denver and Rio Grande Western Railway
Richfield, Utah, 345
Ricker, Robert E., 137, 140
Rico, Colo., 179
Ridgway, Colo., junction of D&RG, Rio Grande Southern, 179
Rifle, Colo., Rio Grande Junction route between Grand Junction and, 171, 173
Rifle Creek, Colo., Rio Grande and Pacific plans to build at, 170
Right of Way Act *(1875)*, 59 n., 61–63
Rio Grande and Pacific Railroad Company, incorporated, 170
Rio Grande Junction Railway Company, formed by D&RG and Midland, 171, 173
Rio Grande Land Company, 332
Rio Grande Motor Way, Inc.: request for airline, 317; D&RGW sale of, 347–48
Rio Grande Motor Way of Utah, 347
Rio Grande River: KP route west of, 3; D&RG route to, 15, 22, 44, 50, 93
Rio Grande River Valley, as agricultural site, 20
Rio Grande Southern: completion, 179; put in receivership, 181; ceases operations, 346
Rio Grande Western. *See* Denver and Rio Grande Western Railway
Ripley, William Z., 251
Risley, Hanson, 56, 143; receiver of D&RG, 82–83; resigns from D&RG board, 133
River Bend, Colorado Springs, and San Juan Railroad, formed, 35
Roaring Fork, Colo.: UP survey at, 157; D&RG construction at, 161; Midland approaches, 160
Robinson, A. A.: captures Raton Pass for AT&SF, 55; control of Canon City and San Juan Railway, 60; escape from Canon City, 62; sends Morley to secure Royal Gorge, 57; starts building between Pueblo and Denver, 85
Rock Island. *See* Chicago, Rock Island, and Pacific
Rockafellow, B. E., 58
Rockefeller, John D., 201, 204, 215, 217; increased holdings in MP and D&RG, 218–19
Rocky Mountain area, economic growth, 352
Rocky Mountain News (Denver, Colo.): support of D&RG, 2, 18, 34–35, 283; cited, 61;

editorial quoted, 80, 240, 254–56; quoted, 187, 215, 217–18, 262, 270, 277, 279–80, 283; support of Moffat Tunnel, 262; criticism of D&RGW, 283
Rocky Mountain states, 187
Rocky Mountains, 335; potential, 6; effect on railroads, 13, 263
Rogers, Andrew N., survey for Rockies tunnel, 165, 261
Rogers, Henry W., decision on D&RG-WP case, 235
Rollins, Pass, Colo., 214, 259; blocked *(1919)*, 267
Root, Elihu, 233
Rosser, Thomas L., 3
Routt County, Colo., 214
Royal Gorge, Colo., D&RG proposed route to, 22; D&RG decision not to route through, 27; D&RG and AT&SF competition for, 27, 29, 53, 57–66, 84, 87–88, 93; suits, 57 n., 58, 60–65, 67, 69, 72–76, 79–80, 82–83, 86–87, 95; as scenic route, 100; Moffat Tunnel as rival route, 266; flooded *(1920)*, 267; route, improvement of, 284; car named for, 353

Sacramento, Cal., 196
Sage, Russell, 85
St. Louis, Mo., 102, 289, 338
St. Louis-San Francisco, 320
Salida, Colo.: D&RG extension to, 101, 106; strike of D&RG at, 151–52; D&RG strike west of, 180; D&RG crash near *(1897)*, 188; narrow-gauge track, 221
Salina Pass, Utah, RGW plans to build over, 115, 117
Salomon, F. Z., 10
Salt Lake and Denver Railroad, 273
Salt Lake and Park City Railway, absorbed by RGW, 115
Salt Lake City, Utah, 185, 244, 336, 353, 358; D&RG plans extension to, 54, 90, 106, 114–15, 124, 133, 170, 188, 192; connection to Denver through D&RGW, 98, 120–22, 128, 190, 218; shipments to Clear Creek, 120; UP and D&RG rate war at, 125–26; CB&Q rumored line to, 165; as transcontinental railroad center, 166; new connections to Pueblo and Colorado Springs, 173; AT&SF extends toward, 174
   growth, 191; desire for transcontinental line, 191, 196; MP-D&RG extension west of, 192, 225; railroad competition for *(1902)*, 201–02; short route to Denver, 231 *(see* Dotsero Cutoff); reaction to WP-D&RG suit, 235; new trains from, 311; U.S. arms plant